Informal Alliance

Informal Alliance is the first archive-based history of the secretive Bilderberg Group, the high-level transatlantic elite network founded at the height of the Cold War. Making extensive use of the recently opened Bilderberg Group archives as well as a wide range of private and official collections, it shows the significance of informal diplomacy in a fast-changing world of Cold War, decolonization, and globalization. By analyzing the global mindset of the postwar transatlantic elite and by focusing on private, transnational modes of communication and coordination, this study provides important new insights into the history of transatlantic relations, anti-Americanism, Western anti-communism, and European integration during the 1950s and 1960s. *Informal Alliance* also debunks the persistent myth that the Bilderberg Group was created by the CIA and repudiates widespread conspiracy theories alleging that Bilderberg was some sort of secret world government.

Thomas W. Gijswijt is Associate Professor in American Studies at the University of Tübingen, Germany.

Routledge Studies in Modern History

For a full list of titles published in the series, please visit www.routledge.com

Informal Alliance

The Bilderberg Group and
Transatlantic Relations during
the Cold War, 1952–1968

Thomas W. Gijswijt

Routledge
Taylor & Francis Group

LONDON AND NEW YORK

First published 2019
by Routledge
2 Park Square, Milton Park, Abingdon, Oxon OX14 4RN

and by Routledge
711 Third Avenue, New York, NY 10017

Routledge is an imprint of the Taylor & Francis Group, an informa business

British Library Cataloguing-in-Publication Data
A catalogue record for this book is available from the British Library

Library of Congress Cataloging-in-Publication Data
A catalog record for this book has been requested

ISBN: 978-0-8153-9674-1 (hbk)
ISBN: 978-1-351-18104-4 (ebk)

Typeset in Times New Roman
by codeMantra

For Andrea, Jakob, and Johanna

Contents

Acknowledgements

This book began as a PhD project at the University of Heidelberg. I am grateful to the Curt Engelhorn Foundation, the Institute for European History in Mainz, and Nuffic for financial support. More recently, the German-American Fulbright Commission and the University of Maryland's English Department enabled me to spend a semester at UMD College Park, where much of the final research and work for this book was done.

Over the course of my archival research, too many archivists to mention have provided essential assistance, for which I am grateful. Many people have provided encouragement, help, or ideas at different stages of this project. Special thanks to: Thorsten Benner, Volker Berghahn, Albertine Bloemendal, Maarten Brands, Simone Derix, Philipp Gassert, Johannes Großmann, Detlef Junker, Holger Klitzing, Hans Krabbendam, Dino Knudsen, Anna Locher, Charles Maier, Bruce Mazlish, Ton Nijhuis, Christian Nünlist, Giles Scott-Smith, Mathieu Segers, Hein van Steenis, Jeremi Suri, Kenneth Weisbrode, Andreas Wenger, and Anne Zetsche. A shout-out to Willi and Piccolo in Tübingen for coffee and inspiration.

My mother, Marijke, was my most faithful reader and even acted as a researcher to track down the latest Bilderberg documents. Thank you!

My wife, Andrea, my son, Jakob, and my daughter, Johanna, have made me happy. To them, with all my love, this book is dedicated.

List of abbreviations

ACG	American Council on Germany
ACUE	American Committee on United Europe
ACUS	Atlantic Council of the United States
AEC	Atomic Energy Commission
ARAMCO	Arabian American Oil Company
BDI	*Bundesverband der Deutschen Industrie*
BVD	*Binnenlandse Veiligheidsdienst*
CCF	Congress for Cultural Freedom
CDU	*Christlich Demokratische Union Deutschlands*
CEDI	*Centre Européen de Documentation et d'Information*
CEIP	Carnegie Endowment for International Peace
CEPES	*Comité Européen pour le Progrès Économique et Social*
CFR	Council on Foreign Relations
CIA	Central Intelligence Agency
DAG	Development Assistance Group
DGB	*Deutsche Gewerkschaftsbund*
ECA	European Cooperation Agency
ECF	European Cultural Foundation
ECSC	European Coal and Steel Community
EDC	European Defense Community
EEC	European Economic Community
EFTA	European Free Trade Area
ELEC	European League for Economic Cooperation
EM	European Movement
ERP	European Recovery Program (Marshall Plan)
EURATOM	European Atomic Energy Community
EYC	European Youth Campaign
FBI	Federal Bureau of Investigation
FTA	Free Trade Area
GATT	General Agreement on Tariffs and Trade
HICOG	High Commissioner for Germany
IAC	International Advisory Committee Chase Bank
IBRD	International Bank for Reconstruction and Development

ICBM	Intercontinental ballistic missile
IFC	International Finance Corporation
IMF	International Monetary Fund
IRBM	Intermediate-range ballistic missile
JAEC	Joint Atomic Energy Committee
JCS	Joint Chiefs of Staff
KVP	*Katholieke Volkspartij*
MIDEC	Middle East Development Corporation
MLF	Multilateral Force
MRBM	Medium-range ballistic missile
MRP	*Mouvement Républicain Populaire*
MSA	Mutual Security Agency
NATO	North Atlantic Treaty Organization
NEI	*Nouvelles Équipes Internationales*
NPG	Nuclear Planning Group
OECD	Organization for Economic Cooperation and Development
OEEC	Organisation for European Economic Cooperation
OPC	Office of Policy Coordination
OSS	Office of Strategic Services
PPS	Policy Planning Staff (State Department)
SACEUR	Supreme Allied Commander Europe (NATO)
SCUA	Suez Canal Users' Association
SEATO	Southeast Asia Treaty Organization
SFIO	*Section Française de l'Internationale Ouvrière*
SHAPE	Supreme Headquarters Allied Powers Europe (NATO)
SOE	Special Operations Executive
SPD	*Sozialdemokratische Partei Deutschlands*
UEF	Union of European Federalists
UEM	United Europe Movement
UN	United Nations
UNDP	United Nations Development Program
WEU	Western European Union

Introduction

At the 1965 Bilderberg conference in Italy, the leading American diplomat George Ball explained the remarkable US decision, first made by the Truman Administration and confirmed by subsequent presidents, to become a 'European power' in peacetime. "Based on a profound inculcation of the lessons of history," Ball said, "and [...] inspired by the desire to avoid the main causes of the two previous European tragedies," the United States had decided to "irrevocably link its own destiny with that of Europe."[1] This linking of transatlantic destinies is arguably the most important reason why Europe, even if divided by an Iron Curtain, developed along peaceful lines in the decades after 1945 – in stark contrast to the 1930s, when a fateful combination of economic distress, racist and anti-Semitic ideology, and aggressive nationalism plunged the world into darkness.

What went wrong during the 1930s was, to a considerable degree, a failure of the industrialized world to cooperate in the face of a global economic crisis, as well as a failure of the civilized world to respond jointly to Italian, Japanese, or German aggression. This, at least, is how many of those involved in rebuilding the world after World War II saw it. These internationalists were determined not to repeat that mistake; accordingly, they developed an interlocking system of multilateral institutions designed for the more effective functioning of international cooperation and coordination.

If the initial thrust of internationalism had been economic and global – with the creation of the United Nations, the International Monetary Fund (IMF), the World Bank, and the General Agreement on Tariffs and Trade (GATT) – the emerging Cold War quickly forced internationalists in the United States and Europe to become more and more Atlanticist, needing to concentrate their attention on questions of regional security in Europe and the Atlantic area. This explains why the Marshall Plan soon turned into a program for military assistance, and it explains why the North Atlantic Treaty of 1949 quickly turned from a paper treaty into an integrated military organization (NATO) with a vast US military presence on European ground. It also explains why, in the late 1940s and early 1950s, the United States became so much more deeply involved in European affairs than anyone had thought necessary at war's end.

Not surprisingly, this deepening American involvement in European affairs caused frequent transatlantic tensions and misunderstandings. European interests, after all, did not always coincide with American interests, and Europe's economic and military dependence inevitably generated anti-American resentment as European prestige and pride took a hit. The need to coordinate policies, moreover, frequently displayed the truth of Churchill's dictum: "there is only one thing worse than fighting with allies, and that is fighting without them." The official institutions and leaders of the Atlantic alliance, for one, turned out not to be very good at dealing with these tensions.[2] In part, this reflected the intricacies of US foreign policy decision-making, which involved such a large number of executive and congressional players that the added complexity of allied consultation frequently proved too much. But it was also the quite natural reaction to the sudden rise of the United States as the superpower chiefly responsible for Western Europe's security.

This is where the Bilderberg Group, founded in 1952, came in. One of the main arguments set forth in this book is that the Bilderberg Group formed an important part of what I call the *informal alliance* – as opposed to the official alliance consisting of NATO, the Organization for Economic Cooperation and Development (OECD), and other multilateral institutions. The informal alliance had its origins in the early Cold War and consisted of a fast-growing group of private or semi-private transnational organizations engaged in fostering and promoting cooperation and understanding within the Western world. The fact that global communication systems and intercontinental air travel were creating what Wendell Willkie, in his 1943 bestseller, had called "One World" made frequent transatlantic contacts and networking physically possible for the first time in human history.[3] As a result, the informal alliance came to play an important role in the difficult process of adjustment to the fundamental shift in power relations between the new world and the old.

Some of the organizations in the informal alliance were continental European undertakings, whereas others were transatlantic or bilateral in nature; some focused on cultural or political issues, while others brought together defense intellectuals or economists. What united them was that they operated transnationally and that their members broadly shared a *global mindset*: the belief that the nations of the 'Free World,' after two devastating world wars and facing a wide range of global challenges, could not confront the modern world in isolation. Needless to say, the exact nature and methods of cooperation – from world government to Atlantic union, from economic functionalism to political federalism – remained the subject of much debate and disagreement.[4]

The Bilderberg Group was one of the first organizations of the informal alliance. Its main purpose was to improve and solidify relations between Western Europe and the United States through secret, non-partisan discussions.[5] The Bilderberg Group's private nature and its high caliber, multifaceted membership made it an ideal platform for engaging in *informal diplomacy* and for developing *transnational connections*. The Bilderberg Group was unique not just in inviting participants from virtually all NATO members (as well as some of the neutral European states) for its yearly meetings but also in bringing together a surprisingly broad range of participants representing various political groupings, trade unions, the business and financial world, civil society, and government. Despite its secretive nature, Bilderberg in fact contributed to a democratization and broadening of the transatlantic foreign policy elite in the 1950s and 1960s. Its organizers were convinced that international understanding would only take hold if as many societal groups as possible were represented.

Given the immense imbalance in power between the United States and Europe in the immediate postwar period, the history of transatlantic relations is often written through the lens of American agency, hegemony, or empire. The term Americanization, for example, implicitly posits a one-directional flow of influence and power. The history of the Bilderberg Group suggests, however, that the actual dynamics of transatlantic relations were much more complex, and that American primacy was not as straightforward as it seemed. US leadership of the alliance, after all, depended upon a certain level of support from European publics and foreign policy elites. This became clear as soon as Western Europe started to recover economically in the early 1950s and a wave of anti-American sentiment swept the continent in the wake of the Korean War and McCarthyism.

Believing that transatlantic cooperation was in jeopardy, this wave of anti-Americanism prompted Joseph H. Retinger, Bilderberg's Polish-born founding father, to create a new type of forum for informal transatlantic exchanges.[6] He argued that "private initiatives" would be more successful than public diplomacy because Europeans were "tired of official [American] propaganda."[7] The Bilderberg Group, in other words, was not an American invention – the group was based on a decidedly European initiative and, though it soon turned into a transatlantic organization, its leadership and direction would continue to come predominantly from Europe.

The story of how the Bilderberg Group, despite initial American reluctance to cooperate, became one of the most important bodies of the informal alliance reveals much about the dynamics of transatlantic relations during the Cold War and provides new answers to the question why, despite its frequent crises, the Atlantic alliance turned out to be resilient as well as enduring. This book tells that story in different ways, focusing more on the political than on the economic dimensions of the Bilderberg discussions. It relates, first of all, the history of Bilderberg's founding and its institutional development. Who organized the Bilderberg meetings? How were they financed? Who set the agenda and sent out the invitations? Why did the Bilderberg Group continue to meet even after European anti-Americanism seemed to have subsided in the late 1950s? And how did the group change over time?

A second, closely intertwined storyline examines how the manifold connections between members of the transatlantic elite led to new modes of communication and a sense of shared, transnational, or global identity.[8] It traces the ideas, values, interests, and emotions that united as well as divided the members of this elite. This can provide us with important insights into how members of the informal alliance perceived and responded to challenges of the Cold War, decolonization, and globalization.

Finally, *Informal Alliance* interweaves the narrative of the Bilderberg Group and the transatlantic elite with the broader history of transatlantic relations, thus bringing in a new perspective that has largely remained out of view because of the dominant state-based historiographies. To a considerable degree, this history was one of crisis and failure – from the European Defense Community (EDC) to the Suez and Sputnik crises, or to the French withdrawal from NATO's integrated military command structure in 1966. An important function of the informal alliance was therefore to keep the basic consensus underlying the institutions of Western cooperation alive as well as to search for new avenues of cooperation. From the American point of view, meanwhile, the informal alliance provided opportunities to legitimize US leadership, as long as a more equal Atlantic partnership remained elusive.

Throughout these different storylines, the question of the Bilderberg Group's influence emerges. I argue that this influence was mainly indirect. The historical record shows that the Group was not involved in decision-making, nor were any specific, actionable conclusions reached. However, the Bilderberg organizers did hope and expect that through the agency of the Bilderberg participants, the discussions would have an impact on decision-makers and public opinion. They did not hesitate to bring the results of their discussions to the attention of government officials and political leaders, yet they had little control over what was done with this information.

The actual power of the Bilderberg Group hence mainly consisted of introducing new ideas, sustaining a sense of community among the members of the transatlantic elite, and enhancing understanding for differences in attitudes and political cultures – in short, *indirect influence*. As the Bilderberg organizers themselves realized, such influence was impossible to measure with any precision. Ultimately, it depended both on how the Bilderberg participants influenced each other and on what they did with the information, impressions, and contacts gathered at the Bilderberg meetings. For the Bilderberg participants themselves, meanwhile, the meetings were useful as a source of information, connections, and status. Of course, they could also be interesting and enjoyable; the atmosphere of the meetings was a key ingredient for their success.

Informal Alliance is the first research-based history of the Bilderberg Group. Although much has been written about Bilderberg, most of it is highly speculative and very little is based on actual archival research.[9] One explanation for the surprising lack of serious research about the group is that Bilderberg's official archives were long closed, governed by a 50-year access rule (meaning that for this book I have been able to access all material up to 1967). In addition, the fact that Bilderberg's membership was so diverse makes the group challenging to study. Even after multilingual archival research in dozens of private and official collections in more than 40 archives in seven different countries, this book inevitably provides only a partial view. The main geographic focus of *Informal Alliance* lies on the United States, Great Britain, France, Germany, Belgium, and the Netherlands, which means that countries such as Denmark, Greece, Italy, Sweden, or Turkey do not get as much attention as they deserve.

The wealth of material in the Bilderberg archives and in a range of other collections does make it possible to write a detailed history of the Bilderberg Group and its role in transatlantic relations in the period until 1968. Particularly, the first three Bilderberg conferences (one in 1954 and two in 1955) are well documented because verbatim transcripts of these conferences are available. Official reports exist for all other conferences; although these detailed summaries of the discussions do not identify the names of most speakers, it is oftentimes possible to reconstruct who said what by combining the reports with the private notes and correspondence of participants.[10] Many participants, moreover, wrote accounts of the meetings for official or private purposes, adding more evidence for analyzing Bilderberg's indirect influence.[11]

Informal Alliance combines a chronological with a thematic approach. The first three chapters examine the origins of the Bilderberg Group. The first chapter begins with the fascinating story of how the penniless London-based Polish writer Joseph Retinger turned into an influential informal diplomat who stood at the origins not just of the Bilderberg Group but also of the European Movement. It then addresses the question of US involvement in funding the European Movement against the background of the Cold War. The second chapter shows how Retinger assembled a leading group of Europeans to analyze Europe's anti-American turn in the early 1950s and how this led to the first Bilderberg conference. It demonstrates that the Bilderberg Group was a decidedly European creation and that, in fact, the Eisenhower Administration was initially reluctant to support Retinger's initiative.

Chapter 3 concludes the first part of the book and gives a detailed account of the first conference held at Hotel de Bilderberg in May 1954. This conference represented a new phase in postwar transatlantic relations as Europe's most immediate dependence on the United States slowly receded. The success of the first Bilderberg conference had much to do, I argue, with the emerging global mindset of an expanding foreign policy elite in the West. The chapter also shows how emotions turned out to be an important category of analysis for understanding the transatlantic alliance and its anti-communist underpinnings.

Chapter 4 takes a step back from the chronological approach and looks more closely at the Bilderberg Group's organization and membership. It addresses the question of influence and elaborates the concepts of informal diplomacy, the transatlantic elite, and the informal alliance. Taking Henry Kissinger and Zbigniew Brzezinski as two prominent examples, it also shows how the informal alliance allowed relative outsiders to become influential members of the transatlantic elite.

Chapter 5 returns to the Bilderberg story and looks at how the Bilderberg Group responded to the failure of the EDC in August 1954. The Bilderberg discussions on European integration provide an important correction to existing explanations of the creation of the European Communities. They show that anti-communist motivations played a much larger role than is often recognized and they underline the profoundly interconnected nature of the many political and socioeconomic motives and interests on which the 1957 Rome Treaties were based.

Chapter 6 turns to the topic of decolonization and asks why the so-called colonial question continued to bedevil transatlantic relations throughout the 1950s, culminating in the 1956 Suez crisis. A mixture of different cultural attitudes, emotions, Cold War pressures, and divergent national interests are part of the answer. At the same time, the emerging global Cold War forced the transatlantic elite to grapple with questions of economic and political development, as well as with the strong wish of many newly independent nations not to be drawn into the East-West conflict.

Chapter 7 deals with a problem that essentially remained unsolved: the question of nuclear strategy and control within NATO. It shows that the Bilderberg meetings provided an important platform for the dissemination of expertise and strategic thinking on nuclear issues and a key venue for transnational criticism of the Eisenhower Administration's doctrine of massive retaliation. This became all the more important after the Sputnik shock of 1957 exposed the increasing vulnerability of the American mainland to Soviet nuclear attack.

Chapter 8 examines how the Bilderberg Group responded to President de Gaulle's return to power in 1958. The discussions about the relationship between the Inner Six of the European Communities – now united in a common market – and the rest of Europe uncovered disturbing challenges to the internationalist consensus of the informal alliance. The debate about the Kennedy Administration's ideas about a NATO defense strategy of flexible response provided further confirmation that nationalism (primarily in the shape of Gaullism) had returned to the European mainstream. The Bilderberg meetings reveal how the debate about the future of transatlantic relations became a struggle between competing concepts of how nations should cooperate.

Chapter 9 analyzes how this struggle culminated in the transatlantic crisis of 1963 (when President de Gaulle vetoed Great Britain's admission to the European Communities) and how it triggered a process of renewal within the Bilderberg Group itself. This process received further impetus from the Vietnam War, the rise of Goldwater conservatism in the United States, and the global upsurge of youth and student movements.

The conclusion returns to the question of the wider significance of the Bilderberg Group and the informal alliance in the history of transatlantic relations and attempts to explain why the Bilderberg Group has become a favorite object of so many conspiracy theories.

Notes

1 Villa d'Este Report, Box 23, Bilderberg Archives, NANL.
2 For the case of NATO, see Milloy, *The North Atlantic Treaty*.
3 See Van Vleck, "The 'Logic of the Air,'" and Zipp, "When Wendell Willkie Went Visiting."
4 For a recent study of the global mindset from the perspective of a number of leading public intellectuals in Europe and the United States and focusing on the 1940s, see Rosenboim, *The Emergence of Globalism*.
5 See the appendix for a list of all conferences and their agendas until 1968.
6 I will use the English 'Joseph' throughout this book, instead of the Polish Józef; this is what Retinger himself did during and after World War II, the period most important to this book.
7 See chapter 2.
8 On the concept of global identity, see Mazlish, *Reflections on the Modern*.
9 Exceptions are the (partly unpublished) works by Aubourg, Black, Bloemendal, Philipsen, Richardson, Wendt, and Wilson.
10 For reasons of narrative convenience, I use quotes from these reports and private notes as if they are direct quotes from the participants. In the case of the verbatim reports, this is of course true; in other cases, the actual wording/phrasing will have been slightly different, without changing the meaning of the contributions. Tapes of most meetings do exist but were not yet available during the research for this book. They will likely need to be restored and digitized before becoming accessible. Transcribing the tapes will be a massive – but I would argue worthwhile – undertaking.
11 Bilderberg participants and steering committee members are identified in the index by the years of their participation in the Bilderberg conferences.

1   Joseph Retinger – informal diplomat

Joseph Retinger was one of the most fascinating figures involved in international relations during the 20th century. During his lifetime, opinions about Retinger ran the gamut from hero to traitor. His friends nominated him for the Nobel Peace Prize and Denis de Rougemont called him the "spiritual father" and "midwife" of the Council of Europe.[1] Paul-Henri Spaak, himself one of Europe's founding fathers, described him as one of the "pioneers of Europe."[2] In stark contrast, his enemies accused him of being a secret agent for the British, the Soviets, the Mexicans, or the Jesuits.

The fact that Retinger's detractors have frequently tainted him with the brush of conspiracy is understandable, as we shall see, but it has had the unfortunate effect of deflecting attention from his real accomplishments and his innovative approach to international relations. Based on the existing evidence, the judgment on Retinger's more controversial activities – particularly during the two world wars – remains undecided. Yet very little credible evidence has emerged to substantiate accusations of spying and dubious loyalties.

Retinger's preferred methods of operation partly explain the abundance of conspiracy theories about him. Retinger's métier was *informal diplomacy*.[3] He never ran for public office, he held few official positions, and he lacked a traditional power base. His diplomatic tools consisted of high-level connections, a talent for personal persuasion, and the occasional bottle of vodka. He was at his most effective outside of the limelight, and he preferred operating in the dining rooms of Europe's finest restaurants and hotels. His footprint in the diplomatic archives is correspondingly small.[4] Arguably, however, his impact on both transatlantic relations and European integration was greater than that of many leading politicians and diplomats of his time. The reason for this was that Retinger's talent for informal diplomacy was particularly well suited to the fast changing post-1945 world of globalization, technological change, Atlantic alliance, and European integration.

Joseph Retinger was born in 1888, the son of a prominent Polish family in Cracow, Galicia. Galicia was part of the Austro-Hungarian Empire, but Retinger was raised as a Polish patriot and educated as a cosmopolitan European. The struggle for Polish independence was the central political cause of his life. Retinger studied at the Sorbonne in Paris and received a PhD in literature at the remarkable age of 20. With the help of his wealthy mentor and family friend Count Władysław Zamoyski, he became an active participant in Parisian high society, befriending André Gide, Maurice Ravel, Eric Satie, Francis Poulenc, and a number of influential political figures such as Marquis Boni de Castellane.

After further studies in Munich and a brief period back in Cracow as the publisher of a literary review, Retinger moved to London. There he worked for the Polish National Council, a small Galician organization working to advance the cause of Polish independence. Retinger published his first political treatise, an analysis of the relationship between Russia and Poland, and became a close friend of émigré-writer Joseph Conrad.[5] In August 1914, Retinger arranged Conrad's first return to Poland in 20 years. They used their visits to Cracow and Lviv to discuss Polish independence with religious and political leaders. Then the outbreak of the World War I forced them to make a hasty retreat. Although the details of his journey are sketchy, Retinger ended up in a French prison, having to rely on Count Zamoyski's contacts to get released.[6]

During the war, Retinger embarked on his first major mission as an informal diplomat. Using his access to high-placed British and French politicians such as H. H. Asquith, David Lloyd George, and Georges Clemenceau, as well as bombarding the British Foreign Office with plans for solving the Polish question – some of them co-authored by Conrad – Retinger convinced London and Paris to allow him to try to negotiate a separate peace with the Habsburg Austro-Hungarian Empire. Supported by Boni de Castellane, Prince Sixte de Bourbon, Lord Northcliffe (the British publisher of *The Times*), and leading Catholic officials, Retinger traveled back and forth between Paris, London, and Switzerland. In his memoirs, Retinger admits to the naïveté of these efforts given the complexities of the Polish situation. Different Polish factions and parties regarded him as too pro-Austrian or suspected him of being an agent for Britain or the Vatican. Conrad, however, expressed his admiration for Retinger's "… brilliant piece of work […] as an unofficial intermediary between the British and French Governments."[7]

The collapse of Retinger's efforts in 1917 left him severely depressed. His marriage dissolved, he started a disastrous affair with the American adventuress Jane Anderson, and he apparently even made a half-hearted suicide attempt.[8] Meanwhile, his opposition to the creation of a Polish exile army in France – which would destroy his hopes of solving the Polish question with the help of Austria – made him persona non grata in Great Britain and France. British diplomat Harold Nicolson noted in September 1918 that Retinger was likely "an international spy."[9]

Despite the failure of Retinger's informal diplomacy during the Great War, his remarkable talent for persuasion and gaining access to decision-making elites stands out, particularly considering his relative youth (he turned 26 in

1914). In terms of strength of personality and relentlessness in pursuit of new ideas and solutions, Retinger resembled another young European first catapulted to prominence during the war: the Frenchman Jean Monnet. Several decades later, their paths would cross in the struggle to unite Europe.

Immediately after World War I, Retinger acted as an advisor to the revolutionary government in Mexico. His role in opposing American oil companies operating in Mexico landed him in a series of American prisons in 1921.[10] A young American intelligence officer named J. Edgar Hoover noted that Retinger might have been a German spy during the war.[11] At some point, Retinger returned to London, married Stella Morel, the daughter of the leftist political philosopher E. D. Morel, and continued his involvement in Polish affairs. One of his political friends in this period was General Władysław Sikorski, who had served briefly as Poland's prime minister in the 1920s. In addition, Retinger was involved in the work of the international trade unions movement.[12]

1940–1945: Wartime diplomacy and the European idea

The outbreak of World War II propelled Retinger back onto the international stage. In June 1940, as German tanks rolled towards Paris, he convinced the British Air Ministry – probably with support from Prime Minister Winston Churchill – to provide him with a plane to rescue General Sikorski from the South of France.[13] Retinger succeeded in bringing Sikorski to London, where the general immediately met with Churchill. As soon as Sikorski became head of the Polish government-in-exile, he named Retinger his diplomatic counselor. In this function, Retinger maintained contacts with the British government and played a key role in negotiating the controversial Polish-Soviet Agreement of July 1941, acting as a translator during the many meetings between Sikorski and Foreign Secretary Anthony Eden. Retinger then briefly served as the first Polish chargé d'affaires in Moscow. Despite the fact that the 1941 agreement obliged Stalin to free all Polish prisoners-in-arms in the Soviet Union, many exiled Poles, united in their hatred of Russia, strongly opposed it.

The upheavals of war set off a global rethinking regarding the nature and future of international relations. New ideas about sovereignty, security, nationalism, and international cooperation found their way into the Atlantic Charter and a number of resistance manifestos in Europe and the colonial world. Wartime London, above all, served as a fertile breeding ground for new ideas, and Retinger was one of the central drivers of change.[14] In order to safeguard Poland's future independence and security, he proposed to establish regional blocs with the ultimate aim of a federated Europe. As he put it in his memoirs:

> In my frequent conversations with General Sikorski before the War,
> I pointed out the advantages for Poland of a federated Europe, and the

impossibility for a small country like Poland to live surrounded by jealous neighbours, since she would be unable to withstand any pressure that might be brought to bear on her by the two big Powers nearest her, Russia and Germany.[15]

In early 1941, Sikorski and Retinger initiated regular meetings with representatives of several other small European powers to discuss future cooperation. The Belgians – represented by Foreign Minister Paul-Henri Spaak, Marcel-Henri Jaspar, and Paul van Zeeland – were the first to show a strong interest in regional federations. The Czechoslovakian leadership, represented by Jan Masaryk, soon joined. By the fall of 1942, Sikorski and Retinger had set up an Inter-Allied Committee on postwar issues for the Polish, Belgian, Dutch, Greek, Norwegian, and Czechoslovakian governments-in-exile. Retinger was the linchpin of these efforts. As Spaak remembered in his memoirs:

> An intelligent, active and slightly mysterious individual, he would have luncheon every day with one British politician or another, or with a member of one of the governments in exile. He knew everybody and no door was closed to him.[16]

Retinger's initiative gave an important boost to the idea of Europe during the war. One indirect result was the postwar Benelux Union, which Spaak had first discussed with Eelco van Kleffens, the Dutch foreign minister, and Pieter Kerstens, the Dutch minister of trade, at Retinger's table.[17] Another result was that, as Retinger put it in his memoirs,

> [t]he Foreign Ministers' meetings, although not publicized, created great interest in Great Britain and America. One of the Americans particularly interested was Mr. John Foster Dulles [....]. I remember spending several hours with him and discussing not only Polish affairs, but also the general idea of the unity of Europe.[18]

The British, however, were afraid of anything that risked complicating their difficult relationship with the Soviet Union. Because the Polish plans were clearly directed not only against future German aggression, but also against possible Soviet meddling in Central European affairs, Soviet diplomats communicated Moscow's concerns to London. As a result, Foreign Secretary Anthony Eden repeatedly warned General Sikorski about the implications of his proposals in terms of relations with the Soviet Union and refused to give strong British support.[19]

As part of their efforts to win support for the Polish government-in-exile and the Polish resistance, Retinger and Sikorski traveled to Washington, D.C. in March 1942. Despite his earlier dealings with American law enforcement, Retinger managed to meet with a number of influential members of the Roosevelt Administration, including W. Averell Harriman and Adolf Berle Jr. In Retinger's telling, his discussions with Berle resulted in a phone call to President Roosevelt and the promise of $12 million in annual assistance to the Polish resistance. Two weeks after their return to London, the American Ambassador to Poland, Anthony Drexel Biddle Jr., showed up with a suitcase containing the first 2 million in cash.[20]

Following General Sikorski's death in a plane crash in July 1943, Retinger lost much of his influence in the Polish government-in-exile. His conservative enemies resurrected old spying stories and suggested that he was a Soviet agent. Despite these attempts to discredit him, in late 1943 Retinger managed to persuade the new Polish Prime Minister, Stanisław Mikołajczyk, to send him on a secret mission to Poland for discussions with the Polish underground. Retinger felt that he could be useful in establishing closer contacts between the government-in-exile in London and local Polish resistance leaders in order to plan for Poland's future. He also felt that these leaders needed to be convinced of the need for cooperation with Soviet forces once the Red Army had crossed the Polish border. This was a highly fraught issue given the revelation, earlier in 1943, of the Katyn massacre and the subsequent breaking-off of relations between Moscow and the Polish government-in-exile. Retinger felt, however, that the Polish should be pragmatic, particularly in view of the fact that the British were unlikely to support any anti-Soviet action taken by the Polish underground or government-in-exile.

Prime Minister Mikołajczyk told Marek Celt, the young Polish officer chosen to accompany Retinger, that Retinger was the right man for the mission because "he has a lot of important English friends; they trust him, they'll believe without reservation whatever he tells them about the state of the Underground in Poland."[21] Of course, Retinger's closeness to British decision-makers also meant that anything he heard from the Polish underground would likely be shared with the British government. Mikołajczyk did not believe that Retinger was a British agent, but he did order Celt to warn the Polish resistance leadership not to tell Retinger anything they did not want the British to hear.[22]

British historians Stephen Dorril and Norman Davies have interpreted Retinger's airdrop over Poland in April 1944 as proof that he was indeed a British agent, employed by the Special Operations Executive (SOE), yet they provide no evidence for their claims.[23] It is far more likely that Retinger, supported by Mikołajczyk, used his excellent connections with SOE – whose director, Major-General Colin Gubbins, had been deeply involved in Polish affairs and considered Retinger a friend – to organize the jump over Polish territory. Moreover, because of the crucial role the British government would play in any postwar settlement, Retinger closely coordinated his plans with the Foreign Office.[24]

A recent study of Retinger's mission based on British Foreign Office records confirms that it was Retinger who approached Frank Roberts, the acting head of the Foreign Office's Central Bureau, and Anthony Eden to win their support. Eden was hesitant at first because he did not "entirely trust M. Retinger." However, Roberts managed to convince his superiors that Retinger's mission served a useful purpose and Eden agreed to meet with Retinger as a result.[25] After the war, Roberts told Harold Macmillan that Retinger had played "a helpful and certainly an important role in Anglo-Polish relations before and even after General Sikorski's death. He certainly showed great personal courage in being dropped by parachute into Poland to make a personal report on conditions there."[26]

Retinger's parachute jump over enemy territory was indeed risky. He was probably the oldest, and certainly the least fit, parachutist of the entire war. Yet he somehow managed to land in Poland without serious injury, met with most of the Polish resistance leadership, and avoided arrest by the Gestapo. He even survived an assassination attempt by opponents within the Polish Home Army, who tried to poison him.[27] Retinger ended up being partly paralyzed, but made it out of Poland alive and immediately briefed Mikołajczyk and the British government.[28]

Retinger and the European Movement

During their weeks of waiting in Italy, before weather conditions allowed for their long-distance flight to Poland to proceed, Retinger had told his companion Marek Celt that he collected two things: "people and world records." Even if he joked about his collection of world records – being the youngest Sorbonne PhD graduate was one – he was certainly serious about collecting people. A keen observer of human psychology, Retinger kept a little notebook with "people's characteristics" and spent much of his time and energy managing his network of friends.[29]

One of his admirers, the Italian diplomat Pietro Quaroni, described Retinger's method as follows:

> One succumbed to his personality without noticing it, irresistibly. He was steadfast in his friendships, as he was in his dislikes. He inspired confidence. Firstly by his discretion. He was no doubt one of the best-informed people in the world, and his views on all problems, big and small, were very reliable and realistic, based on concrete data.[30]

Or as *The Observer* put it:

> He was one of those international figures who have ideas and a genius for finding the means to carry them out. A great joker, he had a cigarette perpetually drooping from his lip, never ate a sausage but seemed to live on whiskey and soda.[31]

Access to the right people had been the basis of Retinger's influence during the war. After the war, he continued to expand his network of contacts and friends, traveling widely across Europe and the United States. His method of informal diplomacy turned out to be particularly well suited to the rapid expansion of *transnational* organizations working towards a more united Europe in the immediate postwar era.[32] This transnationalization of efforts to integrate Europe opened up new channels of influence for people like Retinger, and he jumped at the opportunity.

Retinger publicly outlined his views of a more stable postwar order in Europe during a speech at Chatham House on May 7, 1946. His lifelong goal of Polish independence remained a key concern to him. Having traveled to Poland immediately after the end of the war, Retinger had witnessed the communist takeover of power and had been forced to leave the country. At Chatham House, he warned of the emerging Cold War, arguing that

> the complacency of some of the Big Powers and the rivalries between them have led to the division, in fact if not in theory, of the Continent into two zones of influence and thus sewn the seed, perhaps, of a much greater conflict.

Unless Europe wished to become an "appendage to the Russian empire" or "a free market for Anglo-Saxon expansion," it had to "create a free Continent, economically cohesive and politically unified."[33] It is clear that Retinger regarded such a united Europe as a possible 'third force' between the Soviet Union and the United States – not in the sense of a neutralist Europe but in the sense of a Europe strong and independent enough to overcome the division of the continent in Soviet and American 'zones of influence.'

Not long after his Chatham House speech, Retinger met with Paul van Zeeland in Brussels and made plans to create a European League for Economic Cooperation (ELEC).[34] The League aimed to overcome the economic policies of autarky and protectionism, which had dominated Europe in the 1930s. By increasing economic interdependence within Europe – with the ultimate aim of one large European market – the organizers hoped to pave the way for future political initiatives. Retinger traveled throughout Europe to help set up local sections of ELEC. Sir Harold Butler agreed to chair the British section, which also included Retinger's old SOE friend Major-General Colin Gubbins, as well as leading industrialists and politicians such as Edward Beddington-Behrens, Harold Macmillan, Walter Layton, and Peter Thorneycroft. Daniel Serruys organized the French section and brought in Michel Debré, Edmond Giscard d'Estaing, André Voisin, and others. Pieter Kerstens took charge of the Dutch section.

Retinger did not want to limit the League's efforts to Western Europe. He worked hard to involve Eastern European countries as well, but was thwarted by Moscow's refusal to cooperate. Retinger and Van Zeeland did manage to find considerable backing for ELEC in the United States.

Retinger found Harriman, who served briefly as US ambassador in London, willing to support him. "As a stateless Pole," Retinger remembered,

> I naturally had difficulties in getting an American visa, but Averell Harriman was my sponsor and arranged my visit. He strongly believed in European unification and as Secretary of Commerce and later head of the European Co-operation Administration was responsible for the tremendous support the United States gave to this idea.[35]

Retinger organized an American section under the chairmanship of Adolf Berle Jr., and a number of prominent bankers and businessmen, including Nelson and David Rockefeller, agreed to join.

Retinger was convinced that American support for a united Europe was essential. Accordingly, ELEC's first public initiative consisted of a pamphlet and resolution in support of the European Recovery Program (ERP), which General George Marshall had announced in June 1947. The memorandum stressed the need for the establishment of a European planning board with executive powers and for the reduction of trade barriers.[36] In the following years, ELEC organized several expert conferences and working groups concerning trade liberalization, currency convertibility, and institutional possibilities for European economic cooperation.[37] ELEC's studies on convertibility helped lay the groundwork for the creation of the important European Payments Union in 1950, which did much to stimulate intra-European trade.[38]

In December 1947, Retinger cofounded the Joint International Committee of the Movements for European Unity, an umbrella organization for ELEC, Churchill's United Europe Movement (UEM), the Christian Democratic *Nouvelles Équipes Internationales* (NEI), and several other European organizations. Together with UEM's Duncan Sandys, Churchill's son-in-law, Retinger set out to organize the Congress of Europe at The Hague in May 1948.[39] By all accounts, the Congress was a real turning point in European history. It brought together an impressive group of leading Europeans, including Churchill, Spaak, Paul Ramadier, Paul Reynaud, and Konrad Adenauer, and it received wide coverage in the European press.[40] Retinger firmly believed in the importance of influencing public opinion by means of political, intellectual, and cultural elites. In his view, the Congress had succeeded admirably in doing so: "[it] received enormous publicity and the participants, once dispersed, added to it further and confirmed its impact. As a result the idea of Europe was strikingly brought to the attention of public opinion."[41]

In his memoirs, Retinger claimed that "[a]t The Hague we laid the foundations for all that was to mark the progress of the European Idea in the next decade."[42] Even if this was perhaps somewhat of an overstatement, the Congress did agree to a number of important resolutions, which later found expression in the Council of Europe, the European Convention on Human

Rights, the College of Europe in Bruges, and the European Cultural Center in Geneva. Churchill called the Congress a "milestone," and in the words of the German historian of European integration Wilfried Loth, "[...] the transnational societal consensus on which the later European Communities would rest had become palpable for the first time."[43]

In the wake of the Congress, the Joint International Committee was changed into the European Movement (EM), with Retinger and Sandys acting as secretary-general and president, respectively, of its international committee, and Spaak, Churchill, Léon Blum (leader of the French socialists), and Italian Prime Minister Alcide de Gasperi serving as honorary presidents. Retinger and Sandys worked hard to transform the resolutions of The Hague into reality. Retinger personally met with a large number of European prime ministers, presidents, and parliamentary leaders to keep the momentum going.[44] He focused in particular on the governments of the Brussels Treaty powers (France, the United Kingdom and the Benelux countries had signed a defensive pact in 1948), hoping that they would take the lead. In addition, national delegations of the newly formed EM petitioned parliaments across Europe to take action.

In a letter to Harriman, Retinger emphasized the importance of informal diplomacy. "[P]rivate and independent activities for the Unity of Europe," he wrote,

> are extremely important at this stage, as Governments by definition, especially when they are democratic, must be over cautious and rather timid in dealing with great initiatives in the domain of International policy. We obviously want to go further than the Governments can and to pave the way for the effective Unity of Europe.[45]

In August 1948, Ramadier agreed to present a proposal drafted by Sandys and Retinger to the French government.[46] As a result, French Foreign Minister Robert Schuman officially proposed the creation of a European parliamentary assembly later that year. The British Labour government, however, in what was to become a recurring feature of European negotiations, was unwilling to agree to any sharing of sovereignty. Foreign Secretary Ernest Bevin expressed a preference for intergovernmental modes of cooperation and countered with a plan for a European ministerial council.

Throughout the tricky negotiations that followed, Retinger played an important role as an informal troubleshooter and mediator. One typical episode appears in his memoirs. In October 1948, the Brussels Treaty powers had agreed to form a study group to devise a compromise between the British and French positions. The study group was chaired by Édouard Herriot and included EM members such as Léon Blum, Paul Reynaud, and Pieter Kerstens; on the British side, Hugh Dalton and Sir Gladwyn Jebb were involved. Before the first official meeting of the study group, Retinger decided to bring the heads of delegations together for an informal lunch in Paris. As he put it, "[...] I thought it would be helpful if a friendly atmosphere prevailed among the delegates right from the start of these difficult negotiations. In this we succeeded [...]."[47]

Other contemporary observers (and, it should be noted, friends of Retinger) confirmed Retinger's impact. In the words of Pietro Quaroni,

> It is difficult to imagine all that Retinger did to clear away the stumbling-blocks – arranging meetings between the English and the French, coaxing one side, pleading with the other! In one week, I remember, he travelled four times between London and Paris with proposals from one country to the other. And he succeeded. If the great "stars" of Europe will forgive me [...] I cannot help feeling that if the Council of Europe got on to its feet, a great deal of credit must go to the modest, silent endeavours of Dr. Retinger.[48]

Denis de Rougemont likewise emphasized the importance of Retinger's informal diplomacy, calling him the "midwife of the Council of Europe."[49]

By May 1949, the Brussels Treaty powers, joined by Denmark, Ireland, Italy, Norway, and Sweden, agreed to the creation of the Council of Europe in Strasbourg, with a Consultative Assembly responsible to a Committee of Ministers. Greece and Turkey joined three months later, to be followed by Iceland and the Federal Republic of Germany in 1950.

Transnational Europe

Even if the Council of Europe never fulfilled the initial hopes of Retinger and others, these early steps towards a more united Europe did pave the way for future developments in European integration, including the European Coal and Steel Community (ECSC) founded in 1950, and the 1957 Rome Treaties establishing the European Atomic Energy Community (Euratom) and the European Economic Community (EEC). The Congress of Europe, the Consultative Assembly meetings in Strasbourg, and several subsequent large EM conferences all nurtured a new sense of commitment to the idea of uniting Europe, particularly among a number of European leaders who would later play pivotal roles in creating the European Communities.[50]

As Paul-Henri Spaak recalled in his memoirs,

> Between 1949 and 1954 I devoted myself unreservedly to the cause of European unity and wrote a large number of articles in its support. I made speeches in all the member countries of the Council of Europe. This was a time of lively activity and genuine enthusiasm. My friends and I were convinced that we were fighting for a cause that merited our absolute devotion.[51]

Harold Macmillan wrote about his experience in the Consultative Assembly in similar terms: "[...] we met in a real atmosphere of spiritual excitement. We really felt convinced that we could found a new order in the Old World – democratic, free, progressive, destined to restore prosperity and peace."[52]

The result was a vast increase in transnational contacts and the establishment of a transnational European public sphere – or, to use Macmillan's phrase, a "sounding board" for Europe.[53] Within this European public sphere, debates about questions such as supranational versus intergovernmental or political versus economic integration served to crystallize trends and to provide greater clarity on what was achievable and what not.

Harry Price, author of an early official history of the Marshall Plan, was one of the first to recognize this: "[The Council] furnished [...] a useful channel for continuing intergovernmental deliberations on further measures in the direction of political integration. Its chambers served as a forum for the discussion and clarification of the Schuman Plan."[54] Another case in point was the deeply entrenched British (and Scandinavian) reluctance to commit to the sharing of sovereignty, which became apparent during the long discussions at Strasbourg and which convinced many continental European leaders by late 1951 to concentrate on the Europe of the Six in the hope of bringing the United Kingdom in later. When the British Conservatives returned to power in October 1951 and turned out not to be any more willing to engage in supranational adventures than their Labour predecessors – despite Churchill's important contributions to the EM – people like Spaak resolved to focus their efforts on 'little Europe.'

A further critical feature of the EM and the Council of Europe was that they transcended not just borders but also political parties and ideological divides. To Retinger, nonpartisanship came naturally; he routinely dealt with political leaders from all sections of the political spectrum. But it remains an interesting peculiarity of European integration that both the ECSC and the Rome Treaties were created by politicians who would not normally have sat comfortably at the same table. Two of the main architects of the Rome Treaties, Konrad Adenauer and Guy Mollet, for example, were a conservative German Christian Democrat and a left-wing French socialist.[55] The early phase of European integration had given politicians such as these opportunities to get to know each other, or, at least, to know where others stood on the question of supranational European cooperation. Thus, they developed a greater sensibility for each other's standpoints and backgrounds.

The relative seclusion of Strasbourg – which did not have a large international airport – meant that the long Assembly sessions forced participants to spend much time together. As Macmillan remembered:

> In Strasbourg there were few distractions. We lived together in the Assembly or its committees during many working hours. In our leisure, we shared an agreeable atmosphere of social recreation and informal discussion. During the three years that I sat on this body I got to know almost every distinguished personality in Europe.[56]

As it happened, many of the connections and friendships forged in the Assembly and in the EM would later play an important part in the Bilderberg meetings.

In a similar way, the EM brought together a large number of private organizations and figures from different societal backgrounds, including religious organizations, trade unions, youth groups, and other non-state actors. Retinger called this the "Europe of the people," and, in the words of John Pomian,

> attached great importance to it, for it was in keeping with his understanding of the process of history. Religious, cultural, economic and social forces are more stable than the often ephemeral political ones and in the long run equally, if not more, effective in shaping the course of events.[57]

Retinger remained secretary-general of the EM until April 1952.[58] In this period, he helped set up the European Youth Campaign (EYC) and was deeply involved in the work of the European Cultural Center in Geneva. He also remained active in the Eastern and Central European Commission within the EM, which he had set up with Macmillan with the aim of keeping the European nations beyond the Iron Curtain involved in European affairs.[59] In the first half of 1950, moreover, Retinger was deeply involved in the crisis of leadership concerning Duncan Sandys. Sandys' leadership at the EM was criticized as 'dictatorial' and his reluctance to keep pace with federalist plans led to resentment on the part of continental organizations such as the Union of European Federalists (UEF). In late summer, Sandys agreed to step aside, and Spaak, assisted by Retinger, took over the helm at the EM.[60]

American connections

In the summer of 1948, Retinger and Sandys had traveled to New York City to gain US backing for the new movement. They succeeded in convincing Allen Dulles, the wartime Swiss director of the Office of Strategic Services (OSS), to support the EM. At the time, Dulles had been involved in setting up a committee to support Count Richard Coudenhove-Kalergi's European federalist organization, but the success of the Congress of Europe induced him to shift his support to the EM. Dulles and George Franklin Jr., the director of the New York-based Council on Foreign Relations (CFR), were instrumental in creating the American Committee on United Europe (ACUE) in early 1949.[61] General William Donovan, former head of the OSS, was willing to become its chairman. Franklin served as secretary of ACUE, and General Donovan convinced Thomas Braden, another former OSS operative with close ties to the European resistance movements, to become ACUE's executive director.

ACUE's list of board members reads like a 'who's who' of the US state-private network engaged in responding to the escalating Cold War.[62] Among the people involved were General Lucius D. Clay, David Dubinsky, Arthur Goldberg, George Nebolsine, General Walter Bedell Smith, Charles M. Spofford, and Arnold J. Zurcher. A number of ACUE members ended up serving in important positions at the US Central Intelligence Agency (CIA) after Smith became its director in October 1950. Smith recruited Dulles to become Deputy Director for Plans, and in 1951 Dulles asked Braden to join the agency as well.

The ACUE served two functions. First, it engaged in a range of public and lobbying activities to win support for European unity in the United States. Second, the ACUE responded to an urgent request for financial support by Sandys with a fund-raising campaign set off by a speech and dinner with Churchill in March 1949.[63] Initially, the ACUE relied on private contributions from wealthy supporters, such as Max Ascoli, the publisher of *The Reporter*; Nelson and David Rockefeller; and Walter Washington. The Rockefeller Brothers Fund also contributed $10,000 in August 1950.[64] In the period from February 1949 to October 1951, the ACUE raised a little over $200,000 in private contributions, about half of which had been passed on directly to a number of European organizations, including the EM.[65] The French-based European Council of Vigilance was another major recipient. At some point, the US government stepped in to provide more substantial funding for the EM's EYC.[66]

Although the details of the Truman Administration's financial support for the EM remain murky, many historians have jumped to the conclusion that ACUE was in fact a CIA front organization. The first account of CIA funding for the EM emerged in a sensationalist article published by the British magazine *Time Out* in 1975 in the midst of a British referendum campaign on EEC membership.[67] The only source for the article was a decade-old dissertation on the early years of the EM written by F. X. Rebattet, the son of EM official Georges Rebattet. In the 1990s, the British historian Richard Aldrich picked up the trail and published several influential articles on ACUE.[68] Although Aldrich uncovered valuable new information based on his extensive research in US archives, the Rebattet dissertation again turned out to be the main source for his far-reaching claims about ACUE's CIA connections. As Aldrich put it, "[...] it is the remarkable work of Rebattet, with unparalleled access to European Movement documentation, that confirms that most ACUE funds originated with the CIA."[69]

Rebattet's dissertation, in fact, does no such thing. Based solely on European archives, Rebattet's history of the EM argues convincingly that the Truman Administration stepped in to provide major funding for mainly the EM's EYC (£440,080 – around $1,2 million – in the period from May 1951 to May 1953). However, according to Rebattet, "[t]he resources of the European Youth Campaign came from the American Committee on United Europe which acted in this case as a covering organisation for the American State Department."[70] Aldrich's claim, moreover, that "[t]he CIA had its greatest impact on the European Movement in 1949 and 1950" is not supported by any documentary evidence.[71]

A more likely timeline, supported by evidence from the EM archives, ACUE records, and official US documents, suggests that secret US government funding did not start until late 1951, when the EYC, which had been founded in the summer of 1951, really got going.[72] During the first half of 1951, the ACUE's financial support for the EM remained fairly limited. As Braden told Georges Rebattet in March 1951, total ACUE funding for the EM from August 1950 to August 1951 was projected to be $25,000, a relatively modest amount compared to the $1,2 million provided for the EYC in a two-year period.[73] ACUE funding for the EM picked up during the second half of the year and totaled $61,011 for 1951 as a whole.[74]

Moreover, in 1952, the year that the EYC picked up steam, Spaak decided

> that funds from American sources that had previously been used wholly for the ordinary budget of the International Secretariat of E.M. because they were only a small part of total receipts, would in future be used for specific activities for which special budgets would be opened outside the ordinary budget of E.M.[75]

The "secret State Department funds" mentioned by Rebattet were in all likelihood Marshall Plan counterpart funds, which were used by both the European Cooperation Agency (ECA) and by the Office of Policy Coordination (OPC), an independent outfit within the CIA engaged in covert psychological warfare and paramilitary operations.[76]

Pomian suggests as much in Retinger's memoirs, and Retinger indeed worked with ECA officials on a number of projects.[77] In early 1951, for example, Retinger told Braden that he had met with Roscoe Drummond, the director of ECA's European Information Division in Paris, "and finally arranged the way they will help on our publications on European unity."[78] A few weeks later he asked Braden to "tell the General that Roscoe Drummond is working very loyally and very helpfully with us to the satisfaction, I hope, of both parties."[79] Further evidence for ECA's involvement comes from an early official history of American psychological warfare, which shows that the "ECA also sponsored national youth movements to counter Communist success in this field. In 1950, a European youth organization was fostered to counter-balance the proposed Communist Youth festival for Berlin in 1951."[80]

Of course, ECA, OPC, CIA, and other agencies worked closely together on these matters. As early as February 1949, Retinger had asked his wartime friend Anthony Drexel Biddle Jr. to arrange a meeting at the CIA. Biddle told CIA Director Roscoe Hillenkoetter that as secretary-general of the EM, Retinger had "excellent contacts." Retinger met with the deputy director of the CIA and it was noted that he had "a suggested plan which may be of interest to OSO [the Office of Special Operations] and/or OPC."[81] It is unclear whether the CIA took any action, but a year later, in February 1950, the head of OPC, Frank Wisner, discussed "Dr. Rettinger [sic] and European union" with Hillenkoetter and requested "for permission to brief Harriman et al."[82] Hillenkoetter asked the FBI to check for a file on "Rettinger," and was told there was none.

Wisner then informed W. Averell Harriman, ECA's Special Representative in Europe: "we are presently working on an overall project that will seek to promote Western European political integration with ECA support." Wisner asked for Harriman's guidance on which organizations or individuals to support. Harriman made clear that in his opinion, the EM was "by far the most effective organ for promoting the political union of Europe" and that Coudenhove-Kalergi's group was "practically non-existent." Yet Wisner worried that pinning all hopes on the EM might backfire and mentioned the possibility of supporting people like the pro-European British Labour party member Ronald MacKay and member organizations of the EM like the European Union of Federalists, ELEC, the *Nouvelles Équipes Internationales*, and the Socialist Movement for the United States of Europe.

As Wisner put it, "were we to select the European Movement as the single instrument through which to support unity, would we not risk of confirming the domination of the unity movement by those advocating a slow approach to the problem?" Wisner clearly favored a more federalist approach and noted that the EM was "dominated for the most part by those, including some prominent Britains [sic], who advocate the functional (slow and step-by-step) approach to unity."[83] Harriman's response is unknown, but it seems likely that he shared Wisner's views and no immediate action was taken.

After it became clear that Spaak would take over from Sandys in the summer of 1950, however, these concerns no longer weighed as heavily. "Between us," Braden now told Dulles,

> General Donovan and I talked with Mr. Harriman, Mr. Katz and Roscoe Drummond. When we told them the news about Spaak, they thought that E.C.A. would be prepared to give help previously withheld because of concern over the leadership of the Movement.[84]

It wasn't until early 1951, however, that Spaak and Retinger had a new secretariat in Brussels fully up and running.[85]

In addition to his contacts with ECA and OPC/CIA officials, Retinger decided to ask the US High Commissioner for Germany (HICOG) John McCloy for support for a youth campaign.[86] As High Commissioner, McCloy controlled Marshall Plan funds in Germany and was deeply involved in psychological warfare operations.[87] In early 1951, one of his top concerns was the upcoming World Youth Festival in East Berlin, a massive undertaking bringing together 1.5 million young people over the summer.[88] The American response to the World Youth Festival is important for understanding why the Truman Administration decided to support Retinger's plans for a EYC.

Initially, HICOG and OPC operations in Germany had predominantly consisted of paramilitary training and stay-behind organizations, but after the outbreak of the Korean War in June 1950, a larger campaign of covert political and psychological warfare commenced.[89] One key aim of this campaign was to strengthen anti-communist organizations and attitudes in Germany and Europe. OPC and HICOG activities ranged from sending the Boston Philharmonic on a trip through Europe to giving financial support to non-communist trade unions, political parties, student organizations, and the Congress for Cultural Freedom (CCF).[90] One of OPC's largest operations was the funding, through the National Committee for a Free Europe, of Radio Liberty and Radio Free Europe, with their European headquarters in Munich.[91]

The importance of the Korean War as a turning point for the United States' psychological warfare strategy is evident in HICOG files.[92] Two months after the outbreak of the conflict, McCloy reported to the State Department: "[the] entire HICOG headquarters has been devoting major efforts and attention to up-swelling anti-Soviet campaign [...]" As part of this campaign, he wrote, US officials were working with "publishers and other civic leaders, including youth and women leaders, with [a] view to strengthening [the] German anti-Communist propaganda effort."[93]

European unity now turned out to be an attractive theme for US anti-communist propaganda. A united Europe stood for peace, economic progress, and freedom; it allowed for a *positive* anti-communist message and the kind of "program for positive Western objectives" that McCloy wanted. Recently declassified CIA documents show that a number of covert US operations in Germany in the early 1950s indeed focused on European unity. One recipient of American funds was the German *Europa Union*, a member of the EM.[94] Another was the *Gesellschaft Freies Europa*, an organization close to the Christian Democratic Union (CDU) of Germany and headed by Chancellor Konrad Adenauer's public relations chief Otto Lenz. A briefing for CIA Director Walter Bedell Smith made clear that financing for the *Gesellschaft* was "part of campaign to bring favourable notice of the Schuman Plan to every level of German life [...]"[95]

European unity was particularly appealing to a young generation that had grown up in times of war and economic devastation.[96] Therefore, Europe played a major role in HICOG's response to the youth rally in East Berlin in the summer of 1951. McCloy reported that

> In addition to Europa Zug and Marshall Plan exhibit at ERP pavilion, ECA will definitely: (a) Feature free films in George C. Marshall House, (b) distribute 200,000 copies each of satirical pamphlet (Wir Brauchen Keinen Marshall Plan) contrasting econ[omic] conditions in [the] Sov[iet] Zone and [the] Fed[eral] Rep[ublic] and of ERP pamphlet on Berlin (Berlin Baut Auf) [...][97]

In addition, McCloy favored holding a plebiscite in Berlin on European unity. Such plebiscites had been organized in several German cities and had received much positive attention. The Frenchman Jean Moreau, one of the organizers behind this campaign, would later become the first head of the EYC.

McCloy was satisfied with the "global campaign to counteract and discredit [the] Communist World Youth Festival." Yet he reported to the State Department and ECA that much more needed to be done. Of the World Youth Festival, he said,

> It was a mammoth effort and [if] repeated without any opportunity to counter it, the likelihood that a strong core of youthful adherents will be established by such methods is just as certain as the fact that the Nazis were able to do as much.[98]

In this context, it comes as no surprise that Retinger's plan for a EYC found a receptive audience at HICOG.

Meanwhile, Retinger began telling his partners at ACUE of his new focus on Europe's youth. In March 1951, he informed Braden about plans for a large rally: "we shall have about 50,000 youngsters present and make a really big show out of it."[99] A few weeks later, Retinger added,

> I believe that in a few days' time I shall be able to write you very interesting news about our relations with McCloy and Katz [Milton Katz, ECA special representative in Paris] whom we are meeting in a few days.

Not long thereafter, the EYC was up and running, and Retinger was back to his familiar role of traveling across Europe to convince governments to support it.[100]

Over a period of eight years, the EYC would receive significant US funding, channeled through ACUE, and organize a wide range of conferences, workshops, and other activities. Paul G. Hoffman (who became de facto chairman of ACUE in 1955 as Donovan's health declined) continued to believe that this support was important in later years. In 1957, he wrote,

> The European Movement and the Youth Campaign, which have helped keep alive and vibrant the concept of a united Europe, and to which the Committee has contributed the bulk of its funds, have assured a political climate which has made easier the ratification of the Common Market and Euratom treaties.[101]

The success of the European Communities finally led to the suspension of ACUE's activities in 1960.

So, what does all this mean for the question of the CIA's involvement in ACUE and the EM? The answer is both more complex and more speculative than the existing CIA front explanations.[102] The ACUE undoubtedly had excellent connections to the emerging US intelligence world; after all, the CIA recruited some of its top talent from ACUE. But there is no indication that

ACUE was created by the CIA as a front organization. Moreover, official American backing for EM programs such as the EYC did not start until after the outbreak of the Korean War, and the money likely came from ECA counterpart funds. Based on the available evidence, it is difficult to tell where, when, and by whom exactly the decision to support the EYC was made. One possible scenario is that HICOG (McCloy) and ECA (Katz) agreed to pay for the EYC, while OPC was responsible for delivering the money from counterpart funds – known internally as 'candy' – to the ACUE.[103] This would tally with Braden's recollection that one day a banker with the irresistible name of Pinky Johnson showed up at the ACUE offices with $75,000 in cash.[104] It also fits with Wisner's 1950 memorandum to Harriman describing OPC plans to start promoting European unity with ECA support.

ACUE was obviously so closely aligned with the US government that it was willing to go along with any scheme to provide covert funding for the EYC (as well as other special EM campaigns and projects later in the decade). What remains unclear, however, is to what extent – if any – ACUE followed directions from the CIA or other agencies on how to spend the money. Revelations of CIA funding often imply a high level of CIA control over its 'front organizations.' Most studies of the Congress for Cultural Freedom have noted, however, that the CIA had little say in its day-to-day business.[105] The EM itself, meanwhile, attempted to separate secret US financing of the EYC and other campaigns from its regular budget. In fact, the EM struggled to survive financially in the mid-1950s.[106]

Retinger did not much care about distinguishing between different US departments and agencies. In typical fashion, he established contact with everyone he deemed capable of helping his cause: with McCloy at HICOG; with Harriman, Drummond, and Katz at ECA; and with Wisner at OPC. Retinger did not mind accepting secret US funds, but he must have been aware of their drawbacks. With the benefit of hindsight, it is evident that the EM made a significant mistake in accepting them – despite the desperate need for funds. Ever since the funding was inevitably exposed, both historians and a variety of anti-European conspiracy theorists have used this episode to argue that the CIA played a much larger role in 'creating Europe' than the agency in reality did.

In addition, ACUE's assistance came with certain strings attached. Donovan and Braden, for example, were deeply involved in the campaign to replace Sandys with Spaak in 1950.[107] In early 1951, moreover, they aggressively pushed the EM to denounce any connection with an Atlantic Union declaration proposed by Count Coudenhove-Kalergi. They explained that US public opinion would not look favorably upon any plans for an Atlantic Union until much more progress was made at the European side. When the EM did not immediately respond, Braden wrote an angry letter to Rebattet, asking "What the hell are you doing about it? Let me know at once."[108] Such heavy-handed tactics – supported by the implied threat of withholding further financial support – must have caused resentment on the part of the EM.

By the spring of 1952, Retinger decided that the EM had lost much of its earlier effectiveness, and he stepped down as secretary-general of the EM's international committee, although he continued to support the movement as a general delegate. The British blockade against any supranational political initiatives was an important reason for the EM's loss of momentum. The realization that Churchill's return to power had not led to a fundamental change in the British attitude caused much soul-searching on the part of the continental members of the EM. The Schuman Plan and the proposal for a European Defense Community now shifted the focal point of European integration to the Europe of the Six.

Retinger believed that the EM had moved too strongly in this direction and was unhappy to witness the weakening of the movement's national councils in Great Britain and Scandinavia. In a long conversation with Macmillan in early 1952, he explained his concerns. Macmillan's summary of Retinger's *tour d'horizon* is worth quoting in full:

> Unless England takes the lead, [Retinger argued,] there will be a gradual weakening of European morale and the will to resist. ... '[I]f we [i.e., the British, TWG] take the lead, the British Empire-European bloc can be made independent of American and Russia – a real and beneficent third force. Then a deal can be made and he is convinced that Russia will give in without war – even to the extent of retiring to her frontiers. Nothing could be a greater guarantee to Russia than the emergence of a Europe-Empire group *not* subservient to America. The Russians are absolutely convinced that Britain and Europe are as much satellite states as her own [...]
>
> 'Churchill understands all this – but is too old to break through the prison of English tradition. Eden understands it not so well, but he is too ambitious for the succession (the only thing he thinks about) to risk any bold policy. He is a prematurely aged man. He had moments of genius during the war. Now he is very conventional. He is not sure of himself. This is why he is so jealous. He is an aging woman, with a morbid fear of any younger or more attractive rival.
>
> War is almost certain, unless Britain leads Europe. The Americans have the wealth and the material power – but they have no experience and no patience.

Macmillan "thought it a pretty shrewd summary of the world situation – and a pretty frightening one."[109]

In the face of Britain's continued inaction, Retinger now decided to shift his focus to transatlantic relations. He remained convinced, however, of the overall accomplishments of the EM, writing in 1954:

> The main achievement of the European Movement and the Movements of which it is composed rests on the fact that the idea of the unity of Europe was lifted from the sphere of Utopian dreams into that of a practical reality.[110]

Looking back at the early phase of European integration, there can be little doubt that Retinger's informal diplomacy made a significant contribution to the lifting of dreams into reality.

Notes

1 Retinger was nominated in 1954. See Paul Rijkens to Prince Bernhard, August 20, 1954, Box 186, Bilderberg Archives, NATH. Rougemont, "Esquisse d'une biographie," 480.
2 Spaak, *Combats inachevés*, 24.
3 On the importance of informal or private diplomacy, see the *New Global Studies* 2014 special issue (Vol. 8, no. 1), guest edited by Giles Scott-Smith; in particular, the introduction and article by Scott-Smith and the articles by Johannes Großmann and Albertine Bloemendal. See also the important recent book by Dino Knudsen on the Trilateral Commission: Knudsen, *The Trilateral Commission*, 160 ff.
4 The main source we have on his life is his unfinished memoir, Retinger, *Memoirs of an Eminence Grise*, edited and completed by his longtime assistant John Pomian. Much of the existing literature on Retinger is based on this memoir. The first academic biography, published in 2017, brings together interesting new material; however, most of it concerns the period before 1945. Biskupski, *War and Diplomacy*.
5 On his friendship with Conrad, see Retinger, *Conrad and his Contemporaries*.
6 Retinger, *Memoirs*, 26.
7 Conrad to Richard Curle, August 16, 1916, quoted in Biskupski, "Spy, patriot, or internationalist," 47.
8 Pomian refers to a letter Retinger wrote to a friend "indicating that he even tried to commit suicide." Pomian, *Joseph Retinger*, 38.
9 Biskupski, "Spy, patriot, or internationalist," 58.
10 Retinger tells colorful stories about his time in jail in St. Louis, Houston, and Laredo in his memoirs: Pomian, *Joseph Retinger*, 61–64.
11 See Unrue, *Katherine Anne Porter Remembered*, 40–41. Retinger was involved in a brief affair with the American writer Porter and asked for her help in getting him released from prison. Porter paints a decidedly less flattering portrait of Retinger than emerges from his memoirs.
12 See Biskupski, *War and Diplomacy*, Chapters 3 and 4.
13 Both Retinger himself and Prime Minister Mikołajczyk told the Polish officer Marek Celt that Retinger had gone directly to Churchill to get permission to rescue General Sikorski. See Celt, *Parachuting into Poland*, 41 and 58. See also Biskupski, *War and Diplomacy*, Chapter 5. Biskupski remains unsure whether Retinger was in direct contact with Churchill but does not discuss Celt's memoir.
14 On the exile communities in the United Kingdom and their impact on postwar Europe, see Conway, "Legacies of Exile."
15 Pomian, *Joseph Retinger*, 100. See also: Lane and Wolański, *Poland and European Integration*, 16–17 and 78–98; Biskupski, "Spy, patriot, or internationalist"; Biskupski, *War and Diplomacy*, Chapter 6 and 7; Grosbois, "L'action de Józef Retinger"; Pieczewski, "Joseph Retinger's Conception."
16 Spaak, *The Continuing Battle*, 202.
17 As Harold Macmillan put it in his memoirs,

> During the war itself the European idea had found many sympathizers, both in the underground movements fighting Hitler and among leading members of the exiled Governments. Thus, United Europe to some extent became a

symbol of resistance to Hitler's New Order. One of the most prominent in this work was General Sikorski, the former Prime Minister of Poland, assisted by Dr. J.H. Retinger, who afterwards became an important figure in the European Movement. It was during these terrible years that the first outline of the customs union which was to become Benelux was devised, and two eminent Belgian statesmen, Paul van Zeeland and Paul-Henri Spaak, were equally active in the development of the European ideal.

   Macmillan, *Tides of Fortune*, 152.
18 Pomian, *Joseph Retinger*, 107.
19 On this point, see Polonsky, "Polish Failure" and Biskupski, *War and Diplomacy*, Chapter 8.
20 Pomian, *Joseph Retinger*, 137.
21 Celt, *Parachuting into Poland*, 41.
22 According to Celt, Prime Minister Mikołajczyk told him that it had been Retinger's idea to go to Poland, but that Anthony Eden might be behind it. Celt, *Parachuting into Poland*, 40–42.
23 Dorril, *MI6*, 427; Davies, *Rising '44*, 54. Later, Davies calls Retinger an SOE "asset." Davies maintains that Retinger refused to do a practice parachute jump "for fear of losing his nerve." Given his age (he was 56) and given his frail physique, Retinger's own explanation that he did not want to risk injuries during a test jump is more believable. Accusing Retinger of being afraid of losing his nerve is all the more remarkable because he risked torture and death at the hand of the Gestapo if he had been captured. Gubbins later confirmed Retinger's version of events. Major-General Sir Colin Gubbins, "Joseph Retinger," *The Times*, June 13, 1960, Box 2075, Van Zeeland Papers, *Archives Université Catholique de Louvain* (AUCL).
24 This is confirmed by Gubbins, ibid.
25 See Bułhak, "The Foreign Office."
26 Memorandum by Frank Roberts, March 10 1954, Box 113240, FO 371, TNA/PRO. In his memoirs Roberts writes about Retinger: "Many distrusted him, but I never found cause to do so." Roberts, *Dealing with Dictators*, 56.
27 See Bułhak, "The Foreign Office," 49. Retinger had been aware of the threat but doesn't seem to have connected his paralysis with an attempt to poison him. He blamed the illness polyneuritis. Pomian, *Joseph Retinger*, 178. See also Biskupski, *War and Diplomacy*, Chapter 10 for evidence that high-ranking members of the Polish Home Army suspected Retinger of being a British or Soviet agent.
28 He was saved in part by the fact that the Polish underground had managed to capture a V2 missile; British intelligence was keen enough to pick up the V2 to try several risky landings in Poland.
29 Celt, *Parachuting into Poland*, 54.
30 Quaroni, "Did We Really Know Him?" Box 373–2, Wolff papers, SRWW.
31 "Private Common Market Talks," *The Observer*, July 3, 1962.
32 On transnational Europe, see Bossuat, *Inventer l'Europe*; Dumoulin, *Réseaux économiques*; Kaiser and Starie, *Transnational European Union*; Kaiser, Leucht, and Rasmussen, *The history of the European Union*.
33 The speech (with a postscript dated August 30, 1946) is available at www.cvce.eu/obj/address_given_by_joseph_retinger_on_the_future_of_the_european_continent_london_7_may_1946-en-534c684a-8924-445a-8181-58360f939f56.html. Accessed March 7, 2017.
34 The organization was originally called *Ligue Indépendante de Coopération Européene* – it changed its name in June 1948 to ELEC. See Dumoulin and Dutrieue, *La Ligue Européenne de Coopération Économique*; Lipgens and Loth, *Documents*,186–276; Lipgens, *Die Anfänge*, 331 ff.; and Pomian, *Joseph Retinger*,

209–216. On Van Zeeland, see Dujardin and Dumoulin, *Paul van Zeeland*. Van Zeeland, a prominent member of the Belgian Christian Social Party, was a leading economist who had been Foreign Minister and Prime Minister of Belgium in the 1930s. He held the post of Foreign Minister again from 1949–1954. Van Zeeland had frequently called for the lowering of trade barriers in the 1930s.

35 Pomian, *Joseph Retinger*, 212. Harriman contacted his former subordinates at the British embassy in order to arrange for Retinger's visa. See: correspondence in Box 251, Harriman Papers, LOC.

36 The memorandum is printed in Lipgens and Loth, *Documents*, 202–204.

37 In April 1949, Van Zeeland expressed the broad aims of the League as follows:

> We want to remake Europe, we want to give it peace and prosperity and restore it to what it was. We want to create a huge market in which goods can be exchanged freely, or almost so. We want a large area in which capital can be used wherever it is of most benefit to the masses. We want to see men freed from the present hindrances so that they can move wherever they like.

Lipgens and Loth, *Documents*, 253.

38 See Macmillan, *Tides of Fortune*, 154. In 1949 ELEC also held a conference on a European organization of the coal and steel industries.

39 On the Congress, see Guieu and le Dréau, *Le "Congrès de l'Europe"* and Loth, *Building Europe*, 8–19.

40 To Retinger's regret, the British Labour Party decided to send no official delegation to the Congress. Van Zeeland's involvement in the preparations of the Congress was cited by Labour spokesman Hugh Dalton as a reason to stay away. Dalton described Van Zeeland as a reactionary and a "would-be financier of Fascism before the war." See "Labour Party Congress," *The Times*, May 18, 1948. Ernest Bevin was perhaps more honest when he admitted to Retinger that Churchill would dominate the Congress. Pomian, *Joseph Retinger*, 220.

41 Pomian, *Joseph Retinger*, 221.

42 Ibid.

43 Loth, *Building Europe*, 19.

44 Rougemont, "Esquisse d'une biographie," 480.

45 Retinger to Harriman, April 1, 1948, Box 251, Harriman Papers, LOC.

46 Pomian, *Joseph Retinger*, 223 and Loth, *Building Europe*, 21–22.

47 Pomian, *Joseph Retinger*, 223.

48 Quaroni, "Did We Really Know Him?" Box 373–2, Wolff papers, SRWW.

49 Rougemont, "Esquisse d'une biographie," 480.

50 For a sharply contrasting view, see Kaplan, *NATO 1948*, 48. Of the Congress, Kaplan writes, "But once the cheers died down and the self-congratulation of the delegates wore off, the resolutions went into a black hole. While a Council of Europe did come into being, it was toothless and essentially meaningless."

51 Spaak, *The Continuing Battle*, 207.

52 Macmillan, *Tides of Fortune*, 168.

53 Catteral, *Macmillan Diaries*, 55. On the concept of a European public sphere, see Kaelble, *A Social History of Europe*.

54 Price, *The Marshall Plan*, 354.

55 Of course, the Bilderberg Group would play a similar role. See Chapter 5.

56 Macmillan, *Tides of Fortune*, 167.

57 Pomian, *Joseph Retinger*, 234–235.

58 See Retinger's letter to Tom Braden of the ACUE, February 19, 1952, Box 868, European Movement Archives, EUI.

59 See Lane and Wolański, *Poland and European Integration*, 90–91.

60 Wilford, *The CIA*, 232–233.

61 See the correspondence and memoranda in Box 3, Folder 6, Allen W. Dulles Papers, Princeton University Library. See also: Wilford, *The CIA*, 228–229; Vayssière, *Vers une Europe fédérale*, 233.

62 On the concept of the state-private network, see Laville and Wilford, *The US Government*.

63 Aldrich, "OSS, CIA and European Unity," 195.

64 See the financial statements and letters in Box 3, Folder 6, Allen W. Dulles Papers: Digital Files Series, Princeton University Library (PUL).

65 ACUE Statement of Receipts and Disbursements, February 16 1949 through October 31 1950, Box 4, Folder 1, Allen Dulles Papers: Digital Files Series, PUL.

66 Rebattet, "The European Movement," 206–207.

67 Reprinted in Agee and Wolf, *Dirty Work*.

68 Many authors have repeated Aldrich's claims: Brogi, *Confronting America*, 139; Daddow, *Britain and Europe*, 85; Defty, *Britain, America and Anti-Communist Propaganda*, 192–193; Lucas, *Freedom's War*, 112; Wilford, *The CIA*, 225. Stephen Dorril's much-quoted book on MI6 is hard to take seriously: he fails to back up many of his wide-ranging claims – among them of CIA backing of the EM – with any evidence and makes strange mistakes in the process. His claim, for example, that at the time of the Congress of Europe in 1948 Retinger convinced "one of General Clay's key representatives, Shepard Stone, to support the Congress with a grant of £40,000 from the ECA's 'counterpart funds'" is not backed up by evidence and is difficult to believe since Stone was in the United States working as a journalist at *The New York Times*. Dorril, *MI6*, 463.

69 Aldrich, "OSS, CIA and European Unity," 211–212. In his later book *Hidden Hand* Aldrich provides no new evidence on CIA's involvement.

70 Rebattet, "The European Movement," 206–207. Emphasis added.

71 On the importance of avoiding mythmaking concerning covert funding, see Mistry, "Approaches."

72 See Palayret, "Eduquer les jeunes"; Norwig, "A First European Generation?"; and Norwig, *Die erste europäische Generation*.

73 Braden to Rebattet, March 21, 1951, Box 868, European Movement Archives, EUI. Braden wrote: "I am wiring you tomorrow $5,000 as part payment on the difference between the $25,000 pledged and the amount already paid this year (August 1950–August 1951)." Retinger complained a few weeks later that he had expected more. On ACUE's funding of other non-EM projects such as the European Council of Vigilance, see Cohen, "Constitutionalism Without Constitution."

74 See the ACUE request for an emergency grant to the Ford Foundation, March 6, 1952, 52–155, Ford Foundation Archives.

75 Rebattet, "The European Movement," 206.

76 On the use of counterpart funds by the OPC, see Bissell, *Reflections*, 68–69; Scott-Smith, *Politics of Apolitical*, 71; and Thomas, *The Very Best Men*. When General Walter Bedell Smith became Director of the CIA in October 1950, he quickly established CIA control over OPC. Declassified CIA documents confirm the ECA-OPC deal. See 10 March 1950 conversation DCI with J. M. Andrews, AD/OCD – "The DCI stated that Mr. Hoffman of ECA has made available a large sum of money to this Agency and has stated very firmly that ECA is not receiving from CIA as much information as it should be getting." www.cia.gov/library/readingroom/docs/1950-01-03.pdf. Accessed March 29, 2017. On OPC generally, see Warner, "The CIA's Office of Policy Coordination."

77 Pomian, *Joseph Retinger*, 237–238.

78 Retinger to Braden, February 9, 1951, Box 868, European Movement Archives, EUI.

79 Retinger to Braden, April 2, 1951, ibid.

80 See Edward P. Lilly, "The Development of American Psychological Operations," December 19, 1951, 67, www.cia.gov/library/readingroom/docs/1951-12-19.pdf. Accessed March 29, 2017. The term "fostered" is not precise; it is possible that discussions with the ECA started in 1950, but the EYC was not actually created until the summer of 1951. On overt ECA propaganda efforts, see Ellwood, *Rebuilding Europe*; and Brogi, *Confronting America*.

81 Daily Diary DCI, February 15, 1949, www.cia.gov/library/readingroom/docs/1949-01-03.pdf. Accessed March 29, 2017.

82 Daily Diary DCI, February 23–24, 1950, www.cia.gov/library/readingroom/docs/1950-01-03.pdf. Accessed March 29, 2017.

83 Frank Wisner, Memorandum for the honorable W. Averell Harriman, February 15, 1950, Box 272, Folder 4, Harriman Papers, LOC. The memo is also available in the CIA's online FOIA reading room, www.cia.gov/library/readingroom/docs/DOC_0000138967.pdf. Accessed May 11, 2017.

84 Braden to Dulles, June 27, 1950, Box 3, Folder 6, Allen W. Dulles Papers, Digital Files Series, PUL. See also: Aldrich, *Hidden Hand*, 354.

85 Pomian, *Joseph Retinger*, 249.

86 Ibid., 237–238.

87 On McCloy's control of Marshall Plan funds, see Schwartz, *America's Germany*, 41–42.

88 See Kotek, "Youth Organizations."

89 On some of the more dubious activities, involving former Nazis such as Klaus Barbie, see Bird, *The Chairman*.

90 See Wilford, *The Mighty Wurlitzer*.

91 See Lucas, *Freedom's War*; Lynn, *The Inauguration of Organized Political Warfare*; Bischof and Jürgens, *Voices of Freedom*.

92 The same was true for overt US information programs. See Belmonte, *Selling the American War*, 43. On the Korean War, see Stueck, *The Korean War*; and Cumings, *The Korean War*.

93 McCloy to Secretary of State, August 29, 1950, FRUS, https://history.state.gov/historicaldocuments/frus1950v04/d380. Accessed March 26, 2018.

94 Eugen Kogon, the President of the *Europa Union*, was forced to step down in 1953 during a financial scandal. He ended up owing HICOG DM 286,000. See the conversation between the CIA mission chief in Frankfurt and German *Staatssekretär* Hans Globke, January 19, 1954, www.cia.gov/library/readingroom/docs/GLOBKE,%20HANS_0058.pdf. Accessed May 10, 2017. On the *Europa Union*, see also Conze, *Das Europa der Deutschen*, 291 ff.

95 Director's Log for CIA DCI Walter Bedell Smith, September 21–22, 1951, www.cia.gov/library/readingroom/docs/1951-09-01.pdf. Accessed May 10, 2017.

96 On the importance of youth organizations more generally, see Kotek, "Youth organizations as a Battlefield in the Cold War," and Honeck and Rosenberg, "Transnational Generations."

97 McCloy to Secretary of State, May 28, 1951, https://history.state.gov/historicaldocuments/frus1951v03p2/d346. Accessed March 26, 2018.

98 McCloy to Secretary of State, undated, https://history.state.gov/historicaldocuments/frus1951v03p2/d6. Accessed March 26, 2018.

99 Retinger to Braden, March 8 1951, Box 868, European Movement Archives, EUI.

100 For an interesting case study on Retinger's work to get Irish support for EYC, see McKenzie, "The European Youth Campaign in Ireland."

101 Report by Paul Hoffman to Donovan, August 26 1957, Box 2217, European Movement Archives, EUI.

102 It should be noted that Aldrich is aware of the complexity of the American efforts; however, his strong, unsupported statements on CIA involvement have led other authors to draw the conclusion that the CIA was the dominant actor. Aldrich, *Hidden Hand*, 362.

103 Thomas, *The Very Best Men*, 40.

104 See Wilford, *The CIA*, 229. Note, however, that when the story of CIA funding of the EM broke in 1975, Braden denied CIA involvement, despite the fact that he had already come clean about other CIA operations in support of the CCF and the National Student Association. See Bernard D. Nossiter, "CIA is linked to Funding of European Unity Groups," *The Washington Post*, June 26, 1975. The Pinky Johnson story is also told in: John Meroney, "The Battle for Picasso's Mind," *Playboy*, October 13, 2013, www.playboy.com/articles/cia-cold-war-mission-modern-art. Accessed May 15, 2017.

105 For more on the CCF, see Chapter 4.

106 See J.H. Retinger, "Draft Notes on the European Movement," undated, transmitted to Paul van Zeeland on August 25, 1954, Box 926, Van Zeeland Papers, AUCL.

107 See Vayssière, *Vers une Europe fédérale*, 267; Aldrich, "European Integration," 166–167; Wilford, *The CIA*, 232–233.

108 Braden to Rebattet, March 15, 1951, Box 868, European Movement Archives, EUI.

109 Caterall, *Macmillan Diaries*, 136–137.

110 J.H. Retinger, "Draft Notes on the European Movement," undated, transmitted to Paul van Zeeland on August 25, 1954, Box 926, Van Zeeland Papers, AUCL.

2 Anti-Americanism and the road to Bilderberg

In late September 1952, Joseph Retinger invited a high-powered group of European leaders to a secret meeting in Paris. Present were Antoine Pinay, the conservative French Prime Minister; Guy Mollet, the leader of the French Socialist Party (SFIO); Prince Bernhard of the Netherlands; Paul van Zeeland, the Belgian Foreign Minister; Hugh Gaitskell, a leading Labour politician and former Chancellor of the Exchequer; Major-General Colin Gubbins; Paul Rijkens, the Dutch chairman of Unilever; Ole Bjørn Kraft, a conservative Danish politician and Minister of Foreign Affairs; Rudolf Mueller, a Frankfurt-based German lawyer; and Panagiotis Pipinelis, the Greek ambassador to NATO. No journalists were told of the gathering, nor could any limousines be seen arriving at the Élysée Palace. Instead, the men slipped quietly into a private apartment on the Rue de L'Assomption.

Despite the secrecy, Retinger had not brought this unusual group together to hatch any conspiratorial plots. Instead, he wanted to discuss the worrisome increase in anti-Americanism in many European countries. A corresponding rise in "antipathy towards Europe" in the United States troubled him as well, since it might cause the return of US isolationism.[1] Retinger deemed secrecy for the committee necessary because of the controversial subject matter and because of the composition of the group. News of the political rivals Pinay and Mollet meeting in private would have sent the Paris rumor mills into overdrive; Gaitskell, meanwhile, might have faced uncomfortable questions in his own Labour Party about the company he kept.

The discussions in Paris resulted in the writing of a comprehensive report on anti-Americanism. Retinger and Prince Bernhard shared this report with a number of influential Americans and suggested that a similar group in the United States should produce a response without delay. However, despite their contacts with a number of high-level officials in the Eisenhower Administration, the Americans were hesitant to cooperate. It wasn't until the autumn of 1953 that the nonpartisan Committee for a National Trade Policy agreed to formulate an American reaction. As a next step, the Retinger committee decided to organize a high-level European-American conference for informal discussions of the underlying causes of transatlantic tensions. This off-the-record meeting took place at the Hotel de Bilderberg in the Netherlands, May 29–31, 1954.[2]

The story of how a small gathering in Paris evolved into the elite Bilderberg meetings underlines the significance of European anti-Americanism in this period.[3] In telling that story, this chapter shows how older forms of socio-cultural anti-Americanism fused with the more political anti-Americanism of the early Cold War to form a new and powerful mixture that threatened to severely undermine, if not destroy, NATO and the Atlantic alliance. The Eisenhower Administration was deeply worried about this development, while Communist propagandists attempted to ride the anti-American wave in order to thwart US goals in Western Europe.

At the same time, this chapter reveals that the founding of the Bilderberg Group was the result of a *European* initiative; Bilderberg, in other words, was *not* a creation of the CIA or other US organizations. The fact that the Bilderberg Group was first and foremost a European project reflected a strong current of *pro*-American Atlanticism in Europe.[4] This Atlanticism, which was part of a broader rise of internationalism on both sides of the Atlantic, was grounded in the collective memories of the Treaty of Versailles, the Great Depression, and the subsequent descent into totalitarianism; but also in the years of wartime cooperation, and the American commitment to Europe as expressed in NATO and the Marshall Plan.[5] The inability of the democracies to defend themselves during the 1930s had made the internationalists of the early Cold War all the more determined not to repeat the mistakes of the interwar period.

Retinger and his friends summed up Atlanticism in the first sentence of their report: "We [...] are firmly convinced that the security and development of the Western world cannot be achieved unless the friendship and mutual understanding between the United States and Western Europe are maintained and expanded."[6] On the other side of the Atlantic, David Rockefeller, a Bilderberg member of the first hour, later remembered the sense of moral obligation felt by US internationalists: "Like many in my generation I returned from World War II believing a new international architecture had to be erected and that the United States had a moral obligation to provide leadership to the effort."[7]

Retinger's committee

Retinger was well aware of European traditions of cultural anti-Americanism. In the spring of 1952, however, he was more concerned about the political consequences of a broader rise in anti-American sentiments in many European countries. He warned ominously of "a situation of the gravest danger" if no counteraction was taken.[8] Retinger soon learned that leading European politicians and businessmen, many of whom he knew through his work in the European Movement, shared his concerns and were willing to join his committee.

Retinger, in an inspired moment, decided to recruit Prince Bernhard of the Netherlands to chair his committee. As Retinger's assistant John Pomian later recalled, Retinger saw several advantages in asking Prince Bernhard.[9]

Apart from the benefit of a royal title, the Prince was well known and respected throughout Europe and the United States. During the war, he had earned a reputation as a tireless and creative chief of staff of the Dutch army in exile. As a result, he had many powerful friends in Washington and easy access to the White House. After the war, the Prince had become an effective goodwill ambassador for the Netherlands, traveling to South America, the United States, and Canada to promote Dutch economic interests. The Dutch press started calling him 'Prince Charming' and celebrated his success in securing KLM Royal Dutch Airlines landing rights in Houston.

Prince Bernhard spoke fluent English, French, and Dutch, in addition to his native German, and indeed possessed an easy charm and quick intelligence that would serve him well as chair of the Bilderberg meetings. He was a strong supporter of European integration and had cohosted the 1948 Congress of Europe. He was also active in European cultural affairs, founded the Erasmus Prize, and played a leading role in the *Fondation Européenne de la Culture*. The Prince generally resented the constitutional limits to his activities as a member of the royal family and relished every chance to circumvent them.[10] Besides his many admirable qualities, Bernhard's love of fast cars, airplanes, and women frequently got him into trouble and reflected an irresponsible side to his character, which ultimately resulted in the Lockheed scandal in 1976 and his resignation as Bilderberg chairman.[11]

In addition to the men present at the Paris Meeting in September 1952, Retinger and Prince Bernhard asked three other prominent Europeans to join the committee: Max Brauer, the Social Democratic Party (SPD) mayor of Hamburg; Pietro Quaroni, the Italian Ambassador to France; and Lord Portal of Hungerford, a Barclays Bank director.[12] All members agreed to write a series of reports on anti-Americanism within their respective countries. In Paris, they decided that Retinger would then present a summary of their findings "[...] to Mr. Harriman, so that he might ask some Republican personality to prepare with him another report on the causes of anti-European feeling in America." In addition,

> [...] the members should take action individually, without disclosing the existence of the Committee. In this connection, it was mentioned that useful work could be accomplished through such organisations as 'Friends of Atlantic Union', by informal meetings with editors of newspapers etc.[13]

The United States as a 'European' power

One important conclusion reached by the committee was that the anti-Americanism of the early Cold War was, to a large extent, a response to the global power shift that had started in the late 19th century and that had accelerated as a result of the two world wars. As the United States rose to superpower status, Europe experienced a parallel decline, with its economies reeling after the devastations of World War II and its colonial empires crumbling. "The United States," Van Zeeland observed, "is now unquestionably the richest, most powerful country, exercising hegemonic control over the destiny of the free world. In several ways, the United States have [sic] resumed the role England played during part of the last century."[14] For the first time in its history, the United States had abandoned the Monroe Doctrine to become a 'European' power in peacetime. The initial American impulse to pull out of Europe as quickly as possible in 1945–1946 had given way to a clear commitment to European security embodied by the Truman Doctrine, the Marshall Plan, NATO, the Truman Administration's decision to station four American divisions in Europe, and the Mutual Security Aid (MSA) program.

The central paradox of anti-Americanism in Western Europe was that precisely this US commitment to Europe caused widespread concern.[15] In part, this was simply because of the suddenness of the change. "Most of us who collaborate in this Report," Retinger wrote, "remember the time when the influence of the United States on European politics, economic, financial, or cultural life, was negligible."[16] Now, Europe struggled to adjust to the leading role played by the United States in European affairs. Tensions and resentment were more or less preprogrammed, as the example of Washington's insistence on German rearmament after the outbreak of the Korean War showed. Just five years after the end of World War II, many Europeans were not ready to follow the American lead on this controversial issue.[17]

Several contributors turned to the metaphor of family relations to explain the psychological implications of this power shift. Hugh Gaitskell wrote in the introduction of his report on anti-Americanism in the United Kingdom that

> [t]he alliance means we have to try and agree on common policies, that we have in so many ways to try and march together. The process breeds disputes. You have plenty of arguments inside your family, whereas you only nod politely to the people at the other end of the street.[18]

Likewise, Prince Bernhard compared the position of the United States with that of an eldest brother who should consult his younger siblings when making important decisions.[19]

Not surprisingly, the committee concluded that the emergence of the United States as the leader of the West caused most resentment in the United Kingdom and France. The United Kingdom had been an equal partner to the United States during the war – in part because of the Churchill-Roosevelt relationship – and now had to accept a much inferior position.[20] France, after the humiliation of Vichy, was eager to regain a more independent role in world affairs. The reports by Prince Bernhard on the Netherlands, Van Zeeland on Belgium, and Kraft on Denmark showed that in these smaller countries, anti-American sentiment was less of a problem. Germany, obviously, remained a special case because of the occupation and its division into East and West.

The European fear of war

The committee's report identified "attitudes towards war" as the most important difference between Europe and America. For most Europeans, the memories of wartime misery and destruction were still too vivid even to consider the possibility of a new war. During the September 25 discussions, Hugh Gaitskell stressed "that in his opinion the most important single cause of friction was the fear of war."[21] Guy Mollet agreed, writing in his report that "[s]ix years after their liberation, the French people still feel a deep exhaustion and weariness."[22] Major-General Gubbins likewise concluded that continental Europe was "still largely exhausted" and could not understand public discussions in Washington on the prospects of a new world war. The Korean War was judged to have been a key turning point.[23] Mollet pointed to the resulting "fiscal," "economic," and "military mobilisation" in the United States. Against the background of the Korean War, rising East-West tensions, and a strong push for European rearmament, belligerent statements by "trigger-happy" American generals or congressmen were bound to get a negative reception in Europe, even – or perhaps especially – if they were meant for domestic American consumption.[24]

The psychological impact of the Korean War could be observed in a general coarsening of foreign policy debate in the United States and the rise of McCarthy-style anti-communism. Mollet warned that remarks such as "Let us make haste to crush the USSR while we are the stronger" or "Why aren't we using the atomic bomb in Korea" caused immense concern in France.[25] Prime Minister Pinay similarly emphasized that France was willing to follow a defensive strategy in the Cold War. Whenever American policies appeared to be aggressive, the non-communist French public became worried.[26]

The obvious implication was that public figures in the United States should be more careful in their utterances, or at least should be aware of their probable consequences in Europe. Washington, in other words, needed to take into account that the United States was perceived as a relatively inexperienced and volatile player on the world scene.[27] Retinger himself had told Harold Macmillan in January that the Americans had "no experience and no patience" – more and more Europeans now seemed to share that impression.

Transatlantic misunderstandings and tensions were nourished by Europe's unfamiliarity with the American political system. "[Europeans] are bewildered to find Congress and the Administration often acting independently of each other."[28] They had witnessed the important role Congress could play in such policy areas as the Marshall Plan and East-West trade. "The fact that Congress can take initiatives contrary to the wishes and policies of the Executive," the report argued,

> as was the case with the 'Battle Act', creates a feeling of uncertainty and shakes the confidence of many Europeans in the stability of American policies and of the engagements, particularly the long-term ones, which are entered into by the Administration.[29]

Again, the implication was that as the leader of the Alliance, the United States should pursue a clear and consistent foreign policy that could be understood and relied on by its European partners.

Senator Joseph McCarthy's growing influence in Washington did not make this any easier. Hugh Gaitskell criticized the "anti-communist hysteria" and the "tyranny of the majority" in the United States. He presciently argued that if the full scale of McCarthy's witch hunt became known in Britain, critics of the United States would have a field day. The excesses of McCarthyism, Gaitskell argued, questioned the most basic assumptions about right and wrong in the Cold War. "On the rational plane," he said, "it condemns the main argument of the pro-Americans: that America is, after all, a free democratic country, while Russia is a cruel and ruthless dictatorship."[30]

Europe's cultural superiority complex

Several members of the committee identified what historian Volker Berghahn has called the European cultural "superiority-complex" vis-à-vis the United States.[31] "[T]he average Frenchman," Pinay wrote, "experiences at one and the same time a superiority complex with regard to the Americans, which comes from his history and an inferiority complex in face of the overwhelming material superiority of the New World."[32] Mollet analyzed French perceptions of the United States in similar terms:

> [T]o many people America appears as the land of refrigerators, of vacuum cleaners, and of television – a country in which material comfort and mechanisation have developed to a degree which is enviable, but at the same time frightening. [...] [Q]uite understandably [the Frenchman] tends, on the one hand, to caricature this stereotyped idea of a world he hardly knows and, on the other, to console himself for his inferior condition by persuading himself that it is largely recompensed by an understanding of the intellectual, artistic and spiritual values of which the American, because of too much material comfort, has no idea.[33]

Both Mollet and Paul Rijkens emphasized the penetration of American mass culture into European societies. Hollywood and comic strips enjoyed great popularity; in fact, "by 1951, more than 60% of the films showing in Western Europe were American."[34] But many Europeans worried about the cultural and economic impact of this American invasion. In Mollet's words: "Rightly or wrongly, Americans are considered partly responsible for a real deterioration in taste, and even for a certain moral debasement."[35]

It should be noted that European superiority and inferiority complexes were as much about Europe itself as about the United States. As was so often the case in European history, cultural and socioeconomic anti-Americanism was all about *Selbstthematisierung* – the effort to understand the changes in one's own society by drawing a comparison with the United States.[36] Because knowledge about America in most European circles was very much limited to precisely those products and economic practices that were the result of American mass society, the European image of America tended to be rather one-sided. The tens of thousands of American officials, soldiers, and tourists spending their dollars in European countries only seemed to reinforce European prejudices about American capitalism and materialism.

Such perceptions mattered since they coincided and blended with Europe's disquiet about America's new role as the nuclear-armed leader of the Western world. The United States was no longer just modernity knocking on Europe's door in the form of Hollywood movies, comics, and mass-produced cars; suddenly the United States could involve Europe in a war (instead of the other way around) at a time that European influence on world affairs was on the wane.[37] Different non-communist political movements, from the Bevanite wing in the British Labour Party to the Gaullists in France, tapped into this new form of anti-Americanism for their own political gain. Communist parties, of course, were happy to assist.

Decolonization and free trade

Retinger's committee identified several specific policy areas in which European and American interests and perceptions diverged. America's perceived "anti-colonialism" was a major cause of friction. Paul van Zeeland argued that the United States showed little appreciation for the efforts of the colonial powers in their overseas territories. The fact that Washington almost by ideological default intervened on behalf of those seeking independence was criticized in many European countries. Van Zeeland wrote that "this American intervention has ended more than once in making the fate of masses of people in these backward countries a less happy one."[38] In the case of France, US policies in North Africa caused much resentment. As Prime Minister Pinay put it in his report: "To the French it seems illogical that an ally might try to weaken their position in the Colonies."[39] The committee's final report did not suggest any solutions to this problem, but noted that some Europeans were starting to interpret the American attitude as a manifestation of "American imperialism."

Economic liberalization and free trade in the Western world was another important issue. Hugh Gaitskell returned to the family metaphor to explain that Europe suffered to some degree from a "poor-relation complex." Several other contributors noted the striking paradox that the countries that had received the most American assistance under the Marshall Plan were generally more resentful of American economic dominance than the countries that received less aid. Former great powers such as the UK and France, not used to such dependence, seemed to suffer most from this poor-relation complex.

US-imposed restrictions on East-West trade added to the impression that Washington abused its economic power to bully the Europeans into submission. The fact that the Battle Act – which made aid to Europe dependent on adherence to trade restrictions with the Soviet Union and China – had been imposed on the Truman Administration by Congress did little to alleviate its negative impact on European public opinion. Similarly, the fact that military and economic aid to Europe under the Mutual Security Act was negotiated on a bilateral basis further emphasized European dependence.[40] At the time of the Marshall Plan aid, such negotiations had been organized multilaterally.

The solution to the unhealthy economic imbalance seemed relatively straightforward: Europe should be allowed to earn its own dollars and close the dollar gap. "This means that Europeans should be allowed to export to the United States as unhindered and unhampered as possible."[41] Especially in light of the Battle Act and other legislation preventing East-West trade, Washington should open its borders and lower tariffs. Otherwise the impression would remain that

> [...] it is America which, while closing to Europe traditional export markets, refuses to open her own; it is thus America which is keeping Europe starved of dollars, Britain short of food, France short of coffee, [and] Denmark short of steel.[42]

The committee members were, of course, aware that free trade was not necessarily a popular subject in Congress. Still, they wanted to impress upon their American audience that the current situation was having a highly negative impact on European-American relations. By doing so, they gave much-needed support to those in the United States who were in favor of both the relaxation of export controls and the lowering of American tariffs – and they did so not only in private. Danish Foreign Minister Kraft emphasized the point in a speech to United Nations correspondents in New York in November 1952:

> It must naturally cause irritation in Europe that, at the same time as the United States helps us to stand on our own feet and asks us to conduct a trade policy of liberalization, it prevents us, by import restrictions, from earning the dollars necessary to get along without aid.[43]

The concluding part of the final report consisted of several general recommendations for improving transatlantic relations. First of all, official propaganda was judged to be of little use. Europeans were "tired of official propaganda [...] and public men who are known to be protagonists of America, however genuine they might be, are very often for this very reason distrusted by the public."[44] Therefore, the report argued, "private initiatives" could be much more effective.[45] With respect to policies that concerned all members of the alliance, consultation was of crucial importance: "[...]our chief recommendation directed to both sides would be not to make any change of policy without previous consultation. Any one-sided and sudden change is bound to have unfortunate repercussions." The report suggested that NATO was "a most useful instrument" for timely consultations and should be used more effectively. In the economic field, similar machinery failed. An "overall review" of the "economic problem" was recommended in light of the "very great importance" of this matter to Europe.

The report ended on a general note of caution. If Europe and the United States were to cooperate effectively, mutual understanding was an absolute necessity. In Mollet's words:

> Complete frankness in the exchange of views, more contacts, mutual study of our respective problems, having regard on both sides to national susceptibilities [...] – these seem to constitute the means of removing the mistrust in both our countries, and of strengthening the natural ties that unite us.[46]

The final report did not spell out what the consequences of a failure in American-European cooperation would be. The unspoken assumption, however, was that many European countries were at risk of drifting off towards neutralism, thereby creating a dangerous power vacuum that was bound to be filled by the Soviet Union.

The American response and the 1952 presidential election

By the time the committee finished its report, the campaign for the presidential election in the United States was in full swing. General Dwight D. Eisenhower, who remained popular in Europe as the organizer of D-Day and as the first military leader of NATO, had secured the Republican nomination against the more isolationist Senator Robert Taft. Still, the consensus in the American press was that most Europeans preferred the Democratic candidate Adlai Stevenson. Aggressive Republican campaign oratory about liberation and rollback worried European publics. As *New York Times* columnist Cyrus Sulzberger reported from Europe: "No power on this Continent is prepared to underwrite a war to free the Lithuanians."[47] At the same time, suspicions lingered in Europe that the Republicans would return to their traditional policy of isolationism or would shift resources from Europe to Asia. The so-called 'Great Debate' in early 1951 on the stationing of American ground forces in Europe had not been forgotten. Republicans led by Senator Taft had opposed Truman's decision to send several divisions to Europe.[48]

Quite apart from the European preferences in the race for the White House, the fact that political life in Europe had more or less come to a standstill as a result of the American presidential election was striking. "[T]here is a distinct sense of concern in discovering how completely dependent upon the United States Europe has become," reported Volney D. Hurd from Paris.[49] Anne O'Hare McCormick, using language similar to that of the Retinger committee, blamed the mood in Europe on the "reaction of the poor against the rich, of overstrained economies against the cost of rearmament, of old and long-independent peoples against the nagging compulsions of dependence."[50]

Shortly after the election, Prime Minister Antoine Pinay even publicly rebuked American efforts to influence French colonial and financial policies. In the eyes of the State Department, Pinay wanted to capitalize on the anti-American feeling in his country.[51] Yet, as the conclusions of the Retinger committee show, Pinay's action also reflected a genuine need for a more independent Europe vis-à-vis Washington. Public opinion in France, the UK, and many other European countries no longer accepted a too-visible and overwhelming American role on the continent.[52] The incoming Eisenhower Administration, in other words, faced a new chapter in transatlantic relations.

Two weeks after the presidential election, Retinger and Prince Bernhard separately traveled to the United States to discuss their report with a number of influential Americans. Retinger asked W. Averell Harriman to become the point man for a US response, but Harriman, who had just lost the battle for the Democratic presidential nomination to Stevenson, refused. Retinger then turned to the ACUE network and met with General Walter Bedell Smith and Allen Dulles. General Smith, who had been Eisenhower's Chief of Staff during the war and was known to his friends as 'Beedle' or 'Beetle,' was about to leave his post at the CIA to become under secretary of state under John Foster Dulles; the second of the Dulles brothers, Allen, succeeded Smith as CIA director.[53]

In a letter to Bernhard, Retinger called his visit "completely successful." "General Bedell Smith and Mr. Allen Dulles," he wrote, "[...] have quite decided to help in the formation of an unofficial Committee of four or five people."[54] Adolf Berle Jr., too, had agreed to become a member. Retinger mentioned ACUE members General Lucius Clay and Charles Spofford as other possible participants. In addition, he had approached George Franklin Jr. of the Council on Foreign Relations and ACUE to become the "co-ordinator of the committee."[55] Only John McCloy declined to participate, claiming an overflowing agenda well into 1953.

Retinger's optimism soon turned out to be premature. Dulles and Smith, swamped by work during the transition, didn't follow through on their promises, and Franklin wrote at the end of December that the CFR could not become involved after all:

> Any comparable group organized by us would have to include a number of men who had served in important posts with the outgoing administration, and we doubt whether such men should or would want

to express their opinion on European-American relations at this time, even in the restricted way you suggest. We feel that in this country much more can be done to better European-American relations by the new administration than by any private group on this side of the water, no matter how important or well qualified.[56]

Six weeks later, Prince Bernhard decided to call his friend Bedell Smith and ask him to name at least one American representative who could organize an American response. In a follow-up letter, Bernhard wrote that Pinay, Van Zeeland, Gaitskell, and Rijkens had all contacted him to emphasize the urgency of the matter since "public opinion in Europe is not improving."[57] Yet Bedell Smith remained unwilling or unable to act. In May, Bernhard again urged him to do something:

> You know that I realize how terribly busy you are with all the various problems and I know that on receipt of this letter you will probably curse a couple of times. All the same, I have got to give these people some answer. The problem is definitely not made any easier through Russia's latest attitude. So please write me something definite in any form you like, so that I have it in my hands before May 22nd [...][58]

Bedell Smith now passed the ball to Charles D. Jackson, special assistant to the president for International Affairs. As Jackson later wrote to Ann Whitman, Eisenhower's secretary:

> Beedle was up to his ears in CIA stuff, and then swamped all over again early in '53 by being appointed Under Secretary of State. [...] Finally, in desperation, Beedle asked me, since I knew Bernhard quite well, if I could help him out of his fix, and I agreed to take over the project.[59]

Jackson had been a member of Eisenhower's staff during World War II and knew Prince Bernhard well – so well, in fact, that at some point the "dual control stick" of Bernhard's plane ended up in Jackson's trouser leg, "with considerable inconvenience to aerial movement," as Jackson recalled in a letter to the Prince.[60] Jackson served as president of the National Committee for a Free Europe in 1952–1953 and was one of a number of people involved in the Committee who became active in the Eisenhower campaign and administration (Ann Whitman was another).

There is some disagreement in the literature over Jackson's actual influence in the Eisenhower Administration. He left the Administration in the spring of 1954 to return to Henry Luce's Time Inc. as publisher of *Fortune Magazine*. H. W. Brands places Jackson in the "third rank" of Eisenhower men, responsible for stirring up the bureaucracy and bringing in new ideas.[61] Brands points out that Jackson "possessed one of Washington's lowest batting averages, in terms of ideas accepted and put into practice."[62] Other scholars attach more weight to Jackson's position, labeling him the "chief architect of America's psychological warfare effort during and after World War II."[63] Fact is that even after his retirement from the administration Jackson remained close to President Eisenhower and several of Eisenhower's most important advisers, including the Dulles brothers. Moreover, as the publisher of one of the most influential American magazines and as a confidant of Henry Luce, Jackson was a force to be reckoned with in the molding and influencing of American public opinion.[64]

When Bedell Smith wrote to Jackson asking him to take on the project, he made clear that in his view, the matter held little priority. The only thing that needed to be done right now was to give Prince Bernhard "a crumb of comfort to indicate that something is or will be done on our part to evaluate this survey and possibly to provide its U.S. counterpart [...]."[65] In response, Jackson decided to send Retinger's report to several friends in the Eisenhower Administration, including Allen Dulles and Richard Bissell at the CIA.[66] He reassured Prince Bernhard that "a group of comparable stature" was now being organized in the United States.[67]

By the end of August, no further progress had been made, and Retinger became increasingly despondent. One of the conclusions of his report had been that Washington should pay closer attention to its European allies; now the opposite seemed to be happening. "Our friends in the Group working on the problem of European-American relations," he told Bernhard,

> are very worried about the present state of affairs. Only a few days ago I had a long talk with M. Guy Mollet, who thinks we ought to take some initiative in the matter, as according to our information the relationship between America and most of the European countries is deteriorating very rapidly.[68]

Then an unexpected development came to the rescue. As Jackson later told Ann Whitman, "God intervened in the shape of the newly founded Coleman Committee, which was the citizens' committee to carry the torch for the Randall Commission."[69] The Coleman Committee, officially the Committee for a National Trade Policy, was founded to promote free trade. Its chairman, John S. Coleman, was president of the Burroughs Corporation based in Detroit. Other members included Joseph P. Spang, president of the Gillette Corporation, John McCloy (now at the Chase National Bank), and Henry J. "Jack" Heinz II of ketchup fame. George W. Ball, a Washington-based international lawyer at the firm Cleary, Gottlieb, served as the committee's secretary.

In its first press release, the Coleman Committee announced it would "work for public understanding of the need for an expansion of trade and a reduction of trade barriers."[70] The committee argued that the United States should open its markets to its allies in the free world. Only by permitting these countries to earn dollars through trading, could the economic and military aid programs be terminated. American foreign economic policy could no longer be separated from matters of national security, since the Cold War had made "the building of a free world coalition" imperative: "We cannot draw the free peoples together militarily if we divide them economically."[71]

Given the similarities between this message and the conclusions of Retinger's report, it is clear why Jackson decided to contact Coleman in early September.[72] To Jackson's relief, he received a positive reply by the end of the month. Several members of the Committee, Coleman included, agreed to personally organize the American response to Retinger's report.[73]

The question remains why the American response was so slow. Bedell Smith and Dulles undoubtedly faced more pressing concerns in their new positions in the Eisenhower Administration. But even after Jackson took over, the pace hardly quickened. Jackson's suspicions about Retinger seem to have played an important role. As he told Whitman, he had been informed by people "who are in a position to know better than I" that Retinger might operate as a British secret agent. Jackson's distrust of Retinger was nourished by his obvious dislike of the Pole. He wrote that during his time as President of the National Committee for a Free Europe "no matter where the rug was placed, whether New York, London, Paris, Munich, Rome, or what have you, Retinger always managed to crawl out from under it at the most awkward moment."[74]

In a letter to John C. Hughes, the US Permanent Representative to NATO, Jackson called Retinger "Prince Bernhard's Richelieu" and wrote:

> As you know, I try to use both my head and the seat of my britches (sometimes I can't tell which is which), and the seat of my britches tells me that Mr. Retinger is dangerous medicine, to be taken in very small doses if at all, and then only on the instruction of that prominent international toxicologist, Dr. Hughes.[75]

Jackson asked Hughes for "guidance" on how to handle Retinger, pointing to his connection with Major-General Colin Gubbins, the former SOE chief. Hughes replied that he strongly suspected "that the military figure mentioned at the bottom of the first page of your letter [i.e. Gubbins] has a special interest." He also indicated, however, that he thought Retinger's efforts were not without value, calling the report produced by the group "most interesting."[76]

As it happened, Jackson was never able to move beyond the realm of suspicion. He failed to establish a definite connection between Retinger and the British secret service. The fact that Retinger had cooperated with British intelligence during World War II was no secret and adequately explains his relationship with Major-General Gubbins.[77] Gubbins, moreover, had retired to private life after the war and was no longer involved in British intelligence.[78] When in 1955 Prince Bernhard learned of the American suspicions, he was not overly worried. He asked for evidence and dismissed the matter when none was produced.[79]

The Eisenhower Administration and anti-Americanism in Europe

The fact that official Washington was slow to respond did not mean that the Eisenhower Administration wasn't interested in anti-Americanism. On the contrary, the new administration was quick to identify anti-Americanism as a serious problem in Europe. The State Department and the CIA hurried to produce several memoranda on the issue, and anti-Americanism played an important role in the Administration's review of basic national security policy.

It is not clear whether the CIA made use of Retinger's report, but its analysis of anti-Americanism echoed several of the report's conclusions. The CIA argued that European distrust of US leadership was based on the belief that

> the United States has not had sufficient experience in foreign affairs to offer wise and farsighted leadership. [...] Throughout Europe we are often charged with impatience and impetuosity, with an 'all-or-nothing' approach in the East-West conflict, and with intending to press the present struggle to a conclusion entailing humiliation of or annihilation of the Soviet Union.[80]

In addition, frustration over restrictions on East-West trade and over America's protectionist trade policies severely harmed American standing in Europe.

Since the summer of 1952, two factors had further complicated relations between Europe and the United States. The first, ironically, was Stalin's death in March 1953 and the Soviet "peace offensive" that followed. This had led to a "desire to escape the burdens of armament" as well as the strong wish in Europe to "settle the Cold War by negotiation."[81] The United States, moreover, was often perceived as the obstacle to such a settlement. The second factor was McCarthyism. As Gaitskell had predicted, many Europeans objected to McCarthy's methods, and McCarthyism received much attention in the European press, thus hurting America's public diplomacy. The impact of President Eisenhower's "Chance for Peace" speech of April 16, 1953, for example, was "to some extent lost in the almost simultaneous reaction of mingled ridicule and dismay provoked by the Cohn-Schine investigation of US information centers in Europe and the subsequent 'book burnings'."[82]

In October 1953, the National Security Council approved policy paper NSC 162/2 as the new basic guideline for American security policy. NSC 162/2 explicitly spelled out the dangers of anti-Americanism in connection with the Soviet threat. "The United States cannot [...] meet its defense needs," NSC 162/2 argued, "even at exorbitant cost, without support of allies."[83] The strength and cohesion of the coalition, however, was threatened by the recent decline in US prestige as reported in the CIA memo on anti-Americanism.[84] As NSC 162/2 stated:

> allied opinion, especially in Europe, has become less willing to follow U.S. leadership. Many Europeans fear that American policies, particularly in the Far East, may involve Europe in general war, or will indefinitely prolong cold-war tensions. Many consider U.S. attitudes toward the Soviets as too rigid and unyielding and, at the same time, as unstable, holding risks ranging from preventive war and 'liberation' to withdrawal into isolation.

The NSC paper concluded: "these allied attitudes materially impair cooperation and, if not overcome, could imperil the coalition."[85] To strengthen the coalition, America's allies should be convinced that "our strategy is one of collective security," thereby enhancing the "feeling of a community of interest."[86]

With respect to trade, President Eisenhower turned out to be fully on the side of the Retinger committee. Eisenhower believed that liberalized trade would spur economic growth, thereby making American aid unnecessary and raising the standard of living in Western Europe.[87] Moreover, he believed that East-West trade restrictions on non-strategic goods did more harm than good, since they undermined the unity of the Western world. By the summer of 1954, Eisenhower succeeded in partly reversing export control policies. After negotiations with Britain and France, almost half of the items on the list of prohibited goods were removed.[88]

The American report

Around the same time that NSC 162/2 was approved, the Coleman Committee started working on its report on American attitudes toward relations with Europe.[89] In line with the rules of Retinger's committee, the American memorandum was written anonymously, but George Ball was probably its principal author.[90] Ball was a logical choice, given his extensive experience and knowledge of the European scene.[91] He was energetic and eloquent, and had worked closely with Jean Monnet, at first for the French Supply Council and then in setting up the Organisation for European Economic Cooperation (OEEC) and the European Coal and Steel Community (ECSC).[92] In May 1950, Ball was probably the only American to have seen the Schuman Plan before it was announced to the public.[93] Another of Ball's European clients was the *Patronat Français*, the French industrial association.

Ball's report identified a number of issues on which "Americans are often critical of Europeans." The first concerned (anti-)communism. He acknowledged European criticism of McCarthyism and the "psychotic concern with internal security" in the United States. On the European side, however, many tended to underestimate the communist threat. "To American eyes," Ball argued,

> the Europeans' intense, understandable fear of war, their desire to do everything in their power to avoid it, often leads them to deceive themselves about the nature of the danger that confronts us all. Even sensitive and internationally-minded Americans, who are well aware of the defects of American behavior, are at a loss to understand the neutralism of so many European intellectuals, the facile equating of 'American imperialism' with communist imperialism.[94]

In Ball's view, the Western values of freedom, democracy, and tolerance were superior to those apparent in Soviet behavior. In the struggle between Western and Soviet values, there should be no place for neutralism.

With respect to decolonization, Ball recognized a certain degree of "naive Utopianism" in the United States. On the other hand, the "dispassionate" American position was "that the pressure of popular resistance to colonial status is rising everywhere and that the attempt to contain it, in effect by force, will sooner or later become too costly and will finally fail."[95]

Finally, Ball discussed the connected issues of German rearmament and European integration. He acknowledged that the American public might lack a sophisticated understanding of the many psychological and political reasons for the widespread resistance against German rearmament. Many Americans, however, found it "intolerable that the Germans should be prohibited from contributing their very sizeable resources to the common defense." Aside from the military question, it was the official US view that Germany should be integrated solidly in the Western world, thereby preempting the danger of a future Rapallo. Western Europe should agree to some "pooling of national sovereignties," since

> even the largest nations of continental Western Europe are too small, relative to the USSR on one side and the US on the other, to satisfy their own aspirations or to be fully effective as allies if they maintain their full separateness from one another.[96]

This was also true in the economic realm. Ball was in favor of "trade not aid," but he suggested that the Europeans had a long way to go themselves. Why not begin by reforming at home before pointing a finger at the United States? From the American point of view, it was self-evident that Europe should work toward "the creation of a single market."[97]

Organizing the first Bilderberg conference

After receiving the American report, Retinger and Bernhard immediately called a series of meetings in Paris and Brussels in early 1954. On January 18, several members of the committee got together to discuss a synthesis of the European and American reports as well as possible courses of future action.[98] Although some of the original irritants between Europe and the United States had been resolved, many problems remained.

On the positive side, Gaitskell argued, transatlantic tensions had been reduced as a result of the peace treaty in Korea, and the dollar gap had shrunk. On the negative side, many Europeans were concerned about a possible economic downturn in the United States and its consequences for European economies. The memories of the Great Depression and the difficult years after the war were present in everyone's mind ("Slump would be hell," Prince Bernhard wrote in his notes). Second, the issue of colonialism had become more important since the Soviet Union had set its sights squarely on "the colonial territories."[99] Third, in Europe the issue of overriding importance was the European Defense Community with its highly uncertain prospects. Finally, as the Eisenhower Administration had already recognized in NSC 162/2, the Soviet peace offensive had made it more difficult to reach agreement on a common Cold War strategy. "The apparent or possible change in Russian foreign policy," Gaitskell said,

> has proved an apple of discord between the Allies because there is disagreement about what it portends. It is therefore highly desirable to try and narrow any differences between Europe and America on the tactics to be pursued towards Russia in present circumstances.[100]

Gaitskell and Prince Bernhard suggested that these problems should be discussed at a larger meeting of about 50 high-level personalities. Prince Bernhard still thought the Retinger committee should remain secret and therefore could not be the organizing party. He suggested that the Dutch or the Belgian government might be asked to arrange such a meeting. Yet after consultations with Dutch Foreign Minister Johan Willem Beyen in early February, it was agreed that the Prince would issue the invitations for the conference.[101]

The first meeting with the American representatives Coleman, Ball, and Charles Taft took place in Paris on February 7 and 8.[102] "On entering the room," Ball remembered in his memoirs, "we found not only Prince Bernhard but also Guy Mollet, [...] and Antoine Pinay, [...] – two men who, I thought, would rarely be seen together at a private conference."[103] John Hughes, who joined the committee for lunch, reported to Jackson that the Americans had made "an excellent impression." On the European side Pinay, Mollet, and Van Zeeland had taken "an especially active part in the talks."[104]

Retinger and Gubbins had submitted a draft for the final report, which was discussed extensively.[105] The committee agreed that all participants could transmit the conclusions to their respective governments, yet the identity of the members of the committee would remain secret.[106] Gaitskell again underlined the need for anonymity, with respect to the larger transatlantic meeting as well.[107] He was worried that the prospect of publicity would have "a hampering influence on those attending."[108]

The Americans welcomed the plan to hold a meeting in the Netherlands. Prince Bernhard emphasized that it should be a balanced group "of different shades of opinion."[109] As Paul Rijkens wrote in his memoirs, the idea was to bring together the leaders of the left and the right.[110] Anti-Americanism, after all, was not limited to certain ideological groups or political parties. Moreover, the broader aim of strengthening the Western alliance in face of the Soviet threat implied the need to overcome the social and economic troubles that plagued so many European countries; this could only be done on a bipartisan basis.

During another meeting on February 25 at Van Zeeland's house in Brussels, the final report was finished.[111] It drew heavily on the other reports, but also contained some new points. With respect to communism, it added that communism in Western Europe often should be understood as a protest vote. In Italy, the report claimed, only 1 in 19 people voting for the Communist Party actually wished the establishment of a communist system. Relieving the economic and social discontent that lay at the base of these protest votes would therefore be far more effective than a McCarthy-style persecution of Communists. The report identified European economic integration as the best way of doing so.

Not much time was left to organize the Bilderberg conference scheduled for late May 1954. Retinger, assisted by the members of his committee, took the lead in selecting European participants. He relied on his EM network to do so, inviting pro-Europeans such as Roger Motz, president of the Belgian Liberal Party; Etienne de la Vallée Poussin, a Belgian Christian socialist senator; Jean Drapier, a leading Belgian socialist; and Denis de Rougemont, the director of the *Centre Européen de la Culture* in Geneva. Retinger relied partly on André Voisin, the leader of the pro-European organization *La Fédération*, for recruiting French participants. Voisin rejected Wilfrid Baumgartner for being too hostile to European unification. Retinger did invite politicians such as Maurice Faure, a radical socialist member of Parliament, and Pierre-Henri Teitgen, the president of the Christian-Democratic *Mouvement Républicain Populaire* (MRP).[112]

In Great Britain, Retinger, Rijkens, and Gaitskell could rely on their extensive networks in government and business circles. Retinger contacted Harold Macmillan as well as Frank Roberts at the Foreign Office, asking them to propose several conservative participants. He did not fail to mention that Gaitskell would surely organize a strong Labour presence. Macmillan passed on his request to Anthony Eden; Roberts told Eden:

> Although I did not say this to Retinger, it seems to me that this conference, presided over by Prince Bernhard, will rally a number of important European and American figures and that it would therefore be worth while to take some trouble to encourage appropriate Conservative Party representatives to go to The Hague.[113]

In the end, an impressive British group came to the Bilderberg conference with, among others, Sir Oliver Franks, the former ambassador to the United States; Sir Robert Boothby, a conservative MP; John Foster, the secretary of state for Commonwealth Relations; Denis Healey, an up-and-coming Labour politician; Tom Williamson, general secretary of the National Union of General and Municipal Workers; and Sir Harry Pilkington, the president of the British Trade Federation.

In Scandinavia, Gubbins – who had had close ties to resistance groups in the region – and Kraft did most of the recruiting. They invited Leif Høegh, a wealthy Norwegian shipowner; Finn Moe, the socialist chairman of the Foreign Affairs Committee; and the journalists Terkel Terkelsen and Herbert Tingsten. In Germany, Max Brauer and Rudolf Mueller assisted Retinger. Brauer, for example, made sure that leading trade unionist Ludwig Rosenberg attended the conference.[114] In Italy, Alcide de Gasperi helped arrange the participation of politicians Giovanni F. Malagodi and Raffaele Cafiero, as well as the leading businessmen Alberto Pirelli and Vittorio Valletta, the president of Fiat.[115]

The Coleman Committee was responsible for inviting American participants. Yet after it became clear that Coleman planned to ask mainly businessmen connected to his committee, Retinger and Prince Bernhard intervened. In March 1954, Bernhard spent three weeks in the United States, test-flying some of the newest Air Force planes, and narrowly avoiding a deadly crash in one of them.[116] At the start of his trip he visited the White House and told President Eisenhower of the plans for the Bilderberg conference. Eisenhower assured him that he was interested in the undertaking and that he would like to see the final report on transatlantic relations.[117]

Several weeks later, Prince Bernhard followed up with a letter urging the president to assist in enlisting influential Americans who did *not* come from the business community. Bernhard emphasized that in contrast to the American group, the European list was balanced and of high standing:

> [...] you see my fear is that only U.S. top business people will not be a really good counterpart for the purpose of our discussions – mutual understanding and the spreading of it in our press and especially in our political spheres – parliaments and such.[118]

Prince Bernhard asked Eisenhower whether he could not arrange for the participation of some important politicians, diplomats – Bernhard mentioned John Hughes and James Conant – or trade unionists.

The president referred Prince Bernhard's request to the State Department, where it was promptly turned down. Acting Secretary Robert D. Murphy argued that Ambassadors Conant and Hughes might be drawn into unpleasant discussions on such issues as McCarthyism and the hydrogen bomb and "could hardly divest themselves of their official capacities."[119] Anything they said might be interpreted as an "official statement of the U.S. government."[120] The State Department suggested that participation of several labor leaders might give the American delegation "a more representative character." To Bernhard's chagrin, Eisenhower did not overrule Murphy. Hughes and Conant were not given permission to travel to the Netherlands. Instead, Irving Brown, the European representative of the American Federation of Labor, and his colleague W.F. Schnitzler were found willing to participate.

President Eisenhower told Prince Bernhard that he had also contacted Congressional leaders, but had been advised

> that the Legislative program is at such a critical point in the Congress that it would be extremely detrimental to its successful enactment to have any appropriate members of the Congress leave the country to participate in [the] conference you are calling.[121]

Coleman had reached the same conclusion after talks with several congressmen and senators and pointed out that 1954 was an election year.[122]

In the end, the American delegation included George Ball; Barry Bingham, a newspaper publisher and former Marshall Plan representative in France; Gardner Cowles Jr., the publisher of *Look* magazine; John Ferguson, a Paris-based colleague of Ball at Cleary, Gottlieb; Jack Heinz II; C. D. Jackson; George C. McGhee, a Texas oilman and diplomat; George Nebolsine, a lawyer at the New York firm Coudert & Brothers; Paul H. Nitze, the former director of the State Department's Policy Planning Staff; George W. Perkins, a former assistant secretary of state for European Affairs; David Rockefeller; and James D. Zellerbach, a businessman and former Marshall Plan representative in Italy.

The CIA, meanwhile, was not involved in organizing or financing the Bilderberg Group. The oft-repeated claim that the Bilderberg Group was a CIA-sponsored organization is not only unfounded, it is more or less the exact opposite from what actually happened.[123] As we have seen, neither CIA Director Allen Dulles nor former CIA Director Walter Bedell Smith were willing or able to assist Retinger. In fact, until the success of the first Bilderberg conference, the Eisenhower Administration was surprisingly reluctant to cooperate with the Retinger committee. If not for Prince Bernhard's personal interventions, Retinger's initiative might well have failed altogether. Funding for the first Bilderberg conference, moreover, came almost exclusively from European sources.[124]

This does not mean, of course, that the CIA was not interested in the activities of the Retinger committee. A week before the first Bilderberg conference, CIA Director Dulles noted at a deputies' meeting

> that David Rockefeller was planning to go to Holland to attend a meeting with Prince Bernhard, C.D. Jackson, and others, including Dr. Joseph Retinger, and stated in view of Retinger's background and interest in this meeting its outcome would bear watching.[125]

Both Rockefeller and Ferguson wrote reports on the conference and shared these with the CIA and the State Department.[126]

The decision to organize the first transatlantic Bilderberg conference in the spring of 1954 was important for several reasons. The two continents were more closely aligned than they had ever been in peacetime; in the face of the challenges of the Cold War, decolonization, and globalization, they needed a common outlook on a wide range of issues. Yet the need for close cooperation, combined with Europe's frustrating dependence on the United States, inevitably caused misunderstandings and disagreements. The good news was that these could be overcome, the bad news that the young alliance was not very good at doing so. The fusion of different forms of political, cultural, and socioeconomic anti-Americanism in the early 1950s threatened to undermine the very idea of collective security on which NATO was based.

As a result, new modes of transatlantic coordination and consultation had to be developed concerning issues such as (anti-)communism, East-West relations, the colonial question, trade, and European integration. Retinger's long experience in nongovernmental action and informal diplomacy led him to create a private group to deal with these problems.

Over time, the Bilderberg meetings helped to form and expand the informal transatlantic alliance, consisting of a significant number of private or semi-private organizations and networks. The ripple effects of this informal alliance could be felt on many levels, from personal connections and friendships to transnational consensus building and agenda setting. Given the fact that official US public diplomacy had to some degree become counterproductive – as both the Retinger committee and the Psychological Strategy Board concluded – informal efforts to sustain the transatlantic partnership became all the more important.

In line with Geir Lundestad's "empire by invitation" argument, the decision to organize the Bilderberg conference was very much the result of *European* concerns and *European* actions.[127] The Retinger committee brought together a diverse group of Atlanticist Europeans who were convinced that transatlantic cooperation was indispensable and therefore wished to counter the rise in anti-Americanism in Europe. The result was a greater awareness on both sides of the Atlantic that the United States could no longer expect to push through its preferences. If, in the immediate postwar years, the United States had created, in Charles Maier's words, "a multizonal structure of ascendancy" based on "shared security goals, economic support, cultural policies, and sometimes undercover subsidies," the European partners in this structure now demanded a larger say in the West's global affairs.[128] A new phase in transatlantic relations had started.

Notes

1 Retinger memorandum "European-American Relations," undated, Box 329, Folder 16, Harriman Papers, LOC.
2 On the early history of Bilderberg, see Aubourg, "Organizing Atlanticism"; Aubourg, "Le groupe de Bilderberg"; Black, "The Bitterest Enemies"; Geven, "Transnational Networks"; Philipsen, "Diplomacy with Ambiguity"; Wilford, "CIA Plot."

3 This is a necessary corrective to existing histories of transatlantic relations. Mary Nolan's *The Transatlantic Century*, for example, does not mention anti-Americanism until the chapter on 1968. On anti-Americanism see Behrends, von Klimó and Poutrus, *Anti-Amerikanismus*; De Grazia, *Irresistible Empire*; Gienow-Hecht, "Always Blame the Americans"; Friedman, *Rethinking Anti-Americanism*; Hollander, *Anti-Americanism*; Katzenstein and Keohane, *Anti-Americanisms in World Politics*; Kroes, *If You've Seen One*; Kuisel, *Seducing the French*; Markovits, *Uncouth Nation*; Parmar, *Foundations of the American Century*; Roger, *The American Enemy*; Stephan, *The Americanization of Europe*.

4 Kenneth Weisbrode defines Atlanticism as follows: "Atlanticism meant that Europe and America were more alike than different. The twentieth century would prove, moreover, that the security, prosperity, and culture of each interpenetrated those of the other." Atlanticism was about "convincing both Americans and Europeans of the need for common policies" – a transatlantic consensus. Weisbrode, *The Atlantic Century*, 8. Giles Scott-Smith has put more emphasis on American agency:

> This, then, was Atlanticism – the creation of a solid consensus among the elites in Europe and the USA that worked towards first the acceptance of an American role in European affairs, and then its solidification. Institutions such as ACUE, NCFE, and Bilderberg demonstrate the alignment of significant economic and political interests with the maintenance of this hegemonic framework.

Scott-Smith, *Politics of Apolitical Culture*, 78. See also the edited volumes by Scott-Smith, Bossuat, and Aubourg, *European Community*; and Mariano, *Defining the Atlantic Community*.

5 As Warren Cohen has put it:

> A generation of American leaders had concluded that it was American shirking of responsibility after World War I that had allowed for the temporary ascendency of Adolf Hitler and the Japanese militarists, for the Great Depression, and for World War II.

Cohen, *New Cambridge History*, 237.

6 Report on European American Relations, September 1952, Box 1, Bilderberg Archives, NANL.

7 Rockefeller, *Memoirs*, 406.

8 Retinger memorandum "European-American Relations," undated, Harriman Papers, Box 329, Folder 16, LOC.

9 John Pomian Interview by the author, Saturday January 14, 2004.

10 See Hatch, *HRH Prince Bernhard*. On the controversies surrounding Prince Bernhard's NSDAP membership and his various connections to intelligence services, see the rather sensationalist Dröge, *Beroep Meesterspion*.

11 Van der Beugel Oral History Interview, NANL.

12 Note that Brauer had fled the Nazis in 1933 and had lived in the United States until 1946. Brauer was one of several (future) Bilderbergers with a special American connection, having lived or studied in the United States or having American family members. On the importance of German Émigrés in the development of the Federal Republic, see Greenberg, *The Weimar Century*. Lord Portal, it should be noted, did not remain active in Retinger's committee.

13 "Meeting held in Paris on September 25th 1952," Box C 294, Gaitskell Papers, UCL, and "Meeting September 25, 1952, General Discussion," Box 30, Bilderberg Archives, NANL.

14 Report Van Zeeland, Box 1, Bilderberg Archives, NANL. My translation.

15 A full-text search of four major newspapers (*The New York Times*, the *Christian Science Monitor*, the *Los Angeles Times*, and the *Chicago Tribune*) reveals that in the first half of the 20th century the term anti-Americanism is used only a few times each year. Then, between the years 1950 and 1954, there is a big increase – from eight times in 1950, to 29 times in 1951, 52 times in 1952 and 83 times in 1954. Of course, this is a rather crude way of measuring, but it does indicate that the early 1950s are an important period in the history of anti-Americanism.
16 Report No. 1, September 1952, Box 1, Bilderberg Archives, NANL.
17 Both French reports, from Mollet and Pinay, emphasized this point. Marc Trachtenberg and Christopher Gehrz have argued that the American State Department decided to push through the decision to rearm Germany without much regard for European interests or fears, because otherwise the American military build-up in Europe would not have been accepted in Washington. Trachtenberg and Gehrz, "America, Europe, and German Rearmament."
18 Hugh Gaitskell, "Anti-Americanism in Britain," Box 1, Bilderberg Archives, NANL. Gaitskell's memo is also printed in Williams, *The Diary of Hugh Gaitskell*, 316–320.
19 Memorandum July 1952, Box 1, Bilderberg Archives, NANL.
20 Harold Macmillan, who could not be accused of anti-American prejudice, noted in his diary in September 1952: "we are treated by the Americans with a mixture of patronizing pity and contempt. They treat us worse than they do any country in Europe." Catteral, *Macmillan Diaries*, 187.
21 "Meeting September 25, 1952, General Discussion," Box 30, Bilderberg Archives, NANL.
22 Report No. 1, September 1952, 3, Box 1, Bilderberg Archives, NANL.
23 On the crucial impact of the Korean War, see also Chapter 3 on the first Bilderberg Conference.
24 Report Gubbins, Box 1, Bilderberg Archives, NANL.
25 Mollet Memorandum, July 1952, Box C 294, Gaitskell Papers, UCL.
26 Report Pinay, undated, Harriman Papers, Box 329, Folder 16, LOC.
27 Gaitskell, "Anti-Americanism in Britain," Box 1, Bilderberg Archives, NANL.
28 Report No. 1, September 1952, 4, Box 1, Bilderberg Archives, NANL.
29 Ibid. Note that this type of criticism of American 'adventurism' coincided with diplomatic attempts by the British and others to restrain the United States. The American historian William Stueck has argued that such attempts by European allies may have prevented a further escalation of the conflict. Stueck, *The Korean War*. Secretary of State John Forster Dulles also used the 'allies' argument in his opposition to the use of atomic weapons against China in case of Chinese aggression. See Jones, "Targeting China," 44.
30 Gaitskell, "Anti-Americanism in Britain," Box 1, Bilderberg Archives, NANL.
31 Berghahn, *America and the Intellectual Cold Wars*, 288.
32 Report Pinay, undated, Harriman Papers, Box 329, Folder 16, LOC.
33 Mollet Memorandum, July 1952, Box C 294, Gaitskell Papers, UCL.
34 Behrman, *The Most Noble Adventure*, 315.
35 Mollet Memorandum, July 1952, Box C 294, Gaitskell Papers, UCL.
36 On this point, see Gassert, "Amerikanismus, Antiamerikanismus"; Greiner, "Test the West," 17; and Brogi, *Confronting America*, 7–8.
37 On this point – and the importance of heightened tensions after the Korean War – see Hogan, *Marshall Plan*, 338.
38 Report No. 1, 6, Box 1, Bilderberg Archives, NANL.
39 Report Pinay, undated, Box 329, Folder 16, Harriman Papers, LOC.
40 See Spaulding Jr., "A Gradual and Moderate Relaxation," and Førland, "Selling Firearms."
41 Report No. 1, Box 1, Bilderberg Archives, NANL.

42 Ibid. This sentence originally came from Gubbins' report.
43 *The New York Times*, November 18, 1952, 10.
44 Report on European-American Relations, Box 1336, Van Zeeland Papers, AUCL.
45 The Psychological Strategy Board reached the same conclusion a few months later: "In the free world and especially in Western Europe, specific grievances and generalized discontents continue to find expression in anti-American sentiments and resentments of overt United States propaganda and pressure." Report by the Psychological Strategy Board, October 30, 1952, https://history.state.gov/historicaldocuments/frus1950-55Intel/d133. Accessed March 27, 2017.
46 Mollet Memorandum, July 1952, Box C 294, Gaitskell Papers, UCL.
47 C. L. Sulzberger, "Europe Follows Closely Our Campaign," *The New York Times*, October 19, 1952, E3.
48 On the Great Debate, see Hogan, *Marshall Plan*, 385–386.
49 Volney D. Hurd, "Eisenhower Faces European Challenge," *Christian Science Monitor*, November 10, 1952, 10.
50 *The New York Times*, November 15, 1952.
51 See Kuisel, *Seducing the French*, 22–23.
52 On this point, see also Bossuat, *La France, l'aide américaine,* 840–841.
53 See Crosswell, *Beetle*, 47–48.
54 Retinger to Prince Bernhard, December 16, 1952, Box 2, Bilderberg Archives, NANL.
55 Ibid.
56 Franklin to Retinger, December 31, 1952, Box 181, Bilderberg Archives, NANL.
57 Prince Bernhard to Bedell Smith, February 19, 1953, Box 35, Jackson Papers, DDEL.
58 Prince Bernhard to Bedell Smith, May 4, 1953, Box 183, Bilderberg Archives, NANL. Prince Bernhard refers to the Soviet peace offensive after Stalin's death.
59 Jackson to Ann Whitman, November 19, 1954, Box 41, Ann Whitman File, International Series, DDEL.
60 Jackson to Prince Bernhard, July 15, 1953, Box 35, Jackson Papers, DDEL. Prince Bernhard apparently made a habit of such male bonding: adventures in fast cars and planes are a recurring theme in his correspondence.
61 Brands, *Cold Warriors*, xi.
62 Ibid., 117.
63 Blanche Cook quoted in: Ingimundarson, "Containing the Offensive." On Jackson, see also Osgood, *Total Cold War*, 82–83; and Hixson, *Parting the Curtain*.
64 On this point, see Osgood, *Total Cold War*, 82.
65 Bedell Smith to Jackson, July 9, 1953, Box 35, Jackson Papers, DDEL.
66 Jackson to Allen Dulles, August 6, 1953, Box 35, Jackson Papers, DDEL.
67 Jackson to Prince Bernhard, July 15, 1953, Box 35, Jackson Papers, DDEL.
68 Retinger to Prince Bernhard, August 31, 1953, Box 181, Bilderberg Archives, NANL.
69 Jackson to Ann Whitman, November 19, 1954, Box 41, Ann Whitman File, International Series, DDEL. The Randall Commission reported to President Eisenhower in the spring of 1954, recommending a policy of stimulating world trade by lowering tariffs. At the end of March 1954 President Eisenhower addressed Congress on the issue of world trade and asked for authority to negotiate for lower tariffs.
70 Announcement of Committee for a National Trade Policy, no date, Box 35, Jackson Papers, DDEL.
71 Ibid.

72 Jackson to Bullis/Coleman Committee, September 8, 1953, ibid.

73 Coleman to Jackson, September 23, 1953, ibid.

74 Jackson to Whitman, November 19, 1954, Box 41, Ann Whitman File, International Series, DDEL. In August 1954 Jackson had written Edward Littlejohn, Coleman's assistant, as well about his opinion that Retinger was a British secret agent. He added:

> This of course does not mean that his energy and ingenuity and enthusiasm and experience should not be welcomed by us, and used to the fullest extent in those endeavors where our causes are joint. It does mean, however, that in certain endeavors, and where there is major cleavage between the British and the Americans, he should be handled carefully.

Jackson to Littlejohn, August 5, 1954, Box 35, Jackson Papers, DDEL.

75 Jackson to Hughes, June 25, 1954, Box 60, Jackson Papers, DDEL.

76 Hughes to Jackson, June 29, 1954, Ibid. Hughes and Jackson had cooperated in the National Committee for a Free Europe in the early 1950s. Hughes had also been involved in the American Committee on United Europe and must have known Retinger in this connection.

77 There is nothing in the British Foreign Office and Downing Street files on Retinger to suggest that he was indeed on the payroll of the Secret Service. For a different take, see Wilford, "CIA Plot," 77.

78 See Lett, *Soe's Mastermind*; and Wilkinson and Astley, *Gubbins and Soe*.

79 See Prince Bernhard to Rusk, March 2, 1955, Box 187, Bilderberg Archives, NANL.

80 Special Report "Reported Decline in US Prestige Abroad," September 11, 1953, 5, Declassified Documents Online, CK3100194222.

81 Ibid. 4–5. Of course, Prime Minister Winston Churchill was one of the main proponents of this. See Larres, *Churchill's Cold War*. On the Eisenhower Administration's response, see Leffler, *For the Soul of Mankind*, 84–150.

82 Special Report "Reported Decline in US Prestige Abroad," September 11, 1953, 3, Declassified Documents Online, CK3100194222. On Eisenhower's speech, see Ambrose, *Eisenhower*, 324–326 and Osgood, *Total Cold War*, 63–67.

83 NSC 162/2, October 30, 1953, https://history.state.gov/historicaldocuments/frus1952-54v02p1/. Accessed March 27, 2018. As Osgood rightly emphasizes: "[d]iscounting the danger of overt military aggression, NSC 162/2 defined the Soviet threat overwhelmingly in political and psychological terms." Osgood, *Total Cold War*, 71.

84 In addition to the CIA Report, NSC 162/2 relied on the report of the Jackson Committee on psychological warfare. The Jackson Committee was named after its chairman William H. Jackson, but C. D. Jackson was one of the most influential members. See Osgood, "Form before Substance," 424.

85 NSC 162/2, October 30, 1953, https://history.state.gov/historicaldocuments/frus1952-54v02p1/. Accessed March 27, 2018.

86 Ibid.

87 See Bowie and Immerman, *Waging Peace*, 210.

88 Spaulding Jr., "A Gradual and Moderate Relaxation," 244–245. See also Jackson, *The Economic Cold War*.

89 Report No. 2, December 1953, Box 1, Bilderberg Archives, NANL.

90 On Coleman's letter of transmittal to C. D. Jackson, Ball's name is underlined, along with a hand-written note saying "good report."

91 See Bill, *George Ball*; and DiLeo, "George Ball and Jean Monnet."

92 Looking back on his relationship with Monnet, Ball wrote in 1978: "What Monnet expected from me was someone who could translate his ideas into straightforward English prose – and in the process help him think." Note by George Ball, October 3, 1978, Box 26, Folder 3, Ball Papers, PUL.

93 Bill, *George Ball*, 105.
94 Memorandum on American Attitudes Toward Relations with Europe, no date, 2, Box 1, Bilderberg Archives, NANL.
95 Ibid., 8.
96 Ibid., 5–6.
97 Ibid., 10.
98 Present were: Prince Bernhard, Gaitskell, Mueller, Quaroni, Rijkens and Van Zeeland. See Paul Rijkens, "Observations made at the Paris meeting held on Monday, 18th January," Box 30, Bilderberg Archives, NANL and Prince Bernhard's handwritten notes (8 pages) of the meeting, undated, Box 181, Bilderberg Archives, NANL.
99 Paul Rijkens, "Observations made at the Paris meeting held on Monday, 18th January," Box 30, Bilderberg Archives, NANL.
100 Gaitskell, 'Notes for a Joint Report on European-American Relations,' January 19, 1954, Box 1, Bilderberg Archives, NANL.
101 It is possible that Prince Bernhard was hesitant at first to issue the invitations in his name, given the constitutional limits on his political activities. The Dutch cabinet saw no such objections and supported the conference. Beyen suggested several people as Dutch participants. See Rijkens to Prince Bernhard, February 22, 1954, Box 183, Bilderberg Archives, NANL.
102 See the notes on the meeting "7th and 8th February – PARIS," Box 30, Bilderberg Archives, and Prince Bernhard's handwritten notes of the meeting (13 pages), Box 181, Bilderberg Archives, NANL.
103 Ball, *The Past*, 105.
104 Hughes to Jackson, February 10, 1954, Box 35, Jackson Papers, DDEL.
105 Van Zeeland, Rijkens, Müller and Quaroni had contributed notes for the final report as well. See Retinger to Gaitskell, January 27, 1954, Box 295, Gaitskell Papers, UCL.
106 See Report No. 3, Box 1, Bilderberg Archives, NANL. "Members of the Group, bearing in mind that the group has to remain anonymous, and using their own channels, should ensure that the views contained in Report No. 3 be submitted to the various governments."
107 See his letter to Retinger, February 1, 1954, Box 295, Gaitskell Papers, UCL. In reaction to Retinger's draft of the joint report, Gaitskell wrote: "On page 15, at the bottom, you say 'that our group, etc. must for the present remain private.' This worries me a little. I have always assumed that it would never be anything else but private. I do not think we should give any contrary impression to anybody, and I feel pretty certain that the other members would strongly concur."
108 Gaitskell to Pomian, February 22, 1954, Box 295, Gaitskell Papers, UCL.
109 See Coleman's letter to Jackson, March 17, 1954, Box 35, Jackson Papers, DDEL.
110 Rijkens, *Handel en Wandel*, 138.
111 Pomian to Brauer, February 19, 1954, Box 25-1, Brauer Papers, SH.
112 See Voisin to Retinger, May 5, 1954, Box 30, Bilderberg Archives, NANL. From 1958 onwards, Baumgartner, then the President of the *Banque de France*, became a regular Bilderberg participant.
113 Memorandum for the Secretary of State by Frank Roberts, March 16, 1954, Box 113240, FO 371, TNA. Not all of Roberts' colleagues agreed. Anthony Nutting shared C. D. Jackson's cool feelings towards Retinger, commenting "I'm never very keen on things which involve Dr. Retinger."
114 Brauer to Rosenberg, April 5, 1954, Box 25-1, Brauer Papers, SH.
115 See Retinger to De Gasperi, April 10, 1954, Box 30, Bilderberg Archives, NANL.

116 Shortly after Bernhard had returned from a test-flight with pilot Joseph Lynch in a TF-86 Sabre Jet, Lynch crashed in the same plane. See "Dies in Same Plane He Piloted for Dutch Prince," *The Chicago Daily Tribune*, March 18, 1954.

117 C. D. Jackson sent report no. 3 to Gabriel Hauge at the White House, who in turn informed the President of its contents.

118 Prince Bernhard to President Eisenhower, April 27, 1954, Eisenhower Office Files Part 2 International Files Reel 23 Netherlands (Microfilm collection RSC).

119 Memorandum for Mrs. Ann C. Whitman by Robert Murphy, May 1, 1954, Box 41, Ann Whitman File, International Series, DDEL. On March 1, 1954, the United States had tested a multi-megaton H-Bomb on Bikini Island. A Japanese fishing boat was hit by radiation, causing an international uproar further nourished by the statement of AEC Chairman Lewis Strauss that an H-Bomb could destroy a city as large as New York. See Ambrose, *Eisenhower*, 353–355.

120 This was the formulation used in a May 7 telegram Eisenhower sent to Prince Bernhard, Box 41, Ann Whitman File, International Series, DDEL.

121 Eisenhower to Prince Bernhard, May 13, 1954, Box 41, Ann Whitman File, International Series, DDEL. Eisenhower aid General Persons had indeed contacted House Majority Leader Halleck, who told him "that at this time it would be extremely dangerous to suggest that two Congressmen go to the Netherlands to participate in conference (even a Republican and a Democrat)." See memorandum in Box 41, Ann Whitman File, International Series, DDEL.

122 Littlejohn to Retinger, April 19, 1954, Box 30, Bilderberg Papers, NA.

> We have talked to a number of Senators and Congressmen, all of whom expressed great interest in the meeting. All agreed, however, that it was impossible to get away at the present time. As you know, important matters are currently debated in Congress, and this is an election year. As a result, none of them feels he could leave Washington, even for a brief period, at this crucial time.

123 For Richard Aldrich's claim about the CIA's involvement, see Aldrich, *The Hidden Hand*, 369 and Richard Aldrich, "OSS, CIA," 216. Aldrich's claim has found its way into many other works, for example in Dujardin and Dumoulin, *Paul van Zeeland*, 225; and Lundestad, *The United States and Europe*, 74. The CIA-claim was also made in a thinly sourced article by E. Pasymowski and C. Gilbert, "Bilderberg: the Cold War Internationale" which was put in the *Congressional Record* (Vol. 117, 1971) by the right-wing democrat John Rarick. This is the source Stephen Gill gives for his assertion that the first Bilderberg conference was financed by the CIA: Gill, *American Hegemony*, 129. For an earlier debunking of the CIA's involvement see Wilford, "CIA Plot," 77. Bilkupski claims that Retinger "was in the pay of the CIA" while setting up Bilderberg but provides no proof. *War and Diplomacy*, 456.

124 For details on the financing of Bilderberg, see Chapter 4.

125 Deputies' Meeting, May 21, 1954. www.cia.gov/library/readingroom/document/cia-rdp80b01676r002300150013-9. Accessed June 2, 2017.

126 See Ferguson to Nitze, July 8, 1954, Box 58 Nitze Papers, LOC.

127 Lundestad, *'Empire' by Integration.*

128 Maier, *Among Empires*, 35.

3   The first Bilderberg conference

Cyrus Sulzberger, as sharp an observer of the European scene as anyone, noted in April 1954 that a "fundamental shift in psychological balances between the Old and New Worlds" was taking place. "It derives," Sulzberger wrote in his *New York Times* column,

> from three influences which have been making themselves felt gradually: the evolution of Republican foreign policy in the United States since the inauguration of President Eisenhower; the evolution of the Soviet Union's 'new look' foreign policy since the death of Stalin, and the political and spiritual resurgence of free Europe itself as the happy result of the Marshall Plan, NATO and the resultant receding danger of war.[1]

The changed dynamics of transatlantic relations were on full display during the first Bilderberg conference, held at Hotel de Bilderberg from May 29 to 31, 1954. The first session of the conference was dominated by European criticism of the United States in the context of the tense international situation. Dien Bien Phu had fallen on May 7, and despite strong pressure from the Eisenhower Administration, the British government had opposed a US proposal to consider joint military intervention to assist the faltering French army in Indochina. Meanwhile, Secretary of State John Foster Dulles' threat of an "agonizing reappraisal" of the Eisenhower Administration's European policies had failed to push the French towards quickly accepting the European Defense Community (EDC). The only thing the threat seemed to have accomplished was to reawaken the specter of American isolationism. The Eisenhower Administration's talk of withdrawing soldiers from Europe reinforced these concerns. To make matters worse, Senator McCarthy had just broadened his scorching attacks on US institutions, much to the dismay of many Europeans.

Based on the detailed transcripts of the first Bilderberg conference, this chapter shows how European apprehensions about McCarthyism and the international situation inevitably found their way into the Bilderberg discussions, underlining the highly emotional nature of the transatlantic relationship. Starting with an early intervention by Sir Oliver Franks regarding the powerful emotional impact of the Korean War on the United States, many participants returned to the significance of emotions over the course of the next three days.

Some of these emotions were decidedly negative. After the opening session, C. D. Jackson complained in his diary about the "brilliantly executed British hostility" against the United States, and Chairman Prince Bernhard cautioned the Bilderberg participants that he had "heard little more than expressions of irritation."[2] Nevertheless, the overall atmosphere at the conference turned out to be surprisingly constructive, in part because a strong positive sense of emotional community found frequent expression in the almost ritualized reciting of shared values in the face of the threat posed by Soviet communism. The global mindset of most participants also played a role: time and time again participants emphasized the need for transatlantic cooperation and unity in the face of a rapidly changing world. In the words of Prince Bernhard's opening address, "the national or even the continental viewpoint is inadequate and should give way to a global one."[3]

The global mindset implied a constant effort to understand transatlantic differences in attitudes and approaches. At the first Bilderberg conference, this effort involved a long list of issues on the agenda. The organizers had asked one American and one European participant to prepare a brief paper each to set off discussions: Paul Nitze and Alcide de Gasperi on *communism*, David Rockefeller and Hugh Gaitskell on *economic relations*, Barry Bingham and the Dutch civil servant Hans M. Hirschfeld on the *problem of overseas territories*, George Ball and Etienne de la Vallée Poussin on *European unification*, and James Zellerbach and Guy Mollet on the *EDC*. The Bilderberg discussions laid bare not only many transatlantic differences on these issues, but also many intra-European ones. A three-day conference could do only so much to overcome these differences, but in the end even initial Bilderberg skeptics such as Jackson felt that the effort to develop a better grasp of elite opinions and sensibilities on both sides of the Atlantic had been worthwhile.[4]

Hotel de Bilderberg, May 1954

Hotel De Bilderberg was a medium-sized, family-run hotel, mainly chosen for its quiet and remote location in the forests of the eastern Netherlands. It was not a particularly fancy hotel – old curtains had to be used as tablecloths in the conference room – but security was relatively easy to maintain since there was only one access road. Police protection ensured that no uninvited visitors were able to intrude, and the Dutch secret service screened all hotel employees. Those with communist sympathies were asked to stay home for the week.[5] An additional advantage of the Bilderberg Hotel was that, in the absence of any major cities nearby, all participants were more or less forced to stay at the hotel for three full days.

As Retinger's assistant, John Pomian, later recalled, the idea was to create an atmosphere of trust among the participants by spending a great deal of time together, not only during the official discussions, but also at the dinner table and over drinks.[6]

In terms of practical arrangements, Paul Rijkens made available a team of Unilever employees that prepared the conference and staffed the eight-person conference secretariat. Two Philips technicians operated the specially installed audio system, and four translators provided simultaneous translation in the two official conference languages, English and French. 27 drivers and 20 cars were available for transportation, 23 extra telephone lines were installed at the hotel, and copies of international newspapers were ordered. "I have never seen a meeting which went off more smoothly," Rockefeller told Prince Bernhard afterwards, "[and] I have had enough to do with such affairs to know how much advance thinking and planning this requires."[7]

The conference was largely financed by contributions from a dozen large Dutch companies, including Unilever, Philips, Heineken, KLM, and Hoogovens. Prince Bernhard had personally appealed to them, arguing that it was important to bring the conference to the Netherlands. In addition, Prince Bernhard, Kraft, Mueller, Quaroni, and Van Zeeland contributed between £150 and £1000. Most American participants paid for their own transportation, but all other costs were covered by the funds raised by Prince Bernhard.[8]

Journalists were not allowed to cover the Bilderberg discussions, although several publishers and editors were present. The conference organizers did hold a press conference after the end of the Bilderberg meeting and released a press statement summarizing the results of the discussions.

The first morning session on Saturday, May 29, 1954, served to collect general impressions about the state of European-American relations. Prince Bernhard chaired the session and did so with charm, quickly succeeding in establishing an atmosphere conducive to open discussions.[9] In his opening statement, Bernhard went out of his way to stress the common values and culture shared by Europe and the United States:

> Europeans and Americans are linked by the same basic cultural background, the same basic civilisation, the same faith and to a very large extent by the same blood. We can rightly speak of the Atlantic civilisation of which we all share the origin: the European and still earlier the Mediterranean civilisation. This explains, more than anything else, why during the last decennia, whenever European nations got into a big conflict, America, as a member of the same family, joined in. In the face of a real external threat we find ourselves on the same side. This explained [...] why the United States had twice come to the rescue of Europe and why in response to the Cold War challenges, the Western world should hold together again.

Prince Bernhard went on to explain the internationalist rationale behind the Retinger group and the Bilderberg meeting:

> Since the free countries of Europe, the United States and Canada must act as one, they will need a certain unity of outlook and they must make an effort to think in terms of Western partnership as a whole. That means that we must promote a new way of thinking, transcending the Old World mentality which often has a provincial look about it. This could help Western people realize their common interest. [...] To my mind the inter-dependence of the Western countries makes interest in one's neighbour's affairs not only natural but necessary and vital.

In practice, Bernhard argued, cooperation had to take the form of "multi-lateral agreements" such as NATO. In an indirect appeal to the Americans, he underlined the need for careful consultation. "Uncoordinated action," he said, "unagreed [*sic*] moves, decisions affecting allies which have been uni-laterally taken, all these things carry grave dangers by providing the enemy with the immediate chance and the weapon to try to divide us."[10]

Despite Prince Bernhard's call for unity, the first session – and the subse-quent one concerning communism – soon turned into a contentious transat-lantic debate. The American publisher Gardner Cowles Jr. set the tone early on by expressing his disappointment "that so many Europeans thought that the situation in Asia did not call for immediate action." He referred to two recent speeches on the Indochina crisis to illustrate the different attitudes towards the Cold War:

> In the United States [Chief of Naval Operations] Admiral Carney had said that the United States were now rapidly approaching a crossroad in the final fight to finish with Soviet Russia, whereas Sir Winston Churchill appealed for patience in our dealings with Soviet Russia.[11]

The Bilderberg participants had likely read about Admiral Robert B. Carney's speech in their morning papers. *The New York Times* gave the speech front-page coverage and printed it in full on page 2. According to the *Times*, "the admiral's statement was interpreted authoritatively here and in Washington as a new warning that the United States and its allies must be prepared for the possibility of joining the fighting in Indochina."[12]

The trouble was that no agreement existed on the rationale for joining the fighting. France had fought the deeply unpopular war to maintain its colonial empire, yet other NATO members – the United States in particular – were unwilling to send troops into the jungles of Indochina without the promise of independence for Vietnam. At the same time, the Eisenhower Administration's fixation on the communist threat, as expressed by the president in early April with the analogy of the domino theory, wasn't shared to the same extent in European capitals. The British government, for example, was less worried about dominos falling than about a possible escalation of the conflict, leading to the involvement of China and perhaps even of the Soviet Union. The politics of the Indochina crisis, moreover, differed on both sides of the Atlantic. In the United States, anti-Chinese sentiment, particularly among Republicans, remained so strong that US diplomats were forbidden to shake the hands of their Chinese counterparts. In much of Europe, on the other hand, the Geneva negotiations about Indochina were regarded as a much-needed way out of a further escalation of the conflict.

In response to Cowles, Hugh Gaitskell strongly criticized the lack of consultation and unity within the Western alliance. Given America's much greater involvement in the Korean War, he argued, the American assessment of the Soviet threat naturally differed from European perceptions. However, the open division among the Western powers at the Geneva Conference on Indochina gave "dangerous encouragement to the enemy."[13] NATO had been successful in stabilizing the situation in Western Europe and in preventing "sudden attacks," but consultation between the member governments was inadequate. "Many of the difficulties could have been avoided," Gaitskell said, "if more satisfactory machinery existed for inter-governmental discussion."[14]

Sir Oliver Franks followed with a long statement supporting Gaitskell. He agreed that the Korean crisis in 1950, in particular the Chinese intervention, had been the crucial break in the postwar period. As the British Ambassador in Washington, Franks had been in a position to witness the "massive emotional states" that had arisen in the United States.[15] He worried that "real differences of policy or emphasis could in the long run be solved by hard negotiation, but those emotional states rendered a solution impossible." As a result, many people in the United Kingdom "wondered whether America acted from passion rather than from policy." McCarthyism, Franks added, reflected the psychological gap between the new and the old world that had widened markedly since the summer of 1950. A related problem was the way in which officials voiced their opinions in both countries. Americans "erred on the side of mild exaggeration" whereas the British preferred the art of "understatement." Taking Admiral Carney's speech as an example, Franks joked that the British version would have sounded something like this: "If the Russians continue in this way, I believe we should pay a bit more attention to them." The Bilderberg summary at this point simply noted "(hilarity)."[16]

The Italian liberal Giovanni Malagodi reinforced Franks' analysis of emotional states by contrasting "American impatience" with "European patience" based on the realization that no quick or easy solution to such issues as the EDC was possible. Malagodi noted, in agreement with Gaitskell, that better machinery for consultation was needed and that Article 2 of the North Atlantic Treaty could be used to deepen ties between the NATO allies.

How to deal with communism?

The opening session of the Bilderberg conference left little doubt about the importance of the first topic on the agenda: the attitude towards communism. Several speakers pointed to McCarthyism as proof of the fact that America and Western Europe were drifting apart. On the American side bewilderment at the European reluctance to act forcefully against communist expansionism was expressed in equally strong terms. This was a problem because a common Western policy in the Cold War depended, to a large extent, on a common assessment of the adversary. The constant reports about the excesses of McCarthyism strengthened anti-American sentiments in Europe and undermined US leadership in NATO. Conversely, the perception in Washington that many European countries were both 'soft' on internal communism and unwilling to face the threat of Soviet expansionism had a negative effect on Congress' willingness to pay for the American presence in Europe and reinforced neo-isolationist thinking.

Former Italian Prime Minister Alcide de Gasperi and American diplomat Paul Nitze had prepared papers on the attitudes towards communism. They illustrated the sharply diverging views and perceptions: the American tendency to think in Manichean terms of good and evil contrasted with the European conviction that communism as a political ideology had to be battled with political means and would not disappear overnight.[17] The most basic difference was, of course, that in many European countries communism was a fact of life, whereas in the United States communism never was a major political force.

Senator Raffaele Cafiero had taken De Gasperi's place at the conference because the former Italian prime minister was too ill to be present (he died three months later). De Gasperi's report made clear that Italy had a long and painful history of dealing with communism. The fascist reaction in the 1920s had led to a dictatorship and had been a "costly experience" for Italy. The lesson to be learned was that a successful response had to consist of "democratic education and the improvement of social conditions." De Gasperi argued that McCarthyism was a dangerous mistake, an overreaction comparable to the fascist movement in Italy. High unemployment and a depressed standard of living were the main sources for communist strength in a country such as Italy. Combined with a large and efficient communist organization, considerable prestige dating back to the time of the anti-fascist resistance, and ample funds for propaganda, this had led to election results of over 30% of the vote.

With respect to the international situation, De Gasperi pointed out that the Italian communists had been greatly strengthened by the lack of unity in the Western world that had been a consequence of Moscow's 'peace offensive' after Stalin's death in 1953. At the time of the Marshall Plan and the creation of the North Atlantic Treaty, the democratic front in Italy had been united. In the 1953 elections the democratic forces were hopelessly divided, opening the door to communist success.[18]

Paul Nitze, who would become a regular Bilderberg participant, was an interesting choice for the American report on communism.[19] Nitze had been director of the State Department's Policy Planning staff under Secretary of State Dean Acheson.[20] He was one of the principal authors of NSC 68, a blueprint for American strategy in the Cold War during the Truman Administration and beyond.[21] NSC 68, as Craig and Logevall have put it, called for "a policy of global anti-communism."[22] It advocated a vast military buildup based on the assumption that "the Soviet Union, unlike previous aspirants to hegemony, is animated by a new fanatic faith, anti-thetical to our own, and seeks to impose its absolute authority over the rest of the world."[23] In NSC 68, Nitze had defined the Cold War as a moral struggle between good and evil, between "slavery" and "freedom." He argued that the United States should build up a position of strength in order to deter the Soviet Union from further aggression and to prepare the way for an ultimate settlement. Such a program was also needed to reassure the Europeans; after traveling to Europe in the late 1940s, Nitze had become convinced that the North Atlantic Treaty on its own was not sufficient to rally US allies in Europe.[24]

NSC 68 was presented to President Truman in April 1950. The outbreak of the Korean War two months later ensured that its recommendations were largely accepted.[25] The criticism of Soviet experts George Kennan and Charles Bohlen that NSC 68 exaggerated the expansionist intentions of the Soviet Union and put too much emphasis on a military response fell on deaf ears.

Nitze was offered a high-ranking position in the Pentagon when the Eisenhower Administration took over, but the offer was rescinded when right-wing media and senators started criticizing Nitze as a big-spending Truman acolyte.[26] Nitze remained an important voice on foreign policy in the Democratic Party, usually in tandem with his friend Dean Acheson.

In his Bilderberg paper, Nitze distinguished between American views on communism in general and their specific attitudes towards the Soviet Union. While many Americans still felt "considerable respect" for the Russian performance in World War II, "[c]ommunism is regarded as something immoral, which threatens religion, is inhuman toward the individual, is cynically untrustworthy, and challenges all people and nations not under its control." Nitze repeatedly used terms such as "evil" and "unclean" to characterize how most Americans viewed communism. He acknowledged the "near-hysteria over domestic communism" in the United States, but indicated that McCarthyism was on the retreat. Nitze implied that the moral rejection of communism had made it difficult for some Americans to reach a realistic assessment of the threat it posed. However, "[t]o the more sophisticated [Americans] communism is evil, but only constitutes a threat in so far as it is directed from Moscow and backed by the physical power of Russia and of China." Speaking at the Bilderberg Hotel, he said:

Certainly for the American people the threat is without precedent. During the long century from the Napoleonic wars to the 1st world war, they were protected both by a balance of power in the rest of the world, and by seas controlled by a friendly power, the U.K. Now the seas have shrunk, the world has become polarized, and on top of that totalitarian ideas seem to have progressed in internal consistency and in ruthless efficiency in action from the demonic ideas of Nazism to the coldly calculated ideas of communism.[27]

Despite his passionate rejection of communism, Nitze recognized the necessity of negotiating with the Soviet Union, as did a large majority of Americans. But negotiations, he argued, could only be successful from a position of strength. From the American point of view, too many Europeans wanted to negotiate for negotiations' sake, without being prepared for alternative courses of action. Nitze concluded by saying that Europeans should realize that for the United States, the threat of Soviet communism always came first. With respect to the German question this meant, for example, that they had little patience for those who worried more about the "German threat" than about the broader Cold War struggle.[28]

The different attitudes towards communism that had been identified by Nitze and De Gasperi found confirmation in the subsequent discussion. A first dispute concerned the question of whether Western European communist parties were fully under Soviet control. George Perkins, former Assistant Secretary for European Affairs in the State Department, stated flatly that all local communist parties were "agents of Soviet imperialism." When several European participants expressed dissenting views, C. D. Jackson explained that in the United States, communism had first and foremost been a matter of espionage. He warned that communist parties in the rest of the world were skilled at posing as national or local political forces. Yet the danger always remained that they would cooperate with Moscow once they reached a position of power.

Representatives of the European democratic Left criticized the American reaction to communism and emphasized social progress as the best method to combat the communist parties in Western Europe.[29] Tom Williamson, General Secretary of the British National Union of General and Municipal Workers, questioned Nitze's usage of the word "unclean" and insisted that communism in Europe should only be fought with democratic means. His German colleague Ludwig Rosenberg of the *Deutsche Gewerkschaftsbund* (DGB) supported him, saying that Europe's "best weapon" was "improved social conditions," not restrictive legislation.[30] Rosenberg added that the American socioeconomic model could not be applied directly to Europe. In his view, Europe should develop its own vision of the kind of democratic society and economy it wished to create. Among the European masses, democracy should become "a style of living and not just a form of administration."[31] Hirschfeld similarly argued that the "free world" had to "find the happy harmony" between the systems of "free enterprise" and "social security" in order to "fight communism." Max Brauer "again stressed what the other delegates had already said, that democracy can only improve the standard of living. The elaborate window-display in Western Germany is the best possible anti-communist propaganda."[32]

In contrast, several speakers pointed out how effective communist propaganda had been in taking advantage of divisive issues in Europe. Jean Drapier, chief of staff to Belgian Foreign Minister Paul-Henri Spaak, explained how communists used the German question for this purpose. "Their propaganda," he said,

> is based on the desire of the Western European peoples to retain their independence and therefore they encourage fear of the Germans. [T]he Communists in France are stirring up this feeling with unmitigated cruelty. The French are embittered about the fact that they have lost some of their influence and power and the Communists try to take advantage of their striving for social justice and their fear of war.[33]

Denis Healey, a young Labour foreign policy expert, analyzed the different attitudes towards communism in the context of the world situation. He argued that "[i]n America communism was regarded as a moral evil and an alien thing which had no root in the American sphere at all. [...] In the USA any negotiation with a communist state involved a moral compromise with evil." In Europe, this was not the case. Here, Healey said, the "problem was to maintain unity when the communists relaxed pressure." Many Europeans "underestimate[d] the doctrinal elements of Soviet Communism when thinking of possible settlements." Responding to Soviet Communism, Healey argued, wasn't simply a matter of "power problems" because communism was an expansionist ideology combining "religious fanaticism with imperialism." Echoing Kennan's containment strategy, he said that the West should respond by "trying to create forces of social, economic and military strength adequate to keep the peace."[34] If this strategy was successful, coexistence with the Soviet Union was possible and Russian imperialism might change in the future.

Whether coexistence was possible (or even desirable) was to remain an issue of debate at future Bilderberg meetings. George McGhee reminded the meeting that Secretary of State Dulles had recently said "coexistence was impossible so long as Russia continued her present aggressive policy."[35] It was clear that Europeans and Americans "haven't arrived at a commonly agreed estimate of the danger and sense of urgency."[36] The Bilderberg press release summarized these transatlantic differences in similar terms:

> America sometimes charges its allies with slowness and undue deliberation in meeting the Communist threat. European nations sometimes feel that the United States is unreasonably impatient. The main difference between the European and American attitude towards the Communist threat is a different sense of timing. Both the Europeans

and the Americans understand that Communism is not like the weather, against which occasional local precautions can be taken, but that it is an active enemy requiring positive, energetic and steady opposition.

McCarthyism was not officially part of the Bilderberg agenda. Yet as Prince Bernhard acknowledged in his opening statement, it was inevitable that McCarthyism would come up. To many Europeans, the danger of a right-wing takeover in Washington seemed real at the height of McCarthy's influence.[37] We now know that at the time of the Bilderberg conference, McCarthy was fatally undermining his own position by his abrasive behavior during the televised Army-McCarthy hearings, but this turn of events was not yet apparent. Only days before the Bilderberg conference, McCarthy had openly challenged President Eisenhower by calling on government employees to report subversion in their ranks directly to him. Obviously, many Europeans were worried about this state of affairs. Throughout the first day of the meeting, European participants criticized McCarthy's methods and called attention to the negative impact McCarthyism had on European public opinion. As Brauer, who lived in exile in the United States during much of the 1930s and 1940s, said: "[d]emocracy must not be blinded by McCarthyism – Europe can take everything from the United States but not that. Freedom and security are the two things we must fight for."[38]

C. D. Jackson noted in his diary that he "became aware of fact that the Europeans had been pathologically eager to discuss McCarthy from the first hour, but each time the name came up it was quickly slurred over." He also felt that the American response to criticism of the United States was much too timid. He decided, therefore, to request a 'special session' on the topic on the last day of the conference. He had the "strong feeling that if [the] meeting broke up without allowing Europeans [the] opportunity to indulge themselves, they would claim Americans had deliberately avoided issue [...]"[39]

The McCarthy session indeed did much to clear the air between the European and American participants. Jackson started off with a 15-minute presentation. According to Alden Hatch, Jackson bluntly said:

> Whether McCarthy dies by an assassin's bullet or is eliminated in the normal American way of getting rid of boils on the body politic, I prophesy that by the time we hold our next meeting he will be gone from the American scene.[40]

Nitze supported him, saying that it was wrong and unfair to imply, as several European speakers had done, that a majority of Americans supported McCarthy. "Only a small and diminishing [percentage] of Americans approve of McCarthies [*sic*] methods. The overwhelming majority are dead against it."[41] Jackson noted in his diary that the session was a success – with Oliver Franks whispering "jolly good show" – and indeed, on the subject of McCarthyism the American participants had made a convincing case. They were confirmed the next morning with newspapers all over the world reporting that President Eisenhower had opened the attack on McCarthy.

The transatlantic economy

When Retinger and his friends had been preparing their reports on anti-Americanism in mid-1952, two issues had stood out in the economic parts of their analysis. First was the overwhelming European dependence on the United States and the ensuing frequent tensions. Hugh Gaitskell had called this Europe's 'poor-relation complex.' The so-called dollar gap was its clearest expression. It had led to a situation in which the nations receiving the most Marshall Plan aid paradoxically seemed to be most prone to resenting US economic power. The second issue concerned East-West trade and the far-reaching restrictions the United States' Congress had imposed through the Battle Act.

The Bilderberg discussions showed that by the summer of 1954, the economic situation in Europe had improved significantly, lessening Europe's dependence on the United States. As the Bilderberg press release put it, "economic factors were no longer such a serious cause of friction between the United States and Europe as they were a few years ago." Still, East-West trade remained a controversial topic, the dollar gap had not fully disappeared, and many of the European participants, mindful of the breakdown of the international economic system in the 1930s, still worried about the effects a US recession might have on European economies. On the other hand, the American economic example served as a possible answer to the communist challenge. If only the European nations could achieve the kinds of advances in productivity and economic growth that had made the United States into the world's economic powerhouse, the socioeconomic sources of communist support would disappear.[42]

David Rockefeller was the first to present a report on the state of American-European economic relations. Armed with a series of charts, the 38-year-old scion of the Rockefeller family attempted to ease European concerns. The long-term US economic prospects were excellent, he argued, despite the current economic downturn. In view of rising productivity, increasing wages, and faster than expected population growth, the US economy would soon expand again. Moreover, as a result of New Deal reforms, the important role of the government in the national economy had created a "built-in stability." A repeat of the Great Depression, in other words, was difficult to imagine. Moreover, the United States' growing demand for raw materials would provide Europe with the opportunity to earn dollars outside of the United States, "which would mean a re-establishment of multi-lateral trade."[43] Thus, the dollar gap could disappear even without the assistance of US defense spending and military aid. With respect to free trade, Rockefeller noted, the Randall Commission had proposed a series of efforts to lower US trade barriers, and the Eisenhower Administration would likely succeed in getting some of these recommendations passed in Congress.

Hugh Gaitskell, the author of the European report, agreed with Rockefeller that the economic situation had improved and expressed "faith in the enormously improved change in the influence of the government and in the techniques of economic planning now adopted in the free enterprise economy of the United States." On the issue of East-West trade, he returned to the importance of emotions and the impact of the Korean War. He understood that to many Americans it was difficult to understand why Great Britain would want to "trade with the enemy." On the other hand,

> the Battle Act had created the greatest indignation; it was felt that the United States was using economic power to withhold aid in order to impose a particular foreign policy. He felt this was entirely wrong and that trade restrictions already provided ample fuel for communist propaganda. It was important not to confuse political and economic ideology.[44]

The president of the British Trade Federation, Sir Harry Pilkington, supported Gaitskell and argued "that East-West trade could be used constructively to penetrate the iron curtain and to spread Western ideas on the other side." Even cold warrior C. D. Jackson had to admit that "economic warfare with the East had not been intelligently handled." Foreshadowing the decades-long transatlantic dispute on the issue of East-West trade, however, the arguments in favor of trade with the Eastern Bloc came exclusively from European participants. The Bilderberg final report simply expressed the hope that the list of "controlled exports" would be reduced and that East-West trade would no longer create "the considerable propaganda advantage enjoyed by the Communists during the last few years."[45]

The Bilderberg discussions showed a broad consensus in favor of trade liberalization and currency convertibility. On the American side, this was to be expected, given the fact that the Coleman Committee had been founded to support the findings of the Randall Commission in favor of lowering trade barriers. C. D. Jackson added an official voice to Rockefeller's introduction by arguing that the United States

> needed partners in developing the economic growth of the free world, and the European countries were its natural partners. [...] He was glad to say that in his view there was the beginning of a massive change of opinion in the United States on the subject of import barriers.[46]

On the European side, however, the voices in favor of free trade were just as strong. Some of this simply reflected narrow economic interests. The Norwegian shipowner Leif Høegh, for example, criticized the US insistence on using American shipping for at least 50% of its foreign and military aid.

The Belgian Pierre Bonvoisin, president of the *Banque de la Société Générale de Belgique*, complained about the fact that "customs technicalities presented almost insurmountable difficulties for European countries in developing sound and regular trade with the United States." Meanwhile, both Pirelli and Malagodi emphasized Italy's demographic problem and argued that other Western countries should either invest more to assist in economic development or allow more immigration from Italy.[47]

Beyond such specific issues, however, a broader argument in favor of free trade emerged. Bonvoisin argued that "bilateral trade protected by governments was relatively easy; but the liberal multi-lateral system of trading, based on efficient private initiative, could be much more successful." New York was in a position, he added, to take over the role London had played before World War I as a clearinghouse for multilateral trade. The German lawyer and Bilderberg co-founder Rudolf Mueller linked the issue to the earlier discussion on communism, arguing: "the primary target was to raise the standard of living of the masses by increasing productivity, which could only be done by bringing about a freer movement of goods, labour and money." He added that liberalizing the German economy was critical because "on it depended the integration of Germany in Europe." Pirelli similarly argued that in the struggle to ensure economic growth "a primary remedy would be the unification of Europe."[48]

The Bilderberg consensus on trade and increasing productivity was important precisely because of this connection with European integration. In the summer of 1954, the European project was still concerned with the EDC. Soon, however, the EDC was put to rest by the French Assembly, and European integration took a different course, leading to the Rome Treaties establishing the Common Market. A significant number of Bilderberg participants would play both leading and supporting roles in these events.

Decolonization

Barry Bingham, the owner of the *Courier-Journal* and the *Louisville Times* and a former Marshall Plan chief in France, had written the US report on the "Problem of Overseas Territories." Bingham argued that on the question of decolonization, "[e]motion and reason [...] were in conflict, both in Europe and in America." On the US side, a long tradition of anti-colonialism had caused "a strong and traditional feeling that colonial people should be free." On the other hand, the dangers of "too sudden liberation" had become clear to the American public over the past few years. In Europe, Bingham said, "the pull of emotion, in which national pride was involved, worked in the sense of keeping the colonials under European guidance. Reason, on the other hand, had shown the dangers of too tight a hold." The key issue, therefore, was one of timing. Bingham argued that the European colonial powers should ensure a "steady movement toward independence," otherwise "the great Nationalist storm" would lead to chaos and violence.[49] The United

States might play a role as mediator between the colonial powers and their overseas territories. In the case of Indochina, Bingham argued, this meant that France should declare that full independence would await the nations of French Indochina once order had been restored.

The response to Bingham's introduction fell mainly into two camps: those who defended the colonial powers and argued for patience and those who agreed that colonialism was a thing of the past. The French MP and diplomat Jean-Michel Guérin de Beaumont belonged to the former group and ridiculed Bingham's suggestion that the United States could play the role of mediator. "The United States themselves," de Beaumont remarked sarcastically,

> solved the problem of the Indians in the spirit of the time, i.e. - we have to admit it - by eliminating the Indians, but this method can no longer be applied to-day. [...] It is to be feared that Mr. Bingham will have great difficulty in his own country in fighting against the anti-colonialist mentality, which has been firmly established for such a long time in the minds of his compatriots.[50]

With respect to Indochina, de Beaumont argued that it was difficult to explain to the man in the street why France was fighting a war to end its colonial empire. According to Rijkens, de Beaumont's remarks reflected European frustration with the sanctimonious attitude on the part of some of the American participants and did much to clear the air.[51]

The British Secretary of State for Commonwealth Relations, John Foster, added that in the United States, "politics and emotionalism" shaped anti-colonial attitudes. The British did not question the necessity to "bring colonial countries to independence." However, "the issue was not so much one of colonialism and anti-colonialism but one of tempo." The key test was "the country's ability at self-rule."[52]

On the other side of the debate, people like the Norwegian politician Finn Moe and the German trade union leader Ludwig Rosenberg argued that impatience on the part of the colonial peoples was understandable and opened the door for communist propaganda. As Moe put it,

> if America at the time of her independence, Belgium in the beginning of the last century, Czecho-Slovakia in the first World War, or Norway in 1905 had been told their independence was premature [...] they would all have reacted in the same way. If underdeveloped countries were given premature independence, there was a risk of Communism, but if they were kept in a state of dependence, the danger of Communism was far greater, as those countries would look towards Communism to satisfy their strong desire for independence.[53]

Rosenberg similarly argued that it was "dangerous to allow the communists to be the prime champions of freedom for the colonial peoples."[54] In terms of practical approaches to the problem, he explained that European and American trade unions had cooperated to set up trade union schools in the underdeveloped world.

On the American side, C. D. Jackson emphasized that the United States could not afford to stay out of colonial conflicts since they inevitably involved "the military security of the United States." He could understand why many Europeans distrusted the United States; still, he argued, "America had evolved since Wilsonian self-determination, and had gone a long way since the time when every black with a tommy-gun was looked upon as a potential George Washington." From the American point of view, it was clear that

> there was a trend towards freedom, and colonial powers could either keep the lid on it, which was a bloody and unlasting [sic] solution, allow chaos to spread, or organise an evolutionary development ending in liberty for the native populations and economic advantages for the ex-colonial powers.[55]

The difficulty of organizing such an "evolutionary development" was clear to all. In the words of George Ball, it was "continuously necessary to strike a balance between political independence and the clear danger that it will mean temporary or long-term losses to the indigenous people themselves, since they may be worse off after independence."[56] Ball suggested that technical training and other ways of preparing dependent areas for self-government was crucial and was supported in this view by other participants. Indeed, the strong focus on development and modernization that would characterize US and European strategy toward the Third World during much of the Cold War was already apparent in the thinking of many Bilderberg participants.[57]

What was also clear, however, was that striking the kind of balance that Ball was talking about was made all the more difficult because of the Cold War. The Indochina crisis demonstrated how Cold War pressures tended to hinder a joint Western strategy. Sir Robert Boothby lamented "that in recent weeks the West had been faced with a break-down of Western policies, and what amounted to a temporary collapse of the Western Alliance, which had produced the gravest results." Sir Oliver Franks warned that the United States' strong focus on military solutions risked ignoring the political dimension. As he put it,

> although it might be possible to win battles in S.E. Asia and Indo-China, the aftermath of such battles might mean the loss of 500,000,000 souls to communism if social and political aspects of the problem were ignored. Political judgment was vital to the successful conduct of affairs in those countries and was complementary to the military aspect.[58]

Franks' warning reflected high-level thinking in the British government; at the same time, it was a response to Admiral Carney's speech and to American Bilderberg participants, such as Gardner Cowles, who had called for quick common action in Indochina.[59] Franks' words did not miss their mark: several participants underlined the importance of his intervention and he was quoted verbatim in the Bilderberg press release.

European integration

After two days of intense discussions on communism, decolonization, and economic issues, the time had come to talk about European integration. The topic had been broached several times in the previous discussions, reflecting the fact that a number of participants regarded a united Europe as the solution to many of the problems facing the West. In terms of improving social conditions, a united Europe promised increased trade, productivity, and economic growth; in terms of the ideological Cold War, Europe could serve as a beacon of hope to capture the imagination of people around the continent; in terms of decolonization, Europe could absorb the loss of overseas markets; in terms of transatlantic economic relations, only a united Europe would be able to compete with the United States.

The Bilderberg meeting, however, took place at a trying time for supporters of European integration. The EDC – and with it the Political Community – was in serious trouble. The EDC treaty had been signed by France, Italy, West Germany, and the Benelux countries in 1952, yet two years later the treaty still had not been ratified in France and Italy. In August 1954, two months after the Bilderberg conference, the EDC would finally be voted down in the French assembly. Until that moment, the Eisenhower Administration had strongly supported the EDC and regarded it not only as the best way to accomplish German rearmament, but, even more importantly, as a crucial step towards Franco-German reconciliation. President Eisenhower and Secretary of State Dulles were convinced that only the surrender of national sovereignties to a supranational authority would be a reliable safeguard to prevent future conflicts between the two countries. Moreover, a unified Europe would be responsible for its own defense, thereby relieving the Americans of a heavy financial burden.[60]

In France, opposition to the EDC defied party lines and united Communists, Gaullists, and much of what came in between.[61] Hostility to the EDC was based on a number of reasons. The obvious aversion to rearming Germany was strengthened by the fear that Germany would quickly come to dominate the EDC. The French army was severely weakened by the war in Indochina and tensions in Algeria, and Great Britain consistently refused to become a member of the EDC as a counterweight to Germany. Meanwhile, the strong American pressure for the EDC was widely resented. John Foster Dulles' threat of an "agonizing reappraisal" at the December 1953 NATO meeting had been just as counterproductive as the decision by Congress to make military aid dependent on ratification of the EDC.[62] Finally, the fact that the EDC treaty abolished France's ability to develop its own nuclear force seems to have played an important role outside the public discourse.[63]

The tumultuous affair over an unauthorized speech critical of the EDC by Marshal Alphonse Juin and the subsequent decision by the Laniel government to relieve him of all his functions had shown the extent to which the EDC had torn the nation apart. During the controversy, a majority of the Socialist members of Parliament released a bombshell statement saying that they would vote against the pro-EDC party line. The rebellion was not limited to backbenchers; it included former Defense Minister Jules Moch and other prominent Socialists. In light of this development, it seemed less likely than ever that Premier Joseph Laniel would be able to obtain a majority for the EDC.

The French crisis had left its mark on the French representation at Bilderberg. The most important absentee was Guy Mollet, whose presence was needed at a special Socialist Party congress on the EDC. Pierre-Henri Teitgen was also prevented from coming because of a *Mouvement Républicain Populaire* congress on the same subject. Mollet, the secretary-general of the Socialist Party, was a strong supporter of the EDC and had started a campaign to get the mutinous anti-EDC faction back into line. In a paper written for the Bilderberg conference, Mollet explained the difficulty of this task. Communist propaganda had framed the debate in terms of a loss of French sovereignty in exchange for a revival of German militarism. In addition, the public perceptions of the Soviet threat had changed since the death of Stalin and the armistice in Korea. As Mollet said: "The 'German Menace' has simply taken precedent, for some, over the Russian menace [...]." Urging reticence on the part of Washington, Mollet stated that

> [...] there is no doubt that any pressure from outside, any sign of impatience on the side of our allies [...], tends to provoke unfavourable reactions, to hurt national pride, and, as a result, to play into the enemies' hand.[64]

Every impression that the EDC was an American project had to be prevented.[65]

Apart from the French difficulties over the EDC, the Bilderberg discussion was characterized by a solid consensus on European integration. The question was not so much *whether* to pursue some form of European unity but *how* to do so. Of course, Retinger, Van Zeeland, Prince Bernhard, and other organizers of the Bilderberg conference were well-known supporters of the European idea. Many of the participants they had invited shared their pro-European mindset. Quite a few of the Americans, moreover, were former diplomats or Marshall Planners who had been exposed to the pro-European thinking at the State Department. The broad pro-European consensus, in other words, did not come as a surprise. Most dissenting voices, as so often when it concerned Europe, came from the British participants.

George Ball had been asked to outline American attitudes towards European integration. Ball was careful not to prescribe any particular form of integration. Addressing a common European criticism, Ball stated that although the American federal experience certainly influenced American thinking, "informed Americans" recognized the differences between the situation in Western Europe and in colonial America. He emphasized that it was the *European* experience of the last 50 years that had led Americans to "reject old formulas as totally inadequate":

> Since a continuation of the past experience of Europe with its national rivalries and wars can lead to nothing but disaster, a new formula for organizing Europe must be found – and no really new formula has been suggested except unification in some kind of federal system. Alliances, agreements, international organizations, balance-of-power arrangements, all are mere variations on old and unsatisfactory themes.

Next, Ball addressed the "fear that the political unity may conduce to an insipid cultural uniformity." This part of his statement was aimed at those who feared a predominantly catholic and conservative 'Little Europe.' He said that many Europeans probably overestimated the cultural uniformity of the United States. He tried to set their minds at rest by arguing that political unification would lead to a "cross-fertilization of cultures" not a "cross-sterilization." Technological developments in communications were a far more important factor in the process of "cultural standardization."[66] Ball ended by stating that an Atlantic community that united Europe and the United States with a supranational authority was not yet realistic. Supporters of some form of Atlantic unity had to understand that European unification was a precondition for any such development in the future.

Ball's statement was well received, and several of his formulations were used almost verbatim in the press release after the Bilderberg conference.[67] Not all Americans, however, were as finely attuned to European sensibilities. James Zellerbach, former chief of the Marshall Plan organization in Italy, pointed to the impatient mood in Congress and the possible repercussions of a French failure to ratify the EDC. He did not use the term "agonizing reappraisal," but warned "that there was a strong feeling that if Europe were unwilling to defend herself, the United States should not assume that responsibility."[68] C. D. Jackson argued that Soviet opposition to the EDC was another reason to proceed quickly: "What the Soviets feared they respected, and what they respected the West should ratify."[69] George Perkins added that

> [i]t was possible that one of the reasons for which the Russians had agreed to the truce [in Korea, TWG] was that it would deaden the sense of urgency for Western re-armament, and slow down or even put an end to the creation of the E.D.C. In the American view such a result would be disastrous, since in fact the Russian threat remained the same as before Korea.[70]

In reaction, several European participants urged the Americans to be patient. Belgian Senator Etienne de la Vallée Pousin, who had been responsible for the European report, said the United States should forcefully support European integration, yet "at the same time leav[e] Europe more responsibility in the realization." Italian Senator Cafiero pointed out that the tone of Zellerbach's contribution had been that of a "governess to bad boys."[71] It was exactly this type of language that caused anti-American resentment in Europe. Jean Drapier, the Belgian socialist, also argued that Europe itself should fight this battle – without US interference. On a more positive note, Drapier was able to inform the meeting that at the Socialist Party congress, Mollet had secured a positive vote on the EDC question.

One thing the European and American participants could agree on was that the prospect of a united Europe promised a solution to both the German question and the communist challenge. In the Cold War language of the final Bilderberg report,

> European unity in some form has long been a Utopian dream, but the conference was agreed that it is now a necessity of our times. Only thus can the free nations of Europe achieve a moral and material strength capable of meeting any threat to their freedom.

Or as André Voisin had put it succinctly during the discussion on communism, "the best obstacle to Communism is the idea of the European union."

In his report on European unity, Senator de la Vallée Pousin strongly supported this position, saying:

> It must be clearly pointed out that the European Union is probably Europe's best weapon against Communism. The United States regard Communism as Russian Imperialism but in Europe it must not be overlooked that in the eyes of a great number of people Communism represents a new gospel, that is, not just the solution to economic problems but to all problems. [...] It follows that one can only fight one religious idea with another and on this point Europe does not have a common front. The idea of "Europe" is exactly the idea around which Europe could rally as long as she put it over as a great hope.[72]

Max Brauer also made a passionate appeal for European unity, linking it to the German question. "A United States of Europe," he argued, "represented the only way to safeguard peace." The unification of Germany should be achieved "within the framework of a united Europe." Denis de Rougemont added that not only in Germany but also in France, Belgium, and the Netherlands, large majorities of the population were in favor of European unity. Even Soviet foreign minister Molotov could no longer "openly oppose" the idea of a united Europe and had made a counterproposal for a Europe including Russia and Eastern European at the Berlin conference in early 1954.

Concerning the fears of cultural "standardization" mentioned by Ball, de Rougemont offered the example of Switzerland, where after 106 years of union, the different cantons and regions remained "different in language, dialect, religion and way of living." A European Union was necessary, de Rougemont argued, to assure "Europe's independence." If supported by the United States, such a union would "help to strengthen the Atlantic alliance."[73]

Emotions, anti-communism, and the West

Throughout the three days of discussions at the Bilderberg Hotel, the importance of emotions in transatlantic relations was stressed time and time again.[74] Many of these emotions, ranging from fear to jealousy, pride, or impatience, tended to complicate the transatlantic relationship. One takeaway was that the United States, in particular, needed to consider these emotions in order to be an effective leader of the Atlantic alliance. The kind of overbearing diplomacy that Secretary of State Dulles sometimes engaged in was counterproductive precisely because it clashed with national sensibilities and emotions. On the other hand, the Bilderberg meeting also showed that a subtler kind of American leadership could rely on a strong groundswell of support among Atlanticist European elites. Indeed, the explicit willingness to discuss the 'negative' emotions hampering transatlantic relations reflected a set of 'positive' emotions underlying support for the Atlantic alliance.

In part, these positive emotions were simply implicit in the fact that busy men took the time to get together for a long weekend of discussions. But they also found expression in frequent calls for transatlantic unity. Rhetorically, these calls relied first and foremost on anti-communism and shared Cold War threat perceptions.[75] They boiled down to the proposition that Western unity meant that the West stood a better chance of deterring the Soviet Union. At the same time, calls for unity appealed to a set of values and historical memories that allowed the Bilderberg participants to identify as part of an emotional community loosely defined as 'the West', 'the Free World', or 'the Atlantic Community.'[76] As with any imagined community, this community continuously had to adapt to changing circumstances. The concept of the West or the Free World also carried different meanings for the different people and groups that identified with it. Still, the calls for unity and the appeal to a sense of community and kinship encouraged the Bilderberg participants to engage in dialogues of cooperation, not just recrimination, thus undergirding a worldview in which the Atlantic alliance was more – or aspired to be more – than a narrow defensive alliance.[77]

How this worked in practice at the Bilderberg conference was evident in the rhetoric of the Bilderberg organizers. Prince Bernhard had started the conference by drawing attention to the civilizational and cultural roots of transatlantic cooperation and the necessity for a new type of internationalism – a "new way of thinking." Other Bilderberg organizers of the first hour followed up with similar calls for unity. Hugh Gaitskell, for example, warned that "[i]f relations were bad, the Alliance would break up and the Soviet Union would be encouraged in its aim for world-domination." Max Brauer, using more positive language to define the purpose of the West, declared that "[t]he task of the Western Alliance was to ensure the freedom of all men and to give them a sense of security to face the future." The former Danish Minister of Foreign Affairs, Ole Bjørn Kraft, another member of Retinger's original committee, said during the discussion on decolonization that "the freedom and future of Europe was as much at stake as that of the colonial territories. The world was divided into two hostile camps between which a line of balance would have to be found."[78]

Paul van Zeeland, in another typical example, spoke of "a fundamental solidarity between Europe and America" and of "a common ideal based on liberty and the respect of the human personality." In face of the communist challenge, he argued, "we are all in [the] same boat and will sink or swim to-gether."[79] Van Zeeland, who as a conservative Catholic was deeply involved in various anti-communist organizations, also relied on religion to strengthen the sense of community at the Bilderberg conference.[80] Presiding over the Saturday afternoon session, he announced that Prince Bernhard had received

> a letter signed by four clergymen informing the delegates that they had said a prayer to ask for God's help so that the efforts of the impor-tant personalities here present should lead to a positive contribution to world peace. The President added that in acting jointly these four cler-gymen have provided an example of understanding and intelligence and he hoped that everyone here present would bear this lesson in mind.[81]

The Belgian politician Roger Motz, meanwhile, formulated a European ver-sion of the domino theory and argued that "it has to be realized that if Italy becomes Communist, the whole Western European bulwark against Com-munism will collapse. Therefore the questions which are now worrying Italy concern the whole of Europe."[82]

This kind of rhetoric aimed at defining the West as a common space of freedom in opposition to a Soviet-dominated 'other.' The fact that both so-cial democrats and conservatives were able to rely on analogous rhetorical practices illustrates the integrative power of anti-communism when it was combined with the idea that the 'West' or the 'Free World' was held together by certain common ideals, values, and historical experiences.[83] Even if the Bilderberg participants did not agree on the question of how to deal with communism, they did agree on the seriousness of the threat posed by inter-national communism and on the need for cooperation amongst the nations of the West. In the words of Denis Healey,

> We must maintain the policies of the free nations as expressed in NATO, and build up on the side of the free peoples moral, social and military

forces sufficient to discourage aggression. To do this requires collaboration between Europe and America at the highest and most effective level. There must be real confidence and reciprocal comprehension.[84]

The Bilderberg press release shows how the Bilderberg organizers also used anti-communism and the language of community to legitimize the Bilderberg Group. "The peoples of the free nations of Western Europe and the United States," the press release announced,

> are in full agreement that the combination of Communist ideology and Soviet military power is the paramount threat to individual freedom and free institutions. Faced with the threat of aggressive Communism, the Western nations are in the same boat, although it is a boat with several decks; if the boat sinks all will go down together.

The press release went on to argue that transatlantic differences and disagreements were inevitable but needed to be addressed and understood.

> Criticism, which is an essential ingredient of a healthy democratic society, must also be an ingredient of a healthy democratic alliance. The democratic nature of the alliance of the West is both its strength and its weakness. Since the Western nations cannot act through compulsion or regimentation, progress is sometimes delayed, yet the fact that the Western alliance functions through the free consent of all members endows it with a moral and spiritual unity.[85]

The language of community added an emotional element to the rational arguments in favor of transatlantic cooperation. As a result, those who identified with an Atlantic community were arguably more willing to engage in constructive debate and "mutual responsiveness," to use a concept developed by Karl Deutsch; they recognized that divergent attitudes and perceptions needed to be taken into account in the context of "a healthy democratic alliance."[86] As Rockefeller put it to Gaitskell after the conference,

> I believe that conferences such as the one we attended can be helpful in bringing out and explaining the reasons for our differences which, in turn, tend to reduce feelings of resentment and mistrust even though they may not bring about a complete meeting of minds. From this point of view I felt the Conference was extremely valuable.

Paul van Zeeland resorted to the word "goodwill" to describe the effect of the discussions. "A lot of home-truths had been said," Van Zeeland remarked, "during the debates of these two days which have not always been pleasant to listen to. But they have always been accepted with goodwill."[87]

Of course, imagining a Western community in opposition to a Soviet-dominated, communist other was nothing new. What was new, however, was that this imagining took place in a transnational, bipartisan, and informal setting, connecting trade unionists and business leaders, socialists and conservatives, intellectuals and technocrats. Loyalties to nation, class, or party were shown to be compatible with loyalty to a transnational Western community. As Federico Romero has put it, "anti-communism functioned as the catalyst of a complex process of cultural and political foundation of the West."[88] In Johannes Großmann's recent typology of anti-communism – which distinguishes between anti-communism as (1) a worldview expressed in certain ideas and rhetorical practices, (2) a political reality, and (3) a social movement – the Bilderberg Group seems mainly important in the first category.[89] How the ideas and emotions expressed at the Bilderberg conference translated back into national political systems and movements depended to a large degree on the individual participants.

The global mindset of most Bilderberg participants reinforced their disposition towards cooperation. If there was one broadly shared consensus underlying the whole conference, it was that the challenges of the postwar world – communism, economic development, decolonization, military defense, globalization, the German question, Europe's future – could not be met by any nation in isolation. As Prince Bernhard had put it at the start of the Bilderberg conference, "the inter-dependence of the Western countries makes interest in one's neighbour's affairs not only natural but necessary and vital." Most participants, moreover, would have agreed that the United States as a 'European' power had an important role to play in facing these challenges– they were Atlanticists, in other words, as well as internationalists.

All of this meant that despite all the irritations and conflicting emotions that came to the surface at the Bilderberg conference, the necessity for transatlantic cooperation was uncontested. This was important, because during this new phase in the relations between Europe and the United States, as Cyrus Sulzberger put it, "Europe's reactions whether soundly based or not, are an all-important element in political calculations. Europe has now recovered sufficiently from post-war anemia to have a definite influence in the world-power scales."[90] How Europe would bring this influence to bear, and with what consequences for the Atlantic alliance was a key question that would continue to occupy the Bilderberg meetings for years to come.

Notes

1 Cyrus Sulzberger, "Europe is Reappraising both U.S. and Russia," *The New York Times*, April 11, 1954.
2 C. D. Jackson Log Files, Box 68, Jackson Papers, DDEL, and Bilderberg Record of Meetings, Box 3, Bilderberg Archives, NANL.
3 Both quotes from the Bilderberg Record of Meetings, Box 3, Bilderberg Archives, NANL. The British Palantype Reporting Service was responsible for recording

the meeting. The records of the meetings are extensive and appear to have been close to verbatim.

4 As Jackson told John Hughes:

> The meeting turned out far better than I had expected, as the agenda was very general and no conclusions were called for, all of which was a superb opportunity for a lot of gas and no balloons. However, it turned out extremely well, and I think that both the Europeans and the Americans got quite a lot out of it.

Jackson to Hughes, June 25, 1954, Box 60, Jackson Papers, DDEL.

5 See "Memorandum, Geheim," 8 May, 1954, by W. Veenstra on security measures, Box 30, Bilderberg Archives, NANL. See also the interview with Mrs. E.J. Ogterop, widow of the owner of Hotel de Bilderberg, made for Dutch television (*Andere Tijden*) in 2004. I thank the makers of *Andere Tijden* for providing me with the transcripts.

6 John Pomian Interview by the author, Saturday January 14, 2004.

7 Rockefeller to Prince Bernhard, June 3, 1954, Box 186, Bilderberg Archives, NANL. Many other participants expressed the same sentiment: see the letters to Prince Bernhard and Retinger in Box 30 and Box 186, Bilderberg Archives, NANL.

8 See the correspondence and financial statements in Box 186, Paul Rijkens' financial statement concerning the first two Bilderberg conferences, Rijkens to Johnson, May 4, 1955, Box 33, and Retinger to Coleman, July 12, 1954, suggesting that the Americans would pay for half of the cost of the next conference, Box 30, Bilderberg Archives, NANL. As Joseph E. Johnson, who became the American Honorary Secretary of Bilderberg in 1955, told Norman Buchanan of the Rockefeller Foundation: "There was no organized contribution of Americans to that meeting, although I believe one or two individuals did contribute small amounts, as well as arrange for their own transportation to the meeting and housing." Joseph E. Johnson to Norman S. Buchanan, July 19, 1957, Rockefeller Foundation Archives (RFA).

9 Virtually all 'thank-you' letters sent to Retinger or Prince Bernhard after the conference point to the importance of Bernhard's excellent chairmanship for the overall success of the conference. See, for example: David Rockefeller to Prince Bernhard, June 3, 1954: "I can assure you that your skillful handling of the first session was of great importance in setting the right tone." Box 186, Bilderberg Archives, NANL.

10 All quotes: Bilderberg Record of Meetings, Box 3, Bilderberg Archives, NANL.

11 Ibid.

12 Peter Kihss, "Carney says peril is 'graver' today than in Korea era," *The New York Times*, May 28, 1954.

13 Notes by Paul Nitze, Box 58, Nitze Papers, LOC.

14 Bilderberg Record of Meetings, Box 3, Bilderberg Archives, NANL.

15 Franks was ambassador to the United States from 1948–1952. See Lowe, "The Frustrations of Alliance," and Hopkins, "*Oliver Franks and the Truman Administration.*" Lowe calls Franks one of the "principal figures in directing and influencing British policy" in this period: "Franks was shrewd, industrious, with a realistic grasp of American politics and American public opinion." Moreover, he had a good relationship with the American Secretary of State, Dean Acheson (81–83). For an interesting recent take on the impact of the Korean War on the Cold War as an "imagined reality," see Masuda, *Cold War Crucible.*

16 Bilderberg Record of Meeting, Box 3, Bilderberg Archives, NANL. For official British reactions to Carney's speech, see Johnston, "Mr. Slessor Goes to Washington," 396.

17 On the concept of Manicheism and US foreign policy, see Junker, *The Manichaean Trap.*

18 See Alcide de Gasperi, "The European Attitude Towards Communism," Box 25-2, Brauer Papers, SH.

19 On Nitze, see Callahan, *Dangerous Capabilities*; Milne, *Worldmaking*, and Thompson, *The Hawk and the Dove.* See also Nitze's memoirs *From Hiroshima to Glasnost.*

20 Healey, *Time of My Life*, 198.

21 See May, *American Cold War Strategy;* and Rearden, *The Evolution of American Strategic Doctrine.*

22 Craig and Logevall, *America's Cold War*, 111.

23 NSC 68, www.trumanlibrary.org/whistlestop/study_collections/coldwar/documents/pdf/10-1.pdf. Accessed June 1, 2016.

24 See May, *American Cold War Strategy*, 9:

> Conversations with Europeans had convinced him that they needed reassurance beyond the mere text of the North Atlantic Treaty. They were afraid of the Red Army. If they had to put more money into military forces, their economic recovery might derail.

25 As another 1954 Bilderberg participant who would become a regular, George McGhee, said later: "[...] we determined that we had to strengthen Europe militarily or Europe would suffer the same fate as Korea." George C. McGhee Oral History Interview, June 11, 1975, Truman Library. McGhee held several positions in the State Department during the Truman Administration, among them Assistant Secretary of State for Near Eastern Affairs and Ambassador to Turkey.

26 Milne, *Worldmaking,* 291.

27 Nitze notes, Box 58, Nitze Papers, LOC.

28 Nitze, "The American Attitude towards Communism," Box 296, Gaitskell Papers.

29 On socialist and labor anti-communism, see Angster, *Konsenskapitalismus*; and Luff, *Commonsense Anticommunism.*

30 Bilderberg Record of Meetings, Box 3, Bilderberg Archives, NANL

31 Ferguson and Nitze notes, Box 58, Nitze Papers, LOC.

32 Bilderberg Record of Meetings, Box 3, Bilderberg Archives, NANL.

33 Ibid.

34 Ferguson Notes, Box 58, Nitze Papers, LOC.

35 Bilderberg Record of Meetings, Box 3, Bilderberg Archives, NANL

36 Ferguson Notes, Box 58, Nitze Papers, LOC.

37 On McCarthyism, see Schrecker, *Many Are the Crimes*; and Storrs, *The Second Red Scare.*

38 Conference Notes, Box 58, Nitze Papers, LOC. These notes were probably made by David Rockefeller and sent to several American participants. See John Ferguson's letter to Nitze in which Ferguson mentions that Rockefeller had shown his notes to Allen Dulles. Ferguson to Nitze, July 8, 1954, ibid.

39 C. D. Jackson Log, May 29–31, 1954, Box 68, DDEL.

40 Hatch, *HRH Prince Bernhard*, 242. Hatch uses quotation marks for Jackson's phrase, meaning that he probably quotes from an interview with Jackson.

41 Nitze notes, Box 58, Nitze Papers, LOC.

42 On the importance of the Marshall Plan and the United States' example in changing European perceptions of progress and economic growth, see Ellwood, *The Shock of America. Europe and the Challenge of the Century*, Oxford: Oxford University Press, 2012, Chapters 8 and 9.

43 Bilderberg Record of Meetings, Box 3, Bilderberg Archives, NANL.

44 Ibid.
45 Ibid.
46 Ibid.
47 Ibid.
48 Ibid.
49 Ferguson Notes, Box 58, Nitze Papers, LOC.
50 Bilderberg Record of Meetings, Box 3, Bilderberg Archives, NANL.
51 Rijkens, *Handel en Wandel*, 142.
52 Bilderberg Record of Meetings, Box 3, Bilderberg Archives, NANL.
53 Ibid.
54 Rockefeller Notes Box 58, Nitze Papers, LOC.
55 Bilderberg Report, 33 and Bilderberg Record of Meeting, Box 3, Bilderberg Archives, NANL.
56 Ibid.
57 On this point, see Muschik, "Managing the World," and Chapter 6 on the challenges of decolonizaton.
58 Bilderberg Record of Meeting, Box 3, Bilderberg Archives, NANL.
59 Harold Macmillan, for example, noted in his diary concerning the hurried plan for joint action in Indochina: "it is terrifying to realise how dangerous the Americans can be without good advice." April 26, 1954, Catteral, *Macmillan Diaries*.
60 On this point, see Trachtenberg, *A Constructed Peace*, 121–122. See also Neuss, *Geburtshelfer Europas*.
61 For a good overview of the difficulties of the EDC in France, see Lappenküper, *Die deutsch-französische Beziehungen Vol. 1*, 686–709 and Hitchcock, *France Restored*, 169–202. See also Aron and Lerner, *La Querelle de la C.E.D.*; Cresswell and Trachtenberg, "France and the German Question"; Gavin, "Power through Europe"; Guillen, "The Role of the Soviet-Union."
62 See Krüger, *Sicherheit durch Integration*, 340.
63 See Bariéty, "Die deutsche Frage."
64 Guy Mollet, "The European Defence Community," Box 113243, FO 371, TNA.
65 On the other hand, as Mollet emphasized during the Paris committee meeting in February 1954, far-reaching guarantees concerning the US and British presence were necessary if the EDC was ever to be ratified. See Prince Bernhard Notes, Box 181, Bilderberg Archives, NANL.
66 George Ball, "The American Attitude Towards European Unification," Box 25-1, Brauer Papers, SH.
67 See Bilderberg Conference Statement, Box 113243, FO 371, TNA.
68 Bilderberg Record of Meeting, Box 3, Bilderberg Archives, NANL.
69 Ibid.
70 Ibid.
71 Nitze notes, Box 58, Nitze Papers, LoC.
72 De la Vallée Pousin, "European Unification," Box 296, Gaitskell Papers, UCL.
73 Bilderberg Record of Meeting, Box 3, Bilderberg Archives, NANL.
74 On the fast-growing field of emotions and foreign policy, see Bleiker and Hutchinson, "Fear No More," and Costigliola, *Roosevelt's Lost Alliances*.
75 See Romero, "Cold War Anti-Communism." As Romero puts it:

> The notion of a unitary West [...] had little meaning except in an imperially and racially constructed opposition to peoples who were not white and Christian, or to societies that were not industrialized and modern. Yet, in the discourse of anti-communism it acquired internal consistency, conceptual authority and powerful emotional traction precisely by virtue of its opposition to totalitarianism.

76 On this point, see Hemmer and Katzenstein, "Why Is There No NATO in Asia."

77 On the importance of shared values and communication among the members of a community, see Deutsch, *Political Community*, 36: On the role of collective memories, myths, or historical narratives in creating a sense of shared identity and purpose, see Müller, *Memory and Power*. On the cultural and intellectual history of the Atlantic community, see the contributions by Ronald Steel, Marco Mariano, and Giles Scott-Smith in Mariano, *Defining the Atlantic Community*. On the concept of the West, see Angster, *Konsenskapitalismus*, and Doering-Manteuffel, *Wie Westlich*. On the role of fear in the Cold War, see Greiner, Müller, and Walter, *Angst im Kalten Krieg*.

78 Bilderberg Record of Meetings, Box 3, Bilderberg Archives, NANL.

79 Rockefeller Notes, Box 58, Nitze Papers, LOC. Note that Mollet used the exact same metaphor during his trip to the United States as Prime Minister, arriving in New York on February 25, 1957. See Mollet Statement, Box 77, Mollet Papers, OURS.

80 He had co-founded and served as president of the *Comité International pour le Rayonnement et la Défense de la Civilisation Chrétienne* (CIDCC). See Großmann, *Internationale der Konservativen*, 85.

81 Bilderberg Record of Meetings, Box 3, Bilderberg Archives, NANL.

82 Ibid.

83 On anti-communism and anti-totalitarianism as "*Integrationsideologie*," see Großmann, *Internationale der Konservative*, 55–60; Berghahn, *America and the Intellectual Cold Wars*, 95; Romero, "Cold War Anti-Communism," 301–305. On different forms of (transnational) anti-communism during the Cold War, see Dongen, Roulin and Scott-Smith, *Transnational Anti-Communism*, Scott-Smith, *Western Anti-Communism*; Scott-Smith and Krabbendam, *The Cultural Cold War*.

84 Ferguson notes, Box 58, Nitze Papers, LOC.

85 Bilderberg Press Release, Box 3, Bilderberg Archives, NANL.

86 Deutsch, *Political Community*, 129–133. Deutsch and his team rated mutual responsiveness within the North Atlantic area "rather low" in 1957, but identified "a trend toward greater responsiveness, at least on the part of the major countries in the area."

87 Bilderberg Record of Meeting, Box 3, Bilderberg Archives, NANL.

88 Romero, "Cold War Anti-Communism," 304.

89 Großmann, "Die Grundtorheit unserer Epoche," 553.

90 Cyrus Sulzberger, "Europe is Reappraising both U.S. and Russia," *The New York Times*, April 11, 1954.

4 Organization, membership, and the informal alliance

"The three days with you at Oosterbeek," David Rockefeller told Prince Bernhard after the first Bilderberg conference,

> were really a most fascinating and valuable experience. Regardless of what else comes out of the Conference, it was justified, in my opinion, on the basis of the opportunity to meet and talk with so many interesting and leading personalities from all parts of Europe. Certainly as an American, I felt that I came away from the Conference with a far clearer understanding of the reasons for European attitudes on issues which have caused misunderstandings between Europe and the United States.[1]

With similar letters arriving from many other European and American participants, this much was clear: the Bilderberg conference had served a useful purpose, and the format of informal, high-level transatlantic discussions had been well chosen.[2] As a result, John Coleman urged Prince Bernhard to continue the group's work: "[…] all of us learned a great deal, and we came away convinced that a way must be found to continue what you have so successfully launched."[3] Retinger and his fellow organizers likewise concluded that

> the first Bilderberg Conference proved that understanding between Americans and Europeans can be brought about on all the important problems of the day, and that it is possible to reach a reasonable agreement whenever the difficulty is due to a basic difference in tradition or mentality. The Conference applied itself to the study of the different approaches to these problems and not to the problems themselves. It never tried to assume the responsibility of a policy-making body. Thus, it was easier to arrive at a better mutual comprehension, and at the same time much light was shed on all these problems, which is needed to ensure the good working of the Western partnership of peoples.[4]

In September 1954, George Ball, John Coleman, Gardner Cowles, Jack Heinz, C. D. Jackson, George Nebolsine, and Paul Nitze joined Retinger for a meeting in New York City, and all agreed that "a second Conference should be held as soon as feasible."[5] It took place in Barbizon, near Paris, in March 1955 and was followed later that year by another Bilderberg conference, in the Bavarian mountain resort Garmisch-Partenkirchen, in September. By now the Bilderberg Group had become an established organization and a fourth conference took place in May 1956 in Fredensborg, Denmark; in 1957, the Bilderberg Group organized two more meetings: one in February in St. Simons Island, Georgia, the United States, and the other in October in Fiuggi, Italy. After 1957, one annual Bilderberg conference became the regular pattern, sometimes complemented by so-called enlarged steering committee meetings to discuss urgent issues such as the Berlin crisis or the European Free Trade Area.

The success of the first Bilderberg conference also finally removed the Eisenhower Administration's initial reluctance to become involved. C. D. Jackson told the White House and Bedell Smith that Bilderberg was "a good and highly useful endeavour, definitely to be cooperated with."[6] President Eisenhower now informed Prince Bernhard that he supported a second Bilderberg meeting: "I think that such a meeting would be useful if really functional or action items can be included in the agenda."[7] Allen Dulles had made a similar suggestion to Retinger.[8] High-ranking US officials such as Deputy Under Secretary of State for Political Affairs Robert Murphy and White House economic advisor Gabriel Hauge became frequent participants, and the State Department no longer objected to 'official' US participation. After a French newspaper close to Prime Minister Pierre Mendès-France had criticized the 1955 conference in Barbizon, C. Burke Elbrick at the Division of European Affairs even concluded:

> In view of the evident value of the frank and personal discussions made possible by these meetings and in view of the fact that representation from other countries has usually been top-notch, I do not believe that U.S. participants should be inhibited by trivial press criticisms.[9]

At NATO headquarters in Paris, word also quickly spread about the merits of the Bilderberg Group. After participating in the September 1955 Bilderberg meeting, NATO Secretary-General Lord Ismay informed the NATO council about "the useful purposes served by this conference and the excellent chairmanship of Prince Bernhard."[10] Privately, he told NATO's Supreme Allied Commander Europe (SACEUR) General Alfred Gruenther: "I am glad that we went to Garmisch not only because I thoroughly enjoyed it but because I feel it was good for N.A.T.O."[11]

This chapter takes a closer look at the institutionalization of the Bilderberg Group. The first part examines Bilderberg's organizational structures: its leadership, steering committee, membership, and finances. In the next part, the cases of Bilderberg members Henry Kissinger and Zbigniew Brzezinski illustrate how informal diplomacy and transnational networks changed the nature and composition of the transatlantic foreign policy elite. The chapter then argues that the atmospherics of the Bilderberg conferences were part of the secret of Bilderberg's success and ends with a discussion of Bilderberg's (indirect) influence in the context of the wider informal alliance.

The Bilderberg leadership

As the Bilderberg conferences became an established part of the informal alliance, it was clear that a more permanent organization needed to replace the ad-hoc Retinger and Coleman Committees. The resulting Bilderberg organization came to consist of a steering committee, two honorary secretary-generals in Europe and the United States, two American chairmen, and Prince Bernhard as chairman in Europe. Prince Bernhard continued to serve in this role until 1977, when he was forced to resign because of the Lockheed scandal.[12]

Prince Bernhard had a talent for chairing the meetings, possessing not just the necessary charm and tact to lead the sometimes-heated debates, but also the ability to summarize complex discussions.[13] The Dutch government, moreover, supported his chairmanship, despite objections on the part of his wife. During the so-called 'Hofmans affair,' revolving around the influence of the faith healer Greet Hofmans on Queen Juliana, the royal family lived in a "state of war," as Bernhard later called it.[14] Prodded on by Hofmans – who, as a convinced pacifist, was no fan of NATO – the Queen told Prime Minister Willem Drees that she objected to Bernhard's chairmanship of Bilderberg and to his frequent travels abroad.[15] Pointing to the political character of the Bilderberg conferences and to the press coverage of the September 1955 conference at Garmisch-Partenkirchen, she asked Drees to intervene in order to protect the royal family.

Prime Minister Drees and his cabinet refused. Drees told the Queen that if the cabinet felt that the activities of a member of the royal family affected the position of the head of state, their only course of action was to call on the Queen to try to end this behavior.[16] Yet in this case the cabinet did not object to Prince Bernhard's activities. In fact, Drees and Minister of Foreign Affairs Johan Willem Beyen, both Atlanticists and, particularly in the case of Beyen, advocates for European integration, supported the overall aim of the Bilderberg meetings. Beyen noted in October 1955 that the level of the participants was high and that they "obviously appreciate" the meetings.[17] Beyen, who had a friendly relationship with Bernhard, even contributed a paper on European integration to the second 1955 Bilderberg conference. Prince Bernhard, for his part, kept the foreign ministry fully informed about the meetings and sometimes used his Bilderberg connections to advance Dutch economic interests.[18] He also accepted the presence of Eelco van Kleffens at the Bilderberg conferences as an informal representative for the government, a role later played by Minister of Foreign Affairs Joseph Luns.

Bilderberg's founding father Joseph Retinger served as the group's first European honorary secretary-general until shortly before his death in 1960.

He continued to travel frequently to meet with Bilderberg members and to scout for new participants, assisted by his secretary, John Pomian and by Lieutenant General Terence Airey, a former British military intelligence officer. From mid-1957 onwards, however, Retinger's declining health made it more and more difficult for him to do so.[19] The Dutchman Ernst van der Beugel, vice president of KLM and a former deputy foreign minister, succeeded Retinger in 1960 and served as honorary secretary-general until 1980, assisted by the Dutch diplomat Arnold Lamping. Paul Rijkens served as Bilderberg's first treasurer and was succeeded in 1964 by the chairman of AKU (later AKZO), Johannes Meynen.

On the other side of the Atlantic, John Coleman resigned as American chairman in late 1954 after suffering a heart attack.[20] Prince Bernhard, C. D. Jackson, and David Rockefeller approached several potential successors, starting with Arthur H. Dean and David Bruce. When they declined, Rockefeller and Jackson urged Dean Rusk, the president of the Rockefeller Foundation, to take the job. The combined pressure from the White House – President Eisenhower also put in a word – and one of the most influential Rockefeller Foundation trustees did the trick.[21] Rusk agreed to become American chairman of the Bilderberg Group, joined by Walter Bedell Smith as co-chairman. Prince Bernhard "expressed his keen satisfaction" with this solution.[22] Rusk and Bedell Smith were succeeded in 1957 by Jack Heinz and Arthur Dean, a prominent international lawyer at Sullivan and Cromwell and chief negotiator of the Korean Armistice Agreement.

Joseph E. Johnson, the president of the Carnegie Endowment for International Peace (CEIP), agreed to become the American honorary secretary-general and remained so until 1976. Johnson was a former Williams College history professor who had served as chief of the State Department's Division of International Security Affairs during the war. He was also a well-connected director of the Council on Foreign Relations, where he served on the same membership committee as David Rockefeller. The Carnegie Endowment provided him with secretarial support and acted as a clearinghouse for financial contributions to the Bilderberg Group.[23]

The steering committee

The Bilderberg steering committee was formed to assist in planning the meetings, selecting participants, and raising funds. Since the Bilderberg meetings took place in different countries each year, steering committee members were also involved in the organization of the meeting when it took place in their home country. Retinger's original 1952 committee formed the backbone of Bilderberg's steering committee, although membership in the steering committee fluctuated over the years. During the 1950s, the steering committee met around four times per year. Three or four members participated for the larger countries and one or two for the smaller. In the United States, the number was larger, but since most committee meetings took place in Europe, US members were not always able to participate. In addition to Joseph Johnson and the American chairmen, US members were George Ball, Emilio Collado, John Ferguson, Gabriel Hauge, C. D. Jackson, Robert Murphy, George Nebolsine, James Rockefeller, Shepard Stone, and James Zellerbach.

European members of the steering committee included Otto Wolff von Amerongen, Fritz Erler, Rudolf Mueller, and Carlo Schmid in Germany; Hugh Gaitskell, Denis Healey, Reginald Maudling, and Victor Cavendish-Bentinck in the United Kingdom; Pinay and Mollet in France; Pietro Quaroni in Italy; the industrialist Walter Boveri in Switzerland; the diplomat M. Nuri Birgi in Turkey; the banker Charles C. Arliotis in Greece; Paul van Zeeland in Belgium; Leif Høegh and politician Jens Christian Hauge in Norway; the journalist Terkel M. Terkelsen in Denmark; and the prominent banker Marcus Wallenberg in Sweden.

At the first Bilderberg meeting, NATO members Canada and Turkey had not been represented, but this changed in 1955. Prince Bernhard approached Secretary of State for External Affairs Lester Pearson in late 1954 and asked for permission to invite the Canadian Ambassador to Italy, Pierre Dupuy, to the second conference. Pearson agreed and asked Bernhard to also invite the diplomat Norman A. Robertson. The Canadian businessman James S. Duncan became a steering committee member in 1959. Pearson himself participated in three Bilderberg meetings in the 1960s, as did Paul Martin, another liberal Secretary of State for External Affairs. The first Bilderberg meeting to take place in Canada was in 1961, in St. Castin, Quebec.

Starting in 1957, Turkey was mainly represented by the diplomat M. Nuri Birgi and hosted the 1959 Bilderberg meeting in Yeşilköy, Istanbul. Just six months later, Prime Minister Adnan Menderes, who had been present at the Bilderberg Meeting, was deposed in a military coup and executed. Although these events were not directly connected to the Bilderberg conference, they did illustrate the difficulty of dealing with NATO's nondemocratic members. An invitation to organize the 1964 Bilderberg conference in Portugal was rejected after several socialist Bilderberg members, including Norway's long-time Minister of Foreign Affairs Halvard Lange, called attention to the nature of Portugal's regime.[24] The Bilderberg organizers decided to cancel the Bilderberg conference in Greece in 1968 after the military junta had taken power in 1967.[25]

In 1957, with Retinger's health deteriorating, a small working group was formed to assist Retinger and Prince Bernhard in preparing the conferences. The members of this working group were Johnson, Jens Hauge, Mueller, Rijkens, and Quaroni. In 1959, the steering committee had become too large to meet more than once a year and the working group was reorganized into a small advisory committee. After van der Beugel took over from Retinger, the advisory committee was enlarged and now also included the Governor of the Central Bank of France Wilfrid Baumgartner, Cavendish-Bentinck, Boveri, Christiansen, Healey, Høegh, Valletta, and Wallenberg.

In the early 1960s, the Bilderberg leaders started to consider ways of bringing in new and younger members.[26] Since steering committee members were automatically invited to each conference, the fact that the committee now boasted more than 30 members severely limited the possibility of inviting new participants. This led to the decision in 1964 to create a smaller steering committee and to abolish the advisory committee.[27] Old Bilderberg hands such as Gubbins, Mueller, Pinay, Quaroni, Schmid, and van Zeeland made way for a new generation of steering committee members including Gianni Agnelli, Baumgartner, conservative MP Sir Frederick Bennett, Social Democratic Party of Germany (SPD) foreign policy expert Fritz Erler (succeeded by Helmut Schmidt after Erler's death in 1967), the Canadian banker Anthony Griffin, the Belgian diplomat Jean-Charles Snoy et d'Oppuers, and Healey's Private Parliamentary Secretary Dick Taverne (Healey had become Secretary of State for Defence in the Harold Wilson government in 1964 and returned to the steering committee in 1970).

Financing Bilderberg

In Europe, the steering committee members were responsible for securing a modest yearly national contribution to cover Bilderberg's overhead costs.[28] Those members who did not have the necessary financial means themselves usually sought assistance from industrialists or bankers. Paul van Zeeland and Prince Bernhard, for example, convinced the Comte Jean-Pierre de Launoit, president of the *Groupe Bruxelles Lambert*, to create a fund in support of the Bilderberg Group in Belgium.[29] Otto Wolff von Amerongen and Rudolf Mueller took care of the German contribution; Paul Rijkens was responsible for the Dutch contribution. He asked a similar group of firms that had sponsored the first Bilderberg conference to contribute to the running costs of Bilderberg in 1961, as did his successor Meynen in 1966.[30]

The cost of the conferences themselves was partly covered by large corporations, foundations, and wealthy members in the hosting country. Antoine Pinay, for example, arranged to cover the hotel costs for the 1955 meeting in Barbizon, as did Wolff and Mueller for the Garmisch-Partenkirchen conference.[31] Wolff himself contributed 10,000 *deutschmark* and arranged further contributions from the *Bundesverband der Deutschen Industrie* (BDI) and the well-connected banker Robert Pferdmenges.[32] In 1958, the British steering committee members enlisted the help of party leaders MacMillan, Grimond, and Gaitskell (who served on the committee anyway) to write a fundraising letter to British business circles for that year's conference in Buxton. Unilever, I.C.I. and other firms each contributed £500.[33]

The overall costs for running Bilderberg were limited. For the years 1961 and 1962, the annual costs amounted to around 105,000 Dutch guilders (around $30,000 in 1961), which covered the Bilderberg secretariat in The Hague, printing, and conference costs.[34] Still, it was a constant struggle to collect all the national contributions. As a result, steering committee membership tended towards the type of wealthy businessmen and bankers such as Agnelli, Bennett, Baumgartner, Duncan, Griffin, and Wallenberg ("whose name opens all doors in Sweden," as Lamping noted in 1962), who could arrange for annual payments.[35]

In the United States, the situation was somewhat different. In 1955, the Ford Foundation agreed to give substantial financial support to the Bilderberg Group. As Shepard Stone, head of the Foundation's International Affairs division, wrote: "It is believed that the Foundation should not shun a serious conference of such a broad group of distinguished persons in their studied and dynamic efforts toward a meeting of minds in the Atlantic Community."[36] A first grant of $25,000 was approved for 1956; subsequent grants in 1959, 1963, 1966, and 1968 totaled over $200,000.[37] In 1957 and 1958, the Rockefeller Foundation also contributed two smaller grants of $5,000 and $10,000. The H. J. Heinz Family Trust and wealthy Bilderbergers such as Arthur Dean and George McGhee gave similar amounts.[38]

Membership and participation

In the first 15 years of its existence, almost 600 participants took part in the Bilderberg meetings (I will reserve the term Bilderberg 'members' for those who took part in more than one conference). About 25% of the participants came from the United States, 14% from the United Kingdom, and 9% each from France and the Federal Republic of Germany, followed by Canada and the Netherlands with 8% each. The Scandinavian countries together made up another 8%, Italy 6%, Belgium 4%, and other countries such as Switzerland, Turkey, Greece, and Austria a combined 10%.[39]

Businessmen, bankers, and lawyers formed the largest group of Bilderberg participants with over 30% of the total. Politicians and trade unionists accounted for over 20% of participants, diplomats and other government officials for another 16%. Thirteen percent of the participants were academic experts, think tankers, intellectuals, and journalists. International organizations and institutions formed another important category. High-ranking officials from NATO, the World Bank, OECD, and IMF frequently participated, as did officials from the European Communities. Women were glaringly absent at the Bilderberg meetings. Princess Beatrix, Bernhard's oldest daughter, was the first woman to participate in 1962, and for many years remained the only one – in part because Prince Bernhard apparently resisted female participation. It wasn't until the early 1970s that this slowly began to change.[40]

From the start, the Bilderberg organizers did attempt to create a balanced group of participants in terms of different political parties (governing as well as opposition parties), business, finance, labor unions, and civil society representatives. Overall, the organizers were successful, with the partial exception of labor unions, whose leaders were oftentimes reluctant to participate.[41] By the breadth of its membership, the Bilderberg Group contributed to the opening up of foreign policy elites on both sides of the Atlantic. Although many Bilderberg members undoubtedly belonged to traditional elite groups based on class or societal rank, this was by no means the case for all. It would be misleading, therefore, to describe the transatlantic elite as a capitalist 'power elite' in the sense of C. Wright Mills and others.

The pluralistic, nonpartisan nature of the Bilderberg Group ensured that different attitudes and policy preferences were heard and debated. As the Dutch trade unionist Henk Oosterhuis told Omer Becu, the president of the International Confederation of Free Trade Unions, the Bilderberg conferences "particularly can further the mutual understanding between the various groups of social life."[42] The participation of leading German social democrats such as Carlo Schmid and Fritz Erler, moreover, contributed to the gradual acceptance of Germany's *Westbindung* by the SPD.[43] The fact that important members of the British Labour Party as well as socialists from France, Scandinavia and elsewhere took an active part in Bilderberg helped to underpin the legitimacy of the Atlantic alliance.[44] Active participation by left-of-center politicians and trade unionists also helped to counteract the impression that Bilderberg was purely a "rich men's club."[45]

The Bilderberg organizers mainly relied on their private and official networks for the recruitment of participants.[46] To a considerable degree these networks were shaped during World War II and the immediate postwar period. The war effort by the allied powers had resulted in countless friendships and working relationships among policymakers, diplomats, soldiers, businessmen, and intellectuals. Many of these relationships further deepened during the Marshall Plan, the creation of the Organisation for European Economic Cooperation (OEEC), and the founding of NATO. On the US side, virtually all participants in the first Bilderberg meetings had been part of this Atlantic generation: they had either served in Europe during the war, or had earned their stripes as State Department, Marshall Plan, or NATO officials.[47] In the European context, the European Movement, the Council of Europe, and the OEEC had similarly created a web of linkages on which the Bilderberg organizers could rely.

Although the Bilderberg meetings were secret, participants were encouraged to share important insights and conclusions with relevant people in their respective countries. After each conference, a general report was sent to participants with an anonymous summary of the discussions. "Our Group," Retinger wrote in 1955,

> is composed of men of outstanding authority whose opinions command the respect of large sections of the population of their various countries. It is hoped therefore that, while duly safeguarding the provenance of the views expressed in the accompanying document, recipients who agree with these views will not fail to use the opportunities which they may have to transmit them to public opinion within their own special spheres of influence.[48]

Depending on the topics on the agenda, the Bilderberg organizers asked a number of European and American experts to prepare brief reports for each meeting. These reports were sent to participants in advance and the *rapporteurs* started off the discussion on these topics.

Of course, Bilderberg members had different reasons and motivations for participating. Most participants undoubtedly shared the basic Atlanticist, anti-communist consensus underlying the meetings. But they also benefitted from access to people of influence in an informal, intimate setting over the course of several days. In the words of Charles Maier, "power and influence rest on webs of co-opted sociability. Elites recruit themselves, often through merit but also through friendship and family."[49] The Bilderberg organizers frequently sent lists of participants to all Bilderberg members and tried "to encourage and facilitate contacts between [the Bilderberg participants]," as Prince Bernhard wrote to all Bilderbergers in 1960. Paul Rijkens noted in his memoirs that he knew from personal experience how "useful" such "follow-up" could be.[50]

"For me personally," Otto Wolff recalled, "Bilderberg was of the greatest importance. If the New York banker David Rockefeller said that he owed 70% of his important connections to Bilderberg, for me it was almost 100%."[51] When Kurt Birrenbach traveled to the United States in 1959 as a relatively inexperienced member of the *Bundestag*, many of his meetings were arranged by Wolff, who relied exclusively on his Bilderberg network to do so.[52] In later years, Birrenbach became a Bilderberg regular himself and frequently operated as an informal diplomat for the Adenauer and Erhard governments.

It is hard to tell, to what extent Bilderbergers like Wolff and Rockefeller relied on such connections in their day-to-day business. There can be little doubt, however, that they contributed to the increasing economic interdependence in the Euro-Atlantic area. When Finance Minister Antoine Pinay traveled to the United States in 1959, he asked Retinger for help in setting up informal meetings with "leading financiers and business men so that he could discuss with them the financial and economic recovery of France." As Retinger told Rockefeller and Gabriel Hauge, "[Pinay] will, of course, be received officially, but such private talks would be of great help to him."[53]

Rockefeller himself kept close track of all the people he met in an "electronically operated rolodex," eventually collecting more than a hundred thousand entries.[54] He tapped into his Bilderberg network to recruit members for the Chase Bank's International Advisory Committee (IAC). "John Loudon," Rockefeller remembered,

> the distinguished chairman of Royal Dutch Petroleum agreed to take on the critical job of IAC chairman. John's executive capabilities and diplomatic and managerial skills had brought him recognition as perhaps the world's most prominent and respected businessman. I had met him at Bilderberg and other international gatherings over the years and come to like and admire him greatly.[55]

The two other European members Rockefeller mentions in his memoirs, Gianni Agnelli and Wilfrid Baumgartner, were also Bilderberg steering committee members.

Ernst van der Beugel was another example of a prominent Bilderberger becoming increasingly transnationally connected, through a series of directorships at Warburg Bank, Xerox, General Electric, and Petrofina as well as his chairmanship of the International Institute for Strategic Studies. Van der Beugel himself later acknowledged that his Bilderberg connections played an important role in getting these (often lucrative) positions.[56]

Journalists mainly benefitted from the Bilderberg meetings in terms of information and contacts. Even though they were not supposed to write openly about the Bilderberg discussions, they could use the meetings as any other off-the-record source and they received access to the full list of Bilderberg members. Cyrus Sulzberger, for example, based several of his columns on Bilderberg meetings in the late 1950s and asked Arthur Dean for an invitation in 1966 after not having been invited for several years.[57]

The American journalist Joseph Harsch, on the other hand, wasn't overly impressed with the Bilderberg meeting in 1958. As he told a colleague,

> I can't say that I learned anything of great value to current broadcasting. On the contrary, I came away with a feeling that we journalists are as well informed, and at least as wise, as the supposedly great and near great. Perhaps that is why the great statesmen keep as far away from us as possible.

"Its principal value," he added, "was an opportunity to make the acquaintance of some people of some importance. It may pay off ultimately."[58]

In the period until the late 1960s, the number of journalists participating remained limited. The only journalist serving on the steering committee was Terkel Terkelsen. It was only in later years that journalists from the *Economist*, the *Financial Times*, *Die Zeit*, the *Wall Street Journal*, and the *Washington Post* became regular participants, as continues to be the case today.

Politicians and diplomats also had an interest in being present, not just to stay informed but also in order to influence leading members of the transatlantic elite. When David Ormsby-Gore (later Lord Harlech) became Parliamentary Under Secretary of State in 1956, he was, as Retinger told Bernhard, "very keen on our Group – in fact, he telephoned me a few days ago asking whether he would be invited in place of John Hope."[59] Prime Minister Harold MacMillan asked his Lord Chancellor Lord Kilmuir to participate in the Bilderberg conference in the United States in the aftermath of the Suez Crisis.[60] And several decades later, Prime Minister Margaret Thatcher told Michael Heseltine,

> As you know, the Conference has an extremely distinguished membership and on the occasions which I have attended I have found its

discussions of enormous value. If it is at all possible, therefore, I hope that you will feel able to accept the invitation; it will provide both a prestigious platform and a rare opportunity to influence world opinion.[61]

During his time as Chancellor, Helmut Schmidt personally encouraged cabinet members to attend. He told his Finance Minister Hans Apel in 1977 that the Bilderberg conferences were "very useful, particularly because they take place far away from official governmental meetings, and everyone can speak as openly as they want."[62] Several years earlier, when Schmidt had to cancel his Bilderberg participation because of an election campaign, he told the party leadership that Karl Mommer would have to take his place. "It is absolutely necessary," he wrote, "that social-democrats will be well-represented at this important international conference."[63]

Not surprisingly, a considerable number of active, former, or future cabinet members, ministers, presidents, and prime ministers attended the Bilderberg meetings. The list for the 1950s and 1960s included Dean Acheson, Ludwig Erhard, Tage Erlander, Gerald Ford, Walter Hallstein, Edward Heath, Christian Herter, Ole Bjørn Kraft, Kurt Georg Kiesinger, Joseph Luns, Jens Otto Krag, Guy Mollet, Olof Palme, Lester Pearson, Antoine Pinay, George Pompidou, Dean Rusk, Helmut Schmidt, Henri Simonet, Paul-Henri Spaak, Franz Josef Strauß, Pierre Trudeau, Paul van Zeeland, and Jelle Zijlstra. When the Kennedy Administration took office, active and former Bilderberg members George Ball, McGeorge Bundy, George McGhee, Paul Nitze, and Dean Rusk received prominent positions in the State Department and the Pentagon.

High-ranking officials from international organizations such as NATO, the IMF, the World Bank, the OECD, and the European Commission likewise had an interest in participating. NATO Secretary-Generals Lord Ismay, Paul-Henri Spaak, Dirk Stikker, Manlio Brosio, and Joseph Luns all participated in the Bilderberg meetings. As a reflection of how smaller nations could benefit from active participation in the informal alliance, three Dutch Bilderbergers all served in important international functions at the same time in the 1970s: Joseph Luns as NATO secretary-general, Sicco Mansholt as president of the European Commission, and Emile van Lennep as secretary-general of the OECD.[64]

The fact that up-and-coming politicians such as Bill Clinton and Tony Blair were Bilderberg participants before reaching high office has led to suspicions that they had been 'groomed' by the Bilderberg Group. The simpler explanation, however, is that for politicians such as these, participation bolstered their foreign policy experience and increased their status.[65] They advanced their own careers by going to the Bilderberg meetings, rather than the other way around.[66] The Bilderberg organizers, meanwhile, were always on the lookout for new talent to become part of the transatlantic elite through socialization at the Bilderberg meetings.

The Bilderberg organizers themselves were somewhat ambivalent about active prime ministers or cabinet members participating. On the one hand, their participation reinforced Bilderberg's reputation for attracting high-level participants and meant that the discussions directly reached policy-makers. On the other hand, the Bilderberg steering committee wished to prevent the impression that the conferences had turned into a semiofficial meeting place for government representatives, where frank and open discussions were no longer possible.[67]

Despite the long list of influential Bilderberg participants, it should also be noted that there were limits to the reach of Bilderberg. After all, the meetings mainly attracted those who subscribed to the underlying internationalist consensus. Radical critics of this consensus on the left and right were unlikely to be invited, and, if they were, unlikely to be persuaded by the experience. In terms of elite socialization, the Bilderberg Group was most likely to have an impact on 'future leaders' who were more aligned with the political mainstream. By the late 1960s, however, the Bilderberg organizers worried that – partly as a result of the Vietnam protest movements – the pool of younger talent was drying up and embarked upon an active strategy of rejuvenating the Bilderberg Group.[68]

Foreign policy experts: the case of Kissinger and Brzezinski

Some of the talents recruited by the Bilderberg organizers were foreign policy experts, who could benefit from participation in transnational networks with a boost in reputation, authority, and status.[69] Two prominent examples closely connected to the Bilderberg Group were Henry Kissinger and Zbigniew Brzezinski. Both men were ambitious foreign policy intellectuals with a similar background as immigrants and with a similar talent for self-promotion. Both used their domestic and international networks to build a reputation as leading foreign policy experts, a reputation that ultimately helped pave their way into the White House.[70]

Kissinger first drew the attention of the Bilderberg organizers while running a Council on Foreign Relations study on nuclear strategy. His resulting book *Nuclear Weapons and Foreign Policy* became a surprise bestseller and was read at the highest levels in Washington D.C. and other NATO capitals. David Rockefeller served on the same study group and probably arranged Kissinger's invitations to the two Bilderberg conferences in 1957 and again in 1964. From 1971 onwards, Kissinger participated in virtually all the Bilderberg meetings, and after the end of the Ford Administration he joined the steering committee.

Using the contacts established at Bilderberg and at his own Harvard International Seminar, Kissinger started a habit of frequent trips to Europe to meet with members of the local foreign policy elites.[71] In the Federal Republic of Germany, the scope of his networks was particularly impressive and included leading politicians as well as journalists such as *Die Zeit*'s

Marion Gräfin Dönhoff and Theo Sommer (participant in the 1960 Harvard International Seminar), *Der Spiegel's* Rudolf Augstein, and *Die Süddeutsche's* Günter Gaus (another International Seminar participant).[72] Having met Fritz Erler, Carlo Schmid, and Kurt Georg Kiesinger at the 1957 Bilderberg conferences, Kissinger made sure to stay in touch with them by sending publications such as his *Foreign Affairs* article "Missiles and the Western Alliance."[73] In 1959, Carlo Schmid returned the favor by arranging an extended visit to Germany under the auspices of the *Auswärtige Amt.* Kissinger's schedule included meetings with Chancellor Adenauer, Foreign Minister Heinrich von Brentano, Defense Minister Franz Josef Strauß, Berlin Mayor Willy Brandt, and an impressive number of journalists and academics.[74] Kissinger also became a frequent participant in the biannual German-American conferences first organized in 1959 by the American Council on Germany and the *Atlantik-Brücke*.[75]

Kissinger's first foray into actual policy-making, as a consultant in the Kennedy Administration, turned into a major disappointment. He wrote a number of policy and background papers on Berlin and the German Question, but, in part due to his testy relationship with National Security Advisor McGeorge Bundy, his contract ended prematurely in 1962. Nevertheless, Kissinger remained active as a foreign policy advisor to Nelson Rockefeller and frequently published articles in journals such as *Foreign Affairs* and *The Reporter.* He also made sure that the memoranda on his travels through Europe and Asia continued to reach policymakers in the White House and the State Department.

When President-elect Nixon asked Kissinger to become his national security advisor after the 1968 election, the latter's international reputation and network must have been an important factor. Once in the White House, moreover, Kissinger's network gave him access to information and people in a way that enabled him to be his own little State Department and to engage in the kind of back-channel diplomacy that he and the President delighted in. Kissinger, for example, used the 1971 Woodstock Bilderberg conference to negotiate the parameters of *Ostpolitik* with Chancellor Brandt's foreign affairs advisor Egon Bahr.[76] In the 1980s, when Kissinger and Brent Scowcroft founded the international consulting firm Kissinger Associates, Kissinger relied on his Bilderberg network to enlist leading European Bilderbergers such as Sir Peter Carrington, Sir Eric Roll, and Étienne Davignon as international directors.[77] He also continued to use the Bilderberg conferences themselves to arrange private meetings with other members of the transatlantic foreign policy elite such as Chancellor Helmut Schmidt.[78]

One of the closest friendships resulting from Kissinger's international travels was with the Dutch Deputy Foreign Minister Ernst van der Beugel. The two met in the Netherlands in 1957, shared similar backgrounds, and quickly became friends. Van der Beugel introduced Kissinger to the Dutch foreign policy elite and frequently organized private dinners for him in The Hague. Kissinger, meanwhile, arranged for Van der Beugel to spend time at Harvard and helped him publish his study of US postwar European policies.[79] As Albertine Bloemendal has shown, Van der Beugel did not hesitate to enlist the help of his friend in informal diplomacy once Kissinger had become national security advisor.[80] One prominent case involved the controversial negotiations about KLM landing rights in the United States. In addition, Van der Beugel kept Kissinger informed about the Bilderberg conferences and about Dutch policymakers, advising him how to deal with Prime Minister Barend Biesheuvel and Foreign Minister Norbert Schmelzer.[81]

Brzezinski's road to the White House was similar to Kissinger's, with stations at Harvard's Russian Research Center and Columbia University, participation in Council on Foreign Relations study groups and German-American conferences, a stint at the State Department's policy planning staff, and a role as advisor to Democratic presidential candidates. In 1966, Brzezinski participated in his first Bilderberg conference, and it was during a flight to the 1972 Bilderberg conference that he first discussed the creation of the Trilateral Commission with David Rockefeller. Brzezinski and Rockefeller were both in favor of including Japan in the formal and informal counsels of the West, and Rockefeller had attempted to convince the Bilderberg steering committee to open up Bilderberg to Japanese participation. After the steering committee again refused to do so in 1972, Rockefeller set out to create a new informal organization similar to the Bilderberg Group – although more directly aimed at influencing government policies – and asked Brzezinski to help establish the Trilateral Commission.[82] Not surprisingly, Rockefeller and Brzezinski relied on their Bilderberg network to recruit European and American members for the Trilateral Commission.

When the little-known Governor of Georgia, James Earl Carter, became an early member of the Trilateral Commission, Brzezinski agreed to become his foreign policy mentor. As a result, Brzezinski became foreign policy advisor to Carter's long-shot presidential campaign in 1976. After his surprise victory, Carter named Brzezinski his national security advisor and relied on the Trilateral Commission to fill many of the top foreign-policy positions in his administration.

Transnational networks such as Bilderberg and the Trilateral Commission, as these examples show, helped to create opportunities for relative outsiders to become part of the foreign policy establishment. They stimulated closer links between academia, think tanks, foundations, business, politics, and government, and they enabled foreign policy experts to become internationally connected and recognized authorities. In the case of Kissinger and Brzezinski, this trajectory led to high-level policy-making functions in the White House and the State Department. The fact that Kissinger and Brzezinski were members of the transatlantic elite, it should be noted, by no means guaranteed smooth sailing in transatlantic relations while they were in office. Both men faced serious troubles with their European partners during the 1970s.

In Europe, foreign policy-making remained largely the responsibility of politicians and career diplomats. Yet these politicians and officials could benefit from the Bilderberg network in similar ways. In addition, Bilderberg and other transatlantic networks provided special opportunities for politicians of opposition parties to stay informed about important developments on both sides of the Atlantic. As Helmut Schmidt put it in his memoirs:

> One didn't have to travel to the United States every year, as long as one participated in some of the private international conferences; I remember the yearly so-called Bilderberg conferences with gratitude [...] Thus, the United States was relatively transparent to European politicians.[83]

Based on their transnational access to information and people of influence, European Bilderberg members established or strengthened their reputations as foreign policy experts, frequently publishing books, articles, and speeches on issues such as nuclear strategy, NATO, and European integration. In Germany, Fritz Erler, Helmut Schmidt, and Kurt Birrenbach were prominent examples. In the United Kingdom, Healey and Gaitskell were immensely productive authors and speakers on foreign policy. Ernst van der Beugel played a similar role in the Netherlands and also educated future generations of foreign policy professionals as a professor at Leiden University. Other Bilderberg members who can be regarded as leading voices on international affairs in Europe included Raymond Aron in France, Pietro Quaroni in Italy, and Alastair Buchan in the United Kingdom.[84]

Bilderberg atmospherics

The importance of the atmospherics and private interactions at Bilderberg is apparent in much of the private correspondence about the meetings. "The reception of the German participants," Otto Wolff wrote about the 1955 meeting in Barbizon,

> was very friendly from all sides, but particularly from the American side; the overall atmosphere was that of an old group of friends. Lunch and dinner took place without a specific seating arrangement, allowing for interesting private conversations beyond the official agenda. In Barbizon, there was none of the initial reserve, as is usually the case during such meetings.[85]

Louis Camu likewise wrote about the Barbizon conference:

> This exploration of the situation of the Western world, of its material and moral power, took place during forty hours of discussion, with a sincerity, a straightforwardness, and a high-mindedness ["hauteur de vues"] that are rare in international meetings, public or private. Neither

at Strasbourg, nor at the European Movement or the United Nations, do such objectivity, goodwill and intelligence come together. In addition, the personal contacts established during the meetings are valuable and may be useful in consolidating precarious positions or in speeding up US activities in favor of Western Europe.[86]

After returning from the 1957 conference in Fiuggi, Italy, the Ford Foundation's Shepard Stone reported that the informal discussions over dinner or a drink were as important as the formal sessions, if not more.[87] Looking back at his years organizing the Bilderberg conferences, Ernst van der Beugel likewise argued that at least 50% of the importance of the Bilderberg meetings revolved around what occurred outside of the meeting rooms.[88]

These informal discussions stimulated the kind of transatlantic gossip that allowed Bilderberg participants to play their role as members of the foreign policy elite.[89] As the Canadian Ambassador in Rome, Pierre Dupuy, wrote about the Bilderberg conference in Fiuggi:

> The contacts which took place outside the Conference Room were no less useful. In fact, certain impressions could be more easily exchanged in private conversation. For instance, regarding President Eisenhower's state of health I heard it said repeatedly, by people who had seen him in the last few months, that he was no longer the man he used to be and could not be counted upon to make vital decisions. It was suggested that this might account for the bolder policy followed by the Soviets at the present time.[90]

The clubby atmosphere at the Bilderberg meetings also contributed to a certain sense of kinship and community. "Experience has taught me," as Denis Healey put it in his memoirs,

> that lack of understanding is the main cause of all evil in public affairs – as in private life. Nothing is more likely to produce understanding than the sort of personal contacts which involves people not just as officials or representatives, but also as human beings.[91]

And as a report for the Ford Foundation put it:

> The intimate atmosphere of the Conference, the frequency of the meetings, all of which were plenary, with no division into committees, created an environment of mutual trust and friendship. Thus, when it came to dealing with controversial subjects, more was accomplished than had been expected.[92]

Johannes Großmann has shown a similar effect for Europe's conservative transnational organizations during the Cold War, which resulted in numerous friendships, a sense of community, and a shared European "*Selbstverständnis.*"[93]

An anecdote from the 1962 Bilderberg meeting in Saltsjöbaden illustrates the school trip-like atmosphere that could develop. One of the participants had mentioned a fable-like James Reston column in the *New York Times* in which different animals represented various statesmen or countries: President De Gaulle was a giraffe, Chancellor Adenauer an old fox, Prime Minister Macmillan a lion, and the United States a buffalo. The morale of Reston's story was that if the giraffe and the fox kept the lion out of the forest, this might anger the buffalo that was responsible for defending the forest. Once the buffalo was gone and the old giraffe had died, the foxes took over. The bear in the East did not like this. Together with the tiger (China), the bear thereupon ate all the foxes and the giraffes. It was a rather crude story – the giraffe was proud, "and taller than the Washington Monument, and he thought he could see farther than all the other animals" – but it was a hit at the Saltsjöbaden conference. As C. D. Jackson told the story to Reston, the conference secretariat made copies for all participants, causing the French participants – Wilfrid Baumgartner and Pierre Dreyfus – to protest "against this insult to their Chief of State" (the giraffe died of "a terrible sore throat"). "However," Jackson wrote, "from that moment on, all the representatives referred to international personages by animal name rather than surname."[94]

The venues of the conferences further stimulated close personal contacts and socialization.[95] They were chosen for their relative seclusion to ensure that participants would remain together for the whole time of the conference. If the original Hotel de Bilderberg had been relatively simple, many of the subsequent hotels were more exquisite, from the Hotel Alpenhof in Garmisch-Partenkirchen, to the Palace Hotel near Luzern ("where we will have Audrey Hepburn and Sophia Loren as neighbors in their villas," as one Bilderberg organizer noted), the Grand Hotel Saltsjöbaden in Sweden and the majestic Villa d'Este at Lake Como.[96] An exception was the 1967 conference in Cambridge, where participants had to stay in the rather simpler student accommodations of St. Johns College.

Adding to the allure of Bilderberg, participants such as Jack Heinz and Standard Oil's Emilio Collado sometimes made their private or company planes available for transportation, taking along cases of wine or liquor if necessary.[97] As Heinz told Prince Bernhard in preparation for the 1957 conference at the King and Prince Hotel on St. Simons Island: "The facilities for a conference are excellent. The food, I judge, is simple but good Southern cooking, with plenty of good, clean drinkin' whiskey (and I will play deuxieme sommelier when it comes to the vintage stuff)."[98] Mindful of Retinger's love of good food, Prince Bernhard warned him before the Bilderberg conference in Barbizon that "we certainly should not have lunches of 6 courses etc. In fact I insist, repeat insist, that all luncheons are light, otherwise the afternoon will be a sleeping session!"[99]

The atmospherics of the Bilderberg conferences must have encouraged new participants to fit in in order to be accepted as member of the group. As Ian Richardson has argued, "the selection of participants and the subtle expectations of membership incline [elite] networks towards a broad consensual understanding."[100] The fact that only steering committee members were certain of being invited to the Bilderberg conferences will have induced participants who wished to be invited again to conform to the habitus and core beliefs of the Bilderberg organizers. The resulting socialization process and identification with the transnational foreign policy elite implied a willingness to engage in constructive dialogue, thus developing what might be called transnational empathy.[101]

The Bilderberg Group's influence

The central paradox of the Bilderberg Group was that the conferences were so useful to foreign policy elites precisely because of their private nature and the fact that no decisions were made. The Bilderberg meetings provided an informal diplomatic forum for the kind of candid conversations that were rare at official gatherings. Combined with the prominence of many Bilderberg participants, the meetings allowed participants not only to stay informed about important developments, but also, in the words of Margaret Thatcher, to "influence world opinion."

Widespread suspicions that the Bilderberg Group was – or wanted to be – some sort of secret world government thus miss the point of the meetings. They provided no decision-making apparatus, but rather a space for participants to influence each other. The Bilderberg Group itself had no influence or agency beyond setting the agenda for the meetings, inviting participants, and the resulting socialization effects. The real importance of the Bilderberg meetings was determined by what the participants did with the information and ideas they encountered, with the contacts they established, and with, to use Bourdieu's term, the symbolic capital they assembled.[102] As a result, the Bilderberg meetings revolved around informal diplomacy: the kind of indirect influence that relied on introducing new ideas, shaping transnational debates, nurturing understanding for different attitudes and perceptions, assessing the authority and reputation of other participants, creating a sense of community based on certain shared values and norms, and bringing people with diverse backgrounds and political leanings together in an environment favorable to frank exchanges.[103]

"Influence often works most effectively," as Carl J. Friedrich has put it, "by creating a certain ambience for decisions through its effect on attitudes, beliefs and values unrelated to immediate decisions."[104] Joseph S. Nye's concept of soft power – the power of attraction – relies on an analogous understanding of influence.[105] Soft power can make hard power acceptable or legitimate by giving it a shared moral purpose. Conversely, the illegitimate use of hard power (or the perception thereof) can cause a decline in soft power. In the context of the Atlantic alliance, Christopher Hemmer and Peter Katzenstein have similarly argued that collective identification with the politically constructed North Atlantic region is an important part of the explanation why the United States was willing to participate in the highly integrated multilateralism of NATO in Europe, but not in Asia.[106]

Such collective identities, however, are never stable and depend on constant reinforcement and renegotiation. In view of the changing power dynamics of the transatlantic relationship and the many crises facing NATO in its first decades, this was especially true for the Atlantic alliance. In this constant process of shaping and adjusting collective identities, the Bilderberg meetings could serve as a space for consensus building and crisis management. The first Bilderberg conference, after all, had shown that the meetings could cultivate a strong sense of emotional community based on conceptions of the Free World or the West.

In terms of alliance politics, simply showing up could already have an effect. This was true in particular for leading US participants who, by engaging in informal discussions and by showing an interest in their European partners – in short, by mutual responsiveness, could stimulate acceptance of the United States' leadership role within NATO. As Dean Rusk told Paul Nitze in 1955: "I know that our European colleagues appreciated the interest shown by the American side."[107]

John Lewis Gaddis has argued that "the habits of domestic democratic politics" helped the Americans in managing the alliance: "Negotiation, compromise, and consensus-building abroad came naturally to statesmen steeped in the uses of such practices at home."[108] Martin Shaw has similarly drawn attention to the

> more or less consensual partnership of states and societies in which nearly all gained in security and wealth. The West offered a model of internationalization that was not forced, and, despite manifest inequalities, offered real benefits to allies and friends.[109]

The informal alliance was an important part of this Western model and offered not just American or European leaders a chance to engage in informal diplomacy, but also representatives from international institutions. NATO officials were particularly attuned to the potential importance of the Bilderberg meetings. As General Gruenther told the participants in the 1955 Bilderberg meeting at Garmisch: "I should like to hope that you Gentlemen here would constitute yourselves as a type of general staff that would help develop public opinion."[110] Following the example of General Gruenther and NATO Secretary-General Lord Ismay, a long list of high-ranking NATO officials, including Secretary-Generals Spaak, Stikker, and Brosio, participated in multiple Bilderberg conferences – a practice that has continued to this day.

Meanwhile, the Bilderberg organizers themselves recognized that Bilderberg's influence was difficult to measure. "Given the informal nature of the Bilderberg Meetings," the American steering committee members reported to the Ford Foundation,

> it is almost impossible to cite specific achievements resulting from the conferences. [...] Nevertheless, considering the influential positions held by so many of the participants, it seems likely that the views expressed during the discussions are conveyed to government officials, and may thus have an indirect, but nonetheless significant, impact on policies. One indication of the value placed on these informal exchanges is the continued high caliber of the participants.[111]

An internal report by the Rockefeller Foundation likewise concluded:

> There have been five meetings of the Bilderberg Group to date, and all the evidence points to the conclusion that these meetings have done much to promote international understanding among key persons to their considerable mutual benefit. A wider comprehension by persons in high places – as through the Bilderberg Group – promotes international understanding and relieves international tension in a way that research cannot touch.[112]

George Ball described the importance of his Bilderberg connections in similar terms: "When I joined the State Department in 1961, I was already well acquainted with most Western leaders. [...] I was sensitive to their attitudes and prejudices, while they understood America much better because of exposure to articulate Americans."[113]

If the Bilderberg meetings could serve as a sort of barometer of transatlantic relations, many participants shared their impressions of the discussions with government officials and others. As we have seen, several American participants sent reports of the first Bilderberg meetings to the State Department and the CIA. Although the evidence is fragmentary, we can assume that they continued to do so. Joseph Johnson, for example, sent a summary of the April 1958 extended steering committee meeting to Allen Dulles at the CIA, and Gabriel Hauge wrote brief reports on the Bilderberg meetings for President Eisenhower.[114]

Prince Bernhard, as we have seen, kept the Dutch foreign ministry informed and similar reports show up in official German, Danish, and British archives. In 1963, George Ball even reported on that year's Bilderberg conference to the National Security Council. One year later, Ernst van der Beugel spent several weeks in the United States and told Prince Bernhard: "My general impression is that the work of the Bilderberg is considered of the highest importance in this country not only among the Bilderbergers themselves but also very much at the top level in Washington."[115]

The informal alliance

As the story of Bilderberg's founding exemplifies, the Bilderberg Group was part of a wider process of transnational elite formation during and after World War II. In terms of official institutions, as Geir Lundestad has put it, "the many meetings in the various Atlantic organizations and the establishment of permanent bureaucratic structures for these organizations had to encourage the creation of transnational elites." This development, in Lundestad's view, "far from ended conflicts among the participating nations, but it must have made the chances of resolving conflicts somewhat greater."[116] In terms of private or public-private organizations, Bilderberg was part of a strong movement towards informal transnational interchanges and networks, a movement that reflected the global mindset and internationalism of the emerging transatlantic elite.

Membership in these networks overlapped, creating a dense web of transnational relationships and linkages: an informal alliance.[117] Many Bilderberg participants, for example, were active in other transnational networks and were members of foreign policy think tanks and institutes such as the Council on Foreign Relations, Chatham House, the *Centre d'Études de Politique Étrangère*, the *Instituto per gli Studi di Politica Internazionale*, or the *Deutsche Gesellschaft für Auswärtige Politik*.[118]

The foundation of the Institute for Strategic Studies in London in 1958 was even to some extent a direct result of the Bilderberg meetings. The Institute was co-founded by, among others, Denis Healey and Rear-Admiral Sir Anthony Buzzard, both strong critics of the Eisenhower Administration's strategy of massive retaliation. They had been present at the 1955 Bilderberg conference in Garmisch and used their Bilderberg connections to organize a conference on nuclear strategy in Brighton in early 1957. Later that year Healey approached the Ford Foundation's Shepard Stone at the Fiuggi Bilderberg conference and eventually secured a grant of $150,000 to set up the Institute. Alistair Buchan, the Institute's first director, recalled that "without Denis and his contacts we might never have got the money, and the I.S.S. might never have been born."[119]

Other foreign policy institutes founded in the same period included the Foreign Policy Research Institute (founded in 1955 at the University of Pennsylvania by Robert Strausz-Hupé), the Washington Center of Foreign Policy Research at the John Hopkins University's School of Advanced Strategic Studies (founded by Paul Nitze in 1957 and later turned into the Foreign Policy Institute), and Harvard's Center for International Affairs.[120] In an effort to combat anti-Americanism and to promote Atlantic cooperation and European integration, the Ford Foundation and other American foundations also funded dozens of American and European Studies institutes at European universities, as well as academic conferences such as the Salzburg Seminar.[121]

As air travel became faster and more accessible in the second half of the 1950s, frequent trips and speaking tours across the Atlantic suddenly became feasible. The US government and US foundations were particularly active in organizing and financing visits to the United States.[122] US policymakers and politicians, moreover, were remarkably accessible to European members of the foreign policy elite. Meetings at the White House, State Department, Pentagon, and Congress became coveted features for European politicians, diplomats, and foreign policy experts traveling to the United States. Such visits were by no means limited to those Europeans in positions of power.[123] Oppositional politicians such as the SPD's Fritz Erler or Labour's Hugh Gaitskell could count on being taken seriously in Washington. Given the frequent bureaucratic and political battles over most aspects of US foreign policy, access to top decision-makers and members of Congress could open up avenues of real influence.

The correspondence in the private archives of many Bilderberg members shows that being part of the transatlantic elite also meant keeping abreast of widely read publications such as *Foreign Affairs, Orbis, Encounter,* the *International Herald Tribune, The Reporter,* or *Survival* – thus indicating the existence of a transatlantic public sphere.[124] The Bilderberg organizers regularly sent copies of important articles or speeches to Bilderberg members and distributed overviews of research on the Atlantic Community and European integration compiled by the Carnegie Endowment and the Ford Foundation.[125] Several prominent Bilderbergers, including Prince Bernhard and Paul Rijkens, were also involved in the attempt to create a truly transatlantic review called *Western World.* They launched the first issue in the spring of 1957 with a declaration on the Atlantic Community signed by a large number of Bilderbergers.[126] *Western World* managed to attract influential contributors, yet not sufficient subscribers to become economically viable, leading to its termination after just two years.

At the transatlantic level, the Congress for Cultural Freedom (CCF), founded in 1950 to bring together leading intellectuals and politicians (including Bilderberg members such as Aron, Brauer, Healey, Gaitskell, de Rougemont, and Stone), was an important early part of the informal alliance.[127] Other groups focused on different forms of Atlantic unity, including Clarence Streit's federalist Atlantic Union Committee, the Declaration of Atlantic Unity of October 1954, and the Paris-based Atlantic Treaty Organization, founded in 1955. The NATO Parliamentarians' Conference, which first met in 1955, became part of the informal alliance because of the reluctance on the part of Great Britain and other member states to create an official consultative assembly along the lines of the Council of Europe. Finn Moe, chair of the Norwegian Parliament's foreign affairs committee and an early Bilderberg member, was one of its founders and Denis Healey a participant from the start.[128]

One of the initiatives of the NATO Parliamentarians was the 1959 Atlantic Congress in London, which brought together over 600 delegates from NATO countries and resulted in a call to include the United States and Canada in the OEEC and to create an Atlantic Institute.[129] Prince Bernhard chaired the Atlantic Congress's special plenary session, which featured fellow Bilderbergers Halvard Lange, Hugh Gaitskell, and NATO Secretary-General Paul-Henri Spaak.

After the 1959 Atlantic Congress, the International Movement for Atlantic Union, with Streit at its head, was formed and several prominent Bilderberg members, including Paul van Zeeland and Kurt Birrenbach, were involved in the creation of the Atlantic Institute in 1961.[130] The Atlantic Institute received generous funding from the Ford Foundation and acted as a clearinghouse for information concerning the alliance, publishing frequent studies on Atlantic issues, as well as the *Atlantic Community Quarterly*. However, the Institute's frequent leadership struggles limited its effectiveness. In late 1961, Secretary of State Dean Rusk and former secretaries of state Dean Acheson and Christian Herter encouraged a number of Atlanticist organizations in the United States, including the Atlantic Council, the America Committee for an Atlantic Institute, and the Citizens Commission on NATO, to consolidate in the Atlantic Council of the United States (ACUS).[131] Christian Herter acted as the Council's first chairman and was succeeded by General Lauris Norstad in 1963; General Gruenther and Henry J. Heinz served on its executive committee.

In order to cement the *Westbindung* of the Federal Republic, the American Council on Germany (ACG) and the *Atlantik-Brücke* started organizing the biannual German-American conferences, modeled after the Bilderberg conferences, in 1959.[132] Two years later, Ewald von Kleist organized the first *Wehrkundetagung* in Munich, bringing together US and European politicians and defense analysts specifically interested in strategic debates. The annual *Königswinter* conferences, first organized in the early 1950s, played an important role in the bilateral British-German relationship.[133]

In Europe, the postwar transnational turn went beyond the EM and its associated organizations. A significant number of Christian democratic, conservative, and socialist political and business networks saw the light of day, including the Geneva Circle, the *Nouvelles Équipes Internationales*, the *Centre Européen de Documentation et d'Information* (CEDI), the *Cercle Pinay*, the European Committee for Social and Economic Progress (CEPES), the *Institut d'Etudes Politiques* and the European Roundtable of Industrialists.[134]

In late 1954, Retinger, Denis de Rougemont, Prince Bernhard, Rijkens, and other Bilderberg organizers set up the *Fondation Européenne de la Culture*, or European Cultural Foundation (ECF), in Geneva. Prince Bernhard served as the Foundation's president from 1955–1977. After initial struggles to finance the Foundation, he decided to organize a big European fundraising conference in Amsterdam in 1957 on the theme of "Cultural and Intellectual Unity in Europe." Like the Congress of Europe nine years earlier, the Amsterdam conference brought together a large number of prominent Europeans, including Spaak, Adenauer, Schuman, and Hendrik Brugmans, the first principal of the College of Europe in Bruges. The Foundation announced that it wished to emulate the success of the big American foundations and "to build up a strong European foundation, independent of political and governmental control, which can devote itself specifically to the support of the important aspects of European culture."[135] Further conferences followed, and the Foundation worked with the Council of Europe to promote the European idea through programs such as "Europe at School Day." In 1960, the Foundation moved to Amsterdam, and Prince Bernhard secured funding from the Dutch Lotteries through the Prince Bernhard Cultural Foundation.[136]

Probably the most influential informal organization in Europe was the Action Committee for the United States of Europe, led by Jean Monnet and Max Kohnstamm, which engaged in more direct forms of informal governance than other organizations.[137] The Monnet Committee brought together leading European politicians and trade unionist leaders and regularly passed resolutions on European integration, which were brought up for votes in national parliaments. At the same time, Monnet and Kohnstamm frequently acted as informal diplomats in ways similar to Retinger's efforts in the late 1940s and early 1950s. Like Retinger, they could rely on an impressive network of European and American high-level contacts and they did not hesitate to use it. Monnet was invited to several Bilderberg conferences, but declined to participate. Kohnstamm, however, became a frequent Bilderberg participant from 1961 onwards and was later involved in the founding of the Trilateral Commission.

The dramatic expansion of private and public-private transnational organizations after World War II marked an important change in the makeup and interconnectedness of foreign policy elites in North America and Europe. Similar organizations had, of course, existed before the war, but both the quantity and the quality in terms of influence and participation was different after 1945.[138] This was in part the result of improvements in communication and air travel, but it also reflected the global mindset of foreign policy elites on both sides of the Atlantic.

Since the Bilderberg Group was one of the most prominent organizations of the informal alliance, its meetings and the relationships between its members can tell us much about how the transatlantic elite defined common interests and values, how it perceived and tried to shape the key issues and challenges facing the Atlantic alliance, and how it dealt with the inevitable misunderstandings and conflicts of interest. And in the years after the first Bilderberg conference there certainly was no shortage of challenges and conflicts: the failure of the European Defense Community in August 1954 threw Europe into disarray; the Soviet Union's new strategy of peaceful coexistence severely tested the West's ability to adapt to the changing nature of the Cold War; and the whirlwind of decolonization continued to strain transatlantic relations, resulting in the Suez crisis in late 1956.

Notes

1 Rockefeller to Prince Bernhard, June 3, 1954, Box 186, Bilderberg Archives, NANL.
2 See the correspondence in Box 30, Bilderberg Archives, NANL. The Dutch politician Peter van Walsem wrote:

> In order to keep alive the feeling that we all in the free world belong together, a repetition of such a meeting in some other part of the world seems to be recommendable. For, personal contacts and the interchange of personal experiences and ideas between prominent people from various countries of the Western hemisphere, are the best means to maintain and stimulate the bonds of friendship between the free nations.

Van Walsem to Retinger, October 8, 1954. Drapier similarly told Retinger on June 9, 1954: "I believe that it is necessary to quickly exploit the atmosphere that was created at Oosterbeek." (my translation).
3 Coleman to Prince Bernhard, June 9, 1954, Box 186, Bilderberg Archives, NANL.
4 Draft note on Agenda Bilderberg II, Box 936, Van Zeeland Papers, AUCL.
5 Meeting University Club, September 22, 1954, Box 59, Folder 1, Nitze Papers, LOC. Jack Heinz and David Rockefeller each paid $1000 to finance Retinger's trip to the United States. See Nebolsine to Retinger, July 1, 1954, Box 30, Bilderberg Archives, NANL.
6 Jackson to Bedell Smith, January 7, 1955, Box 35, Jackson Papers, DDEL. When Jackson told his friend and Ambassador to Italy Clare Booth Luce about the first Bilderberg conference, he made sure to report his impression of the Italian participants:

> Malagodi was outstanding – and I mean outstanding. The way that man is able to organize his ideas and articulate them in English is extraordinary, and when you add to that a winning personality and interesting appearance, the combination is unbeatable.

Jackson to Luce, June 24, 1954, Box 70, Jackson Papers.
7 President Eisenhower to Prince Bernhard, November 23, 1954, Box 42, International Series, Ann Whitman File, DDEL.
8 As Prince Bernhard said:

> [...] our friend Retinger has talked to Allen Dulles, who was very enthusiastic and wanted to go quite far, always keeping in mind that we have no governmental function and that all we can do is to make suggestions which can be taken up or not by the governments concerned. But to my surprise there is a great demand for solid suggestion, if I may use the word, from both sides. This is probably based on the fact that independent people who have no axe to grind come together and try to do something.

"Meeting held on Monday, December 6th, 1954, in Paris." Box 30, Bilderberg Archives, NANL.
9 Memo Elbrick, June 29, 1955, Box 611.4/3-2857, RG 59, 1955–1959 Decimal File, NARA.
10 See Cavendish-Bentinck to Rijkens, reporting on his conversation with Ismay, October 31, 1955, Box 189, Bilderberg Archives, NANL.
11 Ismay to Gruenther, September 27, 1955, Box 32, Gruenther Papers, DDEL.
12 The subsequent Bilderberg Chairmen have been Alec Douglas-Home, Walter Scheel, Eric Roll of Ipsen, Peter Carrington, Étienne Davignon, and current

Chairman Henri de Castries. Lawrence Shoup has made much of the fact that most Bilderberg chairmen came from "European nobility." In my view, it is more salient that all chairmen were active members of the transatlantic foreign policy elite; most had served in a variety of official diplomatic and government functions. See Shoup, *Wall Street's Think Tank*, 132–135.

13 As the Belgian banker Louis Camu wrote after the second Bilderberg meeting:

> The success of the meeting is to a great extent due to the authority and intelligence of the chairman. The Prince, in French and English, has led the debates, summarized the interventions, kept the rapporteurs to their topic, and drawn the conclusions with great force and perfect competence.

(my translation)
Conférence de Barbizon, Box 936, Van Zeeland Papers. AUCL.

14 The story is well told in Daalder, *Drees en Soestdijk* (67 for the Bernhard quote).

15 In a memo written in 1956 for the Commission of Three that investigated the Hofmans Affair, Drees said he was convinced that Hofmans had influenced the Queen in the Bilderberg controversy in 1955. Daalder, *Drees en Soestdijk*, 25. Already in 1945, the Dutch politician and later prime minister Jan de Quay speculated that Juliana objected to Bernhard's activities abroad, because she was afraid of his private escapades.

16 See the long quote from Drees' letter to Juliana in Daalder, *Drees en Soestdijk*, 81.

17 Johan Willem Beyen, "Notitie Inzake Conferentie Te Garmisch," October 10, 1955, Box 2663, Ministerie van Algemene Zaken, NAH.

18 See, for example, his letter to Reginald Maudling concerning KLM landing rights at Singapore, December 8, 1958, Box 192, Bilderberg Archives, NANL.

19 See Johnson to Retinger, December 18, 1957, Box 45, Bilderberg Papers.

20 This solved a tricky problem for Prince Bernhard, who thought that Coleman had not been up to the job of American chairman and asked President Eisenhower to replace him: See Prince Bernhard to President Eisenhower, October 30, 1954, Box 41, Ann Whitman File, International Series, DDEL. As he told the president:

> I have a little problem. The man whom C.D. asked to head the U.S. Committee, a businessman called Coleman (Burroughs Machines) is very nice but not quite 'big' enough to carry the job, but of course would not dream of giving it up – so I'll have to find a tactful way to replace him by someone like McCloy or such a type of person.

Eisenhower replied that he could not "undertake, under any circumstances, to reward his disinterested work in this field, and to damage his usefulness in other American fields, by just coldly giving him the sack." He suggested that a compromise solution could be found by appointing an American co-Chairman. President Eisenhower to Prince Bernhard, November 23, 1954, Box 35, Jackson Papers, DDEL.

21 In a 1957 telephone conversation with Norman S. Buchanan, a Rockefeller Foundation colleague, Rusk recounted how he "had been urged by both the US Government (President Eisenhower) and RF Trustees" to take part in the Group. Interviews NSB, 'July 26, 1957, Box 57784, RFA. See also: Retinger to Prince Bernhard, January 25, 1955: "C.D. Jackson telephoned today to say that he and David Rockefeller have persuaded Dean Rusk to accept chairmanship of American Bilderberg Group." Box 187, Bilderberg Archive, NANL.

22 At some point, Retinger had suggested to ask two former American Presidents to sponsor the Bilderberg meetings. The plan was quickly dropped when C. D. Jackson told him how old Hoover was and that many Republicans – Jackson included – would refuse to cooperate with Truman. See: Retinger to Prince Bernhard, July 12th, 1954, Box 30, Bilderberg Archives, NANL.

23 Unfortunately, the archival records of the Carnegie Endowment for the 1950s and 1960s are not open for research (and may have been lost).

24 See Van der Beugel to Prince Bernhard, September 12, 1963, Box 22, Bilderberg Archives, NANL. It should be noted that many conservative anti-communist organizations in Europe were actively seeking cooperation with Spain and Portugal. In view of Bilderberg's non-partisanship and strong representation from the Left, it clearly served a different function.

25 See Van der Beugel's report on his trip to Athens in the summer of 1967, Box 76, Bilderberg Archives, NANL.

26 See also Chapter 9.

27 See Minutes of the Steering Committee held at Williamsburg, March 20 and 22 1964, and Johnson to Prince Bernhard, September 9, 1964, Box 68a, Bilderberg Archives, NANL.

28 In 1962, for example, the larger countries contributed about 10,000 Dutch guilders, and the smaller ones 5,000. See financial statement by Paul Rijkens: Otto Wolff to Fritz Berg, March 23, 1963, Box 188, BDIA. Over time, the fact that steering committee members were responsible for financial contributions did lead to an overrepresentation of businessmen and bankers on the committee.

29 "Strictement confidentiel," March 1, 1956, Box 941, Van Zeeland Papers, AUCL.

30 See Meynen to van der Beugel, March 3, 1966, Box 73, Bilderberg Archives, NANL. Unilever, Holland-Amerika Lijn, Heineken, Amstel Brouwerij, Algemene Kunstzijde Unie, and several Dutch banks contributed between 3,000–5,000 guilders in 1966.

31 Retinger to Van Zeeland, February 18, 1955, Box 33, Bilderberg Archives, NANL.

32 Otto Wolff to Mueller, June 8 and September 2, 1955, Box 373-2, Wolff Papers, RWA.

33 See the correspondence in PREM 11 2317, PRO, NAL.

34 See the financial statements for 1961 and 1962 in Box 188, BDIA.

35 A. Lamping, "Reis naar Zweden en Denemarken maart 1962," Box 22, Bilderberg Archives, NANL. Wallenberg financed the 1962 Bilderberg conference in Sweden out of his own pocket. See also Johnson to Holmes, June 19, 1964, Box 70, Bilderberg Archives, NANL: "both Duncan and the Prince may have been influenced by the belief that Griffin would find it not difficult to raise the necessary funds."

36 Shepard Stone, "Bilderberg Conferences – Recommended Action," March 3, 1955, Box 55-79, FFA.

37 See the financial overview in Box 56-341, FFA.

38 See "Interim Financial Report of Funds Received re Bilderberg Meetings for the Period of June 16, 1964 to June 15, 1965," Box 76, Dean Papers, CUL.

39 Despite not being a NATO member, Sweden was included in the Bilderberg Group from the start. In the 1960s, Finland was represented by the diplomat Johan A. Nykopp. These figures are based on an official list of all Bilderberg participants as well as lists of the separate meetings in possession of the author.

40 Bloemendal, "Reframing the Diplomat," 228.

41 Retinger was very well-connected in the international trade union movement and around a dozen trade unionists like Omer Becu, Irving Brown, Henk Oosterhuis, Ludwig Rosenberg and Sam Watson participated in the period until 1968, but none of them participated in more than one conference.

42 Oosterhuis to Becu and others, August 8, 1955, Box 188, Bilderberg Archives, NANL. "From the conversation with Prince Bernhard and the talk which I afterwards had with Dr. Retinger," Oosterhuis wrote, "I found that a group of international notabilities, who had prepared the Bilderberg and Barbizon Conferences ... highly appreciate the interest and the co-operation of prominent people of the international trade union movement." Becu participated

in the 1956 Bilderberg conference and was asked to become a member of the steering committee but did not take part in further conferences.

43 See Chapter 7.
44 See Black, "The Bitterest Enemies," and Maier, "Privileged Partners." As Maier puts it (29):

> The Atlantic community was constructed indirectly on the solidarity pacts that Resistance coalitions had negotiated even in non-corporatist countries such as Italy, France, and Belgium as well as in the more traditionally solidaristic societies of Scandinavia and the Netherlands. These agreements meant that the post-Second World War Atlantic partners built their international cooperation on domestic alliances with non-communist working class representatives in each participating country. Without that breadth the Atlantic alliance would have remained narrow and fragile.

45 These were words used by Ernst van der Beugel (a social-democrat himself), when he discussed Healey's replacement in the steering committee in 1964 and explained that "the only danger for Bilderberg exists in the undeserved reputation that we're a 'rich men's club' and therefore it is immensely important that we maintain a strong socialist element in the steering committee" (my translation). Van der Beugel, December 7, 1964, Box 68A, Bilderberg Archives, NANL.
46 On this point, see Aubourg, "Organizing Atlanticism," 92–93 and Aubourg "The Bilderberg Group: Promoting European Governance," 39–48.
47 In Priscilla Roberts' terminology, two generations of the transatlantic American foreign policy elite were involved: what she calls the 'wise men generation' – people like Harriman, McCloy, and Acheson, and the World War II generation – people like George Ball, Paul Nitze, and Dean Rusk. See Roberts, "The Transatlantic American Foreign Policy Elite." For a good overview of different generations of Atlanticists and Europeanists in the State Department, see Weisbrode, *Atlantic Century*.
48 Note by Retinger, undated (1955), Box 937, Van Zeeland Papers, AUCL.
49 Maier, *Among Empires*, 33.
50 Rijkens, *Handel en Wandel*, 145.
51 Wolff, *Der Weg nach Osten*, 43.
52 Wolff arranged meetings with George Ball, Henry Heinz II, Paul Hoffman, George Nebolsine, George Kennan, and David Rockefeller. See Wolff to Birrenbach, November 6, 1959, Box 003/1, Birrenbach Papers, ACDP.
53 Retinger letters to Rockefeller and Hauge, April 24, 1959, Box 54, Bilderberg Archives, NANL.
54 Rockefeller, *Memoirs*, 419.
55 Rockefeller, *Memoirs*, 208.
56 Bloemendal, "Reframing the Diplomat," 133.
57 Sulzberger to Dean 8 November 1966, 4100, Box 76, Dean Papers, CUL. Sulzberger wrote:

> I don't know who draws up the list of names for the American contingent but I would certainly like to get my own name added back on the list of those considered if this could be arranged. I find these meetings immensely interesting and stimulating.

58 Harsch to Meyers, September 17, 1958, Box 20, Harsch Papers, WHS.
59 Retinger to Bernhard December 18 1956, Box 42, Bilderberg Archives, NANL.
60 See Chapter 6.

61 Thatcher to Heseltine, January 17, 1983, THCR 3/2/110 f147, Thatcher Archive, Churchill College. Thatcher's letter to Heseltine needs to be put in perspective, however, by the fact that Thatcher herself declined to participate several times.

62 Schmidt to Apel, February 28, 1977, Box 6790, Schmidt Papers, FES.

63 Schmidt to Pettirsch, March 3, 1968, Box 5534, Schmidt Papers, FES.

64 See Gijswijt, "The Bilderberg Group and Dutch-American Relations."

65 For a similar point on the Trilateral Commission, see Knudsen, *The Trilateral Commission*.

66 Richardson, Kakabadse, and Kakabadse have drawn attention in a recent book based on interviews with Bilderbergers to the importance of personal motivations for participating in Bilderberg. *Bilderberg People*, 121.

67 See, for example, Wolff to Mueller, December 20, 1956, on the possible participation of Minister of Foreign Affairs Heinrich von Brentano, Box 376-1, Wolff Papers, RWA.

68 See Chapter 9.

69 On this point, see Großmann, "Winning the Cold War," 88.

70 As Justin Vaïsse has argued, the 'Cold War University' and US government funding of many of the institutes and organizations that Kissinger and Brzezinski were part of played an important role in creating a new foreign policy elite no longer dependent on WASP establishment connections and "social hegemony." See Vaïsse, "Zbig, Henry, and the New Foreign Policy Elite."

71 Most of his biographers have ignored Kissinger's international network. Exceptions are Klitzing, *The Nemesis of Stability*, and Suri, *Henry Kissinger*. Niall Ferguson's recent memoirs-based analysis of Kissinger's "network of power" leads to strange results, ignoring all of Kissinger's German connections (except for Willy Brandt) and listing Mao, Brezhnev, Gromyko, and Salvador Allende as part of Kissinger's "ego network." See Ferguson, *The Square and the Tower*.

72 Klitzing, *The Nemesis of Stability*, 76–84.

73 As Kiesinger recounted in an oral history interview, he had met Kissinger at the 1957 St. Simons conference and "since then a continuous contact existed, not very close, but still continuous, which became very important the moment he became national security advisor to the president." Kurt Georg Kiesinger, Oral History Interview, ACDP.

74 For a full list, see Klitzing, *Nemesis*, 104. For the broader importance of transatlantic elite networks in the German-American context, see also Hoeres, *Außenpolitik und Öffentlichkeit*, 91–96.

75 See Zetsche, "The Quest for Atlanticism," 258. Kissinger attended 6 out of 8 conferences in the period 1959–1974.

76 See Hoeres, *Außenpolitik und Öffentlichkeit*, 380.

77 Shoup, *Wall Street's Think Tank*, 119.

78 In 1977, for example, Schmidt originally planned to be at the Bilderberg conference in Torquay for just one day, but decided to remain longer after Kissinger asked for a private meeting. See the correspondence and memos in Box 6790, Schmidt Papers, FES.

79 Van der Beugel, *From Marshall Aid*.

80 Bloemendal, "Reframing the Diplomat."

81 On the KLM-case, see also Scott-Smith and Snyder, "A Test of Sentiments."

82 Rockefeller, *Memoirs*, 416–417. Knudsen argues that Brzezinski's role was as important as Rockefeller's, *The Trilateral Commission*, Chapter 1.

83 Schmidt, *Menschen und Mächte*, 267.

84 See Colen and Dutartre-Michaut, *Companion to Raymond Aron*.

85 Barbizon Report (my translation), Box 373-2, Wolff Papers, RWA.

86 "Conférence de Barbizon" (my translation), Box 936, Van Zeeland Papers.

87 Shepard Stone, "Bilderberg Meeting, Fiuggi, Italy," Berlin October 13, 1957, Box 56-341, FFA.

88 Ernst van der Beugel, Oral History Interview, 683, NANL.

89 See Berghahn, "Zur Soziologie," 408.

90 Pierre Dupuy, Fiuggi Report, Box 130993, FO 371, PRO, NAL.

91 Healey, *Time of My Life*, 196.

92 Box 56-341, FFA.

93 Großmann, *Internationale der Konservativen*, 558.

94 Jackson to James Reston, May 23, 1962, Box 89, Jackson Papers, DDEL.

95 See Zetsche, "The Quest for Atlanticism," 231 for evidence that the organizers of the German-American Conferences paid close attention to the organization of dinner parties and "tête à tête conversations, corridor contacts, and night-cap talks in the bar."

96 Note on Travel to Switzerland, Arnold Lamping, March 21, 1960, Box 57, Bilderberg Archives, NANL.

97 Collado arranged for "private planes of the Standard Oil Company" to fly the American participants in the 1961 Bilderberg conference to Canada. See Duncan to Lamping, April 6, 1961, Box 19, Bilderberg Archives, NANL.

98 Heinz to Bernhard, July 6 1956, Box 42, Bilderberg Archives, NANL.

99 Bernhard to Retinger, March 5 1955, Box 33, Bilderberg Archives, NANL.

100 Richardson, *Bilderberg People*. See also Philipsen, "Diplomacy with Ambiguity," 134–141. Jeffrey T. Checkel defines socialization as "a process of inducting actors into the norms and rules of a given community," but notes that there are two types of socialization: (1) role playing to fit in or "to act in accordance with expectations" without necessarily agreeing to the norms and rules of a group or community, (2) a deeper process of socialization that "implies that agents adopt the interests, or even possibly the identity, of the community of which they are a part." Checkel, "International Institutions," 804.

101 For an interesting analysis of elite socialization in the NATO Parliamentary Assembly, see Flockhart, "Masters and Novices."

102 See Bourdieu, "Social Space and Symbolic Power." Symbolic capital can consist of reputation, the legitimacy of certain ideas, or the authority to speak for a certain group.

103 For a similar argument about the Trilateral Commission, see Knudsen, *The Trilateral Commission* – although it should be said that the Trilateral Commission (particularly in the case of its US founders Rockefeller and Brzezinski) was more proactive than Bilderberg in trying to directly influence governments. For an older study co-authored by Bilderberg's Joseph Johnson, see Berman and Johnson, *Unofficial Diplomats*.

104 Friedrich, *Man and His Government*, 199.

105 Nye, *Soft Power*.

106 Hemmer and Katzenstein, "Why Is There No NATO in Asia."

107 Rusk to Nitze December 15 1955, Box 59, Folder 4, Nitze Papers.

108 See Gaddis, *We Now Know*, 50. Ikenberry also argues that the United States created legitimacy by accepting certain restraints through international institutions, *After Victory*, 164. The informal alliance could play a similar role.

109 Shaw, "The Political Structure," 25.

110 On NATO's official public relations efforts, see Risso, *Propaganda and Intelligence*.

111 'Final Report to the Ford Foundation on its Grant in support of the Bilderberg Meetings for the period 1 October 1959 - 31 December 1962' Joseph Johnson, Box 56-341, FFA.

112 "Grant in Aid to the Carnegie Endowment for International Peace," August 2, 1957, RFA.

113 Ball, *Past*, 106.

114 Johnson to Dulles, May 21, 1958, CIA, FOIA, www.cia.gov/library/readingroom/docs/CIA-RDP80B01676R003800100015-6.pdf. Accessed, January 12, 2018.

115 Van der Beugel to Prince Bernhard, November 3, 1964, Box 67a, Bilderberg Archives, NANL.

116 Lundestad, *The United States and Western Europe*, 72.

117 On the increasing importance of transnational actors after World War II, see Keohane and Nye, *Transnational Relations*, and Iriye, *Global Community*. For the historiography of transnational history, see Iriye and Saunier, *The Palgrave Dictionary of Transnational History*.

118 On the considerable overlap between Bilderberg and the DGAP, see Eisermann, *Außenpolitik*, 133–134.

119 Williams and Reed, *Denis*, 140.

120 Robert Bowie, who left the State Department for the newly founded Center for International Affairs in the autumn of 1957, had participated in the 1957 Bilderberg meeting in the United States and asked Prince Bernhard for an appointment to discuss the new Center "since its purpose is similar in part to that of the Bilderberg meetings." Bowie to Prince Bernhard, January 29, 1958, Box 192, Bilderberg Archives, NANL.

121 See Gemelli and MacLeod, *American Foundations in Europe*, and Parmar, *Foundations of the American Century*.

122 See Scott-Smith, *Networks of Empire*.

123 On official state visits, see Derix, *Bebilderte Politik*, and Daum, *Kennedy in Berlin*.

124 On the concept of a transatlantic public sphere, see Hoeres, *Außenpolitik und Öffentlichkeit*, 528.

125 Johnson to Van der Beugel, November 21, 1962, Box 65, Bilderberg Archives, NANL.

126 See the documentation in Box 920, Van Zeeland Papers, AUCL.

127 Compared to the Bilderberg Group, the literature on the CCF is vast: Berghahn, *America and the Intellectual Cold Wars*; Coleman, *The Liberal Conspiracy*; Harris, *The CIA and the Congress*; Hochgeschwender, *Freiheit in der Offensive*; Saunders, *The Cultural Cold War*; Scott-Smith, *The Politics of Apolitical Freedom*; Wilford, *The Mighty Wurlitzer*.

128 See the report of the first conference available at the NATO Parliamentarians website, www.nato-pa.int. See also Charman and Williams, *The Parliamentarians' Role*. For the official discussions concerning an Atlantic assembly, see Milloy, *The North Atlantic Treaty*, 119–125.

129 Aubourg, "The Atlantic Congress."

130 See Aubourg, "Organizing Atlanticism."

131 Weisbrode, *Atlantic Century*, 165–170; and Small, "The Atlantic Council."

132 Zetsche has shown that "40 of the participants of the German-American conferences were also frequent participants of the Bilderberg conferences, among them George Ball and Shepard Stone on the American side and Kurt Birrenbach and Fritz Erler on the West German one." Zetsche, "Quest for Atlanticism," 251.

133 See Haase, *Pragmatic Peacemakers*.

134 For recent studies of transnational European networks, see Dongen, Roulin, and Scott-Smith, *Transnational Anti-Communism*; Dumoulin, *Réseaux économiques*; Großmann, *Internationale der Konservativen*; Kaiser, *Christian Democracy*; Kaiser, Leucht, and Gehler, *Transnational Europe*; Orlow, *Common Destiny*.

135 "European Foundation. Theme for the Congress and the Idea behind it." Box 941, Van Zeeland Papers, AUCL.
136 For a short history of the European Cultural Foundation, see the Foundation's website. www.culturalfoundation.eu/about-us/ The history of the Foundation and Prince Bernhard's wider role in European affairs remains to be written.
137 See Gijswijt, "Informal Governance." There is no international history of the Action Committee, but several biographies of Monnet point to its importance. See Duchêne, *Jean Monnet*; and Schwabe, *Jean Monnet*.
138 For the period before 1945, see: De Grazia, *Irresistible Empire*; Rosenberg, *A World Connecting*; and Rodgers, *Atlantic Crossings*.

5   Integrating Europe

The dramatic demise of the European Defense Community (EDC) in the summer of 1954 was still reverberating when the second Bilderberg conference took place in Barbizon, France (March 18–20, 1955). Despite the fact that the EDC had been voted down by the French parliament, the French Socialist leader and Bilderberg cofounder Guy Mollet attempted to convince his fellow Bilderberg participants that the European idea was by no means dead. "Rest assured, friends abroad," Mollet announced,

> the day you will confront us with the problem of European economic integration – transport, agriculture, atomic energy pool or general energy pool – you will find 450 votes in the French parliament; they are there, they are guaranteed, they are certain.[1]

Indeed, two years later, the ratification of the Rome Treaties, establishing Euratom and the European Economic Community, resurrected the European project and created the framework for the later European Union.[2]

Mollet, who was the Fourth Republic's longest-serving prime minister (from February 1956 until May 1957), played a crucial role in the negotiations leading up to Rome, as did a number of other Bilderberg participants, including Walter Hallstein and Robert Marjolin.[3] The Bilderberg discussions at Barbizon and at Garmisch-Partenkirchen (September 23–25, 1955) thus allow for unique insights into the evolving thinking of European and American foreign policy elites during the so-called *relance européenne*. What these insights tell us is that much of the historiography of European integration misses both the complexity and the interwoven nature of the political, historical, social, and economic considerations and motives behind the treaties. As the discussions at the first Bilderberg Conference in 1954 already indicated, European integration was a response not just to Europe's fateful history of violent nationalism, but also to the multiple challenges of the postwar world: the communist threat from the East and from within, the demise of Europe's empires, the economic competition from the United States, the unsolved German question in a divided Europe, the advent of the nuclear age, and the fragility of Europe's societies.

Recognizing the interlinkages between these different motives and reasons allows us to overcome the gap in the historiography between the two competing schools of thought personified by Walter Lipgens and Alan Milward.[4] Lipgens, one of the first historians to study European integration, was mostly concerned with the sociocultural origins of Europe. He dealt more with ideas than with policies. He shared the conviction of many of his study objects that the nation-state had proven its inability to deal with the economic and political challenges of the modern age, thus giving way to new, supranational structures. Milward, in contrast, emphasized the continued importance of the state. His revisionist interpretation explained European integration first and foremost as an effort to stabilize and secure the economic and social foundations of the European nation-states through increased cooperation and trade.

Based on the Bilderberg discussions of 1955, this chapter argues that both schools of thought are, in fact, fully compatible. The first part of the chapter shows that Europe's instability and the fear of communist disruption within Western-European societies was a much more important driving force for a renewed attempt to create a united Europe than has been recognized in the literature.[5] The second part highlights the continued importance of the German question, even after the Federal Republic's admission to NATO, while the third part explains the importance of the United States as the economic inspiration for the Common Market. Taken together, these different elements, combined with the geopolitical impact of the Suez crisis, explain why European integration, initially dominated by conservative Catholics such as Adenauer and Schuman, now benefitted from a much broader, cross-party coalition.

Anti-communist Europe

The idea that a united Europe could act as a bulwark against communism while binding Germany more closely to the West was nothing new. Nor was the idea of a European common market, which had been discussed and proposed by the European League for Economic Cooperation, the Council of Europe, the European Movement, the Organisation for European Economic Cooperation, and policymakers such as the Dutch Foreign Minister Beyen. At the first Bilderberg conference, several participants had underlined the need for further European integration, and the final report had called for Europeans to "achieve a moral and material strength capable of meeting any threat to their freedom." What was different in 1955, however, was the even greater sense of urgency infusing the Bilderberg discussions on Europe. This urgency was not only the result of the EDC's dramatic failure; it was based to a considerable degree on the perception of an unrelenting communist threat. Particularly in the French Fourth Republic – never a model of stability – the risk of a communist takeover seemed real.[6]

The Bilderberg participants spent most of the Barbizon meeting grappling with "the uncommitted people" of the world and with the remarkable success of communist ideology and propaganda in Europe and the Third World. European integration was not even officially part of the agenda, yet every time the discussion turned to the question how Western Europe could build a more effective political defense against the communist threat from within, a united Europe turned out to be part of the answer. Meanwhile, the language employed to make the case for Europe was strikingly similar to the rhetoric of emotional community that had permeated the discussions at the first Bilderberg conference.

The French and Italian participants, in particular, emphasized that the threat of a communist takeover was far from imaginary. The strength of the Communist party in both countries and the fact that the communists controlled many important trade unions led Guy Mollet to conclude that there was a real danger of a communist victory in the Cold War – not by military aggression but by internal subversion of Western societies.[7] Danish Minister of Foreign Affairs Kraft warned that there were indications that the Cominform was preparing "some sort of civil war" in Europe during the summer, in which a massive propaganda offensive would be followed by a wave of political strikes.[8]

The question was how to respond to the internal communist challenge in Europe. Pietro Quaroni and George Ball, who presented introductory papers on this topic, both argued that as the immediate threat of military aggression had receded, the Cold War would be fought mainly on the political and economic fronts. In practice, this meant an ideological battle for the allegiance of the uncommitted people in Europe. The enormous economic and social disruptions caused by war, industrialization, and technological change had created a fertile ground for communism. Ball argued that in order to restore Western Europe's faith in democracy and freedom, the social, economic, and political frustrations of millions of Europeans needed to be addressed.[9] Quaroni made essentially the same point. No war, he said, had ever been won by remaining on the defensive. Moreover, the Cold War was bound to be a long conflict. Only if the Western societies proved capable of restoring their vitality could they count on ultimately winning the Cold War. At present, too many European countries seemed incapable of doing so: "Our weakness as Europeans is that we are dreaming of an impossible restoration of the world of before 1940. We sometimes resemble Dante's the Damned, who march forwards with their heads turned backwards."[10]

Everyone present at Barbizon agreed that a restored belief in democracy and the Western socioeconomic system was urgently needed in this new phase of the Cold War. The Soviet leadership was attempting to decrease tensions with its new slogan of 'peaceful coexistence' and its calls for nuclear disarmament. While talking coexistence, however, Moscow continued to practice a strategy of undermining Western Europe's social and political order. As Major-General Colin Gubbins warned in emotional terms:

> There is in Moscow, as we in this room know, a central organisation
> built up of many country sections, where the head of each section is a

man charged with the disruption of a particular country – the disruption of Great Britian, of the Netherlands, of France, and so on. He may have many subordinates. He is aware of movements in those countries. He gets reports from those countries; he sends instructions; he sends men; he sends money; he recruits new men. There is a man working quietly to destroy us. [...] We are choosing to go, as Mr. Pinay said at our last meeting, to a nice gentle death; and it is certain to come unless we take vigorous, definite and effective action [...].[11]

But what kind of action would be effective against the Soviet-directed campaign of propaganda and disruption? Paul Rijkens' suggestion that communist activities should be forbidden by law met with a mostly negative response. In Italy, Quaroni said, it would be hard to deal with the consequences of such a law, considering there were about 2 million party members. But apart from the practical difficulties, most participants agreed that it was the wrong approach. They regretted the fact that democracies were so ill-equipped to deal with internal threats, but to destroy democracy in order to save it was foolish. Mollet added that communism was similar to a religious movement and that the making of martyrs had never hindered the expansion of a religion.[12]

Rijkens' proposal to establish a common organization to fight communist propaganda – some sort of "democintern" – also found little support.[13] NATO already dealt with international communist front organizations, such as the international peace campaign. On the national level, moreover, a standardized Western response made little sense. Healey warned that a single Western organization would be perceived as an operation run by the Americans, which would destroy its credibility in many European countries. He added that even the Bilderberg Group ran this risk: if the meetings received too much publicity, this "could be extremely damaging to our common desires."[14]

Several speakers now turned to the idea of a politically and economically integrated Europe in response to the communist challenge. The political vision of Europe, they argued, could serve to bring back into the fold all those who were disillusioned with Europe's democratic systems. At the same time, European economic integration would serve to overcome the many national barriers against reform that were still in place in many Western European countries.[15]

Mollet was one of those who made this point. He explained that any reform-oriented government in France was, at present, more or less doomed to failure because of two interrelated factors. First, there was the presence of a good hundred communist deputies in the *Assemblée Nationale*. A group of obstructionist right-wing parliamentarians did not hesitate to cooperate with the communists if it served their needs. The moderate parties on the left were forced to participate in – or support – governments that held so little attraction to working class voters that the situation worked into the hands of the communists. Second, whenever a government came close to realizing a program of true reforms, the right brought it down, either with the help of the communists – as in the case of the EDC – or by invoking the confessional question.[16]

The best way to overcome the national deadlock in France was European integration. Contrary to the impression left by the EDC debacle, Mollet said, European integration was one of the few issues for which a relatively certain majority existed in the French parliament.[17] It was the linking of a political Europe with a military Europe – particularly, of course, with a rearmed Germany – that had been fatal. Anti-German sentiments in France and fears of a renewed German militarism had decisively undermined the pro-European consensus. The British also shared part of the blame because of their failure to participate more closely in the EDC. This did not mean, Mollet emphasized, that Europe was a lost cause; on the contrary, if Europe would now focus on economic integration, a clear majority ("450 votes" as he put it) existed to support it.[18]

Mollet was not alone in envisioning such a role for a united Europe. The Italian industrialist Alberto Pirelli, for example, made much the same point. Pirelli explained that one of the key problems facing his country was the economic development of the relatively backward regions in Southern Italy. What was needed was a combination of government investment and private initiative. At present, however, investment from outside of Italy was not forthcoming. Pirelli argued that such investment was not only economically profitable, but that it could also play a major part "in the sphere of anti-communism." In this context, he continued,

> nothing would help more than an economically united Europe, within which economic conditions [...] would be comparable, to establish solidarity against communism. This would help Europe regain the confidence and optimism which have been her driving force in previous times and be the greatest bulwark against communism.[19]

George Ball, who had already made the case for uniting Europe at the first Bilderberg Conference, agreed. "The cure for the [disease] of neutralism," he argued,

> lies not in words but in deeds; [...] it lies in taking those steps which can give a new element of faith, a new desire to fight for the ideas of the West, and that must necessarily come from the correction of social, economic and political frustrations which tend to create a climate for neutralism.[20]

In the case of France, the causes of neutralism were complex and manifold, but at the heart of it was "a deeply-felt intellectual despair and frustration." To restore faith in the "validity of France," the political instability and ineffectiveness of the Fourth Republic should be dealt with. One way to do so, Ball said, was by creating "a new concept and a new system of allegiances through the creation of [a] Federal Europe."[21]

The discussion at Barbizon shows that the combined ideological and socioeconomic challenges posed by communism served as a catalyst for European integration at a time when the European project seemed to have lost its momentum. Aware of the effectiveness of Soviet propaganda and aware of the widespread lack of faith in Western Europe in the existing economic and political structures, many Bilderberg participants regarded integration as the best way to restore Europe to its former vitality. The Belgian socialist Senator Fernand Dehousse put it most dramatically when he said that uniting Europe amounted to "the rescue of western civilization."[22]

The Dutch Foreign Minister Johan Willem Beyen, who was kept fully informed on the Bilderberg Meetings by Prince Bernhard, will have taken notice of Mollet's promise of 450 certain votes.[23] After the Paris Agreements – which made the Federal Republic a sovereign member of NATO and created the Western European Union (WEU) to safeguard certain limits imposed on West German rearmament – had been ratified in May 1955, Beyen and his Benelux colleagues decided that the time was ripe for another go at building Europe. Paul-Henri Spaak, the Belgian Foreign Minister, and Jean Monnet had already developed a plan for further vertical integration along the lines of the European Coal and Steel Community (ECSC) in the fields of atomic energy, transport, and electricity. Beyen insisted on including a proposal for broad horizontal integration in a European common market. At the Messina conference of the Six in June 1955, the French and Germans reluctantly accepted a Benelux proposal to institute a committee to study these plans.[24]

Shortly after the Messina conference, Spaak himself was named chairman of this committee. The Belgian foreign minister had little interest in the details and intricacies of the economic questions involved, but his lack in expertise was far outweighed by his political experience and his European connections. In April 1956, the committee produced the Spaak report, which would serve as the basis for official negotiations among the Six leading to the Rome Treaties signed in March 1957.

After the Barbizon conference, the Bilderberg organizers were eager to comply with President Eisenhower's call for practical suggestions. Prince Bernhard personally invited a group of international trade unionists, including the President of the International Confederation of Free Trade Unions, Omer Becu, to Soestdijk Palace in order to convince them of the need for more effective action against communist infiltration in trade unions.[25] In addition, Bernhard sent the transcripts of the first day of the Barbizon meeting to Louis Einthoven, the head of the Dutch secret service (*Binnenlandse Veiligheidsdienst*, or BVD), and asked him to draw some conclusions about the most effective means to counter communist propaganda and infiltration.[26] These recommendations would then be sent to SHAPE, the NATO headquarters in Paris.[27]

Retinger had the general report of the Barbizon conference printed as quickly as possible and also prepared a memorandum with definitions of coexistence from different countries.[28] All participants were urged "to use as much as possible the various meetings and conferences they attend to put forward the ideas and suggestions made at the Bilderberg Conferences."[29] Given the "the outstanding quality and influence of the members of the Bilderberg group" Retinger felt that this could have a significant impact on public opinion.[30]

A European common market

At the third Bilderberg conference in Garmisch-Partenkirchen in September 1955, the *relance européenne* was discussed at length. Beyen himself contributed a paper and underlined the Cold War implications of European integration:

> An increasing prosperity of the entire Western world and the discarding of irritating protection are undoubtedly important factors in the present cold war situation. The higher level of prosperity provides an economically sound basis for the defence effort and, on the other hand, deprives communism in the West of its breeding ground of poverty. Specialization in production is likely to lead to interlocking commercial and industrial interests and to close contacts between industries separated by national boundaries, all of which will in the long run further political solidarity.[31]

The discussions at Garmisch also revealed two additional arguments in favor of the Messina initiatives. The first revolved around the economic rationale for a European market. The second made a broader case for European integration, hinging on the German question. During the course of the discussions it became clear that the two were closely related.

Louis Camu, Paul Rijkens, and the Yale-educated French economist and former Secretary-General of the OEEC Robert Marjolin all advanced the economic arguments for a European common market. Camu said that a common market would have a far more profound psychological effect than further vertical integration. Thousands of European firms would be forced to rationalize their operations and raise productivity if they were confronted with larger markets and increased international competition. Echoing David Rockefeller's presentation at the first Bilderberg conference, Camu argued that the result would be a general improvement in living standards and employment. Rijkens agreed and predicted an immediate positive effect on the European economy, even if it would take a decade to establish a common market.[32]

Marjolin also made a strong case for the common market and emphasized its importance for the French economy. Marjolin had resigned in April 1955 as secretary general of the OEEC because he was convinced that further liberalization of trade in the OEEC context was impossible.[33] In the paper he contributed to the Garmisch conference, Marjolin identified expanding intra-European trade since 1947 as "one of the great factors of European stability and progress."[34] Europe was well on its way to regain its former position in world trade, which had a favorable effect on the overall balance of payments situation. However, in order to reach a more stable situation, European dependence on American aid and special expenditures had to be diminished even further. Consequently, a continued expansion of international trade was called for. Marjolin said that at the moment this was essentially a European responsibility. With the exception of France, the liberalization of trade in Europe by means of the abolition of quota restrictions had run its course.[35] The reduction of tariffs should be the next step.

Marjolin argued that the ultimate goal of liberalization should remain a global, multilateral system of free trade and payments. But in order to get there, the European countries first had to raise their productivity. At the moment, Europe was largely incapable of competing with the United States. To overcome the productivity gap, European producers should be progressively exposed to more competition. For this reason, Marjolin strongly supported Beyen's Messina initiative. As he put it: "We want the common market because it will create competition among the European countries."[36]

This applied in particular to France. At the moment, France seemed to fare well enough with an elaborate system of import restrictions and export subsidies. "We may be able to live rather comfortably now," Marjolin said,

> without making much effort, but in the long run our industries are suffering, productivity is lagging, and I am afraid that in France we may look up in a few years and find ourselves outdistanced not only by the United States but by other European countries.[37]

The only way to overcome the French apathy was by confronting producers with increased competition.[38] In reply to critical remarks from British and Canadian participants, who feared the creation of a protectionist continental trading bloc, Marjolin added that a European customs union would have to adhere to GATT rules. This meant that the external tariff of the union would be as low as possible. In addition, multilateral efforts at trade liberalization should continue parallel to the creation of a customs union.

The question of Great Britain and Europe came up repeatedly. The editor of *The Economist*, Geoffrey Crowther, predicted that the United Kingdom would not be willing to join a common market. This was hardly a surprise to most participants. More important was that men such as Guy Mollet, who had long insisted on British participation in Europe, now made clear that the Europe of the Six needed to proceed without the United Kingdom. Amintore Fanfani, the leader of the Italian Christian Democrats, added that a recent meeting of the *Nouvelles Équipes Internationales* in Salzburg had reached the same conclusion.[39] Fanfani reasoned that Europe would have to develop at different speeds. The nucleus of the Six had to lead the way, while leaving the door open to the British and others.[40] Jean Drapier, Spaak's close associate and the chairman of the EM's executive bureau, agreed and called the Europe of the Six the "dynamic center of the construction of Europe."[41]

In contrast with the British participants, the Americans strongly encouraged the plans for a common market – as they had done ever since the Marshall Plan. Under Secretary of State Robert D. Murphy and Paul G. Hoffman, the former ECA director, both emphasized the many advantages of creating a larger market. Hoffman recounted how he had made a speech in 1949 calling for a large European market. It was, in fact, during this speech that Hoffman had coined the term 'European integration,' after his advisers in the State Department told him that the term 'unity' was too much for the politically sensitive Europeans.

At the Barbizon Conference, President Eisenhower's economic advisor Gabriel Hauge had already emphasized the importance of a clear understanding of the American system in view of the communist challenge.[42] Hauge acknowledged that

> there has been a debilitating lack of faith among our own people in the ability of the free economy to be stable, to grow and to meet the needs and the justifiable expectations which our people have placed upon it.

The communists seized on these doubts to predict the inevitable collapse of the capitalist system.

> As far as our own country is concerned [Hauge explained], we are seeking to develop as evidence that our kind of economic system, that you and I and all of us here are generally dedicated to, can work. It is [...] an attempt to devise a fluid economy with a fair chance. It is an attempt to have an economic system in which my more need not be your less and thereby help to cut the ground out from a lot of the propaganda that faces us. I think we, in seeking to achieve this objective in our country, are trying to introduce the maximum amount of freedom to change in our economic system, because growth comes through change and causes change.

The maximum amount of freedom did not mean complete *laissez faire*. Hauge assured the European participants that the lessons of the Great Depression had been learnt. A set of rules and regulations, combined with "sustaining forces" provided by the government, was in place to prevent the normal fluctuations of a free economic system from spiraling out of control.[43] Reporting on the Barbizon conference to President Eisenhower Hauge wrote:

> It was interesting to observe in these discussions how various Europeans, who have their assorted gripes against the U.S., time after time cited our country and our economy as evidence of what the free way of life could produce in contrast to the Communist.[44]

At Garmisch, the American participants added a technological consideration with respect to the plans for an atomic energy community. Walker Cisler, chairman of the board of the Detroit Edison Company and one of the leading American experts on the commercial use of atomic energy, held a long presentation on this point in front of a spellbound European audience and had to answer multiple questions. He argued that the sheer scale of the necessary investments called for an integrated effort. Hoffman reinforced Cisler's argument by saying that much of the United States' gains in productivity since 1900 had come from the development of nonhuman energy sources. Europe needed to catch up to the United States in this respect and should not miss the boat on atomic energy. In the words of Hoffman:

> If nationalism creeps into this situation and each country endeavours to work on its own and develop atomic energy, the result will be that they will lag far behind the United States. On the other hand, I believe that if the European nations pool their brain power and their resources they can compete with us more than successfully, and I assure you that there is nothing that would please me more, because that is the way I believe that you can over the next 50 years write a history entirely different from the history of Europe for the past 50 years.[45]

Prince Bernhard wrapped up the session by saying:

> one thing [...] has emerged from our discussions yesterday and today, very clearly in my mind. From all speeches there has been practically unanimity of all the people present here, that it is of the utmost importance to take the quickest possible steps toward the integration of Europe.[46]

The German question

Two months before the Garmisch meeting, the Federal Republic had been officially welcomed as a member of NATO. This was, no doubt, a vindication of Adenauer's policy of *Westbindung*. Only ten years after the end of the war, West Germany regained its sovereignty (or most of it) and became a member of the Atlantic alliance. This remarkable fact has led many historians to treat West Germany's admission into NATO as the culmination point of the process of *Westbindung*. Not all go as far as John Gillingham, who has argued that by May 1955 "the German Problem had disappeared almost unseen," but there is a tendency to consider the problem as having lost much of its urgency.[47] Such readings, however, fail to take into account the fact that the German question was still wide open in 1955 and, more importantly, that it had the potential to undo all the efforts that resulted in the Paris Agreements. In other words, the *Westbindung* of the Federal Republic was by no means as secure as some historians have assumed.[48]

This, at least, was the prevailing sentiment at the Garmisch meeting: the fear of a second Rapallo was in the air. The fact that earlier in September Adenauer had traveled to Moscow increased concerns about a renewed German turn eastwards in order to achieve reunification.[49] In Denis Healey's evocative phrase: "[...] we must all admit that a western policy which is based on the division of Germany has a time bomb at the very heart of it."[50]

Ambassador Quaroni's paper on the German question left no doubt that a settlement with the Soviet Union was unlikely in the near future. "German unity can only be achieved," Quaroni argued,

> within the framework of a complete and radical transformation of the relations between East and West, or else as a result of complete capitulation by either East or West. Which means, in less diplomatic language, that the reunification of Germany will not be achieved.[51]

Understandably, the German participants at Garmisch found this difficult to accept. Fritz Erler, a leading SPD politician and vice chairman of the *Bundestag* Defense Committee, objected strongly to Quaroni's conclusions.[52] He conceded that in the present circumstances no solution seemed possible, but disagreed with the implication of Quaroni's paper that time would work in favor of the free world. In Erler's view, the massive communist indoctrination of the East German population posed a greater threat. The younger East German generations were in danger of being entirely lost to the democratic world because they had experienced nothing but totalitarian systems since the demise of the Weimar Republic in 1933. Having himself witnessed the effects of totalitarian indoctrination, Erler argued that a speedy resolution of the German question was in the interest of the West.

It followed, according to Erler, that Germany's membership in NATO should not be allowed to block negotiations with Moscow. If the door remained closed to a Four Power agreement, pressures in the Federal Republic to start direct negotiations with East Germany would be hard to resist. In that case, Moscow would have the better cards to decide the future of Germany. Carlo Schmid added that, although no party could say so openly in West Germany, he thought that on the difficult question of the Oder-Neisse line concessions by Germany were unavoidable.[53] Perhaps this could open the door to real negotiations. Schmid underlined Erler's point that from the Soviet point of view, it was no use to talk of reunification as long as the Paris Agreements applied. A reunified Germany within NATO was unacceptable to Moscow.

The debate that followed hinged on the question whether the risk of waiting trumped the risk of reaching a settlement that accommodated Soviet interests. Erler had made the case for rapid action. In contrast, Kurt Georg Kiesinger, a Christian Democratic Union (CDU) politician and chairman of the Foreign Affairs Committee of the *Bundestag*, counseled patience and tried to reassure his audience of Bonn's steady course. Kiesinger drew on his experience in Moscow to indicate that, although a solution at the present time was not in sight, in the longer term a settlement leaving a reunified Germany inside NATO might be possible.[54] The Soviet leadership had told the German delegation in Moscow that they were convinced that the current Western leaders sincerely wanted peace. Yet the communist leaders had not suddenly abandoned their ideology. They still believed in the communist prophecy that "some day the capitalist world will make a last desperate attack against the home of Communism."

The Soviet leaders had also told Kiesinger that they favored a period of détente and peaceful coexistence for two reasons: first, "to finish what they intend to do in Russia," and second, to assist in the development and industrialization of China. Kiesinger thought the Soviet leaders had been "romantic about what they planned and what they wanted to do [...]."[55] He speculated that, by taking account of both the Soviet yearning for security *and* their need for economic development, a combined offer of a security system and economic aid might have success in the future. In the meantime, the West would have to be patient and firm.

Most speakers at Garmisch favored Kiesinger's position. Qualified support for the SPD position came mainly from Paul van Zeeland and Denis Healey, who both emphasized the need to negotiate. Van Zeeland called the German question the neuralgic point of the Cold War. Without solving this problem, a lasting peace was not possible. He agreed with Fritz Erler that time was not working in the favor of the West and that everything should be done to find a solution that satisfied the security needs of both the West and the Soviet Union, without endangering the freedom of Germany. Van Zeeland suggested that German reunification might be attained in the context of a broader "global" deal including a demilitarized zone and a general agreement on disarmament. The Locarno Pact, he thought, should be looked at for further inspiration.[56]

Denis Healey was thinking in similar terms. His "time bomb" simile underlined the inherent instability of the division of Germany and Europe. Healey also made clear that he thought German pressure for reunification would increase, as indeed it had in recent months. He suggested that some form of disengagement might be necessary, adding immediately that he had not made up his mind on this issue and that he was a strong supporter of NATO. Still, the idea of a "buffer zone between America and Russia large enough to subsist on its own" seemed attractive if it solved the German puzzle and if it detached the satellite countries from the Soviet sphere of influence.[57] Healey's intervention was criticized by, among others, the former Dutch Minister of Foreign Affairs Eelco van Kleffens, who pointed to the risk of breaking up the Atlantic alliance. Healey's use of the word disengagement reminded van Kleffens of a line in Goethe's Faust: "*Du sprichst ein grosses* [sic] *Wort gelassen aus.*"[58]

George Kennan had long argued that accepting or even solidifying the continued division of Germany was a dangerous policy.[59] The Germans themselves would, in the long run, not go along with this policy. If they attempted to force the issue by themselves, they might get the United States involved in a general war with the Soviet Union, as Moscow could not be expected to give up Eastern Germany without a fight. Kennan had repeatedly warned that the West did not show enough flexibility in the negotiations with Moscow. Now that West Germany had become a member of the alliance, he privately held a somber outlook for the future.

During the Garmisch discussions, Kennan saw his worries confirmed. He told the conference that Khrushchev had not been joking when he declared that Germany's membership in NATO was unacceptable as a basis for negotiations. Instead of negotiating with the Western powers, the Soviet leaders would try to deal directly with Bonn with tempting economic offers. If Schmid's and Kiesinger's accounts of their Moscow visit were any indication, they were already busy laying the groundwork for such a move. In light of similar experiences in the 1920s and 1930s, Kennan warned the German participants that they should be wary of such offers.[60]

In addition, Moscow would focus on "what they regard as the Achilles Heel of the Western position in Germany, and that is Berlin." Based on the experiences of the first Berlin blockade, Kennan predicted (correctly, as it would turn out in 1958) that Moscow would again use West Berlin as a lever for pressuring the West. Starting with minor encroachments, Kennan thought, the Soviets would make life for the civilian population more and more difficult. All Western efforts to negotiate would be referred to the East German authorities in an attempt to "make an honest and respectable woman out of the East German régime."

"Now the purpose of all this will be, of course," Kennan said,

> initially to obtain for Moscow a voice in the internal councils of Germany, in effect, and I think only when that first goal has been achieved will the second task be approached, with all seriousness, and that is the task – as they see it – of liquidating all West German military ties to the Western Powers.[61]

After Kennan's pessimistic outlook it was up to Walter Hallstein, Adenauer's trusted state secretary in the foreign ministry, to defend the foreign policy of the Adenauer government. Like all West German speakers, he started from the premise that "reunification must be brought about if there is to be lasting order in the international situation."[62] With respect to the Oder-Neisse line, Hallstein said that this problem could only be solved by a reunified Germany. He emphasized, however, that the West German government would not act without the full agreement of its allies. Moreover, Bonn was convinced of the need to combine "patience and initiative," although it would be difficult to keep German public opinion in line.

Like Kiesinger, Hallstein felt compelled to express a more optimistic view on the chances for reaching a settlement with Moscow than he may have believed in private. Hallstein asserted that the West should work with "the assumption that there is a price for which the Russians can be brought to agree to German reunification."[63] Repeating Kiesinger's point, Hallstein indicated that the economic difficulties in the Soviet Union might create the conditions for a deal with Moscow. Based on the recent talks in Moscow, Hallstein had concluded that their economic problems were very serious. It made sense, therefore, "[...] to find out if the interest they have in getting rid of these difficulties – their fear, their economic needs – is big enough to bring them to an agreement on German reunification."[64]

Despite Hallstein's and Kiesinger's efforts, the overall tenor of the Garmisch discussion on the German question remained one of deep concern. Immediately after the Bilderberg conference, a large group of American participants traveled on to Luxembourg for a visit to the ECSC. As Max Kohnstamm, who was about to become Jean Monnet's right hand at the Action Committee for a United States of Europe, confided to his diary, they had left Garmisch worried about the "complete uncertainty with respect to German foreign policy."[65] Kennan told Kohnstamm that Walter Lippmann had been right after all, obviously referring to Lippmann's opposition to the creation of a West German state in the late 1940s.[66]

Back in the United States, Kennan felt compelled to publicize his views, providing Joseph and Stewart Alsop with a copy of his "Letter on Germany."[67] Comparing the letter to his famous 1946 Long Telegram, the Alsop brothers wrote:

> [t]his Kennan letter shatters almost as many happy illusions as the historic Kennan dispatch of a decade past. It suggests, in fact, that the current Foreign Ministers' meeting at Geneva is a mere way station to the grand nightmare of western diplomacy, which is a German reversal of alliances.[68]

After the column was published, George Ball informed Lippmann that Kennan's letter was based on the Garmisch conference. According to Ball, the letter "reflects the reactions which most of us had there to the state of mind prevailing among the Germans returning from Moscow."[69] George McGhee also told Dean Rusk that "one got also the impression that if we were not successful in achieving German unity on the basis we desired, that it would be achieved in some other way."[70]

In his "Letter on Germany," Kennan called the West Germans who had just returned from Moscow "somewhat shaky," adding:

> please don't misunderstand me. These men are as much Westerners, in every fiber of their being, as you and I [...] They know, in the wooing of which they are the objects, that they have to do with a siren, and they are miserably conscious of the frequent and, in this instance, wholly probable wages of sin. And still the lady's image haunts their dreams and they can't get away from it.[71]

In Kennan's almost Freudian analysis, the West Germans were tempted by the thought of direct negotiations with Moscow. They were also "intoxicated" by meeting one-on-one with the Soviet leadership, a leadership

> which speaks with one voice rather than three; which has something to give and is capable of delivering it if it wants to; and, above all, which talks the language of political realism to which Central Europeans are accustomed; brutal, cynical, in one sense crude, but in another infinitely subtle and sensitive.[72]

The Garmisch discussions indicate that despite the ratification of the Paris Agreements, the German question was by no means put to rest. To many Bilderberg participants, the Federal Republic's membership in NATO and the WEU was simply not a sufficient guarantee of Germany's *Westbindung*. The lessons of the 1920s and 1930s formed an additional reason. The prominent Dutch social-democratic politician and member of the Consultative Assembly in Strasbourg, Paul J. Kapteyn, explained why:

> [The Germans] have to import in order to live, and they have to pay for these imports, and they have to export in order to pay for the imports. But that people of 50 million, wanting to work, to strive and to thrive, they have not the pleasure of being a member of the Commonwealth, nor do they belong to l'Union Française, and so there is no territory in the world where they have preferential rights. Today we are living through a boom; all is well in Germany and in Western Europe [...] But is there anybody here who believes that the prosperity of today is eternal prosperity?

If a serious economic crisis developed, Kapteyn argued, other countries would close their borders to German exports. A similar situation to the one in the 1930s could easily develop. As Kapteyn put it:

> That is the moment for radicalisation for the German people. That is what we are afraid of, and that is why I am saying it will not be their fault if anything is going to happen – it will be our fault, if we do not succeed in bringing them together with us in a European union and creating a common market.[73]

Guy Mollet agreed with Kapteyn and added another consideration. In his view, Germany had to be protected against itself and against the temptation of another Rapallo. Mollet argued that German nationalism had not simply disappeared after the war. For some Germans, European integration had been nothing more than a means to an end. Now that the goal of sovereignty had been achieved, they might turn their attention eastwards. Here, inevitably, Moscow held the important trump cards. The Soviets controlled Germany's traditional eastern markets as well as the territories beyond the Oder-Neisse. What if they offered the West Germans a tempting offer of reunification including those lost lands? A repeat of Rapallo and a "renaissance" of German nationalism would be the result, Mollet predicted. In addition, he said, the West would face a catastrophic deterioration of its position vis-à-vis the Soviet Bloc.

The best way to prevent a second Rapallo, Mollet continued, was to tie the Federal Republic as closely as possible to the West. As Mollet put it in the report he wrote for the conference:

> However important the economic questions may be, it would be naive to think that they alone affect the construction of Europe. The German problem is more than ever at the heart of our difficulties and Germany's destiny will seal that of Europe. For me, the aim is still a Germany politically and economically integrated in a European Community which would have authority over Germany in the same way as over the other member-countries. Only such a structure would assure stability and power to Europe, and would not be a stake between two blocs but a factor for peace.[74]

At the same time, Germany should be given the chance to develop its economic potential in a large European market.

As he had done earlier at Barbizon, Mollet argued that the same parliament that had killed the EDC would have ratified a project of economic integration. By forcing the issue of military and political integration in the EDC, opponents of integration had been given the opportunity to create a false dichotomy in the public mind by juxtaposing the terms independence and supranationality. They created the impression that independence equaled sovereignty. Mollet argued that this was a dangerous misperception. In any functioning society, individuals or groups accepted certain limits on their individual freedom in order to protect and enhance the freedom and independence of all. The same was now true for the nation-states of Europe.[75] They were no longer in a position to solve their economic, social, and political problems on their own. To protect and enhance their independence and security, a degree of sharing or transferring of sovereignty was necessary.

Mollet therefore strongly agreed with Marjolin that a common market was an economic necessity in order to make Europe's economies more competitive. He indicated that the common market held out great hopes for "economic expansion," adding that from the socialist point of view it could also become a "means of social progress." On the other hand, he acknowledged the many difficulties involved in establishing a common market. Mollet suggested that it could only be done gradually, starting with measures to harmonize "diverse social regulations" and with the creation of a European investment fund. In France, the "fears of growing external competition" had to be taken into account.[76]

Mollet's message was targeted especially at his fellow social democrats Carlo Schmid and Fritz Erler. The SPD had opposed the ECSC, and important sections of the party were still critical of European integration because it would make German reunification more difficult. To them, Mollet said that reunification could not proceed at the expense of integration:

> For us, if this is about integrating and unifying, we agree, but if this is about choosing between unification and integration, I have to say, on behalf of an important part of French public opinion, that we do not agree; if it is necessary to pay for the unification of Germany with the severance, in the short or long term, of the ties that currently unite the Federal Republic and the Free World, and the stronger ties that need to unite us tomorrow, we say "Non."[77]

This was clear language on the part of the French socialist leader, who several months later formed a left-wing government. It confirms French Foreign Minister Christian Pineau's testimony that Mollet (and a select group of pro-Europeans in his vicinity) were in favor of the common market from the start.[78] It was for tactical reasons that the Mollet government long showed a preference for Euratom. As Marjolin wrote in his memoirs, time was desperately needed to convince different constituencies and interest groups of the necessity for breaking down France's trade barriers. Indeed, Mollet warned at Garmisch that France was not yet ready for the idea of growing competition. He himself was convinced of the need to create a European common market; what needed to be done was to convince the French public and parliament.[79]

With Walter Hallstein, Fritz Berg, Kurt Georg Kiesinger, Carlo Schmid, and several other prominent Germans present, Mollet's and Marjolin's contributions will have been shared in influential circles in the Federal Republic, including Chancellor Adenauer himself. For the conservative chancellor in Bonn, after all, this was a vital piece of information, indicating that the socialist leader from France was a reliable partner in building Europe.

The next two Bilderberg conferences, in March 1956 and February 1957, did not feature extended discussions on European integration. Two pressing issues that threatened to divide the Atlantic alliance – the crisis of decolonization and the approaching nuclear stalemate – dominated these meetings.[80] Both problems showed that despite the overwhelming convergence of interests and values between Western Europe and the United States, important differences remained. Throughout 1956, European fears increased that Washington would decide to return to a 'fortress America' mentality in reaction to the fast-increasing Soviet capabilities to reach the United States with nuclear weapons. Moreover, the transatlantic differences over the colonial question could not be easily bridged, as the Algerian crisis and the Suez affair proved. The fact that Washington did not react strongly to Khrushchev's rocket-rattling during the Suez crisis further fueled European suspicions. Given Europe's dependence on the Suez Canal for oil shipments, the case for Euratom and the common market suddenly looked a lot more convincing to many original doubters.

The overall effect of the Suez crisis on the Rome Treaties negotiations remains in dispute. At the height of the crisis, on November 6–7, 1956, Adenauer paid a controversial visit to Paris. The fact that during this visit a Franco-German compromise on several outstanding disagreements was quickly hammered out has led some historians to conclude that the final decision on the part of the French government to agree to the common market was decisively influenced by the Suez crisis. Others have pointed out that this decision was already made in September 1956.[81]

Both positions have something to speak for them. As we have seen, there can be little doubt that Mollet himself was in favor of the common market well before the Suez crisis. There is also sufficient documentary evidence to trace the final decision of the French cabinet in favor of pursuing the common market to September 1956. On the other hand, it is often conveniently forgotten that the Suez crisis began on July 26, 1956: the day Nasser nationalized the Suez Canal. This means that many of the implications of the Suez crisis played a role in the deliberations of the French cabinet during the summer of 1956. Not coincidentally, the French plan to include the French overseas territories in the common market – to create *Eurafrique* – was launched shortly after the failure of Suez, introducing Europe as a way to salvage France's crumbling empire. Moreover, there can be little question that the dramatic ending of the Suez crisis in November 1956 gave added impetus to the drive for a united Europe.[82]

This was true not only for France but also for the Federal Republic, where Adenauer used the crisis to reign in his Minister of Economic Affairs, Ludwig Erhard, who opposed the common market.[83] The chancellor told Maurice Faure on September 17 that even in Britain, the "Suez shock" seemed to lead to a more positive attitude regarding European integration.[84] In his much-noted Brussels speech on September 25, Adenauer repeatedly referred to the Suez crisis as proof of the impotence of a divided Europe. Europe should finally act, the chancellor said, or risk becoming irrelevant.

The Bilderberg Group and the Rome Treaties

Three points stand out in the Bilderberg discussions concerning Europe at Barbizon and Garmisch. First, it is clear that European elites were deeply concerned about the combined ideological and socioeconomic challenge posed by international communism in the mid-1950s. Few works on the history of European integration take this into account.[85] Yet as the Barbizon discussions indicate, it was precisely this challenge that acted as an important catalyst for European integration after the collapse of the EDC. A united Europe as a bulwark against communism, a united Europe as a way to overcome Europe's structural socioeconomic problems and win back the allegiance of those who had lost faith in democracy – those were the ideas put forward at Barbizon. In the context of the Cold War, politics and economics could not be separated. The Cold War was perceived as a struggle against totalitarianism fought on all fronts: ideological, political, economic, cultural, and military. Seen in this light, the 'European rescue of the nation-state' through political and economic integration was necessary not only to secure the social and economic foundations of Europe, but also to protect democracy and freedom itself.[86] Moreover, in the face of the United States' rise to economic superpower status and the loss of traditional markets because of decolonization, the realization that Europe needed a common market to restore its competitiveness only added weight to the argument.

The second point concerns the German question. Ultimately, the German question was a matter of war and peace and therefore a political concern. As the Garmisch discussions show, however, men like Mollet envisioned an economic solution to this political problem. German economic expansionism was to be absorbed in a European market governed by a supranational authority. This had a double advantage: it minimized the risk of a repeat of Germany's economic isolation during the recession of the 1930s and the resulting policy of autarchy and an aggressive search for *Lebensraum*. At the same time, the integration of West Germany into Europe lessened the danger of another Rapallo. Any Russian offer to West Germany – whether it concerned reunification, economic cooperation, or both – stood less chance of success if the Federal Republic was an integral part of Western Europe. In this perspective, the Rome Treaties reflected important lessons of history.[87] Shortsighted economic policies had led to disaster before.

If we turn to the role of the United States in actively stimulating European integration, the third conclusion to emerge is that the Bilderberg Group was ideally suited for the kind of quiet, informal diplomacy that was required after the heavy-handed US strategy of the EDC had backfired.[88] It gave people like Ball, Hauge, Hoffman, Murphy, and Rockefeller the chance to influence European thinking in more subtle ways than Secretary of State Dulles had employed in 1953–1954. One of their most persuasive arguments concerned the extraordinary dynamism of the American economy. The idea that larger markets and more competition would lead to higher productivity as the key to economic growth was particularly important in view of long-standing European traditions of protectionism.[89] The American experience in developing the peaceful use of atomic energy provided another argument in favor of pooling European resources.

As far as the historiography of European integration is concerned, these conclusions show that juxtaposing political and economic driving forces can be misleading. The question is not so much whether the Rome Treaties were a "political construct" (Wilfried Loth) or whether "the economic foundation of the treaties was more fundamental" (Alan Milward).[90] Rather, we should ask how the *interplay* between economic and political motives, interests, and constraints led to the Rome Treaties.

As the evidence from the Bilderberg Meetings suggests, the communist threat, the dynamics of the Cold War, and the German question were important factors in this equation, bolstered by the lessons of history and a sense of emotional community. As the evidence also suggests, economic and political factors tended to reinforce, rather than contradict, each other. Years of discussions among US and European transnational elites had created wide-ranging support for a further liberalization of trade in order to raise competition and productivity; a European common market, much like the United States' example, would serve this purpose. The strong interlinkage between all these factors goes a long way towards explaining the remarkably broad cross-party coalition that in the end supported the Rome Treaties, from socialists to conservatives and from trade unions to business and agricultural associations.

Notes

1 Barbizon Transcript, French IV, 33 (my translation), Box 9, Bilderberg Archives, NANL. See also Appendix 4, Barbizon Report for the full speech. Box 55-79, FFA.
2 Although it should be noted that the final vote count in the French parliament was 342 in favor, not the 450 promised by Mollet.
3 Mollet remains a controversial figure in the French historiography because of his government's violent campaign to suppress the Algerian independence movement. See Lefèbvre, *Guy Mollet*. For criticism of Mollet within the SFIO, see Orlow, *Common Destiny*, 186–187 and 203.
4 On this point, see Kaiser, "From State to Society," and Parsons, *A Certain Idea*.
5 See Großmann, "Die Grundtorheit unserer Epoche," 587.
6 Already in early 1954, Pinay and Mollet were both deeply worried about the situation in France. During a meeting of the Retinger Committee in Paris, in February, Pinay argued that the low standard of living accounted for much of French communist support. Several others then "stressed the importance of economic integration in view of general conditions in Europe and their influence on Communism." Memorandum, "7th and 8th February – PARIS," Box 30, Bilderberg Archives, NANL and Prince Bernhard, handwritten notes (13 pages), Box 181, Bilderberg Archives, NANL.
7 Earlier, during a steering committee meeting in Paris in December 1954 Antoine Pinay had shared this view. See "Meeting held on Monday, December 6th, 1954, in Paris," Box 30, Bilderberg Papers, NAH. Camu told Van Zeeland that he was impressed with Mollet's performance and worried about the situation in France. Camu to Van Zeeland, March 31, 1955, Box 936, Van Zeeland Papers, AUCL.
8 Barbizon Transcript, English II, 22, Box 4, Bilderberg Archives, NANL.
9 Barbizon Transcript, English III, 3–12, Box 4, Bilderberg Archives, NANL.

10 Barbizon Transcript, French III (my translation), 3, Box 4, Bilderberg Archives, NANL.

11 Barbizon Transcript, English IV, 25, Box 4, Bilderberg Archives, NANL.

12 For Quaroni's statement, see Barbizon Transcript, French IV, 3. For Mollet, see Barbizon Transcript, French I, 27, Box 4, Bilderberg Archives, NANL.

13 Gabriel Hauge, Report on the Barbizon Conference, 1/15, DDE Office Files, RSC Microfilm Collection.

14 Barbizon Transcript, English IV, 14, Box 4, Bilderberg Archives, NANL.

15 On the importance of reforming capitalism and avoiding another Great Depression in the 'economic Cold War,' see Gaddis, *The Cold War*, 115–117.

16 Barbizon Transcript, French IV, 31, Box 4, Bilderberg Archives, NANL.

17 Barbizon Transcript, French IV, 33, Box 4, Bilderberg Archives, NANL.

18 Ibid.

19 Barbizon Transcript, English V, 11, Box 4, Bilderberg Archives, NANL.

20 Barbizon Transcript, English III, 6, Box 4, Bilderberg Archives, NANL. The original transcript reads "the cure for the decrease of neutralism." In Ball's original report the formulation is as follows: "Neutralism as a disease can be cured not by words, but by action." George Ball, "The Struggle With The Communists For The Uncommitted Peoples," Box 4, Bilderberg Archives, NANL.

21 Barbizon Transcript, English III, 6, Box 4, Bilderberg Archives, NANL.

22 Barbizon Transcript, French IV, 43 (my translation), Box 4, Bilderberg Archives, NANL.

23 On Prince Bernhard's friendship and cooperation with Beyen, see Weenink, *Bankier van de wereld*, 285–294 and 335. For the fact that Bernhard kept the Ministry of Foreign Affairs fully informed, see Beyen's memorandum for the Dutch Cabinet, "Notitie Inzake Conferentie Te Garmisch," October 10, 1955, Box 2663, Ministerie van Algemene Zaken, NANL.

24 For comprehensive treatments of the Messina conference and its aftermath, see Bossuat, *L'Europe des Français*; Krüger, *Sicherheit Durch Integration*; Loth, *Building Europe*; Segers, *Deutschlands Ringen*; and Thiemeyer, *Vom Pool Vert*. Gerbet, *La naissance du Marché Commun*; and Küsters, *Die Gründung*, are slightly dated but still useful. The classic edited volume (especially valuable for the testimony from Maurice Faure, Christian Pineau and others) is Serra, *Il Rilancio*. For the economic context, see Brusse, *Tariffs, Trade and European Integration*; Lynch, *France and the International Economy*; and Milward, *The European Rescue*. For transatlantic context, see Giauque, *Grand Designs*.

25 As Prince Bernhard had written in his paper for the Barbizon conference:

> In view of the fact that in various European countries Communist tactics are: causing discontentment in industrial enterprises by means of extensive propaganda, written and verbal, amongst the workers, it is suggested that trade unions consider taking much more active counter-measures than they have taken up to now in that respect.

Prince Bernhard, "The Role of Economy in Winning the Allegiance of the Non-Committed People for the West and its Ideology," Box 35, Jackson Papers, DDEL.

26 Prince Bernhard to Einthoven, May 13, 1955, Box 187, Bilderberg Archives, NANL.

27 It is unclear whether Prince Bernhard's communications with Einthoven played a role in the latter's involvement in the Interdoc organization, which was created at the initiative of the *Service de Documentation Exterieure et de Contre-Espionage* (SDECE), the German BND, and the BVD in order to combat Soviet propaganda in Western-European societies. On Interdoc, see Smith, *Western Anti-Communism*.

28 "Various Definitions of Co-existence," Box 32, Bilderberg Archives, NANL. Not surprisingly, most definitions gave voice to doubts about the Soviet willingness to engage in a real coexistence. As the Italian definition, probably written by Quaroni, put it:

> Co-existence, in the true sense of the word, i.e. living side by side in a sort of mutual tolerance, would only be possible in the communist and democratic worlds when communism is convinced that it cannot achieve universal domination. On that day the Russians and the communists will begin to doubt the real truth of their theory: doubt is the beginning of tolerance.

29 See the memo titled "Conclusions," no date, Box 32, Bilderberg Archives, NANL.
30 "Measures for Fighting Communist Propaganda," June 1, 1955, Box 936, Van Zeeland Papers, AUCL.
31 J.W. Beyen, "A Note on the Political Aspects of Convertibility," Box 298, Gaitskell Papers, UCL. In the very first outline of his views on European integration, in November 1952, Beyen argued that the Western European civilization was in mortal danger. The "virus of totalitarianism" could only be effectively battled by strengthening the "economic and social health" of societies; this, in turn, could only be done by raising productivity in a larger European market. See Weenink, *Beyen*, 323–324. Beyen made essentially the same point at the Messina Conference.
32 Garmisch Transcript, Box 9, Bilderberg Archives, NANL.
33 It was mainly the British refusal to discuss plans for a large European customs union that had led Marjolin to resign. See Marjolin, *Le Travail d'une Vie.*
34 Robert Marjolin, "Aims and Means for a Policy of Developing International Exchanges," Box 5, Bilderberg Archives, NANL. By intra-European trade, Marjolin meant the OEEC area.
35 As Marjolin explained in his paper: "Countries with low tariffs will refuse to go any further in abolishing quantitative restrictions unless other forms of protection are reduced also." Ibid.
36 Garmisch Transcript, English VII, 86, Box 9, Bilderberg Archives, NANL.
37 Ibid.
38 Marjolin added that a monetary adjustment was also necessary because the franc was overvalued: "Only a monetary adjustment accompanied by widespread lifting of restrictions on trade with the other countries of Europe and North America will enable France again to play a large part in the construction of Europe and the Atlantic Community." Marjolin, "Aims and Means for a Policy of Developing International Exchanges," 5. This was, in fact, exactly what Charles de Gaulle and his economic advisor, Jacques Rueff, decided to do three years later, in late 1958. See Lynch, "De Gaulle's First Veto."
39 For documentation on the NEI meeting, including a speech by Fanfani, see Gehler and Kaiser, *Transnationale Parteienkooperation*, 441–459.
40 Fanfani, who had been prevented from coming to the Barbizon conference, also reaffirmed the need for a united Europe in the face of the communist threat. He added that only a united Europe would be able to face the Soviet Union at eye level. Garmisch Transcript, French III, 3–4, and French IV, 46–47, Box 9, Bilderberg Archives, NANL.
41 Garmisch Transcript, French IV (my translation), 57, Box 9, Bilderberg Archives, NANL.
42 Hauge had been instructed by Eisenhower himself to take part in the Barbizon meeting. Bedell Smith had asked the president to send Hauge. See Bedell Smith to Eisenhower, March 03, 1955, 1/15, DDE Office Files, RSC Microfilm Collection.
43 Barbizon Transcript, English V, 28–30, Box 9, Bilderberg Archives, NANL.

44 Gabriel Hauge, Report on the Barbizon Conference, 1/15, DDE Office Files, RSC Microfilm Collection. Camu called Hauge's speech "un remarquable exposé de la situation politique et économique des Etats-Unis." Camu to Van Zeeland, March 31, 1955, Box 936, Van Zeeland Papers, AUCL/GEHEC.

45 Garmisch Transcript, English VI, 47–48, Box 9, Bilderberg Archives, NANL.

46 Garmisch Transcript, English VI, 73, Box 9, Bilderberg Archives, NANL.

47 Gillingham, "The German Problem." Marc Trachtenberg has similarly argued that by 1955 all the major elements for "a stable peace" were present: "[the Germans] could live with the arrangements they and their allies had worked out, even though those arrangements limited their military power and political independence in important ways [...]." Trachtenberg, *Constructed Peace*, 144.

48 Perhaps not surprisingly, many German historians show a greater sensitivity concerning this issue. See Thoß, "Sicherheits- und deutschlandpolitische Komponenten"; Schmidt, "'Tying' (West) Germany to the West"; Krüger, *Sicherheit durch Integration*. See also Sheehan, *Where Have All the Soldiers Gone*, 161. Sheehan identifies the German problem as the driving force behind efforts to unite Europe in 1955 and beyond.

49 Three Garmisch participants – Hallstein, Kiesinger, and Schmid – had accompanied Adenauer to Moscow in mid-September 1955. The chancellor's trip caused many raised eyebrows in the West. Despite previous assurances that he would not establish diplomatic relations with Moscow unless definite progress on the question of German unification could be made, Adenauer did so in return for the release of the remaining 10.000 German prisoners in the Soviet Union. The American Ambassador in Moscow, Charles Bohlen, was enraged by what he considered a huge diplomatic victory for the Soviet Union. He even suspected a secret deal between Adenauer and the Soviets. Felix von Eckardt, a close Adenauer confidant, remembered how it took months to convince the Eisenhower Administration that the Federal Republic could still be trusted. See Eckardt, "Konrad Adenauer." On the Moscow visit in general, see Kilian, *Adenauers Reise*.

50 Garmisch Transcript, English IV, 2, Box 9, Bilderberg Archives, NANL.

51 P. Quaroni, "Replies to Questions Raised in the Note on German Reunification," B 13, Band 9, AA. Emphasis in original.

52 See Soell, *Fritz Erler*.

53 During the discussion, Prince Bernhard announced that Carlo Schmid would give a detailed account of the Moscow trip that evening. There is no record of this session. See Barry Bingham to Dean Rusk, December 23, 1955, 5579, FFA. Bingham wrote about the Garmisch meeting:

> I found the discussion about German-Russian relations and especially the report by Dr. Carlo Schmidt [sic] by all odds the most important of the program. This was not really a part of the regular session but an added attraction which struck me as most valuable to anybody who is trying to understand current European trends.

On Schmid, see Weber, *Carlo Schmid*; and Schmid, *Erinnerungen*.

54 Like Erler, Kiesinger took issue with the conclusions in Quaroni's paper. However, several days later, during a CDU-*Bundesvorstand* meeting, Kiesinger seemed much more in agreement with the Italian ambassador. He told his CDU colleagues that he doubted whether Moscow would ever agree to reunification if a reunified Germany was not safely integrated in the communist camp. It shows that one should be careful with taking statements on the German question at face value. Just as many American, British or French statements were mostly for West German consumption, West German politicians realized they had to keep the issue on the agenda of the West. Buchstab, *Adenauer*, 603.

55 Garmisch Transcript, English III, 22, Box 9, Bilderberg Archives, NANL.

56 Garmisch Transcript, French IV, 3–11, Box 9, Bilderberg Archives, NANL.
57 Garmisch Transcript, English IV, 2–3, Box 9, Bilderberg Archives, NANL.
58 Ibid., 1.
59 In 1948, Kennan argued in his so-called Program A for a negotiated pullback of all occupation forces in the four zones to special enclaves at the borders of Germany. Simultaneously, free elections should be held in the whole of Germany. Kennan's Program A was rejected, however, and the FRG was founded in 1949. On Kennan's Program A, see Gaddis, *We Now Know*, 121–123. See also Botts, "'Nothing to Seek." Botts argues that Kennan's motives for developing Program A also involved his conviction that the United States should not overextend itself abroad, because of the many domestic problems the country needed to face.
60 Garmisch Transcript, English III, 24, Box 9, Bilderberg Archives, NANL. Otto Wolff told Rudolf Mueller privately that the Federal Republic's economy was already too intertwined with the West to make an economic Rapallo likely. Wolff to Mueller, September 6, 1955, Box 373–372, Wolff Papers, RWA.
61 Garmisch Transcript, English III, 24, Box 9, Bilderberg Archives, NANL.
62 Garmisch Transcript, English IV, 9, Box 9, Bilderberg Archives, NANL.
63 Ibid., 11.
64 Ibid., 12.
65 My translation, Kohnstamm Diary, 155, Kohnstamm Papers, EUI.
66 Lippmann wrote on January 30, 1948: "So if we make the cardinal mistake of reconstructing a united German national state [...] we shall have laid the foundation of a German-Soviet alliance against the Western world." Quoted in Schlaack, *Walter Lippmann und Deutschland*, 285. On Lippmann's views, see also Steel, *Walter Lippmann*.
67 See Hixson, *George F. Kennan*, 144.
68 Joseph and Stewart Alsop, "Matter of Fact: The Kennan Letter," *The Washington Post and Times Herald*, November 14, 1955.
69 Ball to Lippmann, November 14, 1955, Box 101, Ball Papers, PUL.
70 McGhee to Rusk, November 8, 1955, Box 55–79, FFA.
71 Joseph and Stewart Alsop, "Matter of Fact: The Kennan Letter," *The Washington Post and Times Herald*, November 14, 1955.
72 Ibid.
73 Both quotations: Garmisch Transcript, English VI, 16, Box 9, Bilderberg Archives, NANL
74 Guy Mollet, "The Unification of Europe," 3, Box 298, Hugh Gaitskell Papers, UCL. He also warned: "The risk of a re-awakening of German nationalism is no myth; if no energetic Europe relance intercedes we shall see the sad confirmation of this, perhaps soon, and not only in the sphere of European politics."
75 Mollet's thinking in this respect was influenced by his fellow socialist Léon Blum. See Bossuat, *L'Europe des Français*, 294.
76 Mollet, "The Unification of Europe," 3, Box 298, Hugh Gaitskell Papers, UCL.
77 Garmisch Transcript, French IV, 17 (my translation), Box 9, Bilderberg Archives, NANL.
78 Pineau was the foreign minister in Mollet's government. See Pineau and Rimbaud, *Le Grand Pari*, 186 ff.
79 Garmisch Transcript, French V, 1, Box 9, Bilderberg Archives, NANL.
80 See Chapters 6 and 7.
81 See Krüger, *Sicherheit durch Integration*, 460 ff.
82 Robert Marjolin and Karl Carstens, the two men who negotiated the November agreement, both recount in their memoirs that the Suez crisis facilitated compromises on points which had led to a breakdown of negotiations a few weeks earlier.
83 See Gijswijt, "Informal Governance," and Segers, *Deutschlands Ringen*.

84 "Conversation entre M.M. Faure, le chancelier Adenauer et Hallstein," September 17, 1956, *Documents Diplomatiques Français*, 1956, Vol. 1, 295–296.
85 In a typical example, Tony Judt discusses the Rome Treaties only in a very narrow economic sense and ignores both the Cold War context and the German question. Judt, *Postwar*, 302–309. Note also that in his excellent overview of Western anti-communism, Romero does not mention European integration as an anti-communist strategy. Romero, "Cold War Anti-Communism," 310.
86 I agree with Milward's basic contention that the purpose of European integration was to rescue (or strengthen) the European nation-states. Milward's almost exclusive focus on socioeconomic factors, however, has resulted in a rather one-sided picture, ignoring most other factors. The evidence from the Barbizon conference adds a new dimension by bringing in the communist challenge.
87 On the relationship between memory and power, see Müller, *Memory and Power*, especially the introduction.
88 On the official American diplomacy concerning European integration, see Lundestad, *The United States and Europe*; Neuss, *Geburtshelfer*; and Winand, *Eisenhower, Kennedy, and the United States of Europe*.
89 On this point see Angster, *Konsenskapitalismus*, 61.
90 Loth, "Beiträge der Geschichtswissenschaft," and Milward, *The European Rescue*, 208.

6 Decolonization and the global Cold War

Throughout the 1950s and 1960s, the so-called Third World appeared frequently on the agenda of the Bilderberg meetings. Most Bilderberg participants agreed that the global Cold War could well be decided there: if the West 'lost' major parts of the newly independent nations to communist expansion, the economic and political consequences could be dramatic.[1] However, given the overwhelming speed of decolonization – in the first decade of its existence the United Nations admitted Thailand, Pakistan, Burma, Indonesia, Cambodia, Ceylon, Laos, Morocco, Sudan, and Tunisia as new members – and the divergent views on the timing and methods of dismantling Europe's colonial territories, it proved impossible to forge a common transatlantic strategy with regard to the Third World. As Dean Rusk put it at the 1955 Barbizon Conference:

> The United States is caught in the middle between nationalist movements in other parts of the world and our friends in Europe. I can only say that there are no more excruciating problems for those who make policy than those arising out of colonial questions.[2]

As this chapter shows, the Bilderberg discussions on decolonization did provide a much-needed forum to air grievances and to draw attention to the difficult political implications of the colonial question in most NATO countries. The Suez crisis was the most dramatic expression of transatlantic differences and led to much soul-searching at the 1957 Bilderberg conference in the United States. In terms of practical solutions to the challenge of decolonization, the Bilderberg discussions focused strongly on economic development and technical assistance. This was important because many Bilderberg participants and members, from World Bank President Eugene Black to Eisenhower speechwriter C. D. Jackson, were engaged in private and public initiatives focused on development of the 'underdeveloped world.'

The Bandung conference and the emergence of the Third World

Starting in the second half of 1954, transatlantic differences over decolonization became more important because of two related developments.

First, the Soviet Union and China increased their efforts to bring the non-aligned countries of the Third World into the Communist bloc. At the very least, they attempted to create a sense of community among these countries based on their colonial experiences, the question of race, and a sense of inferiority vis-à-vis the West. Moscow's leaders started traveling to countries such as India, offering help and advice on industrialization and spreading the communist gospel. The Soviet strategy of peaceful co-existence, in other words, meant the emergence of the Third World as an important new battlefield.

Secondly, Indonesia and several other Asian countries took the initiative to organize a large conference in Bandung, Java bringing together leaders from Asia, Africa, and the Middle East. The Bandung conference took place in the second half of April 1955 – a few weeks after the Barbizon conference – and gave a prominent world stage to neutralist and communist politicians such as India's Prime Minister Jawaharlal Nehru and China's Zhou Enlai.[3] Nonalignment was one of the keywords of the conference, as many of the world's smaller nations considered ways of not being drawn into the Cold War.[4]

There was no shortage of issues on the Bandung agenda with a decidedly anti-Western connotation. The history of colonialism and the remaining de-colonization conflicts no doubt were the most emotional ones, but many politicians, especially in Asia, were also worried about having to choose sides in the Cold War. They resented the fact that the United States had created the Southeast Asia Treaty Organization (SEATO) after the armistice in Indochina, and they wished to see the dangerous conflict between communist China and the nationalist Chinese on Formosa – in which the United States played a key role – brought to an end. Last but not least, there was the question of race. As Antoine Pinay said at Barbizon: "For the first time we will see a Conference, organized at the initiative of communist countries, representing almost one billion people at which no one representing the white race will be present."[5]

The Bandung conference presented China and, indirectly, the Soviet Union with an excellent opportunity to pose as the undisputed champions of national independence. And there were limits to how much the West could do about this – at least through common action. As George Ball argued at Barbizon, the Bandung conference was partly a reaction to the habit on the part of the NATO countries to consult with each other before dealing with developing countries. "When this is done too openly, too obviously and too automatically," Ball said, "it gives an impression of ganging-up which, I think, can have and does have sometimes unfortunate reactions on the part of the Eastern peoples."[6] A complicating factor was the racial question in the United States itself. Ball acknowledged, "[...] the persistence of some degree of racial discrimination in the United States has been an effective and important weapon in the Soviet arsenal."[7]

Denis Healey agreed and added that the West should avoid the impression of treating Asia as part of the Cold War Western camp:

> We always talk about "West" and "East", which in itself is a shocking sound in Asian ears – a Western front in the cold war. I remember once last year, for example, the Assistant Secretary in the State Department, Mr. Robertson, boasting in a public speech that America dominated Asia now. Well, that sort of talk is absolutely disastrous when dealing with these countries.[8]

The Dutch diplomat Eelco van Kleffens, who had just served as president of the United Nations General Assembly in 1954, argued that the causes for anti-Western and anti-colonial feelings in many newly independent countries were primarily psychological. For one, a distinct sense of inferiority existed, based on the technological edge of the industrialized world – what he called "an instinctive insurgence against the material preponderance of the West against which spiritual weapons are of slight avail and which therefore strikes these nations as brute force."[9] This feeling of inferiority was reinforced by the widespread disappointment over the fact that independence had not brought the quick political or economic success everyone had hoped for. As van Kleffens said: "[...] those who carry through great revolutions are very rarely allowed to see them come to full fruition; just as Moses, having led the Jews out of serfdom, was not allowed to enter the Promised Land."[10]

This was, however, hard to accept for many, especially among the Asian and African intelligentsia. As a result, the (former) European colonial powers and the United States with its overwhelming economic power were used as convenient scapegoats. "The 'whites'," van Kleffens argued,

> the 'westerners', the technocratic brutes against whom they feel powerless in spite of their independence and for whom, at the same time, they still feel a sort of intolerable respect, creating violent inner tensions – they are the cause of their impotence, the object of their resentment, the target of their thirst for compensation.[11]

Van Kleffens warned that if nothing was done to analyze and respond to these feelings, the risk of losing many Asian and African countries politically and militarily was considerable. Yet this was something only those Asian and African leaders could do who knew and understood the West and realized that their countries had more to gain from cooperation than antagonism. Two such leaders, van Kleffens said, were General Carlos P. Romulo, the Philippine secretary for foreign affairs, and Sir John Kotelawala, the prime minister of Ceylon.

After the Barbizon conference, Prince Bernhard sent both these men – as well as the Pakistani Prime Minister Chaudhry Muhammad Ali – a letter urging them to do something about anti-colonialist sentiments. "The answer seems to us," Bernhard wrote, "that in Asia and Africa a better insight, psychologically, must be awakened regarding those feelings which superficially are called anti-colonialism." As an analysis from the Western point of view, the Prince appended van Kleffens' statement to his letter, writing:

> The conference was of the opinion that while we should by all means try to show every free country in the world that Communist rule and their way of life would be catastrophic for them, we should not ask them to opt for us or become our allies.[12]

The important point was that anti-colonialist feelings should not be allowed to destroy economic, cultural, and political ties between their countries.

During the run-up to the Bandung conference, American and British diplomats were trying to get much the same message across to the same Asian leaders.[13] Whatever the effect of Prince Bernhard's letters, the outcome of the Bandung conference was not unsatisfactory from the Western point of view.[14] It was especially important that Sir Kotelawala – who belonged in the neutralist camp – put up an effective defense against the attempts by Nehru and Zhou Enlai to preach coexistence and focus primarily on the anti-colonial agenda of Bandung. On the other hand, the crisis of decolonization obviously remained an explosive issue. Prime Minister Muhammad Ali told Prince Bernhard that

> [i]t is very important that the non-communist Western Powers should, by respecting the national aspirations of peoples in areas still subject to their rule, remove the causes of real grievances still existing and give confidence to the independent Asian and African nations that there is no fundamental obstacle to cooperation with Western countries on the basis of friendship and equality.[15]

Ali identified the "continued subjection" of much of North Africa – Morocco, Tunisia, Algeria – as the main area of concern.

The second result of the Barbizon discussion of the 'uncommitted people' was the decision to hold a special conference on Asia. Joseph Retinger had already told Prince Bernhard a month before Barbizon that he thought the situation in Asia should be discussed in detail. Van Kleffens' intervention led Retinger to abandon his usual reticence and make a rare speech to the Bilderberg participants. Retinger proclaimed himself in full agreement with van Kleffens' analysis of the psychological causes of anti-Western feeling in Asia. He argued that preeminent thinkers of the West and Asia should be brought together to discuss this topic. The only question was whether the Bilderberg Group was the right organization to do so. When Prince Bernhard announced that he did not think so, Denis de Rougemont volunteered to pursue the idea and proposed to use his Geneva *Centre Européen de la Culture* for this purpose.[16] It was also decided that the Bilderberg conference in 1956 was to address the question of Asia.

The question of economic development

At Barbizon, the rest of the discussion concerning the Third World was spent mostly on the question of economic development.[17] Several speakers argued that an effort on the scale of the Marshall Plan was needed for the underdeveloped world. As Retinger wrote in a short memorandum for the Barbizon Conference:

> We have a responsibility, which is inherent in our very civilization and in our philosophy, to help them. We have also a vital interest to do so. Unless the Western world helps them effectively, they will accept communist aid, or at best turn away from us.[18]

George McGhee argued that the principal front of the Cold War had moved from Europe to Asia. Economic and technical assistance was only one response to this challenge, but it was an important one, given the Soviet activities in this field and the high expectations in many developing countries. Inevitably, the quick industrialization of the Soviet Union through central planning offered a compelling story to the leaders of these mostly agrarian societies.

The Bilderberg participants were aware that the struggle for Asia, Africa, and, to some extent, Latin America would be partially decided by the comparison between the Soviet and Western economic methods.[19] Moreover, as Bertil Ohlin, Gabriel Hauge, and Paul van Zeeland argued: if the economic gap between 'the haves and the have nots' widened even further, this would only serve to increase anti-Western sentiments. Everyone present agreed that it was in the West's interest to expand economic relations with the Third World as a basis for raising their living standards and keeping them out of the communist orbit.

However, they were also aware that quick successes were an illusion and that it was important not to raise false hopes – despite the wish for rapid development in many Third World countries. McGhee, who had acquired vast experience in this field during his time as a diplomat in Turkey, Greece, and the Middle East, emphasized that fast economic development "is really artificial economic development."[20] Very few examples of massive injections of foreign aid had led to a lasting increase in economic growth or living standards. As Gabriel Hauge added, the Marshall Plan for Europe had been about reconstruction: about rebuilding something that had existed. And unlike Europe, many countries in the developing world lacked the basic infrastructure, technical expertise, and institutions necessary for economic development.

George Ball listed some of the key obstacles:

> ... in many of those areas there are few of the basic conditions present in which a capitalistic system can operate effectively: accumulated

savings are meagre and poorly distributed; legal systems do not make it possible for property transfers to be easily effected, do not provide for the recognition of corporate organisms, or do not contain machinery permitting even land titles to be passed with certainty; manual labour is held in disdain and the prestige-indices of various occupations are wholly different from our own and under [those] circumstances rapid material progress within a capitalistic system may be quite impossible.[21]

It followed, Bertil Ohlin said, that one of the most important questions was how to develop institutions that were "[...] compatible with the fundamental ideas and beliefs of the underdeveloped peoples [...]" yet also provided the framework for expanding trade and industry.[22] The West could not expect to export democratic capitalism to countries with a different political and social tradition. Another great problem, as Ohlin pointed out, was that large population increases caused such pressures in many underdeveloped areas that it was virtually impossible to raise their living standards. Reginald Maudling, a British conservative MP and Minister of Supply, concurred and argued that in Southeast Asia a strategy for birth control was perhaps the most important task of all.[23]

The question how to organize economic assistance was fraught with similar difficulties. Several participants said that a concerted action on the part of the West was bound to be met with suspicion and hostility in Asia and elsewhere. Even foreign technical advisors were often seen – or portrayed by communists – as agents of Western economic colonialism. The best solution was to organize development assistance on a loose bilateral or multilateral basis and to give as much responsibility as possible to international organizations such as the International Bank for Reconstruction and Development (IBRD – also known as the World Bank). In addition, initiatives for economic development should come from the underdeveloped nations themselves.

The Colombo Plan, originating in the early 1950s, was one way of doing so. Maudling explained that the "real secret of the Colombo Plan is that there is, in fact, no such plan. There is no blueprint at all."[24] The participating countries in Southeast Asia, Great Britain, Canada, Australia, Japan, and the United States got together to discuss development ideas and mutual aid. There was no question of certain ideas being imposed on the developing world. The underdeveloped countries were responsible for drawing up their own plans. Subsequently, the financial arrangements took place on a purely bilateral basis.

Prince Bernhard argued in the paper he prepared for Barbizon that the actions of the World Bank and bilateral aid could never satisfy the need for capital in the underdeveloped world.[25] More should be done to involve private investment capital in economic development. Everyone agreed on this point, but again the problems involved were hard to overcome. As Jack Heinz argued in his paper, the "present world instability," the many investment opportunities within the United States, and the lack of guarantees for private investment and property rights inhibited investors from investing in the underdeveloped world.[26] The initiative of Eugene Black – the World Bank president who was widely praised at Barbizon – to create an International Finance Corporation (IFC) in order to channel private capital to the developing world was therefore met with unanimous approval.[27] Gabriel Hauge predicted that Congress would pass Black's proposal without difficulty.

On the whole, the Barbizon meeting showed a broad awareness of the enormous complexity and difficulty of the task of developing the 'underdeveloped world.' This was true not only for Europeans with decades-long experience in these areas but also for some of the Americans. The Cold War cliché of the "Ugly American" – barging in to spread the American dream of free men and free enterprise to the rest of the world – did not apply to Bilderberg participants such as McGhee, Ball, or Hauge.[28] Ball, for example, repeatedly opposed a heavy-handed, interventionist approach to the Third World, both with respect to spreading democracy and capitalism:

> I think it is perhaps a mistake for the West to attempt to sell its own ideology in entirety to the East in competition with communism for the reason that throughout the Middle East and extending in the north of Africa down to Pakistan and Indonesia, the mentality of the people is conditioned by the ideas of Islam; in the Far East it has been shaped by Hinduism, Buddhism, Taoism and Confucianism. To Eastern peoples, Western conceptions of individualism – concepts which we have derived from our own religious systems, from the Renaissance to the Reformation and the Enlightenment – these ideas give a strongly rationalistic and secular character to Western thought which may not be acceptable, at least for a very long time, to the peoples of the East. Western man believes in science and in progress; he believes that the individual is a fluid element in society, free to find a level commensurate with his ambitions and abilities, and I reiterate that to expect Eastern peoples to adjust to these economic and political ideas is not realistic.[29]

Ball added that if any country should understand the wish of newly independent nations not to be involved in great power politics, it should be the United States, with its long history of isolationism. On the subject of economic assistance, Hauge sounded a similar note of caution. "In America," he said,

> perhaps we are capable of great enthusiasm; we probably think we ought to remake every place in the image of Detroit, but I think as our experience grows, we do realize that we should develop the ability not to scorn little things and modest beginnings which have good foundations.[30]

The Fredensborg conference, May 1956

The Fredensborg conference, the fourth Bilderberg meeting, took place from May 11 to 13, 1956. Hakon Christiansen of the Danish East Asiatic Company was responsible for the organization, assisted by Ole Bjørn Kraft. The conference dealt mainly with Asia, but also featured a review of recent events.

The Barbizon discussions had highlighted a simple truth: winning the allegiance of the uncommitted leaders of Asia and Africa had become a crucial objective for the West. It was no longer sufficient to organize the defensive perimeters of the Free World through organizations such as SEATO. Just as the socioeconomic communist challenge in Western Europe necessitated a response that went far beyond military strength, the Third World battlefield also consisted predominantly of economic and political fronts.[31] The emergence of a distinct Afro-Asian identity at Bandung, based partly on both anti-Western nationalism and a neutralist distaste for being drawn into the Cold War, did not make this task any easier. If anti-Western sentiments in the Third World were allowed to gain the upper hand, financial incentives, or technical assistance could do little to reverse the situation.

At the abstract level, therefore, most Europeans and Americans agreed on the importance of the psychology of North-South relations. Yet it was virtually impossible to translate this agreement into actual policy. When push came to shove, the French in North Africa, the Belgians in the Congo, the Dutch in West New Guinea, or the British in the Middle East and elsewhere cared more about their immediate interests in these areas than about forging a common Western attitude acceptable to the Third World. Conversely, many Americans (joined, of course, by quite a few Europeans) had little patience with what they regarded as the last gasps of European imperialism.

Although these differences in outlook and interests were nothing new, the increased importance of good relations with the Bandung powers added to the poignancy of these differences.[32] What is more, Washington could no longer expect to overrule European objections to rapid decolonization as in the case of the Dutch East Indies in 1949. At that time, then-Secretary of State Dean Acheson threatened to withhold Marshall Plan and military aid to the Netherlands, more or less forcing The Hague to accept a deal with Sukarno.[33] An economically resurgent Western Europe was less susceptible to such pressures, and more likely to revert to anti-Americanism, as the first Bilderberg conference had shown. Many Europeans also suspected that American anti-colonialism was partly based on a desire to supplant European interests in the Middle East and elsewhere. Such suspicions reinforced existing anti-American reflexes. Consequently, the Eisenhower Administration had to navigate between the 'Scylla' of Third World anti-colonialism and the 'Charybdis' of Western European interests and NATO cohesion.

Another impediment to a unified Western strategy towards the Third World was the changed threat perception of the Cold War in the context of peaceful coexistence. Although most Bilderbergers believed that the Soviet changes were tactical, and that continued vigilance was necessary, this was a difficult conclusion to sell to the wider public. As Paul Nitze said during the Fredensborg conference:

> [...] since September there has been a further development of the feeling that there is little immediate threat of military aggression from the Communists, a weakening of the bond of fear of a common enemy which holds the non-communist coalition together, and a coming to the surface of tensions on lesser issues among the members of the coalition.[34]

One result – predicted already at the Garmisch conference – was that politicians were experiencing increasing difficulties to finance the defense measures necessary to fulfill the agreed NATO goals. In addition, member states were less inclined to consult on problems that did not officially fall within NATO's area of responsibility. Two of the most important issues – Algeria and Cyprus – were not even strictly out-of-area, to use the modern term, but France and Great Britain resisted any meaningful discussion of these topics in the NATO Council.

The overall effect upon the alliance was bad and the NATO ministerial meeting in early May 1956 failed to give the alliance a new sense of direction. The only decision the NATO foreign ministers were able to make was to install another Wise Men Committee to study political consultation. Proposals for an increased NATO role in the economic field won little support. French Foreign Minister Christian Pineau's ambitious plan to create a world economic development agency under the auspices of the United Nations (and including the Soviet Union) met the same fate. In Washington, Dulles told the National Security Council with a sense of understatement that "a certain lack of solidarity among the NATO powers was quite evident at the meeting." The Cyprus crisis, the withdrawal of French NATO forces from Europe to Algeria, as well as Middle East policy in general had not been discussed in depth. Dulles had warned his NATO colleagues that if such issues continued to be "treated independently and unilaterally" the alliance would fall apart.[35]

At Fredensborg, George Perkins, the US permanent representative to NATO, admitted that the NATO summit had mostly produced confused and rambling discussions. Denis Healey, always prepared to call a spade a spade, said the summit had been an "appalling disaster", and Prince Bernhard quickly decided to move on to the next point on the Fredensborg agenda: "a common approach by the Western world towards China and the emergent nations of South and East Asia."[36]

The discussion concerning Southeast Asia covered essentially the same ground as the Barbizon conference. Again, several speakers made the point that concerted Western action was bound to be regarded as another example of Western domination. Robert L. Garner, vice president of the World

Bank, also confirmed the Barbizon conclusion that economic development took time and could not be imposed. He warned that giving too much money too fast was counterproductive, recalling how Turkey had been given so much money that it had ordered 20 cement plants, none of which were now working. Technical assistance and the development of private enterprise were more effective.

The problem was – as Dean Rusk reminded the conference – that the Soviets could promise quick help and point to their own experience with rapid industrialization. The recent visit by Khrushchev and Bulganin to India, Burma and Afghanistan was a good example. Paul Nitze agreed and argued that the Asian trip of the Soviet leaders "[...] may well be the Soviet move toward widespread economic assistance without strings and economic purchases for political purposes. In other words, the opening up of major political warfare with economic means."[37] Several participants said that countries in the region inevitably compared Soviet activities to American behavior. As Gabriel Hauge told President Eisenhower in his report of the Fredensborg meeting: "The fact that Bulganin and Khruschev stayed three weeks in India was considered a great compliment. The fact that Dulles rushed through nine countries in ten days on his last trip there was viewed dimly for the opposite reason."[38]

A new element in the Fredensborg discussions was the question of communist China. Prince Bernhard had avoided the issue at Barbizon, because of its political sensitivity in the United States. Now, the Europeans no longer held back in their criticism of the inflexible American policy of nonrecognition and a comprehensive trade embargo against communist China. Sir John Slessor's introductory paper was representative of European majority opinion:

> [...] our refusal to recognize the government of, or trade with, the biggest nation in the world (which makes no political or economic sense anyway) not only courts Chinese opposition to anything we do in Asia, but also increases our difficulties in the rest of Asia in that it keeps alive and indeed increases the dislike and suspicion of the West on the part of other Asiatic countries.

Slessor argued that a common approach towards Asia could only be based on recognition of communist China, including giving her a place on the UN Security Council. By isolating communist China, the United States was driving her into the arms of Russia. Thus, any prospect of driving a wedge between the two countries was lost.

Slessor realized that in an election year, it was unlikely to expect such a dramatic change of course in US policy, but any policy based just on anticommunism and resentment over China's role in Korea was bound to be sterile. "It seems necessary," Slessor wrote, "to add that the initiative is as important in politics as in strategy and that demands a positive approach;

the purely negative policy of anti-communism or anti-anything is going to get us nowhere."[39]

Most Americans present at Fredensborg were ready to admit that the Eisenhower Administration's policy towards China had reached an impasse. Still, the political reality in the United States dictated that without an important change of attitude on the part of communist China, no US adjustment was likely. Arthur Dean explained that in the United States, communist China was widely regarded as arrogant. Moreover, a compromise on the part of the United States could be interpreted in Beijing as a sign of weakness. US Assistant Secretary of State for International Organization Affairs Francis O. Wilcox added that the American resentment over Korea could only be overcome if communist China showed more willingness to improve relations with the West. Then there was also the problem of Formosa. Johnson and Rusk emphasized that the United States had an obligation to the defense of Formosa.[40] In reply, Alfred Robens, a leading Labour politician, suggested that some form of UN trusteeship for Formosa could be arranged. He argued that it was important to get communist China in the United Nations, because the West "[c]an't expect her to accept rules unless she is a member."[41]

If the American participants found themselves on the defensive with regard to the Chinese question, many Europeans showed great concern about their position in the Middle East and North Africa. Although these areas were not officially part of the agenda, recent events made it impossible to ignore them. The whole region was in ferment as a result of various nationalist or pan-Arab movements, increasing Soviet activities, Israeli-Arab tensions, and the growing importance of oil for the industrialized economies of the West. Ever since the Egyptian leader, Colonel Gamal Abdel Nasser, had accepted an arms deal with Czechoslovakia in September 1955, the big three NATO powers were increasingly at odds on how to respond.[42]

The Eisenhower Administration was inclined to give Nasser the benefit of the doubt and treat him more as an Arab nationalist than as a communist ally. France and Great Britain, on the other hand, were just as worried about Nasser's pan-Arab ambitions as about Soviet incursions into the Middle East. Different national priorities further inhibited Western cooperation in the region. Great Britain tried to build up its Iraqi ally through the Baghdad Pact, whereas the Eisenhower Administration preferred to rely on Saudi Arabia. For the French government led by Mollet, the Algerian rebellion trumped all other concerns. Nasser's perceived support for the rebels – both materially and in terms of radio propaganda – was deeply resented in Paris. Broader French relations with the Arab world were also severely tested by the fact that France was the only major Western power delivering armaments – including modern airplanes – to Israel.

At Fredensborg, Paul Nitze warned of the Soviet "shift in interest to the Middle East as an immediate theatre of contest." There was "a very definite weakening of the political forces favorable to the West in Syria, in particular, but probably throughout the Arab world." Several European participants – including van Kleffens and Robens – expressed their concern about the pan-Arab rhetoric employed by Nasser. The Egyptian leader seemed determined to resurrect the Turkish Empire, but now under Cairo's rule. The Norwegian shipping magnate Leif Høegh accurately predicted that it was of the "highest importance to study Suez control [because] the Egyptians [are] planning to really exploit it." Meanwhile, everyone agreed that control of the Middle East was crucial because of the increased importance of oil. Arthur Dean exaggerated only slightly when he said: "If [the] U.S.S.R. controls those oil fields [the] U.S.S.R. will control industrial life of the world."[43] While the United States was not (yet) dependent on oil from the region, Western Europe certainly was.

Sir John Slessor argued therefore that Nasser should be told that he could not "interfere with oil." The West should not permit the Suez Canal to be anything else than an international waterway. The key to success, he said, was a concerted Anglo-American policy for the region. As the discussion made clear, however, this was also precisely what had been missing in recent months. Maudling, for example, made a strong appeal to his American colleagues to stop Saudi Arabian mischief in the region, partially directed against the British position in the Gulf States.[44]

The Americans replied that there was little they could do since there were no strings attached to the royalties the American oil company Aramco paid to the Saudis. Wilcox and Dean preferred to focus on a solution for the Israeli-Arab conflict, making several suggestions for developing the region, for solving the refugee question, and for devising a plan for international control of the Israeli borders. Of course, they were right in arguing that much of the instability in the Middle East was caused by the Israeli-Arab conflict. The trouble was, however, that some of those directly involved had little incentive to improve the situation. As John Hope said: "Nasser knows that [the] only issue on which Arabs are united is hatred of Israel."[45] Consequently, it was unlikely that Nasser would accept the American proposals.

The problems in the Middle East and North Africa brought out into the open again the transatlantic and inner-European differences over decolonization. On the whole, the United States favored a much more far-reaching and quicker transfer of power in the remaining colonial territories than the European colonial powers. The Bandung movement undoubtedly strengthened existing American anti-colonial reflexes.[46] The basic Cold War interest to develop good relations with the Bandung powers was sometimes at cross-purpose with interests of European allies. One example of the problems this conflict of interests caused was the French anger over international trade union support for Moroccan trade unions. As Omer Becu explained at Fredensborg, the French had imposed unacceptable conditions on Moroccan trade unions, forcing them into the arms of the communists if international Western organizations did not step in. Confronted with this

choice, Becu and his colleagues had decided to help them. The French regarded this as international interference in their internal affairs.

In a paper written for the Fredensborg conference on American attitudes towards colonialism, Dean Rusk reminded the European participants
that the American preference for self-determination and democracy was a
deeply rooted political fact that could not be easily changed. This explained
the readiness of the American people to support NATO, but it also meant a
strong bias towards ending all remaining colonial relationships. The trouble
was, Rusk wrote, that

> unfortunately, a broad tradition provides few guide-lines for the specific
> question of a quasi-colonial nature which now plague the foreign pol-
> icy agenda. Colonialism in the classic pattern is clearly on the way out,
> much of it already liquidated. Much more difficult are situations where
> (1) mixed populations have violently different views about the nature of
> the political settlement (2) over-riding strategic factors force ideological
> factors in a subordinate role (3) the controversy rages without regard to
> the wishes of the people involved or (4) independence promises an early
> assumption of power by communist elements.

With respect to the "quasi-colonial" crises such as in Algeria, where the population was split, Rusk continued, "there is little disposition in the United
States to go out looking for trouble."[47] Ironically, however, American inaction gave the Soviet Union the opportunity to become the champion of
liberty and national independence. And despite American reticence, the
differences between the United States and many European countries were
displayed for the entire world in the United Nations.[48]

Rusk argued that there was no custom-made solution to these problems.
Still, the British model was by far the most successful and should be adopted
by others as well. Until that time, the only thing that could be done to reduce inner-Western tension was to change UN rules in order to prevent frequent voting on these issues, which only exacerbated transatlantic tensions.
Joseph Johnson, who followed developments at the United Nations closely,
agreed. More often than not, he argued, the West found itself in a minority
position in the United Nations, making it advisable to avoid frequent votes
on colonial issues.

As president of the Rockefeller Foundation, Dean Rusk had made the underdeveloped countries of Asia, Africa, and the Middle East a Foundation
priority. Earlier in 1956, he had been asked by John Foster Dulles to study
the "colonial question" as well as the possibility of a "Bandung Conference
in reverse" – a meeting of pro-Western Asia-African leaders. Dulles hoped
that such a meeting would slow the "racially conscious antipathy now developing in non-white areas."[49] However, discussions with London quickly
showed that such a meeting would only highlight differences with other
European allies, and the plan was abandoned.[50] The Fredensborg conference

could only confirm this difficult state of affairs. Despite attempts to forge a common Western response to the challenges of the new Soviet tactics and the post-Bandung emergence of Third World independence, there was no denying that the Atlantic alliance was deeply divided.

The Suez crisis

On July 26, 1956, Nasser nationalized the Suez Canal in response to the sudden Anglo-American decision not to fund the Egyptian Aswan Dam.[51] British Prime Minister Anthony Eden and French Premier Guy Mollet were furious and demanded swift action against Egypt. The Eisenhower Administration, however, preferred to play for time in reaction to Nasser's affront. Eisenhower and Dulles thought that there was no legal basis for an armed intervention and were concerned about American public opinion. Moreover, armed intervention would lead to a major anti-Western backlash in the region and throughout the Third World, as well as open the door to Soviet intervention.[52]

The problem was that the French and British governments felt they could not 'play it long' as Dulles wanted them to.[53] Eden told Eisenhower that several moderate regimes in the region were in danger of falling victim to Nasserite rebellions. Nasser's prestige increased every day he persisted in defying the entire West all by himself. A scenario in which Nasser, under Soviet tutelage, controlled the oil supplies of Western Europe was unacceptable. Mollet fully agreed with Eden's analysis and was additionally motivated to bring down the Egyptian leader in order to stop support for the Algerian rebellion and halt Nasser's aggressive anti-Israeli policies. In October 1956, Foreign Minister Pineau began saying publicly that he was unable to follow the State Department line.[54] Dulles, for his part, announced on October 2 that with respect to colonial problems the United States had a "special role to play" and could not identify its policies fully with the "so-called colonial powers."[55]

When in October all attempts orchestrated by Dulles to reach a negotiated compromise seemed only to have won Nasser time, the British and French governments – in a secret agreement with the Israelis – decided to force a military intervention. The Israeli army would launch a preemptive attack against Egypt, thereby giving the French and the British a pretext for an armed intervention to safeguard the Suez Canal. Washington was not told of the plan. When the French and the British indeed intervened militarily in early November, Eisenhower and Dulles were furious. Not only did they feel deceived, they deeply regretted that the Franco-British action took place at the same time that in Hungary an anti-communist revolt was being crushed by Soviet tanks – not to mention the fact that the American presidential elections were only days away.

The Eisenhower Administration therefore supported a UN resolution – also supported by the Soviet Union – calling for an immediate cease-fire in Egypt, only to be vetoed by the French and the British – the first veto by the United Kingdom since the founding of the United Nations.[56] In the following days, President Eisenhower pressured the British to call off the invasion of Egypt by denying much-needed financial support to stabilize the precarious position of the pound. Bulganin and Khrushchev, meanwhile, threatened Paris and London with a nuclear response to the Suez crisis. In face of the unexpectedly strong American reaction, the British felt they had to call off the military action on November 6.[57] The French could do little but follow suit.

The Franco-British decision for action without consulting or notifying the Americans was based on a complex mixture of perceptions and circumstances. For one, Washington was in the midst of a presidential election and no quick action could be expected from the United States, even if the Eisenhower Administration had been in full agreement with the Anglo-French battle plan. But, such tactical concerns aside, the French and British governments had reached the conclusion that the Eisenhower government – and the State Department in particular – was fundamentally unwilling to seriously consider European concerns. The whole sequence of diplomatic action taken by Dulles, culminating in the Suez Canal Users' Association (SCUA), seemed designed to thwart Anglo-French attempts to back their diplomacy by the threat of force. Several times, the secretary of state promised to maintain a tough stand against Nasser – or so the British and the French thought – only to back down in the face of strong opposition from Nasser.

Retinger had met with Premier Mollet in early August and offered to travel to the United States in order to test the waters for joint action against Nasser. Mollet's *chef de cabinet* Émile Noël noted that such a mission, although unlikely to succeed, might be useful to educate US opinion on the Suez issue. In the end, Retinger decided not to engage in another adventure as an informal diplomat. He told Mollet that any private initiative would be insufficient to bring around American opinion; only official diplomatic action could do so. Retinger argued that the Americans should be asked for a military contribution in case of conflict with Egypt.[58]

By mid-October, Mollet personally thought that it was useless to wait for the Americans.[59] Ironically, his Bilderberg experiences may have strengthened this conviction. There could have been little doubt in his mind that the American anti-colonial tradition was powerful and deeply rooted. When asked after the Suez crisis about the deliberate deception of Washington, Mollet replied: "We did not tell President Eisenhower about the Franco-British invasion, because if we had, the U.S. would have insisted on our stopping."[60] As Nitze told Dean Acheson later:

> From what Guy Mollet, reported by George Ball, says and from what Douglas Dillon [the American Ambassador in Paris] says, it seems to me clear that the French, from the beginning, intended to use the Canal

Users Association as an excuse for the eventual use of force and that Dulles backed away from it because Dillon accurately reported to him Mollet's intentions. [...] The French were under no illusions as to our probable opposition and were shocked at the British lack of courage in not proceeding in the face of an opposition which both they and the British knew they would have to expect. Our opposition was not in pursuit of virtue but was a judgment of expediency covered by a claim of virtue.[61]

More generally – and this is often neglected in the literature – the Suez crisis took place against the backdrop of a much broader crisis in NATO. The breakdown in relations between France and Great Britain on the one hand and the United States on the other did not arrive completely out of the blue. As we have seen, both the NATO summit in early May and the Fredensborg meeting revealed a fundamental lack of agreement on how to react to the new Soviet tactics in the post-Bandung underdeveloped world.

The Bilderberg conference on St. Simons Island, Georgia (February 15–17, 1957) was the first to take place on American soil. Initial worries that a conference in the United States would draw too much unwanted press interested had been addressed in part by choosing a remote location.[62] The agenda consisted of four points: (1) a review of events since the Fredensborg conference, (2) "nationalism and neutralism as disruptive factors inside the Western Alliance," (3) the Middle East, and (4) the policy of the Alliance towards Eastern Europe. Not surprisingly, the Suez crisis dominated much of the meeting.

The American delegation at St. Simons Island was larger than normal, including Senator William Fulbright, the ranking Democratic member on the Foreign Affairs Committee; Senator Alexander Wiley, a Republican and former chairman of the Foreign Affairs Committee; and congressmen John Vorys and Brooks Hays. Bilderberg regulars Ball, Cisler, Hauge, Heinz, McGhee, Murphy, Nebolsine, Nitze, and Rusk were present, as were Bilderberg newcomers Eugene Black, Assistant Secretary of State Robert Bowie, McGeorge Bundy, former Governor of New York Thomas E. Dewey, and Henry Kissinger.

The European group was plagued by last-minute cancellations. Amintore Fanfani and Giovanni Malagodi were prevented from coming because of the unstable political situation in Italy. Baumgartner, the President of the French National Bank, did not dare to leave his country because of the financial crisis in France. Jean Monnet, who had been invited for the first time, decided at the last minute that he had to stay in France to monitor the final stages of the Rome Treaties negotiations. Robert Marjolin had already canceled for the same reason. This left France represented only by the Secretary-General of the SFIO, Pierre Commin, and by Antoine Pinay.[63]

Great Britain had a stronger delegation, including David Astor, editor of *The Observer*; Denis Healey; Air Chief Marshal Sir William Elliot, the

Chairman of the Council of the Royal Institute of International Affairs; and J. L. S. Steel, Director of Imperial Chemical Industries, Ltd. After a telephone call from Prince Bernhard, Prime Minister Harold Macmillan had also asked the Lord Chancellor, Lord Kilmuir, to take part in the meeting. As Macmillan told Kilmuir: "I gather that the Foreign Secretary thinks that the Bilderberg Group can do quite a lot of valuable work and I wonder therefore whether you yourself could possibly consider attending on our behalf."[64] "Valuable work" in this case meant repairing Anglo-American relations, by far the most important foreign policy aim for the new prime minister.[65] The Foreign Office brief prepared for Lord Kilmuir left no doubt on this matter:

> Our aim in discussing Anglo-American relations in any of its aspects should be so far as possible to demonstrate the strength of the connexion [sic] as it still stands to-day rather than to dwell unduly on the obvious defects in American policy, as shown up in the Suez crisis.[66]

The Foreign Office argued that Eisenhower and Dulles had been more concerned with the "position of the West in the United Nations" than with French and British vital interests in the Middle East. Even though the region did not belong to the straightforward colonial problems, "[...] it is clear, if only from unguarded statements which Mr. Dulles has let drop from time to time, that anti-colonial prejudices have coloured his thinking, certainly about the Suez Canal and probably the whole Middle East."[67] The British, for their part, were happy to leave intact the widespread impression that the United States had been responsible for setting off the Suez crisis by unilaterally withdrawing the Anglo-American offer to finance the Aswan Dam. Commenting on a paper the French political columnist Raymond Aron had written for the St. Simons Island conference, the Foreign Office stated:

> We should not play up Monsieur Aron's point [...] about United States withdrawal of the offer of credits for the Aswan dam. Her Majesty's Government probably share at least equal responsibility for the change of attitude, but, perhaps fortunately, this fact is not apparently known outside official circles.[68]

Raymond Aron, one of France's most respected sociologists and political observers, contributed a highly critical analysis of American policy in the Middle East and the larger impact of the Suez crisis on the alliance. Unfortunately – both for the Bilderberg participants and for later historians – Aron did not make it to Georgia. His plane broke down twice, leaving him stranded in Ireland.[69] Still, his paper was discussed at length and provoked several angry American responses.

Although Aron had opposed the Anglo-French intervention – and almost broke with his newspaper *Le Figaro* over the crisis – he thought that much of the current anti-American sentiment in France and Great Britain was understandable. In his view, the record of the Eisenhower Administration in the Middle East was appalling:

> American policy has provoked or encouraged decisions which have aggravated tension; it has systematically run away from the responsibilities arising from the circumstances; it is only gradually finding out that it cannot look on at the rout of European power and prestige and disassociate itself from the consequences.

First, the United States pressured Great Britain to evacuate the Canal Zone. Washington then decided to cooperate with Colonel Nasser, despite the latter's virulent nationalism and his arms deal with the Soviets. Next, the Aswan Dam offer was suddenly withdrawn, causing Nasser to restore his prestige by nationalizing the Suez Canal, "[A]nd now everything goes on as if American diplomacy saw in this nationalization merely an episode in the anti-colonialist struggle, and had no other objective than to incite British and French passivity."[70]

Even if one disagreed with the Anglo-French intervention, the American reaction, Aron wrote, only made matters worse. On the day of the Anglo-French ultimatum to Egypt, October 30, Aron recalled that Eisenhower had declared: "There must not be one law for the enemy and one for our friends, one law for the strong and one for the weak." Two days later Soviet tanks rolled into Budapest. "The United States," Aron wrote,

> taking command of the Afro-Asian coalition in order not to follow it, showed itself more severe toward its allies (France and Great Britain) than toward its enemy (the Soviet Union), toward the weak (France and Great Britain) than toward the strong (the Soviet Union).

The fact that Washington, according to Aron, had seriously considered intervening militarily against France and Britain could not easily be forgotten.[71]

What were the consequences for the Atlantic alliance? "It is not the first time," Aron wrote, "that the leader of a coalition shows itself to be indifferent to the vital interests of its allies. But this indifference inevitably turns the allies into satellites." Aron argued that in response Europe should become responsible again for its own defense, in both the military and economic sense. Europe's relations with the rest of the world – and its dependence on trade and raw materials from outside – demanded a united Europe greater than the Six: "[...] a unity of all the countries of the Old World, right up to the Russian frontier."[72]

As it was, Aron's paper served a useful purpose for those participants at St. Simons Island who were more concerned with restoring transatlantic relations than with assigning blame for the Suez disaster. It gave the American participants an opportunity to deny the more extreme accusations. Robert Murphy, for one, "solemnly denied" Aron's accusation regarding American plans to use force against its own allies and disputed the Frenchman's history of American involvement in the Middle East. Eugene Black also attacked Aron's version of events concerning the financing of the Aswan Dam.[73] The Canadian Minister of Health, Paul Martin, defended the Eisenhower Administration by saying that any other reaction to the Anglo-French ultimatum might have led to general war involving the Soviet Union.[74]

Paul Hoffman also supported Eisenhower's new line, saying that the president's declaration that "the United States could neither ignore nor condone aggression regardless of its source" had made it possible for the first time to mobilize world opinion against the Soviet Union. Until the Suez crisis, Moscow had been remarkably successful in the Afro-Asian world with its peace propaganda. As a result of Hungary and the American role in the Suez crisis, "the intangible asset of moral force could now be brought to bear on the Western side."[75] In response, several European speakers warned that the West had little to gain from building up world opinion through the United Nations as long as the communists were able to dominate the General Assembly in cooperation with the Afro-Asian bloc. The Norwegian Socialist Jens Christian Hauge even argued that President Eisenhower had established a dangerous precedent by making intervention by force dependent on world opinion.[76]

George Kennan was the only one on the American side who pronounced himself in full agreement with Aron's paper. On November 3, 1956, Kennan had already published a letter highly critical of the Eisenhower Administration in the *Washington Post and Times Herald*. "The British and French have fumbled – certainly," Kennan wrote,

> we, too, have fumbled on certain past occasions; and our friends did not turn against us. Moreover, we bear a heavy measure of responsibility for the desperation that has driven the French and the British governments to this ill-conceived and pathetic action.[77]

On the European side, many felt obliged to soften the impact of Aron's paper. Commin argued that Aron exaggerated the strength of anti-Americanism in France and emphasized the need for a common policy in the Middle East since the communists were experts in exploiting nationalist movements.[78] Astor, Healey and Air Marshal Elliot all indicated their disagreement with the Anglo-French Suez expedition. In Healey's words: "We lit ourselves the forest fire we set out to extinguish in the Middle East." Astor, whose *Observer* had been highly critical of the Eden Government, pointed to the complex situation in the United Kingdom: "There isn't <u>one</u> British attitude on the Suez crisis. It is not a row between all of Britain and all of America. The basic interests of the U.S. and the U.K. are similar."[79] Not long after the St. Simons conference, Quaroni told Prince Bernhard that the Franco-British intervention reflected colonialist attitudes that were no longer acceptable: "Ancient tradition has made us Europeans consider that there is a difference between killing Hungarians and killing Egyptians. The new conscience of the world does not admit this difference."[80]

The participants who defended the Anglo-French Suez strategy could be counted on one hand. Lord Kilmuir made the rather disingenuous claim that it succeeded in finally bringing about effective UN action, and Major-General Colin Gubbins argued that Great Britain had been completely surprised by the American attitude. This view, popular in British conservative circles, could not stand up to closer scrutiny. Nitze was correct in saying that the British government could not have had any doubt about the fact that Washington considered the use of force unwise.[81]

One of the main accomplishments of the St. Simons Island discussions was to address the many transatlantic misperceptions – starting with Aron's various accusations, to Gubbins' claim that Great Britain had been suddenly and unfairly abandoned by Washington. The British Foreign Office noted that Aron's strong criticism could also have an "educative effect" on US readers

> in showing the Americans that they must not take too much for granted in their relationship with Europe and that if they are to retain the full support of Europe in the cold war [...] they must take more account of Europe's special needs, vital interests and individual susceptibilities.

As the St. Simons Island report noted: "Many cases were quoted of distortion and falsification of the facts, indeed many participants were alarmed to find how far this distortion had gone, and how high it had penetrated into the top levels of public opinion."[82] With most of these misunderstandings cleared away – "out of our systems," as Rusk put it in a letter to Retinger – Western divisions during the Suez crisis seemed to concern methods rather than goals.[83] In private, American participants even expressed regret that the Anglo-French action had not been successful in getting rid of Nasser.[84]

Their regret may have been caused in part by an unintended consequence of Suez: the failure of the Anglo-French intervention forced Washington to assume a leading role in the Middle East. The British had been traditionally responsible for keeping the Russians out of the region, but obviously they no longer could do so. The resulting vacuum could either be filled by the Soviet Union or the United States. Presented with this dilemma, Washington's choice was obvious. The Eisenhower Doctrine, made public in January 1957, was the result. It promised military assistance to any state in the Middle East threatened by communism. At the same time it instituted a large program of economic assistance. George McGhee argued that if the Eisenhower Doctrine had only existed in 1955 the Suez crisis would never have occurred.

At St. Simons Island, Senator Fulbright came under fire for his early opposition to the Eisenhower Doctrine. He tried to defend his opposition by referring to the constitutional difficulty of pre-delegating the use of force to the president. But as the Canadian Ambassador to the United States, Arnold D. P. Heeney, said, the reluctance to go along was "disturbing" in view of the quick passage of a similar resolution during the Quemoy and Matsu crisis in 1954–1955.

Ironically, the obvious Cold War rationale of the Eisenhower Doctrine hurt the United States' reputation – so carefully protected during the Suez crisis – among the Bandung powers.[85] Moreover, some participants remained openly pessimistic about the chance for economic development in the Middle East. Marcus Wallenberg, a prominent Swedish banker, warned that "the problems of [the Middle East] may well be with us for a long time. It would seem part of wisdom to increase Western flexibility with respect to energy supply."[86] Eugene Black called the Middle East, the "most difficult" region the World Bank had to deal with.[87] Many governments in the region lacked experience, were corrupt, and were suspicious of the West. Moreover, relations between the oil-possessing countries and those who did not were strained. The only hopeful news was that the Arab League had asked the World Bank to assist in the creation of an Arab Development Bank. This might be an effective means for transferring oil wealth to the poorer countries, and Black appealed to the Bilderberg participants to support this initiative.

As a result, several Bilderbergers, including Fritz Berg, Victor Cavendish-Bentinck, Hakon Christiansen, Leif Høegh, George Nebolsine, Paul Rijkens, David Rockefeller, and Otto Wolff agreed to set up a committee to study the possibilities for an Arab investment bank. In October–November 1957, a delegation of the Study Group for the Near and Middle East led by Paul Rijkens traveled to the region to win Arab support for the initiative. Eugene Black also helped organize meetings with Arab representatives at the World Bank.[88] An international consortium of banks and companies underwrote a starting capital for the Middle East Development Corporation (MIDEC), yet it is unclear how successful MIDEC was in the midst of continued instability in much of the region.[89]

The strong Bilderberg consensus on the importance of economic development and technical assistance, meanwhile, did find its way into official circles, if only because so many American Bilderbergers – including Black, Hauge, Hoffman, Rockefeller, and Rusk – were deeply involved in these issues. One result was President Eisenhower's address to the United Nations in August 1958 calling for "an Arab development institution." The speech had been drafted by none other than C. D. Jackson. Paul Hoffman, meanwhile, published a long article setting out his views on a Marshall Plan for the underdeveloped world in the *New York Times* on the last day of the St. Simons Island conference.[90] One year later, he was instrumental in creating and directing the United Nations Special Fund for development, a precursor of the United Nations Development Program (UNDP).[91] At the 1959 Bilderberg conference in Yeşilköy, Turkey, Hoffman shared his experiences and lobbied for the Special Fund.[92]

The Dutch Ambassador in Washington, J. H. van Roijen, who was present at St. Simons Island, told Prince Bernhard that the overall effect of the meeting had been good. Several American participants had expressed their keen satisfaction with the discussions and van Roijen felt that a better understanding for mutual "complaints and grievances" was important.[93] After the breakdown in transatlantic communications during the Suez crisis, it obviously was a relief to be talking again. Lord Kilmuir told Macmillan that

> [a]s the discussion went on the climate changed from 'how could you do this to your old friends?' to a more reasoned approach that, in every healthy grouping of peoples and states, there must be differences as to the methods to achieve common aims, [...] and that nothing had happened which would prevent full co-operation in the future.[94]

The Polish-born economist Michael A. Heilperin was even more optimistic, telling Prince Bernhard:

> I was impressed by the extent to which the membership of this group, whether Europeans or Americans, whether of right- or left-wing predilections, speaks the same language. They are a fair sample of leadership in some future "Atlantic Community" – indeed they make one feel optimistic (or: make me feel optimistic) about the chances of achieving a community and common-purpose spirit within the Atlantic world. There was a frank and outspoken exchange of views, no punches were pulled, yet there was no recrimination, no antagonisms, and, I think, a real wish to find a common ground, or, failing that, a better understanding of the divergent points of view.[95]

Still, the general goodwill displayed at St. Simons Island could not hide the fact that important differences remained. There could be little doubt that despite the Eisenhower Doctrine, Washington would continue to follow a more anti-colonial line than some European countries wished to see. Given the Eisenhower Administration's wholehearted embrace of the United Nations, the General Assembly in New York was bound to witness more inner-Western conflicts. In addition, American leadership within the alliance had taken a hit. As Terkelsen wrote in a report on the conference:

> It appeared, not least in private conversations, that the mistrust in Foster Dulles, which is widely encountered in Europe, is not alien to the Americans, who considered him a capable and supple advocate of any cause, but feel he lacks the broader vision that would enable him to create a coherent policy, with the result that America to some extent fails to live up to the task of being the leading power in the Western alliance.[96]

With respect to the long-term impact of the Suez crisis, historians such as Geir Lundestad and Irwin Wall have argued that Great Britain and France learned diametrically opposed lessons. London, so the argument goes, decided never again to engage in military adventures without coordination with the United States. Paris, on the other hand, would never again trust the 'Anglo-Saxons' to defend French interests. The Bilderberg conference at St. Simons Island suggests, however, that we should be careful with such a far-reaching conclusion since it transposes Gaullist attitudes of the French Fifth Republic onto the Fourth Republic.

The Mollet government, in fact, was remarkably fast in moving on after the Suez crisis. Premier Mollet not only sent his close associate Pierre Commin to the St. Simons Island conference with a very conciliatory message, arguing strongly for restoring the Atlantic alliance; he also traveled to the United States later in February 1957 with a similar aim, using language reminiscent of the Bilderberg meetings. As he put it upon arriving in New York,

> I intend to state emphatically to President Eisenhower [...] that our country which has been for nearly two centuries your faithful ally does not intend, rain or shine, to change its mind nor its heart. We are always in the same boat and our common ideals command us to stick together.[97]

Both the informal and the formal alliance, in other words, focused their energies on repairing the damage done to the alliance. This also meant dealing with the difficult question of NATO's nuclear defense.

As we have seen, the Suez crisis did give a strong boost to European integration, but the concept of a more independent Europe was not necessarily in conflict with improved transatlantic relations.[98] Quite the opposite: in the view of leaders such as Mollet and Adenauer, a more united Europe would continue to work closely with the United States in a more equal partnership, in spite of all the differences over decolonization or nuclear strategy. Moreover, they repeatedly argued that the United States would lose interest in Europe if they did *not* succeed in furthering integration. At St. Simons Island, Rusk made the same point: if only Europe could be more responsible for its own defense, he said, many of the alliance's problems would be solved.[99] President Eisenhower, for his part, continued to support the plans for European economic integration, telling Mollet and Pineau: "the day this common market became a reality would be one of the finest days in the history of the free world, perhaps even more so than winning the war."[100]

Notes

1 Westad, *The Global Cold War*.
2 Barbizon Transcript, English III, 46–47, Box 4, Bilderberg Archives, NANL.
3 See Acharya, *East of India*.
4 On this point, see Gaddis, *The Cold War*, Chapter 4.

5 Barbizon Transcript, French VI, 23–24, (my translation), Box 4, Bilderberg Archives, NANL. Matthew Connelly has argued convincingly that the Eisenhower Administration – and this appears true for many European Bilderberg participants as well – did not regard Asia and Africa solely through a Cold War prism: "[...] international conflict along racial and religious lines was an appalling prospect even if the communists kept out of it." Connelly, "Taking off the Cold War Lens," 742.
6 Barbizon Transcript, English, III, 9, Box 4, Bilderberg Papers.
7 Barbizon Transcript, English, III, 10, Box 4, Bilderberg Papers.
8 Barbizon Transcript, English, III, 24, Box 4, Bilderberg Papers.
9 Barbizon Transcript, English, III, 27, Box 4, Bilderberg Papers.
10 Ibid.
11 Barbizon Transcript, English, III, 28, Box 4, Bilderberg Papers.
12 Prince Bernhard to Sir John Kotelawala, April 5, 1955, Box 187, Bilderberg Archives, NANL. George Ball, in particular, had argued that countries such as India should be given time to settle their political and economic problems first. He reminded his compatriots that the United States had long avoided foreign entanglements during a similar period of political, economic and social change. Consequently, America should be understanding with respect to Indian neutralism. Barbizon Transcript, English III, 6–8, Box 4, Bilderberg Papers.
13 See Parker, "Cold War II," 878–879.
14 Retinger seemed to believe that the Barbizon discussions did have an impact. Discussing the "welcome trend of Asian opposition" at Bandung, he wrote "whether or not this was in any way influenced by the suggestions that were made previously at Barbizon, the episode shows that there is still open an important line of approach." See Measures for Fighting Communist Propaganda, June 1, 1955, Box 936, van Zeeland Papers, AUCL.
15 Ali to Prince Bernhard, April 17, 1955, Box 187, Bilderberg Archives, NANL.
16 See Retinger to Prince Bernhard, March 15, 1955, Box 39, Bilderberg Archives, NANL. "I hear that the Ford Foundation is more or less prepared to subsidise the projected Asian Cultural Conference..." John Pomian remembered that for lack of interest in Asia, the conference never took place. Pomian Interview by the author. According to Pomian, the Bilderberg discussions did cause De Rougemont to write his book *L'aventure occidentale de l'homme* – an attempt to explain Western civilization, published in 1957.
17 See Engerman, *Staging Growth*; and McMahon, *The Cold War in the Third World*.
18 See "The Economic Aspects of the Fight for the Allegiance of the Uncommitted Peoples," Box 59, Folder 3, Nitze Papers, LOC.
19 On this point, see Engerman, "The Romance of Economic Development."
20 Barbizon Transcript, English VI, 5, Box 4, Bilderberg Archives, NANL.
21 Barbizon Transcript, English III, 12, Box 4, Bilderberg Archives, NANL.
22 Barbizon Transcript, English V, 13, Box 4, Bilderberg Archives, NANL.
23 Maudling became a regular Bilderberg participant and member of the European steering committee. On Maudling's career see Baston, *Reggie*.
24 Barbizon Transcript, English V, 26, Box 4, Bilderberg Archives, NANL.
25 Prince Bernhard, "The Role of Economy in Winning the Allegiance of the Non-Committed People for the West and its Ideology," Box 35, Jackson Papers, DDEL.
26 Henry J. Heinz II, "Economic Aspects of Competitive Coexistence as they relate to the Underdeveloped Areas," Box 297, Gaitskell Papers, UCL.
27 For Black's general views on economic development, which were very much in line with those expressed at the Barbizon meeting, see Black, *The Diplomacy of Economic Development*.

28 See, for example, Westad, *The Global Cold War*. In Chapter 1, "The empire of liberty: American ideology and foreign interventions," Westad portrays the 1950s as a period of a virtually boundless belief "that what had worked for the United States would also work for the world." The Bilderberg discussions suggest that we should be a little careful with such a one-sided image.

29 Barbizon Transcript, English, III, 10–11, Box 4, Bilderberg Archives, NANL.

30 Barbizon Transcript, English, V, 41, Box 4, Bilderberg Archives, NANL.

31 This change of focus was reflected in the public statements of the Eisenhower Administration. See for example James Reston, "Administration Alters Tone of Its Foreign Policy Line," *New York Times*, April 27, 1956, 1:

> Instead of questioning the wisdom of neutrality, President Eisenhower and Secretary of State Dulles are now emphasizing the right of neutrality and promising aid to nations even if they do not align themselves with the Western allies. [...] Instead of emphasizing the military aspects of defense, the Administration is now stressing, as President Eisenhower did the last week-end, the need for "economic and social progress" in the under-developed nations.

32 See Thomas, "Defending a Lost Cause," 241. The French Ambassador in Washington, Maurice Couve de Murville, warned Paris in August 1955 that partly as a result of Bandung, the US government could be expected to follow a more critical policy with regard to North Africa.

33 See Westad, *Global Cold War*, 114.

34 To save money Retinger had decided to stop the practice of having transcripts made of the Bilderberg conferences. Therefore, there is no transcript of the Fredensborg conference. In addition to the Fredensborg report, I have relied mainly on notes made by Paul Nitze, who luckily was an experienced and precise note taker. For the quotation, see Speech by Paul H. Nitze, Box 59, Folder 6, Nitze Papers, LOC.

35 National Security Council Meeting, May 10, 1956, Box 7, Ann Whitman File, NSC Series, DDEL. For a good analysis of NATO's troubles see Felken, *Dulles und Deutschland*, 341–403.

36 Nitze Fredensborg Notes, Box 59, Folder 6, Nitze Papers, LOC.

37 Speech by Paul Nitze, Box 59, Folder 6, Nitze Papers, LOC.

38 Gabriel Hauge, Memorandum for the President, May 23, 1956, 1/15, Office Files, DDEL, RSC Microfilm Collection.

39 Sir John Slessor, "China and the Emergent Nations. The Common Approach," Box 59, Folder 7, Nitze Papers, LOC.

40 Although Rusk did note in his memoirs that Dulles approached him during this period to study ways of building bipartisan support for a recognition of Communist China. See Kochavi, *A Conflict Perpetuated*, 3.

41 Nitze Fredensborg Notes, Nitze Papers, Box 59, Folder 6, LoC. Wilcox had been an assistant to Senator Arthur Vandenberg and the first chief of staff of the Senate's Foreign Relations Committee. He was reportedly close to Dulles. See "Carl M. Macy, chief of Staff, Foreign Relations Committee, 1955–1973," Oral History Interviews, Senate Historical Office, Washington, D.C., 72–73.

42 Good overviews are: Ashton, *Eisenhower, Macmillan*; Hahn, *The United States, Great Britain*; Little, *American Orientalism*; and Wall, *France, the United States*.

43 Nitze Fredensborg Notes, Nitze Papers, Box 59, Folder 6, LOC.

44 Since 1952 Britain and Saudi Arabia were entangled in a conflict over the Buraimi Oasis. The British felt that the Americans – especially the Arabian American Oil Company (ARAMCO) – took the side of the Saudi's. They also complained about Saudi financing of anti-Baghdad Pact demonstrations in Jordan. See Ashton, *Eisenhower, Macmillan*, 74–75.

45 Nitze Fredensborg Notes, Nitze Papers, Box 59, Folder 6, LOC.
46 See Parker, "Cold War II," 884 ff.
47 The number of Algerians of European origin was about 1,200,000.
48 Rusk, "A Comment on So-Called Colonial Issues," Folder 7, Box 59, Nitze Papers, LOC.
49 Quoted in Cohen, *Dean Rusk*, 83.
50 Parker, "Cold War II," 886.
51 See Kunz, *The Economic*; Kyle, *Suez*; Laron, *Origins of the Suez Crisis*; Louis and Owen, *Suez 1956*; Nichols, *Eisenhower 1956*; Lucas, *Divided We Stand*; Vaïsse, *La France et l'opération de Suez*.
52 Concerning their worries about an anti-western backlash see Kyle, *Suez*, 155 and Westad, *The Global Cold War*, 125.
53 As Eden wrote Eisenhower at the height of the Suez crisis, on November 5, 1956:

> I know that Foster thought we could have played this longer. But I am convinced that, if we had allowed things to drift, everything would have gone from bad to worse. Nasser would have become a kind of Moslem Mussolini and our friends in Iraq, Jordan, Saudi Arabia and even Iran would gradually have been brought down.

Boyle, *The Eden-Eisenhower Correspondence*, 183.
54 See "Pineau Sees Need for Broader NATO," *The Washington Post and Times Herald*, October 17, 1956, A12. On the difficulty of NATO consultation on out-of-area problems – including Suez – see Milloy, *The North Atlantic Treaty*, 157–161.
55 See the transcript of Dulles's press conference, *Documents Diplomatiques Français*, Vol. 1, 1956, 493.
56 One factor influencing the behavior of Dulles was his serious illness – he had to be operated at the height of the Suez crisis. On his deathbed, Dulles told Dean Rusk that he would have acted differently if he had not been so ill. Rusk, *As I Saw It*, 165.
57 Geelhoed and Edmonds, *Eisenhower, Macmillan*, 5.
58 Noël Handwritten Note, August 8, 1956, Box 80, Mollet Papers, OURS and Retinger to Mollet, August 16, 1956, Box 39, Bilderberg Archives, NANL.
59 See: Bar-on, "Three Days in Sèvres."
60 Quoted in "Beginning of an End," *Time Magazine*, December 17, 1956. In the discussions with the Israeli Prime Minister David Ben-Gurion on October 22 Mollet also argued that while Eden was in favor of military action, it was questionable how long he could maintain this position in view of his increasingly weak domestic position. Bar-on, "Three Days in Sèvres," 175.
61 Nitze to Acheson, September 4, 1957, Box 17, Nitze Papers, LOC.
62 Joseph Johnson was responsible for the overall organization, assisted by other members of the American steering committee. See Johnson to Norman S. Buchanan (Rockefeller Foundation), July 16, 1957, Rockefeller Foundation Archives (RFA): "I took the direct responsibility of organizing and making arrangements of the conference that was held in the United States in February of this year."
63 In the first half of 1956 Commin had taken part in highly secret negotiations with the Algerian rebels. See Wall, *France, the United States*, 53.
64 Macmillan to Lord Kilmuir, January 31, 1957, Box 11/1965, PREM, NAL.
65 Kilmuir called the rebuilding of the Anglo-American alliance "[...] Macmillan's first, and in many ways most important achievement [...]" Kilmuir's trip to St. Simons was part of this endeavor. Kilmuir, *Political Adventure*, 294. The point that Macmillan's overriding aim was to restore Anglo-American relations is well-established. See for example: Geelhoed and Edmonds, *Eisenhower,*

Macmillan, 11 ff. It should be noted, though, that MacMillan was not overly impressed by Lord Kilmuir's intellect and political acumen.

66 "Notes on Memorandum by Monsieur Aron," February 5, 1957, Box 130993, FO 371, NAL.

67 Ibid.

68 Ibid.

69 See Aron to Retinger, February 18, 1957, Box 42, Bilderberg Archives, NANL.

70 Raymond Aron, "The Actual Causes of Tension between Europe and the United States," 2–3, Box 37, Jackson Papers, DDEL.

71 Ibid., 3. The Alsop brothers had reported this in the New York Herald Tribune cursive on November 2, 1956. Apparently, this was based on a conversation Dulles had with Admiral Arleigh Burke, the chief of naval operations, on whether the Sixth Fleet could stop the Franco-British bombardment of Egypt. See Nichols, *Eisenhower 1956*, 217.

72 Raymond Aron, "The Actual Causes of Tension between Europe and the United States," 5–7, Box 37, Jackson Papers, DDE. Aron publicly announced his support for a European or French deterrent on December 11, 1956 in a Figaro column titled "La leçon militaire de la crise."

73 See the report on the St. Simons Island meeting by Michael A. Heilperin, "The Fifth Bilderberg Conference," Box 37, Jackson Papers, DDEL. Heilperin was a well-known American economist and frequent contributor to Time Magazine cursive.

74 See the handwritten notes by Kurt Georg Kiesinger: Kiesinger Notes, Box 710, Kiesinger Papers, ACDP. I thank Philipp Gassert for drawing my attention to these well-hidden notes.

75 Report St. Simons Island Conference, Box 37, Jackson Papers, DDEL.

76 Kiesinger notes, Box 710, Kiesinger Papers, ACDP.

77 George Kennan, "Breach in the Alliance," *Washington Post and Times Herald*, November 3, 1956, A8.

78 See Jackson Notes, Box 37, Jackson Papers, DDEL.

79 Heilperin, "The Fifth Bilderberg Conference," (emphasis in original), Box 37, Jackson Papers, DDEL.

80 Quaroni to Prince Bernhard, April 30, 1957, Box 45, Bilderberg Archives, NANL. Quaroni argued that in the face of the global Cold War, the West should pay more attention to the moral aspects of foreign policy. As Quaroni put it: "It is quite possible that the Cold War will remain Cold. If so, we can only win it if we are really better than others, also from the moral point of view."

81 See Nitze Notes, Box 60, Folder 1, Nitze Papers, LOC.

82 Report St. Simons Island Conference, Box 37, Jackson Papers, DDEL.

83 Rusk to Retinger, March 11, 1957, Box 45, Bilderberg Archives, NANL.

84 See the St. Simons Memorandum by Lord Kilmuir, "Prime Minister," February 19, 1957, Box 11/1965, PREM, NAL.

85 See Gaddis, *The Cold War*, 128.

86 Nitze Notes, Box 60, Folder 1, Nitze Papers, LOC.

87 Jackson Notes, Box 37, Jackson Papers, DDEL.

88 Nathan Citino notes that U.N. Secretary General Hammarskjöld's plans for Arab development may also have been influenced by the study group. See Citino, *Envisioning the Arab Future*, 86.

89 See the information on MIDEC in Box 192, Bilderberg Papers. Fritz Berg informed the BDI *Präsidium* of the plan and was authorized to participate. See Präsidialsitzung BDI May 16, 1957, Box 784, Folder PRO 5/1, BDIA. See also Annex A of the Bilderberg Report of the Fiuggi Conference.

90 Paul Hoffman, "Blueprint for Foreign Aid," *The New York Times*, February 17, 1957.

91 See Murphy, *The United Nations*, 62–63.
92 See Address of Mr. Paul G. Hoffman at the Bilderberg Conference Istanbul, Turkey, September 1959, Box 194, Bilderberg Archives, NANL.
93 Van Roijen to Prince Bernhard, March 4, 1957, Box 190, Bilderberg Archives, NANL.
94 St. Simons Memorandum by Lord Kilmuir, "Prime Minister," February 19, 1957, Box 11/1965, PREM, NAL.
95 Heilperin, "The Fifth Bilderberg Conference," Box 37, Jackson Papers, DDEL.
96 Quoted in Philipsen, "Diplomacy with Ambiguity," 157.
97 Statement made by Premier Guy Mollet on his arrival in New York, Monday, February 25, 1957, Box 77, Mollet Papers, OURS.
98 See Chapter 5.
99 As Rusk put it: "We would feel more comfortable if we could leave Europe more initiative in taking care of their vital interests." Nitze Notes, Box 60, Folder 1, Nitze Papers, LOC.
100 Memcon, February 26, 1957, https://history.state.gov/historicaldocuments/frus1955-57v27/d40. Accessed February 12, 2017.

7 NATO, nuclear strategy, and the Cold War

As the Bilderberg participants gathered for the fifth Bilderberg conference (October 4–6, 1957) in Fiuggi, near Rome, news quickly spread that the Soviet Union had just launched its Sputnik satellite into orbit. According to Denis Healey, the Sputnik shock left the Bilderbergers (particularly the Americans) "flabbergasted," and it was immediately clear that this was an important development for the nuclear defense of NATO.[1] Given both the overwhelming Soviet advantage in conventional military forces and the immense financial costs of keeping under arms the number of divisions necessary to defend Europe conventionally, NATO relied strongly on nuclear weapons for its defense. However, since the United States controlled the vast majority of the nuclear weapons assigned for this defense, the inevitable question arose whether the United States could be relied upon to defend Europe now that Soviet missiles were clearly able to reach the American mainland.

In the resulting transatlantic debate over 'massive retaliation' and 'flexible response,' the indirect influence of the Bilderberg Group becomes apparent. This chapter argues that the Bilderberg discussions on nuclear strategy, disarmament, and Soviet intentions served to disseminate information and expertise that was hard to get by, particularly for participants from the non-nuclear nations. The first part follows the informal alliance's response to the Eisenhower Administration's New Look strategy, as high-ranking NATO officials used the Bilderberg meetings to persuade the transatlantic elite of the necessity of NATO's nuclear turn. The second part shows how the Bilderberg conferences also provided an important forum for critics of the Eisenhower Administration's strong reliance on nuclear weapons. One of these critics was the young foreign policy expert Henry Kissinger. The final part of this chapter examines how the criticism of massive retaliation slowly made its way through the networks and publications of the informal alliance and ended up influencing decision-makers, NATO officials, and politicians on both sides of the Atlantic - both in the form of alternative strategies and in the form of different proposals for the denuclearization or neutralization of Europe.

The Eisenhower Administration's New Look

The NATO strategic doctrine set out in NATO document MC 48, which for the first time integrated the use of nuclear weapons, had been accepted at the December 1954 NATO Council meeting and reflected the strategic thinking of Eisenhower's New Look.[2] The New Look promised a more effective defense at a smaller cost by relying more on nuclear weapons for deterrence: more bang for the buck. To some extent, the policy change was a rationalization of political and economic realities within the alliance.[3] Eisenhower believed that the West was not capable of matching or even approaching the Soviet conventional superiority without threatening its own way of life and economic health. He disagreed, therefore, with the efforts by the Truman Administration at the February 1952 Lisbon NATO summit to achieve a massive buildup of NATO forces. Eisenhower, at that time still SACEUR, was shocked by the resulting force goal of approximately 65 first-line divisions. He told his subordinates at NATO headquarters that the end of NATO was near since he was convinced that the agreed force levels could never be reached.[4] As a result, public confidence in NATO's ability to defend Europe would decline, weakening NATO and strengthening neutralist and communist forces in Europe.

When Eisenhower entered the White House, he was determined to create a more sustainable balance between military and economic needs, a strategy for the 'long haul.'[5] Eisenhower was convinced that nuclear weapons, becoming available in ever increasing numbers and sizes, could close the wide gap in conventional forces between NATO and the Warsaw Pact (which was founded in 1955). The ultimate goal of the New Look was to end the deployment of large numbers of American forces in Europe and to reach a situation in which the Europeans themselves would provide for local defense, reinforced by US air and naval power.

In the short term, however, the redeployment of American forces was out of the question. The European military buildup was much slower than expected – mostly because of the long delay in getting a German contribution – and any hint of an American pullback would have caused political upheaval in Europe. The dilemma of redeployment divided the Eisenhower Administration throughout the 1950s, with Admiral Arthur Radford of the Joint Chiefs of Staff (JCS) consistently arguing for a reduction in force levels abroad and the State Department emphasizing the political ramifications in Europe. Moreover, the right wing, isolationist and anti-European faction of the Republican Party always kept pressure on the Eisenhower Administration to 'bring the boys back' from Europe.

Eisenhower picked his friend and favorite bridge partner General Alfred Gruenther as SACEUR to implement the New Look in NATO. Educating European publics about the new strategy was crucial to its eventual success and this probably explains why General Gruenther accepted the invitation to participate in the September 1955 Bilderberg conference in

Garmisch-Partenkirchen. General Gruenther used the conference to explain the thinking behind MC 48 at length, emphasizing two key arguments: first, that a forward defense required a German contribution of 12 divisions; second, that only with the use atomic weapons an all-out Soviet attack could be repelled.

NATO's reliance on nuclear weapons implied that the West should be willing to use these weapons first. In Gruenther's words: "[...] let us be sure that we understand that we use atomic weapons whether the other side uses them or not."[6] He acknowledged that this reliance on nuclear weapons created a whole range of psychological and political problems. Most importantly, it enabled Moscow to take advantage of the public's natural aversion against weapons of mass destruction and to score propaganda points with calls for nuclear disarmament. Gruenther warned that the Western public should be educated in this respect:

> It creates an entirely new situation for us if the atomic bomb be outlawed, and we feel it represents a tremendous public opinion problem that people should recognise that what the North Atlantic Treaty Organisation is trying to do is to prevent a war from taking place, and that the evil is not weapon A or B or C, but war itself.[7]

This was an important point, going to the heart of President Eisenhower's views on deterrence.[8] The crucial paradox was that only by being willing to plan for the unimaginable could one avoid it. By planning for nuclear war, NATO forced the Soviets to think twice about the possible consequences of aggression. President Eisenhower firmly believed that the Soviet leaders were responsive to the logic of deterrence, as long as they were convinced that the United States would respond to aggression against themselves or their allies – with nuclear arms if necessary. The threat of massive retaliation, combined with an effective forward defense of the NATO territory, therefore more or less ruled out a war in Europe.

The Eisenhower Administration's declaratory policy on the New Look, however, was sometimes misleading. The first speech by Dulles on the subject, on January 12, 1954, introduced the concept of massive retaliation and seemed to imply that the new strategy foresaw an atomic answer to any Soviet aggression, no matter where and no matter how small. Subsequent efforts to clear up this misunderstanding were not entirely successful.[9] Indeed, at the Garmisch conference, Admiral Anthony Buzzard, one of Great Britain's foremost strategic thinkers, claimed that the strategy amounted to

> threatening to blow the world to pieces for any aggression beyond the power of our small conventional forces, for that is what our present policy undoubtedly amounts to so long as we do not establish any distinction between the tactical and strategic uses of nuclear weapons.[10]

Yet as General Gruenther tried to explain, the deterrence of Soviet aggression in Europe rested not solely on thermonuclear weapons. Those weapons were only part of a much broader strategy. In fact, MC 48 stated that Soviet aggression against NATO territory should be deterred not only by the threat of massive retaliation, but also by convincing the Soviets that "[t]hey cannot quickly overrun Europe."[11] The purpose of the German military build-up and the deployment of tactical atomic weapons to NATO forces, in other words, was to deny the Soviets the possibility of a quick military victory.[12] Thus a forward defense with strong shield forces, reinforced by tactical atomic weapons, was seen at SHAPE, NATO's headquarters, as contributing to a credible deterrence.

Gruenther was remarkably candid about these issues. In reply to a question from the Swedish journalist Herbert Tingsten, he left no doubt that a war directly involving NATO and the Soviet Union would quickly turn into total war. All bets would be off: "[...] the general concept is, if a war does occur you will use whatever force is necessary to win that war." The aim would be to destroy Soviet nuclear forces as quickly as possible. On one of his maps, Gruenther pointed out the airfields with tactical Soviet forces that would have a high priority for NATO tactical aircraft. But he also indicated that, although it was not his direct responsibility, in his opinion the major part of the American counterattack would target Soviet strategic forces. Using his map, Gruenther explained what he meant:

> the keystone of the Soviet attack, namely the North American Soviet potential, will come from much deeper, from here, here and here – and not from here. Should you go after those fields or not? My guess is that they [Strategic Air Command, TWG] will go after those fields before you can count to ten, and if they can before you count to five, they will go after those fields before you count to five. They would be the ones that ran the only chance of knocking out North American war potential, and those would be on a very, very high priority.[13]

This was a terrifying scenario and Tingsten wanted to make sure he had understood Gruenther correctly. "May I just add," Tingsten said,

> that there is a certain line of thinking, both in the United States and in Europe, that it would be possible perhaps to have a great war without using this type of bombing against production centres and so on. But as far as I understand you now, we must think of a new world war as a so-called "total" war. Both sides will use all their weapons from the beginning and will not wait until the other begins, so to speak, from the Western side?

"Yes," Gruenther replied, "that is what I think."[14]

It was on this point that Admiral Buzzard put up the most forceful challenge to the new NATO strategy.[15] "Morally, massive retaliation," Buzzard said,

> is [...] far too drastic to be justified any longer than is absolutely necessary. Politically, as Russia's strategic air power grows it becomes increasingly akin to bluff, as a deterrent against any aggression between all-out attack and a very minor one, leaving much room between these two for communist exploitation and misunderstanding and miscalculation.[16]

Massive retaliation should be modified as quickly as possible to a strategy of "graduated deterrence," by which Buzzard meant a recognized difference between tactical and strategic nuclear weapons. Once NATO was confident it could repel a Soviet attack with ground forces equipped with tactical nuclear weapons, the West should unilaterally declare it would not be the first to use the H-bomb. Following that, a declaration should be made that the West would not be the first to attack centers of population. As Buzzard put it: "I maintain that graduated deterrence will assist both in nipping a small war in the bud and in preventing the spreading quite so rapidly into an all-out war."[17]

Denis Healey and Paul Nitze, both keenly interested in nuclear strategy, were intrigued by Buzzard's ideas. They supported his plea for the minimum use of force necessary in reaction to local or limited aggression. Yet they did not agree with his suggestion to announce a no-first-strike policy with regard to thermonuclear weapons. As Nitze put it, he did not see any advantage in "a declaration which ties your hands behind your back." Most other speakers at Garmisch expressed similar doubts about such a declaration. The British Secretary of State for Commonwealth Affairs, John Foster, stated that ever since 1945 he was convinced that Moscow would avoid a direct confrontation with the West, but this was the case solely "[...] because we have been prepared to use our weapons to the full." Foster continued:

> I also believe that, far from quieting public opinion in the world, if we announce to the world that we would not ourselves use all our weapons public opinion would be disquieted, and not quieted, and that our proper policy is to say to the Russians that we will use all our weapons in what in my definition I call a 'total' war – one in which Russia was directly engaged – and in one where Russia was not directly engaged we should pursue what I call the 'Korean policy.'[18]

Several participants pointed out that Admiral Buzzard misinterpreted NATO strategy. Indeed, Buzzard seemed to share in the confusion that had existed ever since Dulles' massive retaliation speech in January 1954. Nitze remarked that, despite some of the rhetoric of massive retaliation, a policy of "graduated retaliation" was actually in effect. "Certainly the fact that we limited the Korean War to Korea is an instance of this. Certainly it is not to the interest of the West to have a general atomic war."[19] Joseph Johnson similarly accused Buzzard of posing "somewhat of a false issue."[20]

Part of the problem was that Buzzard made no distinction between the areas where American and NATO power was committed and 'grey areas,' such as parts of Asia. Buzzard also assumed that the strategy of massive retaliation did not distinguish between different levels of aggression. When Denis Healey pointed out that once "equivalence" in nuclear capabilities was reached, massive retaliation was not a credible response to a "small probe or nibble," General Gruenther hastened to clarify his position:

> I was not talking about a probing attack when I said we were going to use atomic weapons to repel an act of Soviet aggression. [...] I am talking about all-out aggression; the brush-fire war, Korea, Indo-China, I am not discussing.[21]

Of course, Gruenther's response now raised the question what type and what level of aggression amounted to "all-out aggression." Gruenther was quick to acknowledge this problem: "What constitutes an all-out attack I recognize may again back me in a corner very quickly – I cannot tell you what are the gradations."[22] He also said that the difference between tactical and strategic use of nuclear weapons was difficult to establish. What about an atomic bomb on a city of 75,000 with a sizeable army base within its borders? "[I]s that a tactical use of the atomic bomb or is that a strategic use of the atomic bomb? I do not know." As far as SHAPE planning was concerned, centers of population were not used as targets "not only for humanitarian reasons but also because we do not have the bombs to waste [...]."[23]

If General Gruenther did not spell out what amounted to an all-out attack in Europe, he did emphasize that in the end it was not up to the military to decide on an appropriate reaction. This was a decision that should be made by the political leadership, taking into account the political, economic, and psychological consequences.[24] It was impossible to decide beforehand how to react to aggression short of all-out war. In the final analysis, it was a decision for the American Commander in Chief, to be taken when the situation arose.

With respect to public opinion, the Eisenhower Administration's New Look posed serious difficulties. Healey warned that NATO strategy seemed to amount to "swopping the bombs bang off." "The fact that we appear to rely wholly and solely on the H-Bomb," he said, "makes us appear in a very odd light to many people in Europe, not to speak of Asia." He added that,

> so long as any one of the members of the alliance has control of the weapon on which the security of the whole depends it is very difficult to persuade the other countries of the need to make sacrifices for conventional defence [...].

Republican Senator Ralph Flanders also welcomed Buzzard's efforts to come up with an alternative to massive retaliation. "Disarmament is still in the air in America," Flanders argued,

> and that aspiration will still have to be reckoned with. Now, the state of public opinion in my country is thousands of miles away from the general conclusion which has been stated as coming out of this meeting. It is still further away, I believe, if General Gruenther will forgive me, from the vague and disturbing reliance placed on atomic weapons which I gather from his remarks.

Joseph Johnson, another keen observer of American public opinion, added: "I do not think there is a possibility of getting agreement on general disarmament, and I think there is a danger [...] that there may be some disarmament on our side unilaterally if we do not watch out [...]."[25]

After the Garmisch conference, Retinger told General Gruenther that, in his opinion, no more than 10% of the participants had subscribed to Admiral Buzzard's theory.[26] Even Buzzard himself abandoned his call for a no-first-strike declaration after the criticism at the Garmisch conference.[27] Still, the Garmisch discussion highlighted the political sensitivity of nuclear strategy and set the stage for the debate over massive retaliation versus flexible response. In an article for the January 1956 issue of *Foreign Affairs*, written in reaction to the Garmisch discussions, Nitze fired one of the first shots in this battle, arguing that instead of relying on nuclear weapons, the West should be able to react to local aggression with conventional forces.[28] "We should endeavor," he wrote, "to meet aggression and restore the situation without the use of atomic weapons wherever this is possible."[29]

The nuclearization of NATO had been designed to increase the alliance's trust in a credible defense of Europe without destroying the economic and political basis of the West. The Garmisch discussions showed, however, that the Eisenhower Administration's nuclear rhetoric might have exactly the opposite effect. As early as December 1954, during a steering committee meeting in Paris, Quaroni had pointed to the political dangers of MC 48: "When that document [...] becomes public," he predicted, "you will have a tremendous flare-up here in Europe of neutralism."[30]

The Garmisch discussions on NATO's nuclear strategy did allow the European Bilderberg participants to familiarize themselves with strategic thinking on the other side of the Atlantic – where, after all, most technical knowledge and experience concerning nuclear weapons resided – and within NATO. Conversely, the American participants who participated in the Bilderberg conferences developed a greater sensitivity for the political and psychological consequences of nuclear strategy in Europe.

In addition, personal contacts established at the Bilderberg meetings turned out to be consequential for the transatlantic strategy debates. Nitze, Healey, and Admiral Buzzard remained in touch after the Garmisch conference and regularly exchanged articles.[31] Buzzard also kept SHAPE informed about his thinking, which had undergone a significant change as a result of the Garmisch discussions. In January 1957, moreover, Healey, Buzzard, and a few like-minded people organized a conference in Brighton on nuclear strategy and the problem of limited war.

As a result of the conference, Healey and Buzzard decided to create a new think tank to raise the level of strategic debate within the UK, and Healey relied on his Bilderberg contacts to secure funding for the Institute for Strategic Studies.[32] During the 1957 Fiuggi conference, Healey asked Shepard Stone, the director of the Ford Foundation's European program, for financial support for the continuation of the Brighton conference effort and was able to secure a substantial first grant.[33] Over time, the Institute (later renamed the International Institute for Strategic Studies) became an important part of the informal alliance.

Debating massive retaliation

In the first half of 1956, 'peaceful co-existence' and the apparent relaxation of East-West tensions put increasing pressures on defense budgets in most NATO countries. Even to those who did not necessarily believe in a genuine Soviet wish for co-existence, the Cold War seemed to have reached a new phase in which socioeconomic competition had a larger part to play. The British government therefore decided to make drastic cuts in conventional forces and to concentrate on modernizing the British nuclear deterrent. Not only would this save money; the UK would also maintain a 'special relationship' in nuclear matters with the United States and protect its 'big power' status.[34] The conservative government justified this move with the 'trip-wire' strategy, which boiled down to the argument that a small number of conventional forces in Europe sufficed as a trip-wire to set off the West's nuclear response to a Soviet attack in Europe.

While rumors about the British plans were making the rounds, *The New York Times* reported that Admiral Radford, the chairman of the Joint Chiefs of Staff, called for an 800,000-man cutback in American conventional forces.[35] Radford argued that the introduction of tactical nuclear weapons would make up for the loss in manpower. The State Department quickly denied that any such plan was under consideration, but the damage was done: both the Radford plan and the British trip-wire strategy implied a major departure from the kind of forward defense that General Gruenther – and his successor as SACEUR, General Lauris Norstad – advocated.[36] This raised fears in Europe – particularly in Bonn – that the United States and Great Britain would pull out completely from continental Europe and rely on a peripheral strategy, known in the United States as "fortress America."[37]

And then the Suez-Hungary double crisis intervened. The crisis further undermined the willingness in Europe to rely on the American nuclear guarantee. Raymond Aron was not the only one who concluded after Suez that Europe needed its own nuclear deterrent. Even Guy Mollet, who had long opposed the French nuclear program, now agreed that France should accelerate its own nuclear program – although the final decision to build a *force de frappe* wasn't made until later.[38] In addition, the specter of a Hungary-style rebellion escalating into a broader conflict raised the question of whether NATO was prepared to deal with the issue of limited war. Healey, somewhat provocatively, called the Suez-Hungary crisis "the revolt of the satellites – on both sides of the Iron Curtain. It saw nationalism reestablished as the dominant force in world politics, disrupting alliances and confusing the simple bipolarity of the Cold War Decade."[39]

As a result of the Suez crisis, the questions of nuclear control and limited war featured prominently at the NATO summits in December 1956 in Paris and in May 1957 in Bonn. During the first of the two summits, the NATO Council agreed to a Political Directive to clarify NATO's nuclear threshold. This reflected the fear in Bonn that tactical nuclear weapons would be used even in small, local conflicts, resulting in the devastation of large parts of Germany – a matter of great public concern in the country ever since the *Carte Blanche* NATO exercise in 1955 had revealed the destructive power of tactical nuclear weapons.[40] The Political Directive, echoing Nitze's *Foreign Affairs* article, called for shield forces able "to deal with incidents such as infiltrations, incursions or hostile local actions by the Soviets, or by Satellites with or without overt or covert Soviet support" and to do so "without necessarily having recourse to nuclear weapons."[41] On the other hand, the new NATO strategy document MC 14/2 of April 1957 stated that,

> if the Soviets were involved in a local hostile action and sought to broaden the scope of such an incident or to prolong it, the situation would call for the utilization of all weapons and forces at NATO's disposal, since in no case is there a NATO concept of limited war with the Soviets.[42]

The tension between these two statements illustrates how difficult it remained for NATO to deal with different scenarios of possible aggression in Europe.

In response, the Eisenhower Administration now started considering ways of sharing tactical nuclear weapons with NATO allies. Before this could be done, however, Congress had to be convinced to change the Atomic Energy Act.[43] This promised to be a tough fight, as Chalmers Roberts, the foreign policy commentator of the *Washington Post*, wrote in a paper for the Fiuggi conference:

> The Anglo-French venture at Suez increased the reluctance of the Congress even to alter the law so as to permit American nuclear weapons to be put in the hands of NATO allies prior to the outbreak of war. There is a broad American concern that such weapons, if made

available, might be used for reasons considered contrary to American interests just as American-supplied weapons were used in Suez and are being used in Algeria.[44]

Kissinger on nuclear weapons and foreign policy

Not surprisingly, the informal alliance was deeply involved in the transatlantic debates over nuclear strategy. Several Bilderberg members, including Joseph Johnson, Paul Nitze, and David Rockefeller, took part in a Council on Foreign Relations study group on nuclear weapons and foreign policy. Rockefeller had suggested that Henry Kissinger, then a Harvard lecturer in government, should serve as study director.[45] Kissinger had just finished his dissertation on Metternich and Castlereagh and was eager to apply his knowledge of grand strategy to contemporary debates. After the Council on Foreign Relations study group finished its work in mid-1956, Kissinger set out to synthesize its conclusions. Even before Kissinger published the resulting volume, *Nuclear Weapons and Foreign Policy,* in June 1957, he participated in the St. Simons Island Bilderberg conference and contributed a paper on nuclear strategy. Yet because the debate about the Suez crisis took up so much time, the discussion on nuclear strategy was postponed until the next Bilderberg conference in Fiuggi in early October.

Given the fact that US and NATO nuclear strategy was very much in flux, the timing of *Nuclear Weapons and Foreign Policy* could not have been better. Not only did Kissinger provide an incisive analysis of the reasons why massive retaliation was no longer valid; he also contributed several suggestions for solving the strategic puzzle which divided both the alliance and the Eisenhower administration.

Kissinger argued convincingly that American strategic doctrine had been dominated by technical and economic considerations, leading to a dangerous reliance on the threat of massive retaliation.[46] The most important reason why massive retaliation was no longer credible was the rapidly developing Soviet nuclear arsenal. As Kissinger argued in his paper for the Fiuggi conference (a condensed version of his book):

> No matter how vast our remaining margin in number and technological refinement of nuclear weapons, henceforth every objective in all-out war must be weighed in terms of the destruction of American cities. It is not that we will refuse to fight for what we consider our vital interests, it is that the line between what is essential and what is peripheral will shift if we must weigh all objectives against the obliteration of Chicago, New York or Washington. Moreover, even if we are willing to pay the price, it is doubtful whether victory in an all-out war retains any concrete meaning.[47]

Under the current strategic doctrine, Kissinger wrote, the president of the United States would be faced with the choice between surrender and all-out war in case of Soviet aggression. To increase his range of options – and thereby to increase the overall credibility of the deterrent – Kissinger called for an enhanced capability to wage limited war (in direct contradiction to NATO strategy MC 14/2).[48] He argued that a limited war using tactical nuclear weapons was possible, because the threat of thermonuclear warfare would induce the enemy to accept defeat in a local war rather than risk general devastation. In practical terms, this meant that the American military forces should be reorganized into one strategic force, responsible for thermonuclear warfare, and a tactical force required for conducting limited war. At present, the lack of a clear strategic doctrine meant that the Air Force, the Army and the Navy were engaged in an expensive and unnecessary inter-service competition in which all three services attempted to develop a capability for all-out war.

Kissinger was not the first to criticize massive retaliation or to introduce the idea of limited war. He had borrowed heavily from Admiral Buzzard's writings on graduated deterrence and from American strategic thinkers such as Bernard Brodie and William Kaufmann.[49] But he was the first who managed to popularize the notion that massive retaliation had become highly problematic and to call for a reassessment of the relationship between foreign policy and nuclear weapons.[50] As Chalmers Roberts, the reporter who did most to bring Kissinger's book to the attention of a wider public, wrote:

> [...] this volume for the first time marries the two sides of the central problem of American policy: the nature and military meaning of nuclear weapons and the problem of conducting a foreign policy in the light of the nuclear facts of life.

In his review of *Nuclear Strategy and Foreign Policy*, Roberts called it the most important book of the year, adding:

> This is a book which, if one may say so, President Eisenhower should curl up with over a long weekend in the quiet of his Gettysburg farm and Secretary Dulles in the isolation of his Duck Island retreat. It should be read by every top civilian and military leader in the nation.[51]

In early September, Roberts reported that Secretary of State Dulles had followed his advice and "agreed with at least the Kissinger thesis that a small nuclear war is possible." The book could be spotted on a good many Pentagon bureaus and the Joint Chiefs of Staff had discussed it. "All in all," Roberts wrote, "this is a remarkable tribute to the written word in a time of hurry-hurry and an Administration not noted for its egghead approach to public affairs."[52]

What Roberts did not know was that President Eisenhower had already read the book – or at least the summary prepared by his aide, General Andrew Goodpaster. Henry Cabot Lodge, the US representative to the

United Nations, had recommended it to Eisenhower in late July, saying that it was "so clear-headed, profound and constructive that I think it is most important that you should know about it."[53] The president, in turn, sent a memorandum on Kissinger's book to his Under Secretary of State, Christian A. Herter. Eisenhower told Herter that

> [...] there are flaws in his arguments and, at the very least, if we were to organize and maintain military forces along the lines he suggests, we would have what George Humphrey always calls 'both the old and the new'.

But Kissinger's book was important, the president added, because of his analysis of "some general or popular conceptions and misconceptions."[54]

The fact that Dulles had authorized Roberts to report that he, Dulles, agreed with Kissinger's view on limited nuclear war was telling.[55] The secretary of state hoped that small and relatively clean tactical nuclear weapons, which appeared technically feasible in the near future, would help to solve the basic problem which had haunted NATO since the early 1950s: how to diminish the reliance on massive retaliation while keeping defense costs at an acceptable level. In an article for *Foreign Affairs* Dulles wrote that by 1960 it might be possible to defend NATO countries against a full-scale conventional attack without having recourse to massive retaliation.

> Thus the tables may be turned, in the sense that instead of those who are non-aggressive having to rely upon all-out retaliatory power for their protection, would-be aggressors will be unable to count on a successful conventional aggression, but must themselves weigh the consequences of invoking nuclear war.[56]

Nuclear strategy and the 1957 Fiuggi conference

The *Foreign Affairs* article by Dulles appeared just before the Fiuggi conference in early October, 1957. Combined with all the media attention for *Nuclear Weapons and Foreign Policy*, there could be little doubt that Kissinger's book was having an impact. As Admiral Buzzard told Nitze: "I need hardly say that we are all greatly encouraged by Dr. Kissinger's book and Mr. Dulles' latest article, both of which almost make people like me respectable over here!"[57] Accordingly, the conference at Fiuggi featured a long debate on Kissinger's ideas. The one thing everyone agreed on was that Kissinger's basic conclusion about massive retaliation was right on the mark. In the words of the Fiuggi report: "[...] it was generally agreed that Russia's capacity for thermo-nuclear attack on American territory had made the threat of massive thermo-nuclear retaliation less convincing as a deterrent."[58] But this was about as far as the consensus went. On the crucial issues of limited war and nuclear control opinions were divided.

Kissinger argued that future wars would be "short, sharp clashes" and "as much a test of will as of power."[59] The threat of escalation – meaning all-out nuclear war – would keep a limited war from expanding. To make sure that a war could be ended in time, Kissinger argued, the West should make its limited aims clear through continued diplomacy during a conflict. In practical terms, Kissinger proposed a zone of 500 miles on both sides of a demarcation line in which tactical nuclear weapons could be used. Cities without military installations could be declared open cities with a 30-mile radius in which no nuclear weapons were to be used. But Kissinger did not make clear whether these open cities would be exposed to conventional attack.

Several European participants rejected Kissinger's arguments about limited nuclear war. Reginald Maudling argued that it was highly unlikely that any war between the United States and the Soviet Union would remain limited. The West should therefore continue to rely primarily on its capacity for massive retaliation.[60] Fritz Erler also disagreed with Kissinger, but for slightly different reasons: Erler thought that only a *large-scale* Soviet attack on Europe could not remain limited. If NATO used nuclear weapons in defense of a major conventional attack, the Soviet Union would do so as well, and a "global war" would break out. In addition, Erler warned that a war in Europe fought with tactical nuclear weapons would end up destroying the continent. "For Europe," he argued, "every application of nuclear weapons becomes close to self-destruction." Even tactical weapons in the 1–20 kiloton range "would destroy what should be defended."[61]

Paul Nitze had still another reason for rejecting Kissinger's views on limited nuclear war. Kissinger, in Nitze's view, had failed to understand some of the basic technical facts about nuclear weapons. Just before the Fiuggi meeting, Nitze had published a scathing review of *Nuclear Weapons and Foreign Policy* in *The Reporter*. He pointed out that Kissinger miscalculated the increase in blast and heat effects of nuclear weapons compared with conventional explosives. According to Kissinger "the blast effect of the twenty-kiloton bomb exploded over Hiroshima was only ten times greater than a twenty-ton TNT blockbuster," whereas in reality it was one hundred times greater. "This may possibly explain," Nitze remarked dryly, "why Kissinger thinks that five-hundred-kiloton weapons are appropriate for inclusion in an arsenal for a limited nuclear strategy designed to spare from annihilation the inhabitants of a geographic area in which the campaign is to be fought."

Nitze also called Kissinger's plan for a limited zone and open cities completely unrealistic. There were few areas in Europe where two cities were further than 60 miles apart. It was to be expected, therefore, that all cities would simply be declared open cities. "We are then right back where we started from: either the Russians under threat of massive retaliation foreswear aggression against Western Europe or the war Kissinger contemplates is a conventional war."[62]

Nitze later recalled that when Kissinger heard about Nitze's review from the editor of *The Reporter*, he threatened a libel suit.[63] Nonetheless, Nitze decided to publish it, after carefully checking for any mistakes. The Fiuggi conference was the first occasion when the two met after this unpleasant episode; in Nitze's version of events, Kissinger used it to apologize. He told Nitze that he had negotiated a deal with *The Reporter* giving him unlimited space for a reply to Nitze's review. Having reached "page 149" of his reply, Kissinger said, he realized there must be something wrong with his original ideas.[64] Not surprisingly, Kissinger abandoned the idea of limited nuclear war in his next book, *The Necessity for Choice*, published in 1960.[65]

Apart from the many question marks concerning limited nuclear war, the Fiuggi discussions revealed a more general problem with Kissinger's book. As Eisenhower had said, Kissinger analyzed several "general misconceptions." In fact, Kissinger perpetuated the most tenacious misconception, namely that NATO relied only on a thermonuclear response for its defense. As we have seen, the Eisenhower Administration itself was to blame for this perception, but actual NATO strategy embraced strong shield forces as an important part of deterrence. Kissinger ignored this aspect of MC 48 as well as the subsequent development of NATO nuclear strategy – the 1956 Political Directive and MC 14/2. As a Foreign Office analysis of Kissinger's Bilderberg paper, prepared for Lord Kilmuir, put it:

> [...] it is worth mentioning that Mr. Kissinger, in referring to the 'shield forces' does not refer to its two main objectives: to hold a Soviet attack until the strategic counter attack becomes effective, and to deal with border incidents to ensure that they do not spread.[66]

To put it differently, by ignoring the actual NATO strategy, Kissinger could pretend that a 'pure' version of massive retaliation fully dictated NATO strategic doctrine.

At the same time, Kissinger was undoubtedly correct about the strong tendency in the Eisenhower administration to rely on massive retaliation. Moreover, the deficiencies of NATO's shield forces were such that, in practice, the West still very much depended on the US Strategic Air Command and the British Bomber Command. As Nitze put it at Fiuggi:

> If we look at the trends of the last few years certain things seem to stand out: (1) a decreasing allocation of resources expressed in percent of G.N.P. to defense; (2) an increasing reliance on nuclear weapons for that defense, and (3) an increasing posture of covering tactical weakness with a willingness to take great strategic risks.

Major General James McCormack Jr., another member of the CFR study group and a former director at the Atomic Energy Commission (AEC), responded that the economic limits imposed on defense budgets had to be accepted. But Nitze disagreed, arguing: "[t]his point of view is sound for those who must carry out military policy within the resources which they are given. It seems to me that a group such as this, however, can take a different view."[67]

To reverse these trends, Nitze submitted an ambitious program, "elaborated" the previous evening with Giovanni Malagodi "over several bottles of Mr. Malagodi's [Soave] wine." The plan prefigured the much more activist line in transatlantic relations the Kennedy Administration would take in the early 1960s. It contained seven elements: (1) an increase in US defense spending from $38 billion to $48 billion by 1960; (2) a reversal "of the trend toward sole reliance on nuclear weapons" by a conventional buildup; (3) "Suggest to the European powers that they increase their conventional forces while we also make nuclear weapons available to them;" (4) the United States should join the European Free Trade Area or the Common Market; (5) NATO should move towards a semi-federal structure; (6) on the periphery, countries such as India should be assisted in their economic development; and (7) "Expanded exchange program with U.S.S.R. and satellites – negotiations in the future from posture of strength and psychological penetration."[68]

The ambitious scope of Nitze's plan was perhaps partly alcohol-induced, but it also reflected the genuine sense of crisis within NATO, exacerbated by the Sputnik shock. To pull the alliance together in the wake of Suez and Sputnik, Nitze and Malagodi obviously thought that a concerted effort in all these different areas was necessary. Whether the idea of NATO moving in a federal or semi-federal direction was feasible or not could be debated, but bold action was necessary to restore confidence in the alliance. As Malagodi said, the "equilibrium of terror" had led to fears in Europe that the United States "would not attack [the] Russians with [the] ultimate weapons if Europe were attacked."[69] According to Malagodi, the West needed to "recapture some of the mood of [the] Marshall Plan, Truman Doctrine and NATO." More ground and sea forces would be necessary to counter the "great wave of fear" that engulfed Europe. The "reciprocal lowering of [trade] barriers" between Europe and the United States should secure the economic base necessary to sustain an increased defense effort.[70]

Nitze made clear that he thought too much reliance on massive retaliation would lead to "a dispersion of nuclear defense capabilities among further members of the alliance and a tendency toward increased reliance on one's own forces rather than on the common forces of the alliance."[71] Nitze did not outline how a program of nuclear sharing should be organized, but he implied that if nothing was done to address Europe's nuclear worries, NATO's collective security system would be in danger. Lincoln Gordon strongly supported Nitze on this point. If the Soviets succeeded once in breaching NATO's defensive line, the thermonuclear deterrent would be little more than a "paper tiger." Thermonuclear weapons, Gordon argued, were "[...] not appropriate for border instances or far away fracas." Therefore, it was essential to strengthen conventional forces in Europe and provide the European allies with tactical atomic weapons.[72]

Evidence to substantiate Nitze's argument about nuclear proliferation was readily available in a much-noted paper written by the French General Pierre M. Gallois. Gallois maintained that massive retaliation continued to be a credible deterrent for the nuclear powers if they kept their nuclear forces dispersed and strong enough. If the Soviets could not count on destroying virtually all of the opponent's retaliatory forces, Gallois wrote, any rational cost-benefit analysis would produce a decision against an attack. Gallois agreed with Kissinger, however, that for the non-nuclear countries, the American nuclear guarantee lost much of its credibility in the face of increasing Soviet air power.

> For each of the powers of the alliance which do not possess nuclear weapons the question is this: Might it find itself in such a situation that an incident of major importance for its own security or independence might be considered minor not only by guaranteeing atomic powers but also by the other member countries of the alliance?

The Soviet Union might embark on a strategy of small probing actions in order to undermine the Western nuclear line of defense. If the West did not react strongly enough to such probes, Moscow would be in a position to engage in nuclear blackmail and to repeat the kind of aggressive policy Hitler was able to pull off without real opposition in the years preceding World War II.[73]

In response, Gallois opted for what he called the "decentralisation of nuclear weapons" in Western Europe, writing:

> If the deterrent was only likely to operate on the national level – and not if it is the tool of one of the members of the defensive coalition used on behalf of others – then it would be at the national level that the nuclear weapons would have to be decentralised.

National deterrents might be the only way both to reassure Western European countries that their vital interests would not be sacrificed on the altar of (American) public opinion and to reduce the chances that Moscow would attempt nuclear blackmail. The Suez crisis was clearly on the general's mind.[74]

Gallois, who had worked at SHAPE himself, did not suggest any kind of NATO solution. He only mentioned "individual possession" of nuclear weapons or "the possession by groups of nations with very closely connected interests" – implying that NATO did not fit this definition.[75] During the Fiuggi discussion, only Etienne de la Vallée Poussin openly agreed with Gallois. De la Vallée Pousin argued that the Western European Union should be transformed into a European nuclear deterrent using Great Britain's nuclear weapons. Several other speakers agreed that Europe should have more control over nuclear weapons, but the Fiuggi discussion was inconclusive about how to cover Europe's strategic nakedness. Kissinger, for example, argued that: "[t]he United States must take the initiative in developing a capability and a doctrine for the local defense of Europe and in making available the necessary weapons."[76] But Kissinger, Nitze, Gordon, and Malagodi were all unable to make any detailed suggestions on the best way of doing so.

Even if the Fiuggi conference did not deliver any ready-made solutions, the discussions did help to make several things clear. First, continuing the trend already apparent at Garmisch, nuclear strategy had become a political issue of the first order. The unsolved problems about nuclear control and limited war could no longer be contained by informal agreements or by simply ignoring them. The crucial question – which would continue to haunt NATO for many years to come – was how to decide beforehand at what point a conflict in Europe warranted a nuclear response and who should make this decision. This question had major implications for the structure and size of NATO's forces, for NATO strategic planning, and, consequently, for national defense budgets.

But most important were the political implications. Would public opinion in the West accept an overwhelming reliance on thermonuclear weapons for its defense when all-out war would equal suicide? Would European governments continue to accept the American monopoly on nuclear weapons? As Quaroni wrote in a steering committee paper not long after Fiuggi:

> A fair and reasonable solution of the question who gives the order for pressing the button of the I.R.B.M.; the absence of discrimination and a considerable revision of the MacMahon [sic] Act are three political questions to which I think I have the duty to draw the attention of our American friends. For if the Government of the United States insists on maintaining the position it is holding now there is a real danger that all these will simply strengthen a threat which is already strong towards a helpless neutralism.[77]

Yet what were the alternatives? Strong NATO shield forces - even if reinforced by tactical nuclear weapons under SACEUR control – might not be sufficient for some European powers. The clear implication of Gallois' paper was that Europe should have its own strategic deterrent, whether owned nationally or controlled by the WEU or some other organization.

These conclusions reached official circles on the North American continent in several different ways. On October 15, Dana Wilgress sent Lester Pearson a lengthy memorandum on the state of NATO. Wilgress' analysis was based to a large extent on the Fiuggi discussions.[78] The Canadian Ambassador in Rome, Pierre Dupuy, also wrote a report on the Fiuggi meeting. He confirmed that during the discussion of Kissinger's paper,

> [...] a number of the European participants were under the impression that in the process of re-adapting their military establishments to the

needs of nuclear warfare, the United States was slowly moving away from Europe. [...] No one among our U.S. friends present was in a position to give any assurances on behalf of Washington, but reports have since very probably reached the proper authorities in the State Department.[79]

Nitze indeed sent his report on the Fiuggi meeting to his former colleagues at the State Department's Policy Planning Staff (PPS).[80] The PPS had become a hotbed of opposition to massive retaliation, with staff members such as Henry Owen, Leon Fuller, and their boss Assistant Secretary of State for Policy Planning Gerard Smith arguing for a much more flexible strategy along the lines of Nitze's thinking.[81] The report by Nitze supplied them with further ammunition and confirmed a Policy Planning analysis of July 1957 regarding the effects of the approaching nuclear parity on European attitudes. Increasing doubt about the credibility of the US deterrent, the PPS concluded, "[...] inclines some of our major allies to consider the creation of nuclear capabilities of their own. It also contributes to neutralism and a disposition toward accommodation with the USSR."[82]

At the time of the Fiuggi conference, Nitze was also engaged in the writing of the Gaither Report. Officially known as the Security Resources Panel, the Gaither Committee, headed by H. Rowan Gaither, the chairman of the boards of the Ford Foundation and the RAND Corporation, had been appointed by President Eisenhower in April 1957 to study the most effective ways of protecting the American civil population against nuclear attack.[83] The report, which was presented to President Eisenhower in early November 1957, made the case for vastly increased defense spending. By late 1959, the report stated, the American deterrent would be extremely vulnerable to a surprise attack by Soviet missiles if nothing was done to make US forces more secure by improving early warning systems and by speeding up US ballistic missile programs – in other words, by creating a secure 'second-strike capability.'[84]

Officially, Nitze was only an advisor to the Gaither Committee, but since he was responsible for writing large parts of the report, he did influence its message and alarmist tone – which, in any case, reflected the general dissatisfaction with Eisenhower's defense strategy among key members of the committee.[85] The Gaither Committee argued that US and allied limited war capabilities should be improved. This was, of course, another way of saying that massive retaliation was outdated. The report called for a concerted effort to embed the defense measures in a broader foreign policy program for the free world.

If not so integrated into our foreign policy, any substantial program to reduce the vulnerability of the United States might be widely interpreted as signaling a retreat to 'Fortress America.' The USSR would be sure to fully exploit the resulting uncertainties.

The Gaither report listed three general areas of concern for such a program:

1   Measures, some of which are already under way to pool and make more effective the economic, technological and political resources of ourselves and our allies.
2   Supplying NATO with nuclear weapons, to remain in U.S. custody in peacetime, for use in wartime under NATO command – as a means of increasing confidence.
3   Measures designed to assure the uncommitted nations that their national interests are truly a matter of continuing concern to us.[86]

Taken together, these three points, and the calls for increased defense spending and stronger limited war capabilities are strikingly similar to Nitze's proposals at the Fiuggi meeting. President Eisenhower, however, continued to resist many of the more far-reaching (and expensive) recommendations of the report, although his public rhetoric reflected some of its conclusions.[87]

Disengagement, China, and the Berlin crisis

Meanwhile, Khrushchev did all he could to reap the propagandistic fruits of Sputnik. With a mixture of threatening messages and calls for disarmament and a summit meeting he kept Western audiences spellbound. One of the Soviet proposals involved a plan for a nuclear-free zone in Germany, Poland and Czechoslovakia, originally proposed by the Polish Foreign Minister Adam Rapacki on October 2, 1957 and endorsed by Moscow in December. Similar ideas had in fact been discussed at several Bilderberg meetings, and British and West-German social-democrats such as Healey, Gaitskell, and Erler were in favor of a military disengagement in Central Europe. Healey had presented a plan at the St. Simons Island meeting involving the creation of a neutral zone in Central Europe and the mutual withdrawal of NATO forces from West Germany and Soviet forces from Eastern Europe. Most Bilderberg participants, however, had rejected Healey's proposal because it might well mean the end of NATO.[88] As the report of a Bilderberg steering committee meeting in early January 1958 put it: "European demands for disengagement might revive isolationist feelings in the United States and similarly American interest in negotiating a European settlement with Russia might revive Europe's traditional fears of an American withdrawal."[89]

One Bilderberger who agreed with what C. D. Jackson called the "Healey Doctrine" was George Kennan, and not long after the Fiuggi meeting, Kennan reached a large, worldwide audience with his own plans for disengagement through the BBC's Reith Lectures. The informal alliance now became deeply involved in the transatlantic response to Kennan's Reith Lectures. The American Council on Germany, in particular, orchestrated a major publicity campaign against Kennan's ideas, featuring, among others, Kennan's former boss Dean Acheson in a fierce put-down of Kennan's lectures.[90]

The Bilderberg organizers, meanwhile, organized an enlarged steering committee session in the original Bilderberg Hotel to discuss what they perceived as the increasing risk of neutralism in Europe. Two first-time participants were NATO Secretary General Paul-Henri Spaak and New York Times cursive columnist Cyrus Sulzberger.[91] Spaak strongly opposed any proposal for the neutralization of Germany, but acknowledged that the West needed to offer positive ideas to deal with disarmament and a possible East-West summit. As long as the complete withdrawal of US forces from the continent could be avoided, Spaak was even willing to discuss the Rapacki Plan.

Sulzberger wrote two columns about the Bilderberg meeting. Addressing the Soviet calls for a summit meeting, which had found such a receptive audience in Europe, he argued that enthusiasm was limited in the United States after the disappointments of Geneva, Potsdam, and Yalta. However, if a summit was to take place, a "coordinated but flexible approach" by NATO was necessary. Sulzberger mentioned Spaak's conditions (no neutralization of Germany and no withdrawal of US forces) as a possible basis for agreement and added that Spaak would introduce them to NATO's foreign ministers.[92] Sulzberger added that "local Socialists" – presumably Fritz Erler – argued that "if all Germans are convinced the West has made a serious effort to disengage only to be rebuffed, Adenauer's NATO policy would at last be supported by the opposition." In the Federal Republic, the debate about disengagement had been especially virulent because of the parallel discussions concerning the nuclear arming of the *Bundeswehr*. Therefore, the fact that Erler offered the possibility of support for Adenauer's NATO policy was important. Despite the SPD's fundamental opposition to the nuclear arming of German soldiers, the party's general attitude towards NATO was changing.

In fact, during the Fiuggi conference, Erler and Carlo Schmid already had indicated that the SPD was moving away from its plan for a Europe-wide security system through the abolishment of NATO and the Warsaw Pact. The devastating defeat the SPD had suffered in the September 1957 elections, they told the Bilderberg participants, would have consequences for the SPD's foreign policy agenda. As Shepard Stone put it, "Fritz Erler and Carlo Schmid said the Bilderberg contact would have influence on SPD foreign policy ideas in future."[93] Although the SPD's official acceptance of the Federal Republic's *Westbindung* and NATO commitments did not come until the famous speech by Herbert Wehner on June 30, 1960, it was clear that the Bilderberg discussions were having an effect.[94]

By the same token, Erler and Schmid were also influencing Western attitudes towards the SPD. In the late 1950s, the German social-democrats increasingly came to be regarded as a viable alternative to the CDU and Adenauer. When John F. Kennedy became President in 1961, the traditional US support for Adenauer was no longer a given.[95] With regard to the German problem – for example, the recognition of the Oder-Neisse line – the new Democratic administration undoubtedly stood closer to the views of Erler and Schmid than to Adenauer and the majority of the CDU.

The 1958 Bilderberg conference in Buxton, UK (September 13–15) did not feature another detailed discussion of the various disengagement plans. However, the debate on the Soviet Union and the future of East-West relations left no doubt that a great majority of Bilderberg participants remained convinced that a negotiation with the Soviet Union about disengagement stood little chance of success and would severely undermine NATO unity. As several speakers said, all the indications were that the West should expect a period of heightened rather than lessened tensions. Philip E. Mosely, director of studies at the Council on Foreign Relations and professor at the Russian Institute of Columbia University, warned that "The Soviet Union has achieved a position as a nuclear power which would enable it, in the absence of a well-organized and determined opposition, to impose its will on all of Western Europe and on free Asia." Dean Acheson, the former secretary of state and architect of containment, underlined in a paper for the Buxton meeting:

> The [task] of political leadership in the West is to persuade the peoples of the West to develop their power position to the point where intentions hostile to their interests can be frustrated. Without this capacity, and without resolution of purpose, there seems no possibility of achieving two other ends which occupy much of the public discussion in the West: finding some accommodations with the Soviet state; and conducting successfully the cold war, the so-called battle for men's minds.[96]

General Cortlandt Schuyler, the chief of staff at SHAPE, was present to give a special presentation on MC 70 and current NATO strategy. General Schuyler gave an "admirable account of the present state of affairs," in David Ormsby-Gore's view. "He made a strong plea for countries to make every effort to achieve the target set in MC 70. He estimated the increased effort required would amount to an increase of 10% to 15% of existing defence budgets." Schuyler reacted to several questions about the threshold for the use of nuclear weapons in response to aggression by emphasizing the deterrent purpose of strong shield forces. "The task of the shield is to hold an initial attack, and it must be of sufficient strength to meet and hold an aggressor, so that the onus of deciding to extend the conflict would rest with the enemy."[97] Schuyler's message was clear: with an extra effort to strengthen its shield forces, NATO's defense strategy was valid, despite the recent doubts caused by Sputnik. NATO would be wise to put its own house in order instead of hoping for a far-reaching settlement with Moscow.

The review of recent events at Buxton was dominated by the Quemoy-Matsu crisis. In August 1958, Communist China had started shelling these small islands, only a few kilometers off the Chinese mainland's coast, after Chiang Kai-Shek had started reinforcing the nationalist Chinese forces occupying the islands.[98] Mao claimed that Chiang intended to use the islands as a forward base for attacks on the communists and that they belonged to the

Chinese mainland. The United States, meanwhile, was committed to the defense of the islands since the first Quemoy-Matsu crisis of 1954–1955. Despite the fact that Eisenhower and Dulles were annoyed at Chiang's behavior, they felt that they had to respond to what they regarded as Communist China's aggression. Right before the Buxton conference, President Eisenhower had announced live on television that his administration would not abandon the islands.

Quaroni raised the question why Mao had chosen this particular moment to start the crisis. He noted that Mao had not been enthusiastic about Soviet efforts to bring about a summit conference. The shelling of the islands might amount to an attempt to sabotage Soviet designs. Moreover, a "stiffening" of internal policies in the Soviet Union and the satellites was visible. Was this a reaction to Mao, Quaroni asked? At the Garmisch conference, Quaroni had compared the Soviet Union to malaria: "[i]t is wrong to believe oneself dead when the fever is rising very high. But it is an error even greater to believe that one is cured because the attack has ended."[99] Now he asked: "Are we in for another malaria attack?"[100]

Whatever the dynamics of Soviet-Chinese relations, all European Bilderberg participants thought that the case for defending the islands was a bad one – "military nonsense," as Gaitskell put it – and they worried about a military escalation, perhaps even involving nuclear weapons. Gaitskell argued that the island had no defensive value whatsoever for Formosa.[101] Healey added that no one thought that the case for defending the islands – and risking a wider war, perhaps even including the use of nuclear weapons – was "politically or morally justifiable." It was a "good principle applied to a poor case."[102] A quick poll of the participants confirmed that virtually all American and Canadian participants agreed.[103] As Joseph Harsch, political commentator for the *Christian Science Monitor* and NBC, told his editor at NBC: "on a secret poll one vote only was cast in full favor of our Quemoy policy (we were all trying to guess whether it was by C.D. Jackson, Gab Hauge, or Senator Case)."[104] Ormsby-Gore noted that "none of the Americans present seemed the least bit surprised at the European reaction to the situation."[105]

In fact, many of them agreed with the European assessment and could do little more than explain the political sensitivity of the Chinese question in the United States.[106] Harsch criticized that the Eisenhower Administration's response distracted from the real danger in the world: the alliance between the Soviet Union and China. With Russian help, China was fast becoming a major military power. "This conception," Harsch argued, "should govern our every thought and action."[107] Arthur Dean and David Rockefeller, perhaps influenced by the Fredensborg conference, thought that it made little sense not to accept the existence of Communist China, and John McCloy, chairman of the board of the Chase Manhattan Bank and a first-time Bilderberg participant, shared this assessment. At Buxton, he found himself in agreement with much of the Europeans' criticism of the Eisenhower Administration.[108]

After McCloy had returned from Buxton, Secretary of State Dulles asked him to go to Taiwan to convince Chiang to back down over the islands. McCloy refused, in part because of his disagreement with the Eisenhower Administration's course, but also because of the likely treatment of the feared right-wing China lobby in Washington. He did make sure, however, to inform Dulles and President Eisenhower of the state of opinion in Europe he had encountered at the Bilderberg meeting. As Harsch told Retinger:

> I can report to you, under the rules of "Bilderberg secrecy", that Jack McCloy's confidential report at the White House on his return from Buxton was a major, perhaps even the decisive, factor in causing American Far East policy to swing over from a "one-China" to a "two-China" line. He had been startled by the unanimity of view he encountered at Buxton on the subject of Quemoy, and conveyed his reaction to the White House. I learned from several high sources that his report had a profound effect in the National Security Council.[109]

The journalist Marquis Childs also learned about the Buxton discussions on China and warned of the negative impact of the Taiwan crisis on transatlantic relations. Quoting Acheson, who had pointed to "the threat to the Atlantic alliance inherent in the American stand," Childs reported that the Buxton conference "was an important factor" in changing US policy on China.[110]

Dulles ended up flying to Taiwan himself, where he convinced Chiang to renounce the use of force to reach his objective of 'freeing' mainland China.[111] In effect, this amounted to the acceptance of a 'two-China' policy, as *The New York Times* noted, even if it would take another 13 years before Kissinger and Nixon would engineer their opening to China.[112]

Two months after the Buxton conference, Khrushchev issued his ultimatum on Berlin. The Berlin crisis did not immediately end all hopes for some sort of disengagement. However, no one could deny that the likelihood of a settlement in Europe and a solution to the German question had become more remote. Then in March 1959, a visit to Moscow by Fritz Erler and Carlo Schmid put a temporary end to their hopes for disengagement.

Schmid gave a full account of his nine-hour conversation with Khrushchev during a special Bilderberg steering committee meeting on March 21–22, 1959, in Knokke, Belgium. Khrushchev had left no doubt that he was uninterested in any disengagement or reunification proposals until the question of a peace treaty with East Germany was settled. Reunification had to be a matter of negotiations between the two Germanys, Khrushchev argued. Since all disengagement proposals hinged on a Soviet willingness to negotiate, this was a lethal blow to the SPD's attempts to develop a realistic plan for reunification. In addition, Schmid was deeply impressed by the vigor and conviction with which Khrushchev argued his case on Berlin. Schmid concluded that the Soviet leader was not bluffing and would use nuclear weapons in the event of an armed conflict. Khrushchev repeatedly told Schmid that the closest bases to the Soviet Union would be the first ones to be hit.[113]

During the steering committee meeting, Schmid argued that nuclear war "was too high a price to pay even to save the people of West Berlin."[114] The conservative British MP Sir Frederic Bennett and the French socialist Jacques Piette both strongly opposed Schmid on this point. Piette warned that the West should not make unnecessary concessions in the face of Khrushchev's nuclear threats. As Prince Bernhard summarized Piette's words in his handwritten notes:

> if we have to make concessions re Berlin why the hell make more re disarmament of Germany & disengagement? This sort of thing has been ruinous before! It leads to neutralism which means national & international disaster and the end of NATO.

Kraft likewise repeated what Spaak and many others had said at previous Bilderberg meetings: "Here we should agree that US troops must not leave Europe!!! That would be the end of NATO."[115]

The Bilderberg discussions on nuclear strategy and disengagement were important on several different levels. For one, the Bilderberg participants themselves were exposed to information and expertise – from General Gruenther's candid talk on NATO strategy to the debate over Henry Kissinger's influential study – that was difficult to find in most European countries. Experts such as Nitze and Buzzard were prompted by the Bilderberg discussions to develop their thinking and publish the results in *Foreign Affairs* and elsewhere. The transnational contacts established at Bilderberg, moreover, led to the creation of new organizations such as the Institute for Strategic Studies. Taken together, the Bilderberg Group contributed to the development of a transatlantic strategic culture and thus helped to "develop public opinion" (as General Gruenther had put it at Garmisch) about nuclear strategy within the alliance.

On the political level, the Bilderberg discussions exposed important differences between those in favor of some form of military disengagement in Europe and those more concerned with NATO's future and the dangers of neutralism. Again, the informal alliance had an important role to play and paved the way for the NATO-skeptical German SPD to basically accept Chancellor Adenauer's strategy of *Westbindung* by the end of the 1950s. The fact that high-ranking NATO officials frequently participated in the Bilderberg meetings shows that they recognized the relevance of the informal alliance in shaping attitudes in the member countries.

In the United States, the State Department's PPS played a crucial role in translating these transatlantic debates into policy change. As Policy Planning's head Gerard Smith put it in his memoirs: "The Policy Planning staff served as a conduit for ideas from outside the State Department. We consulted many such outside experts, such as Paul Nitze, Jerome Wiesner, Dean Rusk, Ernest Lawrence, Arnold Toynbee, Admiral Rickover, and Albert Wohlstetter."[116] Smith himself became convinced that a more flexible strategy relying much more strongly on the conventional defense of NATO was necessary and did much to educate Dulles on the weaknesses of massive retaliation.

By the end of the 1950s, however, one thing was clear: the magic bullet to solve NATO's nuclear dilemma had not been found. In the context of the Berlin crisis and strong pressures throughout the Atlantic world for disarmament, nuclear strategy would remain high on the agenda of transatlantic relations.[117] Meanwhile, the fact that General Charles de Gaulle returned to power after the collapse of the Fourth Republic ensured that the question of independent nuclear forces in Europe (coupled with the general's skepticism of NATO's integrated military) would continue to occupy the formal and informal alliance.

Notes

1 Healey, *Time of My Life*, 238. On the effect of Sputnik on NATO, see Johnston, *How NATO Adapts*, 84–85.

2 On the New Look and MC 48, see Bowie and Immerman, *Waging Peace*, 178–201; Craig and Logevall, *America's Cold War*, 145–153; Dockrill, *Eisenhower's New-Look*; Freedman, *The Evolution of Nuclear Strategy*, 76–84; Greiner, "Die Entwicklung"; Rosenberg, "The Origins of Overkill"; Thoß, *NATO-Strategie*; and Trachtenberg, *Constructed Peace*, 151–178.

3 This was recognized at the time. See, for example, Slessor, "Air Power and World Strategy."

4 The story is told by Robert Richardson, who was on the staff of the Standing Group at the time of the Lisbon summit. See "The Eisenhower Administration and NATO Nuclear Strategy: An Oral History Roundtable, 10 May 1989," Parallel History Project.

5 See Trachtenberg, *Constructed Peace*, 152.

6 Garmisch Transcript, English I, 58 (a), Box 9, Bilderberg Archives, NANL.

7 Garmisch Transcript, English I, 59–60, Box 9, Bilderberg Archives, NANL.

8 On Eisenhower's views on nuclear weapons, see Bowie and Immerman, *Waging Peace*, 49–52; Craig, *Destroying the Village*; Erdman, "War No Longer"; and Nash, "Eisenhower, Nuclear Weapons."

9 For an effort to do so, see Dulles, "Policy for Security." To a certain extent the confusion was deliberate: the Eisenhower Administration wished to leave the Soviet Union and China guessing about the place, time and means (including nuclear weapons) of an American reaction to Korea-style aggression, thus restoring American control over the deployment of its forces. As John Lewis Gaddis concludes, however: "[...] the gains derived from unsettling adversaries hardly compensated for the damage Dulles's inflated rhetoric inflicted on alliance relationships, and on public presumptions of official common sense." See Gaddis, *Strategies of Containment*, 162. For evidence that Dulles was aware of the negative consequences of a public emphasis on nuclear weapons, see Gaddis, "The Unexpected John Foster Dulles."

10 Garmisch Transcript, English II, 56, Box 9, Bilderberg Archives, NANL.

11 See Pedlow, *NATO Strategy Documents*, 232.

12 In the words of MC 48:

> In planning the future development and organization of NATO forces it is essential not to lose sight of the primary aim of the Alliance which is to prevent war. Within this aim the primary role of the NATO forces in Europe must be that of an effective deterrent. These forces must, therefore, be so organized, disposed, trained and equipped that the Soviets, in taking account of them in their plans, must come to the conclusion that, even with superior numbers and the advantage of surprise, their chances of obtaining a quick decision in the European theater are small and that such an attempt would involve grave risks to the Soviet Union.

Pedlow, *NATO Strategy Documents*, 240.

13 Garmisch Transcript, English II, 19, Box 9, Bilderberg Archives, NANL.
14 Ibid., 20. Trachtenberg has called this a strategy of "extremely rapid escalation," *Constructed Peace*, 159.
15 Admiral Buzzard contributed a paper to the Garmisch conference titled: "Must we continue to threaten the destruction of civilization?" On Buzzard's role in the strategic debate of the 1950s, see Baylis, *Ambiguity and Deterrence*.
16 Garmisch Transcript, English II, 56–57, Box 9, Bilderberg Archives, NANL.
17 Ibid., 62. Buzzard even argued that if the distinction between strategic and tactical nuclear weapons had been established at the time of the war in Korea and if "we had the ability to come down with atomic weapons in Korea, I do not think it would have started, and if it had started it would have been over in a week." Ibid., 87.
18 Ibid., 60–61.
19 Ibid., 47.
20 Ibid., 67.
21 Ibid., 27–28. Note that Eisenhower and Dulles had used the threat of nuclear weapons to bring an end to the Korean War. They also publicly contemplated the use of nuclear weapons in the two Quemoy-Matsu crises in 1954–55 and 1958. For the nuclear threat in Korea and Formosa, see Gaddis, *Strategies of Containment*, 168–170.
22 Garmisch Transcript, English II, 29, Box 9, Bilderberg Archives, NANL.
23 Ibid., 30.
24 Gruenther had said earlier:

> [w]e are not the ones who would make a decision whether they would be used in an actual case: that is a political decision, but as far as the military realities are concerned our military judgment is that they must be used.

Garmisch Transcript, English I, 59, Box 9, Bilderberg Archives, NANL.

25 Garmisch Transcript, English II, 71, Box 9, Bilderberg Archives, NANL.
26 Untitled Memo by HGW to General Schuyler, 5 January 1956, Box 4, NATO Series, Gruenther Papers, DDEL.
27 Buzzard to Gruenther, February 25, 1956, Box 24, Gruenther Papers, DDEL.
28 See Interview with Paul H. Nitze 7 April, 1982, by Steven Rearden and Ann Smith, Box 118, Nitze Papers, LOC. While discussing the value of the Bilderberg meetings, Nitze remembered the discussion at Garmisch-Partenkirchen with Admiral Buzzard: "... as a result of that debate I wrote that article [in] Foreign Affairs..." The Bilderberg secretariat sent Nitze's article to all Bilderberg members. See the correspondence in Box 40, Bilderberg Archives, NANL.
29 Nitze, "Atoms, Strategy," 196.
30 "Meeting held on Monday, December 6th, 1954, in Paris." 24–25, Box 30, Bilderberg Archives, NANL.

31 In his memoirs, Healey calls Nitze "our most important associate in Washington" and also mentions Senator Ralph Flanders' support for his criticism of massive retaliation. Healey, *Time of My Life*, 236. In the autumn of 1956 Healey, Buzzard and others published the volume *On Limiting Atomic War.*
32 As discussed briefly in Chapter 4.
33 Healey, *Time of My Life*, 239.
34 On British thinking, see Baylis, *Ambiguity and Deterrence*; and Melissen, *The Struggle*, 18.
35 Anthony Leviero, "Radford Seeking 800,000-Man Cut; 3 Services Resist," *The New York Times*, July 13, 1956, 1.
36 In a January 1957 speech Norstad argued:

> if our line is being held in reasonable strength, and if the enemy knows this beyond doubt, then any inclination on his part to cross the line makes him face the terrible decision of detonating World War III, with a sure prospect of his own annihilation. The defensive forces deployed on our eastern boundary thus become an essential part of the deterrent.

(Emphasis in original)
"Remarks by General Lauris Norstad Before the American Council on NATO," New York City, January 29, 1957, Box 190, Bilderberg Archives, NANL.
37 On the Radford Plan, see Felken, *Dulles und Deutschland*, 364–375; and Osgood, *NATO*, 121–130. For the reactions in the Federal Republic see Schwarz, *Adenauer*, 292–296. Adenauer not only opposed the Radford Plan because it would lead to the redeployment of US forces from Europe, he also thought that an over-reliance on nuclear weapons would increase the risk of nuclear war and make any disarmament agreement more difficult.
38 See Pagedas, *Anglo-American Strategic Relations*, 14.
39 Denis Healey, 'Nationalism and Neutralism in the Western Community,' Box 304, Gaitskell Papers, UCL.
40 *Carte Blanche* had shown the likelihood of the Federal Republic being completely destroyed under a barrage of tactical atomic weapons in case of war. See Greiner, "Die Entwicklung," 132.
41 For the text of the Political Directive C-M(56)138 see Pedlow, *NATO Strategy Documents*, 269–276; quote on 275.
42 Ibid., 291. See also Trachtenberg, *Constructed Peace*, 188–189 and Craig and Logevall, *America's Cold War*, 171–172 on President Eisenhower's conviction that a war with the Soviet Union would quickly escalate into general nuclear war.
43 Trachtenberg, *Constructed Peace*, 208.
44 Chalmers Roberts, "The Limitation of Armaments and the Possible Effects on NATO," Box 60, Folder 4, Nitze Papers, LOC. A good indication of Congress's exasperation about French policies was the *Foreign Affairs* article by Democratic Senator John F. Kennedy, published in October 1957. Kennedy called for a more active policy against "Western imperialism" and criticized French policy in Algeria, writing: "When Morocco and Tunisia are free states, Algeria cannot be kept an armed camp." Kennedy, "A Democrat," 52.
45 See Interview with Paul H. Nitze, April 7, 1982, Box 118, Folder 10, Nitze Papers, LOC. This interview was part of a series of interviews held by Stephen Rearden and Ann Smith in preparation for Nitze's memoirs.
46 On the reception of Kissinger's book, see Ferguson, *Kissinger*, 373–379; Hahnimäki, *The Flawed Architect*, 8–12; Kuklick, *Blind Oracles*, 190–192; Milne, *Worldmaking*, 340–344. For a highly critical evaluation of Kissinger's views on nuclear strategy, see Craig, "The Illogic." For Kissinger's reception in Germany,

where he was called 'America's Clausewitz,' see Klitzing, *The Nemesis of Stability,* 96–102.

47 Henry A. Kissinger, "The Impact of Technological Progress in Armaments on Strategy and Diplomacy both National and Collective," 2, Box 60, Folder 4, Nitze Papers, LOC.

48 Of course, MC 14/2 was secret and not known to Kissinger.

49 See Craig, "Illogic," 548–549 on Brodie and Kaufmann.

50 Kuklick makes the same point: Kuklick, *Blind Oracles,* 191.

51 Chalmers Roberts, "A Recipe Against Annihilation," *The Washington Post,* June 30, 1957, E6.

52 Chalmers Roberts, "Kissinger Volume Stirs a Debate," *The Washington Post,* September 1, 1957, E4.

53 Henry Cabot Lodge to President Eisenhower, July 25, 1957, Ann Whitman Files, DDE, RSC Microfilm Collection.

54 President Eisenhower Memorandum for the Acting Secretary of State, July 31, 1957, Ann Whitman Files, DDE, RSC Microfilm Collection.

55 I also suspect that Robert's barrage of articles on Kissinger's book reflected his own views on nuclear weapons and the dangers of massive retaliation. As an officer in the Strategic Bombing Survey Roberts had witnessed the horrific effects of the atomic bombs in the autumn of 1945. See Roberts, *The Nuclear Years.*

56 Dulles, "Challenge and Response," 31.

57 Buzzard to Nitze, October 3, 1957, Box 19, Nitze Papers, LOC.

58 Fiuggi Report, Box 12, Bilderberg Archives, NANL.

59 Henry Kissinger "The Impact of Technological Progress in Armaments on Strategy and Diplomacy both National and Collective." Box 60, Folder 4, Nitze Papers, LOC.

60 Kissinger's book was also studied extensively in London. P. E. Ramsbotham of the Foreign Office sent Macmillan's Private Secretary, Philip de Zulueta, a critical analysis of the book in December 1957:

> Much of Dr. Kissinger's book is highly persuasive in its rational presentation of the balance of advantage to both sides of limited over all-out war. But the rationality also seems to be its major defect. For the possibility of keeping any war limited is made to depend entirely upon the continuous, rational calculation of each side that to spread it would be more disastrous than to lose it. In the clamour and confusion of war this seems to be placing too much faith in human reason. In particular, Dr. Kissinger ignores the pressures of fear, anger, prestige and personal pride. Both popular demand and personal involvement of the leaders in success or failure would surely provide a powerful impulse to hit as hard as possible.

Box 11-4223, PREM, NAL.

61 Notes Nitze, Box 60, Folder 4, Nitze Papers, LOC.

62 Paul H. Nitze, "Limited Wars or Massive Retaliation," Box 215, Folder 4, Nitze Papers, LOC. Nitze's review was published in the September 5 issue of *The Reporter.* I have quoted from the original manuscript in the Nitze Papers.

63 See Milne, *Worldmaking,* 341–342. Milne suggests that jealousy may have played a role in Nitze's reaction.

64 Interview with Paul H. Nitze, April 7, 1982, Box 118, Folder 10, Nitze Papers, LOC.

65 Typically, Kissinger was not entirely straightforward about this change: he maintained that a limited nuclear war capability was still necessary, but that most efforts should be concentrated on conventional forces. At Fiuggi, Kissinger argued that the dangers of escalation were the same in a limited conventional war

and in a limited nuclear war. By 1960, he acknowledged that "[e]ven with the best intentions on both sides, a nuclear war will be more difficult to limit than a conventional one." Kissinger, *The Necessity for Choice*, 82.

66 J. M. O. Snodgrass, September 27, 1957, "Item 2 (a): The Impact of Techno-logical Progress in Armaments on Strategy and Diplomacy," Box 130993, FO 371, TNA. Note that two days before the Fiuggi meeting Norstad briefed the NATO Council about MC 70 – his memorandum about future force require-ments based on the 1956 Political Directive. Norstad again strongly emphasized the need for effective shield forces:

> This last point Norstad elaborated at considerable length, stressing that it was up to governments concerned to decide whether they wished to avoid situation in which, if NATO line were breached without use of force (which might be result of too thin a shield), they would have to make hard decision of being first to use force in order restore position. He stressed point that, if NATO has only token shield forces, NATO invites local action, and further, NATO would have to depend principally on massive retaliation.

Norstad briefing on MC 70, FRUS, 1955–1957, Vol. IV, No. 57, 170–171.
67 Notes Nitze, Box 60, Folder 4, Nitze Papers, LOC.
68 Ibid.
69 Handwritten Notes Shepard Stone, Fiuggi, Box 56-341, FFA.
70 Notes Nitze, Box 60, Folder 4, Nitze Papers, LOC.
71 Ibid.
72 Ibid. and Handwritten Notes Shepard Stone, Fiuggi, Box 56-341, FFA.
73 As Gallois put it: "Experience of the past years has shown the vulnerability of Western policies to the pressures of public opinion, which is almost systemati-cally wrong when the very conditions of its existence are concerned." See Pierre M. Gallois, "Modern Weapons and Disarmament in the context of Western Security," Box 60, Folder 4, Nitze Papers, 8–9.
74 Ibid., 8.
75 Ibid., 11.
76 In a subsequent article in *Foreign Affairs*, Kissinger argued that a European IRBM force "[...] should not be under United States but under NATO control [...]." Kissinger, "Missiles," 392.
77 Ambassador Quaroni, "Review of the political situation since the Fiuggi Con-ference," Box 191, Bilderberg Archives, NANL.
78 Wilgress to Pearson, "The Present Position of NATO," October 15, 1957, *Documents on Canadian External Relations*, Vol. 24, No. 184.
79 Pierre Dupuy, "Conference of Bilderberg Group," Box 130993, FO 371, NAL.
80 There is a reference in the Policy Planning Staff Files to Nitze's Report in Henry Owen's Files, Box 181, Lot 67D548, NARA.
81 See Smith, *Disarming Diplomat*. The Policy Planning staff kept a voluminous "Nitze File."
82 "Memorandum on S/P Discussion of NATO and Related Problems, July 11 and 15," July 19, 1957, Box 175, Lot 67D548, Chronological File Leon Fuller, NARA.
83 On the Gaither Report, see Divine, *The Sputnik Challenge*; Kaplan, *The Wizards of Armageddon*; Roman, *Eisenhower and the Missile Gap*; and Snead, *The Gaither Committee*. For a contemporary account based on leaks from members of the Gaither Committee, see Chalmers M. Roberts, "Enormous Arms Outlay Is Held Vital to Survival", December 20, 1957, *The Washington Post*, A1. For the first attempt to analyze the impact of the report, based partly on interviews

with Nitze, see Halperin, "The Gaither Committee." On Nitze's thinking, see Milne, *Worldmaking*, 298–299 and Thompson, *The Hawk and the Dove*, 165.

84 The term 'second-strike' was made famous by Albert Wohlstetter, a RAND Corporation analyst, who had advised the Gaither Committee on the vulnerability of the US retaliatory forces. For Wohlstetter's views, see Wohlstetter, "The Delicate Balance of Terror."

85 Snead comes to the conclusion that Nitze's influence on the final report was not as large as is often said. Steven Rearden, who after all co-wrote Nitze's memoirs, supports Snead on this point. See Rearden, "Feature Review," 155.

86 "Deterrence and Survival in the Nuclear Age," November 7, 1957.

87 On this point, see Divine, *Sputnik Challenge*, 39 ff. Eisenhower knew that the threat of Soviet ICBMs was exaggerated, but he decided not to make this information public because it came from highly secret U-2 plane flights over the Soviet Union.

88 For a detailed look at the Bilderberg discussions on disengagement, see Gijswijt, "The Bilderberg Group and the End of the Cold War."

89 Meeting of the Steering Committee, London, January 10–12, 1958, Box 46, Bilderberg Archives, NANL.

90 See Zetsche, "The Quest for Atlanticism," on the role of Christopher Emmet and the American Council on Germany.

91 Labour MP George Brown was another newcomer. Other participants included Fritz Erler, John Ferguson, Sir Colin Gubbins, Jens Hauge, Denis Healey, Michael Heilperin, Lord John Hope, Antoine Pinay, Pietro Quaroni, Paul Rijkens, Shepard Stone, Paul van Zeeland, and James Zellerbach. See Enlarged Steering Committee Meeting, April 25–26, 1958, Box 47, Bilderberg Archives, NANL.

92 Cyrus Sulzberger, "'Incompossibility' and the Summit", *The New York Times*, May 4, 1958, 28.

93 Shepard Stone, "Bilderberg Meeting, Fiuggi, Italy", Berlin October 13, 1957, Box 56-341, FFA.

94 This has been recognized in the literature. See Grabbe, *Unionsparteien*, 252.

95 See Soell, *Erler*, 368–369.

96 Dean Acheson and Marshall Shulman "The Western Approach to Soviet Russia," Box 13, Bilderberg Archives, NANL.

97 On the other hand, General Schuyler did admit that it was doubtful whether an attack directly involving Soviet forces could remain limited.

98 See Craig and Logevall, *America's Cold War*, 179–183; and Tucker, *The China Threat*.

99 Quaroni, "A Survey of International Events," Box 298, Gaitskell Papers, UCL.

100 Nitze Notes. Box 60, Folder 5, Nitze Papers, LoC.

101 Ormsby-Gore, "Bilderberg Conference Group Meeting 13–15 September 1958," Box 137746, FO 371, NAL.

102 Nitze Notes, Box 60, Folder 5, Nitze Papers, LoC.

103 Buxton Report, 3, Box 13, Bilderberg Archives, NANL.

104 Harsch to Meyers, September 17, 1958, Box 20, Harsch Papers, WHS.

105 Ormsby-Gore, "Bilderberg Conference Group Meeting 13–15 September 1958," Box 137746, FO 371, NAL.

106 For a detailed look at how the Bilderberg discussions on China influenced US elite opinion over time, see Banyan, "The Bilderberg Connection." Banyan notes that several US Bilderbergers, including Dean and Johnson, were involved in a number of important think tanks studies concerning China.

107 This quotation comes from a report written by one of the British participants, Henry Tiarks, that he sent to the Foreign Office. Henry Tiarks Report, Box 137746, FO 371, NAL.

108 Bird, *The Chairman*, 474. Note that Bird is wrong about the location of Buxton, calling it a North Carolina oceanside resort.

109 Harsch to Retinger, October 31, 1958, Box 20, Harsch Papers, WHS.

110 Marquis Childs, "Washington Calling," *Ocala Star-Banner*, October 9, 1958, quoted by Banyan, "The Bilderberg Connection." McCloy told Prince Bernhard in March 1959:

> I very much enjoyed my visit to Buxton but I felt it was regrettable that some of those who were in attendance there seem to have spoken rather freely before some newspaper people. Accounts did appear in the papers which purported to give some of the exchanges which had taken place during our discussions. I do not believe great harm was done but inasmuch as it was the first time that I am aware of any comments appearing in the newspaper regarding your meetings, I thought you might have felt concerned.

Box 193, Bilderberg Archives, NANL.

111 The official documents contain many references to the importance of allied opinion. As Dulles himself said on October 8, 1958: "Chiang must realize, or be made to realize, that he has just had a narrow escape. We have had to strain our relations with Congress and with foreign governments to almost the breaking point to save him this time." https://history.state.gov/historicaldocuments/frus1958-60v19/d169. Accessed March 10, 2018. The harmful impact of the Taiwan Straits crisis on US relations with NATO also received prominent attention in the American media. Max Ascoli, for example, argued in the October 16 issue of *The Reporter*: "Our country cannot afford to jeopardize its system of alliances for the sake of placating the American constituency of the Kuomintang."

112 E. W. Kenworthy, "Taiwan in effect accepts two-China policy," *The New York Times*, October 26, 1958.

113 Schmid's 7-page account was sent to all Bilderberg steering committee members. "Compte rendu d'une conversation récente avec Monsieur N. Krushchev," Box 1640, Carlo Schmid Papers, FES. Prince Bernhard's handwritten notes of the meeting are in Box 194, Bilderberg Archives, NANL.

114 See Bennett to Ormsby-Gore, March 23, 1959, Box 146257, FO 371, NAL.

115 Prince Bernhard Handwritten Notes (emphasis in original), Box 194, Bilderberg Archives, NANL.

116 Smith, *Disarming Diplomat*, 59–60.

117 On the public pressure for disarmament, see Nehring, *Politics of Security*; and Wittner, *Resisting the Bomb*.

8 The return of nationalism
From de Gaulle to Kennedy

Until the late 1950s, most Bilderberg participants probably agreed that European integration generally strengthened the Atlantic alliance. However, after the end of the French Fourth Republic and the return to power of President Charles de Gaulle in May 1958, this slowly changed. De Gaulle's vision of a more independent, French-led Europe clashed with the supranational political ambitions of Europe's founding fathers. Moreover, de Gaulle's refusal to accept the United States' leadership position within NATO, coupled with his determination to disentangle the French military from NATO integration, questioned the basic Atlanticist consensus underlying the Bilderberg Group.

This chapter explores the resulting tensions in the period 1958–1962, revolving around three key issues: the plans for a Free Trade Area (FTA) linking the Common Market to the rest of the OEEC countries, especially Great Britain; de Gaulle's proposals to create a French-British-American leadership council to deal with global issues; and the nuclear question. The Bilderberg discussions reveal how closely interrelated these issues were. At the same time, the global Cold War kept the Western alliance on edge, with crisis points ranging from Berlin to Algeria, and from New Guinea to the Congo.

For the Bilderberg Group, President de Gaulle's authoritarian nationalism meant a serious challenge to the internationalist, global mindset of most of its participants. Perhaps even more important than de Gaulle's ideas were his style and methods of communication. De Gaulle's preference to deal only with fellow leaders, his tendency not to inform even his closest advisors of important decisions, and his Hobbesian conviction that nations do not have friends, only interests, were hardly compatible with Bilderberg's reliance on informal discussions and international understanding. As a result, French interest in Bilderberg seemed to be in terminal decline right at the moment that Retinger retired as secretary general in 1959.

The Free Trade Area, 1958–1960

General de Gaulle returned to power in May 1958, after the French Fourth Republic seemed unable to stop its slow slide into a civil war over the

Algerian crisis. De Gaulle was perceived to be the only statesman possessing the prestige and toughness necessary to bring the Algerian war to an end. As a result, even socialists such as Guy Mollet voted for a new constitution giving the president of the Fifth Republic far-reaching constitutional powers, especially in the fields of foreign and defense policy.

President de Gaulle did not hesitate to make use of these powers. He quickly and determinedly challenged many of the assumptions on which the Atlantic alliance and the European Communities were founded. De Gaulle's fundamental purpose was to return France on the world stage as a great power. This corresponded with his deeply held views about the historical role France had to play in the world. But it was also de Gaulle's answer to the difficult question of how France could restore its self-confidence after a prolonged period of national failure. The guiding principle of all his actions was simple: "France is only France when she is in the first rank."[1]

One of the most important implications was that de Gaulle could not tolerate the predominant American leadership position in NATO. Furthermore, with respect to the European Economic Community (EEC), de Gaulle refused to accept the supranational political aims Mollet and the other founding fathers had associated with the Brussels communities. In May 1958, of course, no one knew exactly what de Gaulle planned to do. But one thing was clear: as Dulles told Spaak after his first conversation with de Gaulle in July 1958, "We shall have a rough time."[2]

Not surprisingly, many feared first and foremost for the future of the EEC. De Gaulle had consistently opposed plans for supranational integration and could easily wreck the newly founded Common Market. After all, the first six years of the EEC were a crucially important period, since many of the most difficult issues – including a common agricultural policy – had been left unresolved; the most far-reaching measures to eradicate trade barriers and abolish the veto in the decision-making process of the European Communities would not come into force until the mid 1960s.

Unexpectedly, however, President de Gaulle accepted the Common Market as an important device to modernize and strengthen the French economy. Moreover, his financial advisors Antoine Pinay and Jacques Rueff – who both participated in the September 1958 Bilderberg conference in Buxton – convinced him that France needed to devalue the franc, reign in her budget deficits, and open up her economy to foreign competition in a concerted effort to restore confidence in the currency, reverse the balance of payments difficulties, and bring down inflation.[3] By pushing through this program, de Gaulle made it possible for France to take part in the first scheduled reduction of trade barriers among the Six in January 1959 and in effect saved the Common Market.[4] Both de Gaulle's acceptance of the EEC and his courageous economic program earned him a great deal of political capital in pro-European circles.

De Gaulle took a less benign view of the Free Trade Area proposed by Great Britain in the fall of 1956. He announced in November 1958 – more or less at the same time as Khrushchev's Berlin ultimatum – that he did not expect the FTA negotiations with Great Britain and the other members of the OEEC to succeed.[5] These negotiations had gone on for over a year in an OEEC committee chaired by Bilderberg steering committee member Reginald Maudling.[6]

The French position angered not only Great Britain, but also most governments of the other five EEC members. Particularly in the Netherlands and in West Germany, many worried about the prospect of a protectionist, French-dominated EEC causing a dangerous split in Europe. In the case of West Germany, however, proponents of the FTA like Ludwig Erhard were held in check by Chancellor Adenauer, who gave priority to building a good relationship with de Gaulle in order to secure French support in the Berlin crisis and the preservation of the Common Market.[7]

The Bilderberg organizers quickly decided to organize another enlarged steering committee meeting at the Bilderberg Hotel (January 17–19, 1959) to discuss the FTA crisis. As Retinger told Johnson:

> we believe that the collapse of negotiations between the "Six" and the rest of Europe may be extremely dangerous and possibly lead to an economic war in Europe; this situation may bring about the collapse of a number of European official organisations, such as the European Payments Union, the Common Market itself, the Council of Europe and may also influence the future of NATO. I have had an opportunity of consulting a number of people in authority and members of the governments of different European countries and in the eyes of many the situation looks disastrous. On the other hand, there is some hope that our private and confidential exchange of views may have some fruitful influence on the final deliberations of the official bodies. Incidentally, Reginald Maudling told me yesterday that some members of the OEEC are trying to postpone their meeting on 15th January until after our own meeting in the hope that our discussions may clarify people's minds.[8]

The steering committee meeting was probably the most direct attempt by the Bilderberg organizers to engage in informal diplomacy, and it brought together several of those directly involved in the FTA negotiations: Ernst van der Beugel, a high-level Dutch diplomat close to Foreign Minister Joseph Luns; Reginald Maudling; Alfred Müller-Armack, the secretary of state in Erhard's economics ministry; and Jean Rey, the Belgian member of the EEC Commission responsible for external trade relations. Walter Hallstein, the president of the EEC Commission, planned to come, but had to cancel because of illness. In addition to the FTA negotiators, the heads of the French and German employers' organizations, George Villiers and Fritz Berg, and the Overseas Director of the Federation of British Industries, Peter Tennant, were all present, as was Hubert Ansiaux, the president of the Belgian National Bank.

The other European participants less directly involved in the FTA negotiations were Gianni Agnelli, Raymond Aron, Louis Camu, Hugh Gaitskell, Viscount Kilmuir, Jens Otto Krag, Giovanni Malagodi, Bertil Ohlin, Alberto Pirelli, Jacques Piette, and Otto Wolff. From the United States, George Ball, Arthur Dean, John Ferguson, Jack Heinz, Joseph Johnson, and George Nebolsine were present. They had been briefed on the US position with regard to the FTA by the State Department. Given the sensitivity of the issue, it was agreed that George Ball would prepare a position paper that would guide the American participants in the discussion.[9]

Just before the Bilderberg meeting, Gaitskell travelled to France – in his own words, in order "to find out what I could about the background of the Free Trade Area – Common Market negotiations." He met with President de Gaulle, Prime Minister Debré, Foreign Minister Couve de Murville, and a number of politicians and journalists. With respect to the general political situation in France, Gaitskell remained concerned about extreme right-wing forces in the country: "Some say that Soustelle, with the help of the Army, will get rid of de Gaulle; others that de Gaulle will allow himself to become the instrument of the Fascists; others that de Gaulle will become more authoritarian." With respect to the future of the European Communities, Gaitskell asked de Gaulle directly "if he thought the Common Market would lead to political union." The French president pointedly answered that it was "a purely commercial affair."[10]

De Gaulle's refusal to accept the EEC as a political project was at the heart of the central paradox that would determine the European scene for a decade: the ever-present possibility of destroying the European Communities enabled de Gaulle to basically blackmail pro-European forces – from Jean Monnet to Konrad Adenauer – into supporting him on all developments concerning the Common Market. Because decision-making by the Six was unanimous, there was little the other Five could do about this.

Raymond Aron was mainly responsible at Hotel de Bilderberg for trying to explain the French position. He argued that the breakdown in the negotiations was partly based on France's long history of protectionism. At the same time, the fact that the Common Market was much more than a simple free trade area explained why Paris was reluctant to give preferential treatment to the other eleven OEEC members without a harmonization of social policies, a common external tariff, or the coordination of economic policies.[11] Fritz Berg had contributed a paper arguing for a gradual, sector-by-sector approach to the FTA question and Maudling and several others attempted to push this as the basis for new negotiations. Aron, however, doubted whether the French government would be interested. Moreover, any halfway solution was likely to breach existing GATT rules. In addition, many in the French political and administrative class continued to regard the common market as "morally and politically" different from a classic free trade area.[12]

Several of the French and Italian participants, including Malagodi, Piette, and Quaroni, underlined Aron's point about the political importance of the common market. As Quaroni put it, the idea of Europe had a certain "mystic content":

> I don't think that 99% of the people in Europe have the faintest idea what the common market means. They simply think of the common market as something which will stop French, Germans, Italians to look at each other like dogs, or worse, and think in terms of facing the common danger. And if when the European Army failed, we could more or less fill the gap. If the common market fails, I really don't know what we can invent to fill this gap. I am very much afraid of the consequences, the moral consequences in most European countries when the youth cannot hope anymore for European integration.[13]

Malagodi likewise emphasized the political importance of the Six and drew attention to the Cold War context of the Common Market, which had been discussed at length at previous Bilderberg meetings:

> The community is coming to represent in [terms of] political feeling, and I would like to underscore the word 'feeling' of the 6 countries, certainly of our own country, something which is irreplaceable. If tomorrow we were confronted with a breakdown of the community, we would all feel that something very dangerous was happening to each of our countries. We are under tremendous pressure from the East; altogether at our Eastern frontier, and in the case of some of us, the French and ourselves, also internally. The community does represent today the feeling of many of our people, the ultimate guarantee, internal guarantee, against that.[14]

Van der Beugel acknowledged the political importance of the Six but warned that the French attitude carried grave dangers for the future of the European community. In a community of six nations, he argued, certain compromises were necessary; however, it was not acceptable for one of its members to continuously impose its will on the other five. As Van der Beugel put it:

> the compromises we have reached until now are compromises which have asked very much from those partners in the 6 who are very positive towards the Free Trade Zone and the moment may come, if that is going on, that the life of the community itself may be in danger.[15]

Other FTA proponents, including Maudling, Gaitskell, and Ohlin, added that the political and economic consequence of failure would be dramatic. Gaitskell warned that Great Britain would likely form its own free trade area if the Six refused to compromise.

Jean Rey, reflecting the difficult position the newly founded European Commission found itself in, called for patience and understanding for the French position. The Commission was responsible for coming up with a plan for future negotiations in April, but it could ill-afford to start a fight with one of the most powerful members of the Six before it had really started functioning. Meanwhile the German participants found themselves in between the two fronts, calling for a pragmatic approach.

Although the enlarged steering committee meeting did not bring a solution to the FTA controversy any nearer, it did result in several new diplomatic channels: Jean Rey proposed informal discussions between Maudling and the Commission and Van der Beugel and Müller-Armack promised to keep each other informed about their dealings with the Commission.[16] "I have just come back from Paris," Retinger told Johnson, "where I had long talks with Pinay and Baumgartner about our last meeting. They both think that it will prove to be helpful and Maudling thinks that some progress is being made."[17]

Perhaps the most important result of the meeting, however, was a crystallization of attitudes concerning the European implications of President de Gaulle's return to power. Ernst van der Beugel's report on the meeting for Minister Luns was particularly revealing. After emphasizing that the discussions had been more open and informal than would have been possible at an official gathering, Van der Beugel expressed grave worries about the French position regarding Europe:

> I have come to the conclusion that France has attached itself to the Europe of the Six, not because it wants integration, but because it wants to achieve leadership of this group. Villiers and Professor Aron, who are both close to the government, have left absolutely no room for misunderstanding about this.

Van der Beugel was convinced that France had no intention of accepting the FTA even if every single one of her economic demands was granted. The European Commission would support Paris because of the political importance of the Europe of the Six – the "European mysticism," in Van der Beugel's words. Ironically, however, "the French government will never agree to a form of political integration that is acceptable to the other partners. Only a political integration under complete French leadership."

Ambassador Quaroni, Van der Beugel wrote, had confirmed this analysis, saying "we, Italians, Germans and Dutchmen have to choose between integration under French hegemony or no integration at all." Van der Beugel added that there was little hope for support from Bonn, since Adenauer "no longer pays attention to any advice and will, so it is expected, accept every French condition as long as the Europe of the Six exists." Van der Beugel concluded that The Hague had to prepare for an extremely difficult period in European affairs. He emphasized that to him personally "the Europe of the Six as an instrument of French hegemony is completely unacceptable." Finally, Van der Beugel pointed out that all political life beneath President De Gaulle had ceased to exist and called the French Fifth Republic an "absolute monarchy without the mistresses."[18]

Van der Beugel's report is significant not just because he would soon succeed Retinger as secretary general of the Bilderberg Group, but also because it already contained the essential arguments and positions that would later fuel the Dutch opposition to de Gaulle's proposal for a confederal European political organization. This so-called Fouchet Plan – named after the French negotiator Christian Fouchet – ultimately failed in 1962, largely because of suspicions in The Hague and Brussels about de Gaulle's intentions and his authoritarianism.[19] Van der Beugel, who remained close to Luns after returning to private life in 1959, and many other Dutch diplomats thought that the alliance between the pro-Europeans and General de Gaulle was a marriage of convenience, which would only last as long as the deep-seated political differences between the two groups could be ignored. The long-term Gaullist political design, they were convinced, was fundamentally incompatible with the integrative aims of the pro-Europeans.

Fritz Berg returned from the meeting a little less pessimistic than Van der Beugel. He told the BDI *Präsidium* that his proposal for a flexible solution to the FTA problem had been well received.[20] Peter Tennant, on the other hand, broadly shared Van der Beugel's views, telling Maudling that neither the French nor the Commission would agree to a compromise solution acceptable to the UK. Tennant underlined the essentially political nature of the problem, writing: "[t]he Rome Treaty is a political document disguised in economic jargon." Based on the Bilderberg discussions, he concluded that there remained a "deep suspicion" on the continent that the British were "merely paying lip-service to European unity."[21] Therefore, any British pressure on the Five or threats of British economic reprisals against France only served to rally the Six together.[22]

"There seems to be little doubt," Tennant continued,

> that with de Gaulle in the position of a benevolent despot in France he is the only man who can exert any influence at all. His Ministers and Civil Servants are treated as lackeys and are expected to do what they are told, even if it involves sudden changes of policy.[23]

Given the political nature of the problem, a meeting between Macmillan and de Gaulle might be the only way to produce a solution. If no progress turned out to be possible, the UK should first disengage temporarily in order to build up its own economic activity and put additional pressure on the Six. At the same time, the UK should attempt to create a wedge between the Commission and the member governments of the EEC. "Personally," Tennant told Retinger ten days later, "I think the auguries are now fairly hopeful and there now seems every chance of a meeting between Macmillan and de Gaulle."[24]

The assessments by Van der Beugel and Tennant carried several implications for all diplomatic dealings with France. First, any negotiation involving Frenchmen other than de Gaulle would always be subject to sudden reversals or changes depending on the general's attitude. Second, the weakness of democratic political life in the Fifth Republic was bound to be resented by France's Western partners in the long run. For now, many in the West accepted de Gaulle because he was widely judged to be the only one capable of bringing the Algerian war to an end. But this could not be expected to last forever.

Bilderberg and the Gaullist challenge to NATO

For the Bilderberg Group, the French situation posed a serious problem. If political life under de Gaulle had ceased to exist, as Van der Beugel put it, then how could France continue to make a serious contribution to the Bilderberg meetings? Moreover, French interest in the Bilderberg Group seemed to have declined considerably since de Gaulle had become president. At the same time, President de Gaulle had been remarkably successful in raising France's international standing as a result of his much-noted state visits to Great Britain and the United States in April 1960, his insistence on equal treatment within NATO, and his unruffled handling of the 1960 Paris Summit (not to mention the first major French nuclear explosion in February).

De Gaulle's first challenge to NATO had come in September 1958, when he secretly proposed a tripartite Franco-British-American directorate in NATO to Eisenhower and Macmillan. De Gaulle wished both to achieve recognition of France's global interests and to end the American de facto control of NATO nuclear policy.[25] He was not prepared to accept anything less than equal status of France in the alliance. Moreover, he expressed his fundamental opposition to military integration in NATO. De Gaulle maintained in his memoirs that the September memorandum was the first move in a process of disengaging France from NATO in order to restore her freedom of action.

Whatever de Gaulle's exact motives in 1958, his memorandum inevitably caused great consternation within NATO. The fact that he sent the West Germans and Italians versions of the memorandum that were different – and less offensive – than the original only increased the opposition of these and other, smaller NATO members to de Gaulle's plans.[26] President Eisenhower, however, was in fact willing to go quite far in accommodating de Gaulle's wishes. In December 1959, the president even agreed to hold secret tripartite meetings.[27] He also indicated that the US was prepared to assist the French nuclear program.

Yet Eisenhower's hands were tied by Congress and internal divisions within his administration. The JAEC vetoed an American offer to sell France a nuclear-powered submarine. Moreover, by late 1959 both the State

Department and General Norstad strongly opposed giving bilateral nuclear aid to France. De Gaulle's record, after all, seemed to indicate that such aid would not secure a more positive French attitude towards NATO. In the summer of 1958, de Gaulle had refused the deployment of intermediate-range ballistic missiles on French soil if they were not at least partly under exclusive French control. In March 1959, the French president announced the withdrawal of the Mediterranean fleet from NATO's integrated command. Later that year, he declined to give approval to the stockpiling of US nuclear weapons in France – forcing Norstad to remove all American fighter planes from France – and refused to participate in NATO's integrated air defense system. Dulles' prediction of a "rough time" for the alliance had been right on the mark.

A new team of Bilderberg organizers now had to deal with the question of French participation after Retinger's retirement in 1959. At the 1959 Bilderberg in Yeşilköy, Turkey, the steering committee unanimously accepted Prince Bernhard's proposal to ask Ernst van der Beugel to be Retinger's successor in the role of honorary secretary general.[28] As Rijkens told Healey:

> We all know how difficult it will be to replace [Retinger], and also how few people there are who can approximately approach Joseph's merits in the Bilderberg set-up. It was therefore something like general relief when Mr. van der Beugel accepted the nomination.[29]

Van der Beugel had earned his stripes as a diplomat in the 1940s working on the Marshall Plan and the founding of the OEEC, and he remained a committed Atlanticist for the rest of his life.[30] He had also been deeply involved in the Rome Treaties negotiations and was convinced that the Europe of the Six should develop as a liberal, outward-looking group. His resulting critical attitude towards Gaullist France was evident at the 1959 steering committee meeting. Van der Beugel left government in 1959 and joined KLM as a vice-president. After four not altogether successful years at KLM, Van der Beugel decided to leave and combined his Bilderberg activities with a professorship in Atlantic Studies at Leiden University.

Van der Beugel was much less of a Europeanist than Retinger, with his long history in the European Movement. This probably explains why Retinger, who would have preferred Van Kleffens to Van der Beugel as his successor, was not happy about the decision to move the Bilderberg secretariat from London to the Netherlands and to replace his assistant Pomian with another Dutch diplomat: Arnold Lamping, a former ambassador in Bonn.[31] Retinger's attempt to prevent these changes failed, however, after Prince Bernhard asked him rather sternly to refrain from further involvement.[32]

In terms of personality, Van der Beugel was certainly a worthy successor to Retinger, with a similarly well-developed sense of humor, a deep love of culture (opera in particular), and a talent for dinner-table story telling. As his friend Kissinger wrote about him upon Van der Beugel's retirement from Bilderberg in 1980: "I know no one who is a more reliable human being, a steadier companion, a more charming conversationalist." Prince Bernhard called him "perfect for this difficult job, thanks to his outstanding talents, his great enthusiasm, and his gift to inspire and stimulate people – the right man on the right place."[33]

The 1960 Bilderberg conference at the Bürgenstock near Luzern, Switzerland (May 28–29), was the first to be organized by Van der Beugel and Lamping, and they immediately faced the problem of French participation.[34] Since Mollet and Pinay no longer played an active role in the steering committee, Wilfrid Baumgartner was the main Bilderberger responsible for suggesting French participants. However, because Baumgartner had just become minister of finance, he had little time to assist the Bilderberg organizers.

Lamping, frustrated after weeks of not being able to get hold of Baumgartner, noted in early May that only two Frenchmen had participated in the last two Bilderberg conferences and called the "decline of French interest remarkable." This was unfortunate, he thought,

> because the prestige of de Gaulle – and therefore of France – has grown considerably in recent weeks and no international problem can profitably be discussed without hearing the voice of France. If we will have to accept another weak French delegation this year, this will be more worrisome than in past years when France wasn't taken fully seriously.[35]

On the other side of the Atlantic, Heinz and Ball too had expressed their concerns about French participation in the upcoming conference. As Lamping put it:

> we may personally lament what is going on in France, we may think of de Gaulle's behavior and policies whatever we want; politically and strategically France remains a decisive factor on the world stage. Our American friends are completely right when they point to the eminent importance for the Bilderberg-combination tied to a strong and representative French participation.[36]

In the Federal Republic, Wolff and Mueller agreed that it would be "pointless" to continue the Bilderberg meetings without French participation.[37]

In the end, after the Dutch Ambassador in Paris, former Minister of Foreign Affairs Beyen, intervened with de Gaulle personally, French participation in the Bürgenstock conference was acceptable. Frequent Bilderbergers Aron, Baumgartner, and Piette were joined by first-time participant George Pompidou, a Gaullist close to the French president.[38] Still, the problem of French participation would continue to trouble the Bilderberg organizers in years to come. In addition to a certain Gaullist reluctance to engage in transatlantic meetings, French political sensitivity seemed to be part of the problem. As Lamping noted: "The French shouldn't get the impression that they will be faced with a crushing Anglo-Saxon majority, in the face of which even their continental friends will melt away: this in itself would suffice to annoy the French."[39]

The Bürgenstock conference, May 1960

The first part of the Bürgenstock conference was devoted to the failed East-West Summit in Paris, broken off by Khrushchev ostensibly because of the shooting down of an American U-2 spy plane over Soviet territory a week earlier. C. D. Jackson acknowledged that the Eisenhower Administration had botched the public relations aspect of the U-2 affair, calling it "unfortunate" that the President initially denied knowledge of the U-2 overflight. Tongue slightly in cheek, Jackson explained the episode by saying that "for a whole variety of reasons, we [Americans] suffer from a boy scout complex and there is nothing more distressing than when a boy scout is caught in the jam closet."

On a more serious note, Jackson argued that the real reason for the Summit's failure had been that Khrushchev had recognized that the Western position on Berlin was firm: "he wanted to come back to Moscow with a Berlin concession from us, and when he discovered that that was not likely to take place, the summit became very unattractive to him." The U-2 incident simply "furnished him with a gold plated excuse having tremendous propaganda advantages, which he could use to torpedo the summit." President Eisenhower, meanwhile, was "terribly disappointed, terribly hurt and terribly angry." In the last phase of his presidency, Jackson argued, Eisenhower "really deep in his heart wanted to emerge, wanted to leave the White House as a President who had really brought some kind of peace to the world."[40]

Opinions at the Bilderberg meeting were divided over how to judge Mr. K. – as Khrushchev was called, almost affectionately, in the conference report. NATO Secretary General Spaak mentioned his recent talk with Yugoslav leader Tito, who was convinced that Khrushchev had to deal with substantial opposition to his leadership in Moscow. Spaak also thought that the fact that it took Khrushchev a week to respond to the U-2 affair indicated that he initially hoped to prevent a breakdown of relations with Eisenhower. Apparently under pressure from Soviet hardliners, Khrushchev was forced to change tactics after Eisenhower took full responsibility for the U-2 overflights in a press conference. Spaak added that he thought Khrushchev was something of a communist heretic, more pragmatic than ideological. In terms of the West's posture towards the Soviet Union, this meant, Spaak argued, that firmness should be combined with a certain flexibility.[41]

Several speakers agreed with this assessment, but others, including Raymond Aron, voiced doubts and maintained that Khrushchev's aims were broadly the same as Stalin's. Pierre Dupuy reported the impression of many diplomats in Paris that Khrushchev was a sick and tired man. Some even speculated that he might be gone in a few months' time. Again, Aron sounded a note of caution, reminding everyone that Khrushchev was still in the driving seat and that the "temperature of Cold War is a function of what Mr. K. wants." Heilperin contributed the view that Khrushchev had "out-promised" himself in the domestic field – he could not deliver the increase in living standards promised to the Soviet people, so what better way to retreat than "stepping up the cold war."[42]

With respect to future Soviet tactics in the Berlin question, Pietro Quaroni and Carlo Schmid both warned that the Berlin problem would not go away by itself and that a new Soviet initiative was only a matter of time. C. D. Jackson agreed and delivered a typical call for common action:

> there is no question but that there is going to be another [Soviet] move. The West has fallen into the habit of scoring points by getting out of tight fixes, heaving a great sigh of relief, and then going off to have a Martini at 5.30. That 5.30 whistle never blows in the Kremlin, and these gentlemen are hard at work at the moment preparing the next 'sale coup' which is sure to come and probably very soon.[43]

Jackson blamed the West as a whole, but many participants at Bürgenstock thought that a primary cause for Western weakness was a lack of American leadership. Denis Healey said so openly and was only opposed by Robert Murphy.

The second day of the conference was reserved exclusively for the rift between the Six and the UK-led Seven. After the final breakdown of the FTA negotiations in March 1959, the British had decided to organize the Seven into a counter-group to put pressure on the Six. The European Free Trade Area (EFTA), which also included Austria, Denmark, Norway, Portugal, Sweden, and Switzerland, was up and running by the time of the Bürgenstock meeting. The schism in Europe many had feared was now a reality. The proponents of the Common Market, however, were unapologetic at Bürgenstock. If anything, they were on the offensive.

Paul-Henri Spaak and Robert Marjolin, now a member of the Commission in Brussels, put forward several arguments in favor of the Six and did so in the strongest possible terms. Supported by other pro-Europeans such as the Dutch politician Pieter Blaisse (KVP), they emphasized three points. First, contrary to what Great Britain might have hoped and expected, the EEC "was now an accomplished, irreversible fact" – as the Bürgenstock report put it. The fact that the Commission had proposed plans for an acceleration of the transition to the Common Market had proven that the Six were determined to proceed quickly. In other words, attempts by the British to dissolve the EEC in a wider European trade area could not succeed. Second, the political aspect of the European Communities was crucial. The Six should be regarded as the nucleus of a politically united Europe open to other countries. The political nature of the EEC was embodied in the fact that the Rome Treaties "were an indissoluble whole." The common external tariff was "only one element of a vast political, economic and social system, from which it could not be detached."[44] Spaak in particular underlined this point, calling the Rome Treaty a "stage in the movement toward European unification" and attacking the position of the Seven as "fundamentally and radically false."[45] Finally, they defended the EEC against the often-heard accusation that it was a protectionist, inward-looking bloc. They emphasized that the Six were not only committed to the reduction of trade impediments, but also welcomed any new members.

The American delegation at Bürgenstock mainly supported the Marjolin-Spaak line. The American *rapporteur* on the topic – probably George Ball – explained that the Common Market had been hailed in the United States as an important step toward a politically unified Europe. "On the other hand, the European Free Trade Association did not represent the same aspiration, at least not in the political field, and this had led to a certain American hesitation with regard to it."[46] Edward M. Martin, who was shortly to become assistant secretary of state for Economic and Business Affairs, highlighted the importance of lowering trade barriers in view of the US balance of payment deficit of the last two years. The United States would either have to increase its exports or diminish its expenditures abroad. As a result, Martin said, both the EEC and EFTA would be pressured to further open their markets to American products, as well as to conform to GATT rules. Moreover, to strengthen the economic ties between Europe and North America, the United States and Canada would join the OEEC countries in the Organization for Economic Cooperation and Development (OECD) which was to replace the OEEC.[47]

By all accounts, the Bürgenstock discussion of the Six and the Seven was extremely frank. After the conference, Jackson told Prince Bernhard, who had spent the second day of the conference sick in bed:

> I am sure that you got a report about the fascinating discussion on the Six and the Seven. It was so good that I would not be a bit surprised if this particular Bilderberg did indeed affect history, inasmuch as both sides heard some very plain and forceful truth to which they appeared to be paying considerable attention.[48]

Eelco van Kleffens was also impressed. In a letter to the President of the ECSC, he reported that the Americans were clearly in favor of the Six. "For the case of the Seven," he wrote, "it was a bad day."[49]

Another report on the meeting was written by Kurt Birrenbach, a first-time Bilderberg participant. Birrenbach was a prominent member of the CDU and an industrialist with close ties to Krupp and the BDI.[50] He was accomplished at international networking, an active member of the DGAP and someone frequently used by the Bonn government for discreet diplomatic missions abroad. Birrenbach favored a flexible solution to Europe's trade difficulties and was obviously shaken by the Bürgenstock discussion. He sent his notes to Adenauer, Foreign Minister Heinrich von Brentano and others, writing:

> The speeches by Marjolin and Spaak, as well as to a lesser degree some of the other interventions by participants from the Six, showed an attitude towards the solution of the European trade problem that could not be detected before. Marjolin rejected the idea of a Free Trade Area in the strongest possible way, even on the basis of participation by the EEC as a whole, and demanded a similar political goal as a nonnegotiable justification for association with the common market. Spaak went even further, both in the sharpness of the manner in which he presented his thoughts, and in the explicit way in which he demanded the acceptance of full political integration in return for the solution of the European trade issue.[51]

In general, two conclusions could be drawn from the Bürgenstock discussion. First, the British had obviously failed in their attempts to force a purely economic solution to the European trade problem. Despite strong support for a free trade area in several member states of the EEC, there could be little doubt that the Six remained intent on forging an economic and political union. The Bürgenstock meeting also confirmed that the Six could count on strong support from the United States in this respect. The Americans treated the EEC as an entirely different entity than the British-led EFTA. No doubt this led to fears in the UK that the special relationship with the United States was in danger of crumbling with the advent of a strong, united grouping on the continent.[52] To make matters worse – from the British perspective – the unholy alliance between pro-Europeans and Gaullists showed no signs of faltering.

The second conclusion followed logically. In these circumstances, the only way to overcome the economic split in Europe was for the United Kingdom either to become a full or an associate member of the EEC. This was exactly what Frederick M. Bennett, a conservative MP and Maudling's principal assistant, took away from the meeting. Bennett indicated privately during the Bürgenstock conference that London was ready to accept the political purpose of the EEC. He told Kurt Birrenbach that the British were willing to consider an associate membership along the lines sketched by Birrenbach in his response to Spaak's statement. Birrenbach had opposed Spaak's position with regard to a political entrance fee for British participation in the Common Market. Instead of full membership, Birrenbach argued, the UK should only accept the harmonization of most tariffs, the inclusion of agriculture, and the coordination of trade and economic policy. Some kind of institutional framework could then be found, which would allow the Six to deepen their political cooperation and which would allow the British to maintain their special relationship with the Commonwealth countries.[53]

Bennett's interest in Birrenbach's proposals was an indication of the change in British thinking that took place around this time. Shortly after the Bürgenstock conference, both *The Economist* and *The Observer* spoke out in favor of full British membership in the EEC.[54] Meanwhile, a high-level review of Britain's European policy, headed by Permanent Secretary at the Treasury Sir Frank Lee, had reached the conclusion that the UK could not afford to remain aloof from the Europe of the Six.[55]

As a result of his Bürgenstock conversations with Bennett, Birrenbach traveled to London in early July, for meetings with Maudling, Bennett, Ormsby-Gore, and others. It is unclear whether Adenauer specifically asked Birrenbach to undertake this mission to London, but Birrenbach kept the chancellor fully informed.[56] As he told Adenauer after his visit, the Macmillan Government was moving in the direction of closer ties with Europe. Prime Minister Macmillan was still undecided, but members of the Conservative Party and several high-placed officials in the Foreign Office were interested in his proposal.[57]

When the British government announced on July 25 that it recognized the impossibility of negotiating a simple Europe-wide FTA, Adenauer quickly indicated that West Germany favored preliminary discussions with London on several of the outstanding problems, including agriculture and the Commonwealth. Yet the German-British rapprochement – partly based on Adenauer's increasing doubts about the reliability of both de Gaulle and the United States – was rather short-lived.[58] By early 1961 it was clear that neither France nor the European Commission were willing to consider an association of Great Britain with the Common Market.

The *coup de grâce* to Birrenbach's association scheme was delivered by none other than George Ball. After John F. Kennedy's election victory in November 1960, Ball had been named under secretary of state for Economic Affairs. Ball's intimate knowledge of the European scene quickly made him the point man responsible for most European questions in the Kennedy Administration, and he was soon promoted to the number-two spot in the State Department. The fact that Ball and the new Secretary of State, Dean Rusk, were "Bilderberg brothers" enabled them to quickly develop a good working relationship.[59]

Ball now pushed through an important change in American policy to-wards the Six and the Seven. In March 1961, he was in London for a meeting of the Development Assistance Group (DAG), an organization inspired by the frequent Bilderberg discussions concerning the Third World and set up by the OECD members with the aim of increasing and coordinating Western development aid. While in London, Ball also met with Edward Heath and Frank Lee, two of the top officials responsible for British policy towards Europe. They asked Ball point-blank whether the Kennedy Administration was in favor of Great Britain joining the Common Market. As Ball later recalled, "this was the first time the question had ever been raised in those terms and there was no such thing as an American policy on the issue."[60] Nonetheless, Ball answered in the affirmative. If Britain was prepared to become a full member and accept the political aspirations of the Six, he said, the United States would regard this as a welcome strengthening of the West.

To Ball's delight, his straightforward talk with Heath and Lee showed immediate effect. During Macmillan's first official meeting with President Kennedy in early April 1961, Britain's relations with Europe and the United States stood high on the agenda.[61] Kennedy had approved the position Ball had taken in London and now left it to Ball to explain US policy to Macmillan. Ball repeated his views about the political importance of full British membership. He argued that it was uncertain what would happen in West Germany and France after Adenauer and de Gaulle left the scene. Therefore, it was highly desirable that the United Kingdom would "help cement the German ties to the West and provide cohesion."[62]

Macmillan asked and received assurances from President Kennedy and Ball that British membership in the EEC would not harm British relations with the United States. In reply, the president emphasized that he regarded British membership as an important step towards a more viable Atlantic Community.[63] During dinner the following evening, Macmillan took Ball aside and told him: "we are going to do this thing." It would not be easy – Macmillan expected major trouble from de Gaulle – but he was now determined to apply for British membership. Ball used the 1961 Bilderberg meeting in Canada two weeks later to underline the attitude of the Kennedy Administration towards the EEC-EFTA issue. In a fifteen-minute *tour d'horizon*, he explained that the United States regarded EFTA as a group "devoid of political overtones" and was in favor of "the largest possible number of the Seven joining the Common Market. That would be a very helpful step."[64]

The Kennedy Administration

For obvious reasons, President Kennedy's election in November 1960 drew much attention in Bilderberg circles. A key feature of the Bilderberg Group – namely that a sizeable number of its participants were drawn from those not currently in power – seemed to have paid off: several influential new members of the Kennedy Administration were (former) Bilderbergers, from Secretary of State Dean Rusk to George Ball, Paul Nitze (who became assistant secretary of defense for International Security Affairs at the Pentagon), George McGhee (who first headed the Policy Planning staff and later became ambassador to Germany), and National Security Advisor McGeorge Bundy. Dean Acheson and Henry Kissinger, moreover, served as advisors on NATO and the Berlin crisis.

Whether the new administration would succeed in providing the kind of leadership in the alliance that had been missing in the final Eisenhower years was a different matter. As Lamping wrote, many Europeans had noted with some trepidation that many of the "new men" seemed to

> have a markedly greater interest in the United Nations and the uncommitted countries than was the case during the Eisenhower Administration. It has been noted that during the campaign, Kennedy talked little of the relationship with Europe, and much more about the underdeveloped nations.[65]

This could easily exacerbate existing transatlantic disagreements over decolonization. As Van der Beugel had told Johnson just before the presidential election:

> I think that one of the basic problems now is that there is a general feeling in Europe (not, repeat not shared by me personally) that Europe suffers from the ambiguity of the U.S. foreign policy towards its European partners: support in Europe; no support in the rest of the world. This brings us approximately to the topic of global U.S. responsibilities, compatible or not compatible with its European alliance.[66]

The 1961 Bilderberg conference in St. Castin, Canada, provided an important opportunity for the Kennedy Administration to present itself to the informal alliance.[67] In Healey's view, "The Americans were clearly anxious to use the meeting for a trial run of some of the new Administration's ideas."[68] Leon Fuller of the State Department's Policy Planning Staff prepared a general memorandum on the agenda of the St. Castin meeting and argued that there was no alternative to an effective Atlantic community to counter the Soviet-Sino threat and to deal with the challenge of the developing nations. Apart from the economic and military strength of the Atlantic nations, Fuller emphasized the importance of shared values within the alliance. "We have a priceless asset," he wrote,

> in the natural, historically derived, affinity of the Western nations for each other and in their sense of being a real community. Despite all obstacles, this makes possible to an exceptional degree a common viewpoint and common policies in international affairs.[69]

These shared values, however, were not in evidence during the Bay of Pigs debacle that unfolded just days before the Bilderberg meeting and prevented Rusk and McGhee from coming to St. Castin. Healey was particularly galled over the American-sponsored intervention in Cuba. He and Gaitskell had spent considerable political capital in trying to convince the Labour Party that the Kennedy Administration was different from previous American administrations and should be cooperated with.[70] At St. Castin,

Healey said the invasion violated the UN Charter, drew a parallel with the Suez crisis, and emphasized that the effect on the alliance and particularly on the developing world was disastrous. The Kennedy Administration had shown that in its "sphere of influence," the United States felt entitled "to overthrow governments of which they disapproved." How could the alliance be expected to follow American leadership, he asked, if the US showed such poor judgment?[71]

Baron Snoy et d'Oppuers, an influential Belgian civil servant, presciently argued that the failure of the invasion had strengthened the Soviet position and invited dangerous counteractions. Earl Jellicoe, a British conservative MP, regretted the lack of consultation on Cuba and asked whether there should not be more consultation on another area of great concern: Southeast Asia. The American participants acknowledged, in the words of Democratic Senator Mike Monroney, the "body blow to U.S. prestige."[72] At the same time, they tried to play down the extent of American involvement. Joseph Johnson rejected the comparison with Suez by pointing out that no Americans were involved in the invasion. In addition, several American participants pointed to the danger of the Communist takeover in Cuba, which might spread to other countries in Latin America.

In a one sense the comparison with Suez was valid: like the Suez crisis, the Cuban invasion proved again how difficult the out-of-area problem was for NATO. Not surprisingly, therefore, the St. Castin discussion of "the role of N.A.T.O. in the world policy of the member countries" was as inconclusive as earlier Bilderberg debates. Lester B. Pearson, the leader of the Canadian Liberal Party, started off the discussion on this point. The fact that the Cold War battlegrounds had shifted from Europe to Asia and Africa created difficulties, he argued, aggravated by the global disruptions of the decolonization process. Because of the "bedeviling influence of colonialism,"[73] Pearson said, certain countries "were pro-Atlantic in Paris but not in New York."[74] The troubles in Angola, Algeria and the Congo divided the NATO member states in the United Nations, and Pearson foresaw no improvement as long as the colonial question remained unsolved. Most participants agreed that apart from better consultation, there was little that could be done.

In contrast, Olivier Guichard, a Gaullist member of the French National Assembly, argued for the establishment of a three-power organization within NATO, consisting of France, Great Britain and the United States, to deal with global issues. He argued that this was not an attempt to establish a 'directorate,' as was often said, but simply recognition of France's interests outside NATO.

Not surprisingly, the strongest opposition to Guichard's attempt to revive de Gaulle's September 1958 memorandum came from the Bilderberg participants of the smaller NATO members. An unidentified Canadian participant thought that what Guichard described sounded very much like a directorate. Snoy et d'Oppuers maintained that such a directorate would be "worse for the small countries than imperfect consultation in NATO," and the Dutch Social-Democrat and former Minister of Justice Ivo Samkalden pointedly inquired how Guichard's proposal for a directorate was compatible with the close association between France and Germany.[75] As Lamping summarized the St. Castin discussion in his notes:

> The French argued that N.A.T.O. cooperation in Europe would depend on its members coordinating their policies in other parts of the world and in the United Nations. The impact of this argument was weakened by their incompromising [sic] insistence that France could not cooperate effectively even in N.A.T.O.'s strategic tasks in Europe unless she obtained assistance from the U.S.A. in producing her own atomic striking force. Participants from all the other European states both great and small (and Canada) rejected the French proposal for a Three Power Political Directorate in N.A.T.O., though some of the British believed it might be desirable and possible to arrange for some sort of N.A.T.O. Inner Cabinet in which the Great Powers were permanently present while the smaller powers took turns.[76]

Beyond the discussion of out-of-area issues, the Bilderberg meeting suggested two main conclusions about the new Kennedy Administration. First, the administration seemed determined to decrease NATO's reliance on nuclear weapons for its defense through a strategy of flexible response. Second, the new president wished to start a serious attempt to negotiate an effective disarmament agreement with the Soviet Union.

The Ford Foundation's Shepard Stone, a long-time associate of John McCloy, informed the Bilderberg participants about the efforts of the Kennedy Administration in the field of disarmament. McCloy had just been named advisor to the president on disarmament, and Stone left no doubt that Washington was serious about trying to make progress on disarmament. "I can not emphasize too much," Stone said, "the fact that those dealing with disarmament in Washington are deeply attached to the NATO alliance. But exposed to the overall problem of the arms competition, they believe that we must try to find solutions in the disarmament area."

In his Bilderberg presentation, which was printed in the final report, Stone gave a detailed overview of the various problems involved in disarmament and the present state of the test ban negotiations. He urged the European participants to develop their own thinking on these matters because Western Europe seemed to trail the United States in this respect. A strong argument in favor of disarmament was that it would make resources available "for peaceful purposes." Stone ended with an appeal for more Western self-confidence:

> Some of the speakers said here, and this seems to me to be essential, that we ought not be afraid of Soviet competition in the peaceful area. If the Western nations, 500–600 million strong, with their great resources,

talents and skills, are not convinced, as they should be, that they can
win the competition with the Communist states in the non-military
area, then indeed we are going to lose out. We have every reason to have
confidence in ourselves. It must be the assumption of this group that
it is in the Atlantic Community – if we put together the Community's
resources – that we really have the answer to the Communist challenge.[77]

The question of NATO nuclear strategy took up the largest part of the discussion at St. Castin. Many of the arguments were familiar to those who had
participated in the Bilderberg conferences at the time of the Sputnik shock,
but an important difference was the rapid developments in US rocket technology. Lamping noted that July 1960 represented an important milestone
with the launching of the first solid-fuel Polaris missile. Although the Polaris
missiles were expensive and had a range of only about 2,000 kilometers, they
had one overwhelming advantage: they could be launched from submarines.
Combined with the successful testing of the Minuteman ICBM (range:
6,500 kilometers), the United States would soon no longer be dependent on
European bases for the effectiveness of its nuclear deterrent. Lamping wondered whether this development "will make Europe less important to the
United States' strategy with far-reaching consequences for the international
political realm."[78]

On the American side, an impressive group of experts was present to answer this question, including Christian Herter, Paul Nitze, Isidor I. Rabi,
the former chairman of the General Advisory Committee of the Atomic
Energy Commission, and Albert Wohlstetter, a RAND Corporation analyst. Nitze and Wohlstetter had been involved in the drafting of the Acheson
Report, which provided the basis for Kennedy's NATO policy; Wohlstetter,
moreover, had just published an influential article in *Foreign Affairs* on
"Nuclear Sharing: N.A.T.O. and the N + 1 Country."[79] Wohlstetter opposed
Eisenhower's policy of nuclear sharing and argued that unified control of the
nuclear deterrent was safer than a proliferation of national nuclear forces.
For the same reason, he opposed the creation of a NATO nuclear force.[80]

Not surprisingly, Nitze also strongly argued in favor of less reliance on
nuclear weapons in the defense of the West. He told the Bilderberg participants that NATO's conventional forces should be capable of holding NATO
positions long enough "for significant political consultation within NATO,
and long enough for the Soviets to reassess the effect upon themselves of our
determination to react." At the same time he reassured his European audience that the new administration stood behind the US nuclear guarantee:
"It is firmly determined that any nuclear attack upon a NATO power, or any
major non-nuclear attack which involves, or presages, a determined Soviet
effort, must be met by a full nuclear reply." As soon as NATO's territory
was thus secured, Nitze argued, "we can then turn our major disposable
energies to meeting the threat where it is most imminent, Asia, Africa and
the Western Hemisphere."[81]

Not all participants, however, were willing to leave the nuclear defense of Europe to the United States. French participants Olivier Guichard and General François Croisillier argued that France, as a world power, needed its own nuclear force and would insist on building it with or without US assistance. Guichard suggested that given existing arrangements for US–British nuclear cooperation, a similar deal with France would make sense in the context of a tripartite nuclear directorate. With such a solution, he suggested, the French attitude on NATO cooperation would become more positive.[82]

On the question of increased conventional forces, most participants agreed that an effort to strengthen the NATO shield was necessary. Continuing earlier attempts by NATO officials to influence Western opinion, Raymond Thurston, an aide to General Norstad, presented a paper on NATO strategy that again underlined the importance of a strong shield.[83] Some doubts were expressed, however, about the willingness of the member states to pay for this effort.

The rest of the discussion focused on the role of tactical and strategic nuclear weapons. According to Earl Jellicoe, it was unrealistic to expect conventional forces alone to hold a major attack. In view of Nitze's strong emphasis on non-nuclear forces, he also warned that the Soviet Union should not be given the impression that NATO had turned away from the use of nuclear weapons. This would undermine the credibility of the overall deterrent.

Several participants wondered whether NATO could be given control over all tactical nuclear weapons in Europe. At present they were either controlled by American forces, or by a double veto of the United States and the European host country. If NATO had control over these weapons, however, the question was whether there would there be sufficient time for a collective decision. And would not fifteen fingers on the trigger undermine the credibility of the deterrent in Soviet eyes?[84] The Canadian Chairman of the Chiefs of Staff Committee, General Charles Foulkes, suggested that an ideal solution to the control problem was virtually impossible. "Perhaps," he said, "fuzziness is the best solution."[85]

As in earlier discussions of nuclear weapons, a fundamental problem was whether one thought in terms of deterrence – preventing war – or in terms of fighting a war. In case of the former, the presence of tactical nuclear weapons was crucial both to strengthen the NATO shield and to force the Soviets to take into account the risk of a nuclear response to any aggression. If one started thinking about the actual occurrence of war, however, tactical nuclear weapons seemed to pose great risks.

Both Fritz Erler and Healey argued that tactical nuclear weapons should not be part of frontline forces. In case of attack, these forces might be quickly overwhelmed, putting them in the position of either giving up their weapons or using them. And most participants – including Herter, van Roijen, and Erler – agreed that it was highly likely that the use of tactical nuclear weapons would lead to general nuclear war. Rabi added that small nuclear weapons were expensive to develop compared to larger weapons. This raised the question of how Soviet forces were equipped. Rabi doubted whether they had at their disposal the same range of weapons as the United States. In other words, chances were that the Soviets would respond to tactical nuclear weapons by firing back big ones.[86]

With respect to strategic nuclear weapons, there was a remarkably strong feeling that the United States should be responsible for their use. The St. Castin report was unambiguous on this point:

> As regards the use of the major deterrent, there was no difference of views among the speakers: the survival of the West in the face of the Soviet peril depended on the Strategic Air Command, and only the United States could decide when to use that.

Ultimately, it was a "question of the Allies' trust in the wisdom of the United States Government, and it was up to the Americans to do everything possible to justify that trust."[87]

In this context, the American suggestion to base several Polaris-armed submarines in European waters was welcomed by most participants. Herter, who had first made this proposal to the NATO Council in December 1960, explained that the primary purpose of the Polaris submarines was to show that part of the US strategic forces was "irrevocably committed to Europe." The control question had been left undecided to give NATO the opportunity to discuss different scenarios. But with remarkable candor, Herter said that in his view, NATO should decide it was best that "we keep our finger on [the] trigger." There could not be the slightest doubt, he added, that SAC would be used in defense of NATO if necessary. The only one who seriously questioned the American guarantee was General de Gaulle.[88]

Visiting the White House after the St. Castin conference, Prince Bernhard briefed President Kennedy on the Bilderberg discussions and said that in his view, "there should not be a tripartite control over the use of nuclear weapons nor a 15-nation control through NAC, but rather he felt that the sole control should rest with the President of the United States."[89] The smaller NATO countries, Prince Bernhard said, clearly preferred US control to the Gaullist suggestion of a tripartite directorate. Kennedy replied that he regarded the Polaris proposals as a way of "discouraging the development of an independent nuclear capability on the part of the French and eventually the Germans."[90]

Meanwhile, the St. Castin report concluded that "none of the speakers threw any formal doubt on the value of the American guarantee, which had been reaffirmed by the new President." Yet this ignored the problem of national nuclear forces in Europe.[91] Guichard and Croisillier had left little doubt that France would build its own nuclear force. This inevitably raised the question of whether West Germany would accept an inferior position in the alliance. The last-minute absence of two important German participants, State Secretary for Foreign Affairs Karl Carstens and Defense Minister Franz Josef Strauß, was part of the explanation for the relatively straightforward acceptance of US dominance in the nuclear field.[92] The only German politician able to speak with authority on nuclear strategy, Erler, was generally in agreement with the Kennedy Administration's line on NATO and did not wish to see a greatly enhanced German role in the nuclear field. However, the Adenauer Government was unwilling to accept long-term discrimination against the Federal Republic and strongly supported SACEUR General Norstad's proposal to create an integrated NATO nuclear force – including land-based medium-range ballistic missiles (MRBMs) – not controlled by a veto of the American president.

All in all, the relatively weak German presence at the St. Castin conference was unfortunate, since a German-American crisis of confidence was very much in the making.[93] The Kennedy Administration's reluctance to make NATO into the fourth nuclear power was understandable, but as Max Kohnstamm, one of the new Bilderberg participants in Canada, noted in his diary, it was imperative to prevent discrimination against West Germany in the nuclear field. Kohnstamm, who as Jean Monnet's principal assistant in the Action Committee was an important player in the informal alliance, correctly foresaw that the German government would be reluctant to accept the United States' more or less unilateral control of the nuclear deterrent and the reversal of Eisenhower's policy of nuclear sharing.[94] Strauß was soon to become the strongest critic of the Kennedy Administration's new NATO strategy.

President Kennedy did reaffirm Herter's proposal to commit five Polaris submarines to NATO in a speech in Ottawa in May 1961. The president also mentioned "the possibility of eventually establishing a NATO seaborne force, which would be truly multi-lateral in ownership and control." However – and this was important – he added that NATO's non-nuclear goals should be achieved first.[95] This was an unmistakable retreat from Herter's offer, since it was unlikely that the non-nuclear build-up would be finished before 1966. It was clear, therefore, that for the moment President Kennedy saw the multilateral Polaris proposal mainly as a way to deflect attention from General Norstad's continued calls for land-based MRBMs. Kennedy believed that the Europeans would be unable to come up with a feasible proposal for control of a multilateral force and would eventually decide to leave the strategic deterrent in the hands of the United States.[96]

President Kennedy's assessment, based on advice from Dean Acheson, was certainly plausible. Moreover, as long as the British membership negotiations with the EEC continued, the Kennedy Administration was reluctant to inject the nuclear issue into the mix. This meant, however, that the new administration provided strong arguments to all those who said that US leadership in the alliance amounted to unacceptable dominance. Combined with the construction of the Berlin Wall, which started in August, 1961, and the fact that President Kennedy advocated a much more flexible Western posture in the Berlin crisis than President de Gaulle and Chancellor Adenauer found acceptable, this meant that the early 1960s turned into a struggle for leadership in Europe between Gaullists and Atlanticists, culminating in the transatlantic crisis of 1963.[97] Reflecting the increased importance of television and mass media, this struggle unfolded partly in the public view, through speeches, press conferences, state visits, and public diplomacy.[98] Yet of course the informal alliance also had a major role to play.

Notes

1 Lüthy, "De Gaulle: Pose and Policy," 568. On President De Gaulle, see Lacouture, *De Gaulle*; and Roussel, *Charles de Gaulle*. For an overview of de Gaulle's foreign policy, see Vaïsse, *La grandeur*. For the international dimension, see Bozo, *Two Strategies*; Conze, *Die Gaullistische Herausforderung*; Großmann and Miard-Delacroix, *Deutschland, Frankreich*; Martin, *General De Gaulle's Cold War*; Nünlist, Locher, and Martin, *Globalizing De Gaulle*; Paxton and Wahl, *De Gaulle and the United States*; Winand, *Eisenhower, Kennedy*.
2 A. de Staercke to P. Wigny, July 7, 1958, Box 294, No. 5476, Spaak Papers, FPHS.
3 See Lynch, "De Gaulle's First Veto," and Vaïsse, *Grandeur*, 169–170.
4 See van Lennep, *Emile van Lennep*, 95. Van Lennep, the Treasurer-General in the Dutch Finance Ministry and Secretary-General of the OECD from 1969–1984, argues that without the Rueff Plan, the Common Market would probably have failed. Van Lennep was a frequent Bilderberg participant in the 1960s and 1970s.
5 On the Berlin ultimatum, see Smyser, *From Yalta*.
6 See Camps, *Britain and the European Community*; Giauque, *Grand Designs*, Chapter 2; Kaiser, *Using Europe*, 61–107; Ludlow, *Dealing with Britain*; Lynch, "De Gaulle's First Veto"; Mangold, *The Almost Impossible Ally*, 100–116; Milward, *Rise and Fall*, 302 ff.
7 See Schwarz, *Adenauer*, 465–467.
8 Retinger to Johnson, December 24, 1958, Box 54, Bilderberg Archives, NANL.
9 "Meeting of American Members, Bilderberg Steering Committee, Lunch Club, New York, 8 January 1959," Box 36, Jackson Papers, DDEL.
10 Gaitskell Report on visit to Paris, Box D47, Gaitskell Papers, UCL.
11 Verbatim Report, Box 17, Bilderberg Archives, NANL.
12 Ibid.
13 Ibid.
14 Ibid.
15 Ibid.
16 See Memorandum "Mr. Clark," January 28, 1959, Box 234/358, Treasury Files, TNA and Ernst van der Beugel, "No. 180," January 19, 1959, Box 2, Van der Beugel Papers, NANL.
17 Retinger to Johnson, February 5, 1959, Box 54, Bilderberg Archives, NANL.
18 Ernst van der Beugel, "No. 180" and "No. 181," Box 2, Van der Beugel Papers, NANL (my translation). Louis Camu reached the same conclusion as Van der Beugel concerning the French aims in Europe. He told Baron Snoy et d'Oppuers that "[...] France intends to use the Treaty of Rome to promote its own global leadership. This is a very different idea from that which is acceptable to Benelux." Quoted (and translated) in Grosbois and Stelandre, "Belgian Decision-Makers," 134.
19 On the Fouchet Plan, see Vanke, "An Impossible Union," and Segers, "De Gaulle's Race."

20 See BDI Präsidialsitzung, March 3, 1959 and the attached proposal, Box 781, Folder PRO 7, BDIA. The BDI accepted the political importance of the EEC, but wished to avoid a schism within Europe. The BDI proposal suggested that many of the French worries about unfair competition could be solved. The British would have to accept that without including agriculture, the FTA was not only unacceptable to France, but also to other agricultural exporters in the OEEC. Berg had also sent the BDI proposal to Chancellor Adenauer. See Präsidialsitzung, December 3, 1958, Box 784, Folder PRO 5/2, BDIA.

21 See Tennant to Maudling, January 22, 1959, Box 337/8, Treasury Files, NAL. Tennant also called on Ormsby-Gore to inform him about the Bilderberg meeting. See C. S. L. Cope to J. E. Killick, January 20, 1959, Box 146257, FO 371, NAL.

22 The British Embassy in Rome quickly provided evidence of this, reporting on a conversation with Malagodi:

> Recently he had attended a meeting in Holland of the Committee presided over by Prince Bernhard and had there met the Lord Chancellor, the Paymaster General and the leader of the opposition. He had gone to this meeting considerably prejudiced against the French. After hearing statements by the British ministers, and particularly by Mr. Gaitskell, he found himself equally prejudiced against the British. The Italians were completely nonplussed by the present situation. The French were pressing for a pragmatic solution, while the U.K. were standing on principle. This was so unusual on both sides that they assumed there were hidden motives. They believed the French were seeking political concessions, and that the U.K. was trying to wreck the Common Market.

K. Uwin (Embassy Rome) to L. G. Holliday, Esq., C.M.G., February 7, 1959, Box 234/359, Treasury Files, NAL.

23 Tennant to Maudling, January 22, 1959, Box 337/8, Treasury Files, NAL.

24 Tennant to Retinger, February 3, 1959, Box 54, Bilderberg Archives, NANL.

25 The French president had been rattled by the fact that an Anglo-American intervention in Jordan and Lebanon in the summer of 1958 had taken place without prior consultation and in an area where France traditionally had great influence. On the September memorandum, see Vaïsse, *La Grandeur*, 114 ff and Trachtenberg, *Constructed Peace*, 242–244.

26 Either this was an intentional move on the part of de Gaulle – but it is difficult to see what purpose it served to snub two European neighbors – or it reflected a complete lack of understanding of how NATO worked. Perhaps de Gaulle really thought he could get away with his deceit; however, NATO Secretary General Spaak showed the Germans and Italians the original memorandum. The Belgian Permanent Representative to NATO, André de Staercke, called the situation "burlesque." A. de Staercke to P. Wigny, October 7, 1958, Box F294, No. 5496, Spaak Papers, FPHS.

27 For the following, see Pagedas, *Anglo-American Strategic Relations*, 48 ff.

28 Steering Committee Meeting, Yeşilköy, September 17 and 20, 1959, Box 194, Bilderberg Archives, NANL.

29 Rijkens to Healey, December 17, 1959, Box 194, Bilderberg Archives, NANL.

30 On Van der Beugel's career, see Bloemendal, "Reframing the Diplomat."

31 See Retinger to Rijkens, January 5, 1960, Box 2 XXVIB, Retinger Papers, Polish Library, London. Retinger told Rijkens:

> I believe that all the Europeans, without any exception, who may accept the fact that three Dutchmen are the officers of the Group, will certainly not accept the fact that the international Secretariat is in Holland. As a matter of fact, you have already had a letter from Denis Healey to this effect and I myself

have heard the same kind of remarks not only from Reggie Maudling, but also from Quaroni and the Germans.

32 See Prince Bernhard to Retinger, January 30, 1960, Ibid.
33 See "Book on Ernst," Series 6, Box 27, File 1, Shepard Stone Papers, Dartmouth College. I thank Albertine Bloemendal for providing me with a copy.
34 Walter Boveri, president of the Swiss electrical engineering company BCC, was responsible for the organization in Switzerland.
35 Lamping, May 7, 1960, Box 57, Bilderberg Archives, NANL.
36 Lamping, November 9, 1960, Box 56, Bilderberg Archives, NANL.
37 See Wolff to Mueller, February 2, 1960, Box 377-3, Wolff Papers, RWA.
38 De Gaulle had also suggested Valéry Giscard-d'Estaing, who did not come. See De Graaff to Lamping, April 4, 1960, Box 57, Bilderberg Archives, NANL.
39 Lamping, undated (1960), Box 57, Bilderberg Archives, NANL.
40 Speech of Mr. C. D. Jackson, Box 18, Bilderberg Archives, NANL.
41 Spaak transcript, 1960, Box 18, Bilderberg Archives, NANL.
42 Jackson Handwritten Notes, Bürgenstock, Box 36, Jackson Papers, DDEL.
43 C. D. Jackson "Summing Up," Box 36, Jackson Papers, DDEL.
44 Bürgenstock Report, 19, Box 18, Bilderberg Archives, NANL.
45 Paul-Henri Spaak (my translation), Box 18, Bilderberg Archives, NANL.
46 Bürgenstock Report, 18, Box 18, Bilderberg Archives, NANL. The political reasons for American support for European unity were the same as in the mid-1950s. Under Secretary of State C. Douglas Dillon told C. D. Jackson, who had sent Dillon a report on the Bürgenstock discussions:

> The U.S. has consistently and warmly supported the formation of a common market because of the political advantages which we see accruing from this organization, not the least of which is tying Germany to the West and helping to end the centuries-long strife between France and Germany. Such political advantages more than outweigh, in our view, the discrimination inherent in a customs union.

Dillon to Jackson, July 1, 1960, Box 47, Jackson Papers, DDEL.
47 The OECD was a rather transparent device developed by Jean Monnet and his American partners to prevent a merger of EFTA and the EEC. In addition, the Americans hoped to get a larger contribution from Europe in assistance of the underdeveloped world. See Winand, *Eisenhower*, 131 ff and von der Groeben, *The European Community*, 56–58.
48 Jackson to Prince Bernhard, June 2, 1960, Box 34, Jackson Papers, DDEL.
49 Van Kleffens to Wehrer, May 31, 1960, Box 17, Kohnstamm Papers, EUI.
50 See Hinrichsen, *Der Ratgeber*.
51 Birrenbach to Brentano, June 3, 1960, Box 50, B1, AA.
52 On this point, see Camps, *Britain*, 283.
53 For a summary of Birrenbach's speech at Bürgenstock, see Birrenbach to Brentano, June 3, 1960, Box 50, B1, AA.
54 Camps, *Britain*, 287–289.
55 For the official history of the UK's European policy in this period, see Milward, *The Rise and Fall*.
56 It is likely that the chancellor did encourage Birrenbach to travel to London. Initially Birrenbach had not sent his Bürgenstock report to the chancellor. In late June, however, Adenauer asked Birrenbach to forward him a copy. The timing of Birrenbach's trip to London – one week later – suggests that Adenauer at least did not object. In late 1961 Adenauer also sent Birrenbach on a mission to the United States to find out how the political situation was before Adenauer's own trip to Washington.

57 Birrenbach to Adenauer, July 8, 1960, Box 076/1, Birrenbach Papers, ACDP.
58 On Adenauer's doubts, see Schwarz, *Adenauer. Der Staatsmann*, 562–580.
59 Bill, *Ball*, 63.
60 George Ball, Oral History Interview, April 12, 1965, JFKL.
61 Winand, *Eisenhower, Kennedy*, 266–270.
62 This is how Ball put it in a conversation with Senator Fulbright, in which he reported on the Macmillan talks. Telcon Fulbright-Ball, April 7, 1961, Box 1, Folder Britain 3/31/61-11/20/62, Ball Papers, JFKL.
63 See Telcon Dillon-Ball, April 7, 1961, Box 1, Folder Britain 3/31/61-11/20/62, Ball Papers, JFKL. Ball expressed his amazement to Dillon, who had become Secretary of the Treasury, at "the directness" with which Kennedy had given these assurances.
64 Van Kleffens to A. Wehrer, April 23, 1961, Box 1279, CEAB-5, ECSC Archives, EUI. Emphasis in original.
65 A. Lamping, "Benoeming van Dean Rusk," December 31, 1960, Box 58, Bilderberg Archives, NANL.
66 Van der Beugel to Johnson, October 20, 1960, Box 57, Bilderberg Archives, NANL.
67 Steering Committee member James Duncan was responsible for the organization, assisted by the director of the Canadian Institute of International Affairs John Wendell Holmes. See also Gijswijt, "Beyond NATO."
68 A. Lamping, "Report on European American Assembly on Disarmament," August 29, 1961, Box 19, Bilderberg Papers.
69 L.W. Fuller to Mr. McGhee, "Agenda for the Bilderberg Meeting, April 21–23," Box 1, Folder 8, Series XIII, McGhee Papers, GUL.
70 See Arthur Schlesinger, "Memorandum for the President; Reactions to Cuba in Western Europe," May 3, 1961, DDRS, No. CK3100447239. Healey told Schlesinger: "I've staked my whole political career on the ability of the Americans to act sensibly."
71 Nitze Handwritten Notes St. Castin, Box 61, Folder 5, Nitze Papers, LOC and St. Castin Report, 15, Box 19, Bilderberg Archives, NANL.
72 Nitze Handwritten Notes St. Castin, Box 61, Folder 5, Nitze Papers, LOC.
73 Ibid.
74 St. Castin Report, 9, Box 19, Bilderberg Archives, NANL.
75 Nitze Handwritten Notes St. Castin, Box 61, Folder 5, Nitze Papers, LOC.
76 Notes on the Bilderberg Meeting at St. Castin, Box 58, Bilderberg Archives, NANL.
77 Stone Statement, Box 19, Bilderberg Archives, NANL.
78 Lamping Memo, April 14, 1961, Box 58, Bilderberg Archives, NANL.
79 National Security Advisor Bundy put the article in President Kennedy's briefing book for his first trip to Europe in May, Box 398, NSF, JFKL.
80 See St. Castin Report, 23, Box 19, Bilderberg Archives, NANL. The fact that the St. Castin Report contained a 6-page summary of Wohlstetter's article indicates its importance.
81 Remarks by Paul H. Nitze at Bilderberg Meeting, Box 61, Folder 5, Nitze Papers, LOC. Nitze sent these remarks to Secretary of Defense Robert McNamara.
82 Nitze Handwritten Notes St. Castin, Box 61, Folder 5, Nitze Papers, LOC.
83 "The Role and Control of Atomic Weapons Inside NATO," Box 38, Norstad Papers, DDEL. See also Norstad's letter to Prince Bernhard, March 20, 1961, ibid.
84 St. Castin Report, 27–28, Box 19, Bilderberg Archives, NANL.
85 Nitze Handwritten Notes St. Castin, Box 61, Folder 5, Nitze Papers, LOC.
86 Nitze Handwritten Notes St. Castin, Box 61, Folder 5, Nitze Papers, LOC and St. Castin Report, 25, Box 19, Bilderberg Archives, NANL.
87 St. Castin Report, 27, Box 19, Bilderberg Archives, NANL.

88 Nitze Handwritten Notes St. Castin, Box 61, Folder 5, Nitze Papers, LOC.
89 Meeting between Kennedy and Bernhard, April 25, 1961, Box 18, NSC Country Files, the Netherlands, JFKL.
90 Ibid.
91 St. Castin Report, 27, Box 19, Bilderberg Archives, NANL.
92 Carstens had to cancel at the last moment; it is not clear why Strauß, who was invited, did not come. In fact, two earlier attempts to get Strauß to participate had failed. Carstens' suggestion to send Kurt Birrenbach in his place did not work out. See Carstens Telegram, April 12, 1961, Box 76, B 2, AA.
93 See Smyser, *From Yalta*; and Münger *Kennedy*.
94 Max Kohnstamm Handwritten Notes St. Castin, Box 19, Kohnstamm Papers, EUI.
95 President John F. Kennedy, Address Before the Canadian Parliament in Ottawa, May 17, 1961.
96 As President Kennedy told Richard Neustadt in April 1963:

> Originally [...] it had been the idea – Acheson's to begin with – that we drag out a multilateral force proposal and let the Europeans wrestle with it for a while, until they saw all the bugs in it and decided they'd be better off to leave nuclear forces to us – at least until 'Europe' really developed with someone in charge, which obviously wasn't going to be soon.

Memorandum of Conversation with the President, April 27, 1963, Box 21, Neustadt Papers, JFKL.
97 On the Cold War background, see Beschloss, *Crisis Years*; and Leffler, *For the Soul*. For a dramatic account of the Berlin Crisis in 1961, see Kempe, *Berlin 1961*.
98 On these changes, see Großmann and Miard-Delacroix, *Deutschland, Frankreich*, 13–34; and Daum, *Kennedy in Berlin*.

9   Alliance in crisis

The Bilderberg conferences from 1963 to 1967 were dominated by the crisis in the Atlantic alliance set off by President de Gaulle's refusal in early 1963 to accept Great Britain's EEC membership application, his simultaneous rejection of President Kennedy's proposal for a multilateral solution of the nuclear question, and the signing of the Franco-German Treaty of Friendship less than two weeks later. The crisis continued with the controversy over the Multilateral Force (MLF) and the European empty chair crisis, only to culminate in the French withdrawal from NATO's military integration in 1966. Throughout these years, the Bilderberg organizers had to face a dilemma: on the one hand, they clearly saw a role for Bilderberg in responding to de Gaulle's nationalism and his undermining of some of the basic internationalist assumptions underlying the alliance; on the other hand, they realized that Bilderberg as an informal transatlantic forum could hardly function without a French contribution.

All this led to emotional debates about the future of Europe and the alliance and a decision by leading US officials to use the informal alliance to defend the American leadership position and to respond to the French accusation of hegemonic domination. In the end, no solutions were found to overcome the Gaullist-Atlanticist rift; at the same time, the much-feared disintegration of NATO did not come about. The French, moreover, despite their obvious dislike of being criticized in a transatlantic forum such as Bilderberg, never fully cut their ties to the informal alliance. Meanwhile, Germany became more and more important as a key voice in the struggle for the future of transatlantic relations. Without German support, after all, President de Gaulle's ambitious plans for an independent Europe were doomed to failure.

Another consequence of the transatlantic crisis was that the Bilderberg organizers realized they had to bring in new and younger participants into the group. In the face of strong movements in favor of nuclear disarmament, the rise of student activism, and the Vietnam War protests, the internationalist Bilderberg consensus seemed to be under attack not just from Paris, but also from university campuses and protest marches around the globe. The Bilderberg Group responded by bringing in new faces and by making a serious, although not entirely successful, effort to understand the spirit of 1968.

The 1962 Saltsjöbaden conference

1962 was a year of transition in transatlantic relations. Not long before the 1962 Bilderberg Conference in Saltsjöbaden, Sweden (May 18–20), Luns and Spaak rejected President de Gaulle's plan for a confederal political Europe (the Fouchet Plan) after de Gaulle had unilaterally deleted references to the continued importance of NATO. The Dutch and Belgians feared not only French domination of the new structure, but also a weakening of the existing institutions of Atlantic and European cooperation. On May 5, De Gaulle reacted with one of his famous press conferences – fulminating against a supranational Europe dominated by the United States as the external federator. The five MRP ministers in his cabinet resigned in protest.

For the first time, the Kennedy Administration decided to publicly respond. A day before the Saltsjöbaden conference, President Kennedy warned:

> We cannot and do not take any European ally for granted and I hope no one in Europe would take us for granted either [...] American public opinion has turned away from isolationism but its faith must not be shattered.[1]

Further complicating the situation, however, was the fact that the British membership negotiations were still dragging on, and the US-Soviet Berlin negotiations had led to a serious crisis of confidence between Adenauer and Kennedy, involving German leaks of secret negotiating documents and the de facto US dismissal of the German ambassador in Washington. Secretary of Defense Robert McNamara further added to transatlantic tensions with a speech at the NATO ministerial meeting in Athens in early May arguing that indivisibility of control was crucial in the nuclear deterrent and that small, independent nuclear forces were useless at best and dangerous at worst.

At Saltsjöbaden, these developments overshadowed the first day's discussion of the United Nations (which was "rather dull" in Erler's view) and led to a renewed focus on the fact that despite Europe's economic resurgence, a huge gap in military and technological power still existed between Europe and the United States. Max Kohnstamm was one of those strongly arguing in favor of an Atlantic partnership of equals to overcome the present difficulties. "A partnership of a large group of nations," Kohnstamm argued,

> dominated by a single power or tied together by rules and institutions would always be weak and vacillating. Therefore, equal partnership between a United Europe and the United States is the necessary prerequisite for the strength and solidarity of the Atlantic Alliance.[2]

Kohnstamm continued by arguing that the three fundamental tasks of the alliance – deterrence, to find a durable "modus vivendi" with the Soviet Union, and to help the developing world – could only be reached if the West was closely united. "Such unity," Kohnstamm argued, "depended on an equal partnership between the United States and Europe." Kohnstamm went to great length to emphasize that such a partnership should extend to the military field. He argued that this was the only way to counter the "idea of a third force" – meaning, of course, a Gaullist third force.[3]

The practical problems of such an equal partnership, however, were evident at Saltsjöbaden. In the first place, a successful completion of the British membership negotiations was a precondition, yet after de Gaulle's most recent press conference, there was little cause for optimism. In addition, the question of how the rest of Europe would have to adjust to EEC enlargement remained unanswered. The Scandinavians were particularly anxious about this and were prominently present to make their case with, among others, Swedish Prime Minister Tage Erlander, Swedish Minister of Trade Gunnar Lange, Norwegian Foreign Minister Halvard Lange, Erik Boheman, Ole Bjørn Kraft, Bertil Ohlin, and Marcus Wallenberg. As Erler told Nitze:

> George Ball had a good case for Britain's membership, but a bad one against the association of the European neutrals. In this problem he had just one companion: Mr. Kohnstamm from the Monnet team. All the other participants were in favor of finding a fair association for the European neutrals. Putting them back to the same status as Japan or Latin America in relation to Europe would not correspond either to their geographical position nor to their political sympathies and cultural heritage.[4]

Many participants at Saltsjöbaden were worried that rather than an Atlantic Partnership, "the formation of a Paris/Bonn axis" was more likely. An agreement between de Gaulle and Adenauer to keep the United Kingdom out of the European Community was generally felt to be unacceptable. Joseph Harsch, who participated in the Saltsjöbaden conference, reported two days later that George Ball was in Europe to tell Bonn that West Germany "must choose between General de Gaulle and the American alliance."[5] As a result, the German participants – Fritz Berg, Max Brauer, Fritz Erler, Carlo Schmid and Otto Wolff – found themselves in an awkward position. Stressing the importance of Franco-German friendship, one of them said that creating "conditions which would force Germany to make a choice between friendship with France and friendship with the other Western countries" should be avoided.[6]

One month after the Saltsjöbaden conference, the Monnet Committee decided to publish a declaration along the lines of Kohnstamm's speech.[7] Having kept their many American friends fully informed about their thinking, Monnet and Kohnstamm were happy to learn that President Kennedy, prodded along by Ball and others in the State Department, adopted their basic concept in his July 4, 1962 speech in Philadelphia.[8] As Kennedy put it in this speech:

> We do not regard a strong and united Europe as a rival but as a partner. To aid its progress has been the basic object of our foreign policy for

17 years. We believe that a united Europe will be capable of playing a greater role in the common defense, of responding more generously to the needs of poorer nations, of joining with the United States and others in lowering trade barriers, resolving problems of commerce, commodities, and currency, and developing coordinated policies in all economic, political, and diplomatic areas. We see in such a Europe a partner with whom we can deal on a basis of full equality in all the great and burdensome tasks of building and defending a community of free nations.

Both Kennedy and Monnet believed that a partnership on an equal footing was only feasible if the UK joined the European project. In Kennedy's words: "The first order of business is for our European friends to go forward in forming the more perfect union which will someday make this partnership possible."[9] This was, of course, also the great weakness in what later became known as Kennedy's Grand Design. By directly challenging de Gaulle's concept of an independent Europe, the president hoped to create sufficient pressure in Europe – especially in Germany – to drive de Gaulle into accepting Great Britain in the EEC. Beyond such pressure, however, there was little either Kennedy or the Monnet Committee could do to force the General's hand.

The transatlantic crisis of 1963

On January 14 1963, President de Gaulle's publicly announced decision to unilaterally end the British membership negotiations, coupled with his refusal to explore a NATO nuclear deal based on the US-British Nassau Agreement, plunged the West into a deep crisis, made worse by the nationalist tone in which it was done.[10] De Gaulle warned that an enlarged European community risked losing its cohesion as part of a "colossal Atlantic community under American dependence and direction." He also questioned the trustworthiness of the American nuclear deterrent for Europe, pointing to the Cuban Missile Crisis as evidence that "the defence of Europe" had become a "secondary consideration" for the United States because of the fact that the Soviet Union now possessed the nuclear forces "to threaten even the life of America."[11]

De Gaulle also made much of the fact that the Nassau offer, which had been extended to Great Britain and France in the form of Polaris missiles, made no sense for France, since she lacked the necessary submarine and thermonuclear technology. Here, the French president seems to have purposely ignored that the offer from President Kennedy implied that France could receive help beyond what the British needed.[12] Given the improvised nature of the Nassau Summit and the internal divisions of the Kennedy administration, this message was somewhat muddled, but US Ambassador Charles Bohlen made clear to de Gaulle in early January that far-reaching US assistance was on the table if the French president accepted some sort of NATO multilateralism.[13] On the other hand, the French president had been disappointed before by American offers of nuclear assistance, and the fact that Kennedy's offer was made at an Anglo-American summit without consultation with France would surely have annoyed him.[14]

McGeorge Bundy, Kennedy's national security advisor, argued that de Gaulle's press conference was very much part of a pattern. The Gaullists seemed to be using every opportunity in the battle for the hearts and minds of Europe to undermine trust in US leadership. "Our emphasis on conventional weapons," Bundy told President Kennedy,

> has been distorted to imply a lack of firmness in our nuclear guarantees of Europe. Our insistence upon communications with Moscow has been distorted to mean that we may sacrifice the interests of others for the purpose of accommodation among the giants. Even our final and decisive confrontation in Cuba has been read as a demonstration that while we will not risk our nation for Europe, we will risk Europe to meet a local threat at home.

All this was immensely frustrating to Kennedy and his advisors because they felt that after the Cuban Missile Crisis, a singular opportunity existed to move beyond the Berlin crisis. As Bundy put it: "we are in a better position for serious negotiation with the Soviet Union than at any time since the war." At the same time, European concerns about nuclear strategy had to be taken seriously:

> The victory of Cuba has increased our stature--but it has also increased the fear that by our own local action we might quite literally bring an end to Europe. These questions are spoken only by our opponent de Gaulle, but they are felt among our friends, and we owe them an answer.[15]

In the Federal Republic, Adenauer wasn't pleased with de Gaulle's press conference, but decided that he could not postpone the signing of the Franco-German Treaty ten days later.[16] The fact, however, that the treaty read very much like a bilateral Fouchet Plan and contained a provision on defense cooperation that seemed likely to undermine NATO caused concern not just in Washington but also in Bonn. Privately, President Kennedy and others worried that a secret nuclear deal between France and Germany might be in the working as well.[17] Moreover, by signing the treaty at this particular moment, Adenauer could not prevent the impression that he supported de Gaulle's decisions.

In response, members of the informal alliance on both sides of the Atlantic started a public and private campaign to add a preamble to the Treaty making clear Germany's continued alliance loyalties.[18] Bilderbergers Erler and Birrenbach were closely involved in this campaign; Birrenbach in particular worked intensively with Monnet and Kohnstamm to formulate such a preamble and to win political support for it. While Birrenbach was primarily responsible for organizing the CDU opposition to the Franco-German Treaty as it stood, Monnet and Kohnstamm kept in close touch with various members of the Kennedy Administration as well as the SPD, FDP and DGB leadership.[19] They even considered the possibility of a nationwide strike to underline opposition to Adenauer's Gaullist policy.

On the US side, members of the transatlantic elite like Acheson, McCloy, the American Council on Germany's Christopher Emmett, and General Lucius Clay started a letter-writing campaign to convince their German contacts that Adenauer had gone too far.[20] In official contacts with German diplomats, a similar line was taken by the Kennedy Administration. In early February, the American Ambassador in Bonn told Kennedy that with "discreet action" the ratification of the Franco-German Treaty could be influenced. In addition, the Kennedy Administration started promoting the MLF, hoping to prevent a German push for a Franco-German nuclear deal.

Meanwhile, George Ball used friendly reporters such as *The New York Times*' James Reston to send a strong signal of disapproval. "Adenauer is now being asked to act upon de Gaulle's vision," Reston wrote in a column passed on for local use by US embassies in Europe,

> to rely on French atomic power when France will not rely on American, and to reject British membership in the community on the theory that Britain would be a kind of Trojan horse in Europe for the United States. This amounts to the preposterous suggestion that the United States Government would not only abandon its allies in Europe after a Soviet attack but would abandon its own armies standing closer to the Red Army than does France.[21]

Most striking about the response of the informal alliance was its emotional nature – almost reminiscent of the way Bilderberg participants talked of the Soviet-Communist threat in the mid-1950s. McCloy told his old friend Adenauer:

> I am more disturbed by the turn of events than I have been at any time since the end of the war. I have the fear that unless steps are deliberately taken, the goals of European unity and Atlantic partnership toward which you have always directed your policies may be fatally disrupted.[22]

Birrenbach, using similar language, told a friend that just before de Gaulle's press conference he "began to realise that our cause was in mortal danger." Monnet, in turn, warned the US diplomat Livingston Merchant "that de Gaulle on January 14 had invoked ancestral memories and loyalties which struck a responsive chord widely, not only in France but in Germany and Italy as well. Hence we must start moving promptly."

Bilderberg responds

Against this emotionally charged background, the 1963 Bilderberg conference in Cannes, France (March 29–31) took on extra importance.[23] Van der
Beugel warned Prince Bernhard that it would not be easy:

> There is absolutely no doubt that this will be one of the most difficult
> conferences that Your Royal Highness will have presided over in the
> context of Bilderberg. The situation is explosive; the issues are explosive;
> the participants are explosive and in addition my conversations have
> made clear that nobody knows what needs to be done after the General's
> intervention. The only ones who have a clear line, are the French. Both
> the Americans and the British lack a strategy; the Germans are drifting
> more than ever and the state of the Alliance is, in my view, more seri-
> ous and more confused than it has ever been since 1945. All this makes
> the Bilderberg conference extremely important, since it is the first time
> since de Gaulle dropped his bombshell that this type of group gets to-
> gether. However, if the meeting is not managed well, it carries grave
> risks, in part for the future work of Bilderberg. It is not difficult, after
> all, to offend all the French in the first half hour, but it is difficult to have
> these days end on a somewhat positive note.[24]

As a result, the Bilderberg organizers decided that Prince Bernhard would
give a special introduction, drafted by Van der Beugel, reiterating the central idea behind the Bilderberg meetings. "During the long years we have
met," the Prince announced at the start of the conference,

> we have never tried to solve problems. What we have always tried to do
> is to analyse and to discuss problems of mutual concern and in our dif-
> ferent jobs try to influence our friends outside Bilderberg with the aim
> of strengthening the Western Community and of fostering a better un-
> derstanding not only between Europe and our North American friends
> but also inside Europe itself.

He went on to call for a civilized discussion: "Without wishing to put a brake
on the frankness of our discussions I think we should try to analyse rather
than to attack and finally try to define what should happen from now on."[25]

The run-up to the conference had been nerve-racking for Van der Beugel
and Lamping. It had started with the French government insisting that the
Bilderberg meeting in France should avoid "acutely controversial issues."[26]
Apparently, President de Gaulle had felt the Saltsjöbaden meeting to be
overly critical of France (perhaps annoyed at being called a giraffe with a
sore throat in the widely quoted Reston column).[27] The Bilderberg organizers, however, had refused to allow any outside interference in setting the
agenda of the Cannes meeting. Wilfrid Baumgartner – who had issued the

French invitation – had to convince de Gaulle that the conference could only take place if the French government refrained from trying to influence the discussions.[28] By November 1962, de Gaulle agreed to welcome the Bilderberg Group without any conditions – perhaps because by that time he had greatly strengthened his domestic position after settling the Algerian war and after winning a surprisingly large majority in a referendum on his policies.

Cooperation between the Bilderberg organizers and Baumgartner, however, remained difficult. The choice of hotel wasn't settled until two months before the conference, and only after it became clear that the non-Gaullist camp in France would be well-represented at Cannes ("You're inviting all our enemies," Foreign Minister Couve de Murville told Baumgartner) did the Gaullists confirm their participation.[29] To keep control, however, they designated "one 100 percent Gaullist as their speaker: [Jacques] Baumel, on whom the General was sure he could count."[30]

In addition to Baumel, the secretary-general of the Gaullist Party *Union pour la Nouvelle République*, the French participants in Cannes were Wilfrid Baumgartner, Maurice Faure, André Fontaine (foreign affairs correspondent of *Le Monde*), René Massigli, Guy Mollet, Jacques Piette, Antoine Pinay, René Pleven, Jacques Segard, and former OEEC Secretary General René Sergent. On the American side, Ball, McGhee, and Nitze represented the Kennedy Administration, with the State Department's Director of Atlantic Policy Studies, Harold van B. Cleveland, also present. In addition, virtually all American Steering Committee members came to Cannes, as well as Republican Senator Bourke B. Hickenlooper, Congressman Cornelius Gallagher, Cornell University President James A. Perkins, and former NATO Ambassador Charles Spofford.

Prime Minister Macmillan decided to send Lord Privy Seal Edward Heath, who had been responsible for the Common Market negotiations, to Cannes.[31] In addition, the Bilderberg regulars Bennet, Cavendish-Bentinck, Gubbins, and Healey were joined by Labour MP James Callaghan.[32] For Germany there were two new participants: Hans-Heinrich Herwarth von Bittenfeld, the secretary of state to the West German president, and Franz Josef Strauß, who in January had been forced to resign as defense minister because of the *Spiegel* controversy but who remained a force to be reckoned with as leader of the Bavarian CSU. The other Germans present were Fritz Berg, Max Brauer, Fritz Erler, Carlo Schmid, and Otto Wolff von Amerongen.

The fact that the smaller nations were similarly well-represented, complemented by a strong list of 'international participants' – Henrik Beer (secretary general of the League of Red Cross Societies); Guillaume Guindey (general manager of the Bank for International Settlements); Max Kohnstamm; Emile van Lennep (chair of the OECD's Monetary Working Group); EEC Commissioner Sicco Mansholt; SACEUR General Lyman Lemnitzer; and Pierre Uri of the Atlantic Institute – illustrated the importance of the moment. As George Ball put it in his report to the National Security Council, the meeting had "brought together for the first time since de Gaulle's press conference of January 14 the leaders of major European States."[33]

From the Gaullist side, Jacques Baumel put forward the Gaullist case in a way that was widely taken to be the official position of the French government. Baumel asserted that it was necessary to "restore the balance of the very foundations of this Alliance on both sides of the Atlantic in a more suitable manner." Europe had recovered in 15 years' time, he said, whereas NATO was still "a predominantly American organization." In this respect, the nuclear question was the most important one, Baumel argued,

> for everyone knows perfectly well that the world of tomorrow will be dominated by the atom and [...] only nations having the atom at their disposal will tomorrow be modern nations, strong nations with which it will be necessary to reckon.

For the moment, he added, nuclear forces could only be national forces

> for there is no nuclear force that is not in the service of political power. And that political power, for the time being, is a national power, and, considering the tragic consequences of the use of this force, only States may take the crushing responsibility of being able to use it.

Baumel suggested that if the United States decided to help the French nuclear effort – alongside the other European power with "a world position," meaning the UK – then "frankly everything will be possible," including "very close cooperation and a genuine full coordination." [34] This last remark was clearly aimed at those in the Kennedy Administration who favored giving France nuclear assistance.[35]

Baumel went on to accuse the United States of trying to maintain its nuclear monopoly. "Everything proposed [by America] on the subject of nuclear forces," he argued, "and now in a different form of multinational or even multilateral force, consists in giving their allies the impression of [possessing] a certain amount of responsibility, but in sovereignly [*sic*] retaining the sole right to press a button!" The American emphasis on conventional forces, Baumel said, was meant to keep the Europeans in the role of "footsloggers." The Nassau agreement and the cancellation of Skybolt, moreover, were proof that the United States did not always take the interests of its allies into account.

Baumel's speech, carefully designed to appeal to all those who either distrusted US aims in Europe or who thought that Europe should become more responsible for its own defense, made a deep impression on many participants. Ball had the speech translated and sent it to Bundy, McNamara, and Rusk. A report of the Cannes meeting for the Ford Foundation described it as "the most forthright presentation of the Gaullist point of view ever put forth in any forum."[36]

During the subsequent discussion of the nuclear question, most support for Baumel's position came from other French participants. With respect to the French national nuclear force, three counterproposals were advanced during the Cannes discussion: (1) the multilateral force; (2) an independent European nuclear force, perhaps based on the French and British forces; and (3) a much greater sharing of information and knowledge about the American strategic deterrent and targeting.

George Ball used the MLF to defend the US position and argued that the present course of events would inevitably lead to further proliferation of nuclear weapons. The United States thought this was a dangerous prospect given the increased risk of accidents. Therefore, a different solution had to be found to the nuclear problem in NATO. Ball said that the MLF, with "joint possession of certain nuclear devices with power of decision being held on an equal footing," was the best possible solution for the moment. This might not be the perfect solution, but Europe had "not yet reached a stage where it could speak with a single voice." And not only would the non-nuclear NATO members have the possibility of a greater participation in their nuclear defense, they would also "share America's experience in the management of such a force."[37]

In response, Baumel did all he could to undermine the American MLF proposal. "I am quite certain," he said, "that our British friends, who have accepted the Nassau Agreements on the basis of a multinational force are much less enthusiastic now about the establishment of a multilateral force with mixed crews and under a single command." He also ridiculed the Polaris offer made to France at the time of the Nassau Summit, saying "[w]e were being offered ball-point pens without the ball points and without ink [...]." Moreover, the multilateral force, Baumel maintained, "has no chance of becoming a fact." He called the MLF mission to Europe of US diplomat Livingston Merchant a failure and argued that the only possibility for a multilateral force would be a German-American force.[38]

Ball privately favored the concept of an MLF evolving into a truly European force, without an American veto. If he could have said so during the Cannes conference, he would have deflected much of Baumel's criticism, which clearly resonated with some European participants. The trouble was, however, that President Kennedy was not prepared to relinquish the American veto.[39] Moreover, even if he was, Congress had to agree to such a decision, and congressional reluctance to loosen US control over nuclear weapons was considerable. When Kohnstamm asked Ball privately why he had not reacted more forcefully to Baumel's remarks about the American veto, Ball answered: "How can I answer with Senator Hickenlooper present at the meeting?"[40]

The amount of support for the second proposal – a European nuclear force – showed that the Gaullist rhetoric about a more independent Europe appealed to many Europeans. Pierre Uri advanced a proposal for a merging of the French and British nuclear forces. Pleven, Mollet, and Fontaine all spoke out in favor of an independent European deterrent. Fontaine pointed out that with the increasing number of intercontinental ballistic missiles, the strategic importance of Europe for the United States had decreased. Consequently, the idea of a nuclear-protected "fortress America" had become a realistic possibility. With the Suez crisis in mind, Fontaine said that in case of a different assessment of vital interests between Europe and the United States, Europe would need its own deterrent as a "safety parachute."[41]

Strauß presented a similar argument. He stated that a real Atlantic partnership could only be built on the basis of a united Europe with its own nuclear force, not one dependent on the United States. At the same time, he rejected Baumel's argument that a nuclear force could only be national. In the nuclear age, Strauß said, national sovereignty was "obsolete." This was somewhat disingenuous since as defense minister, Strauß had privately argued that West Germany would have to develop its own nuclear force if no satisfactory NATO nuclear force came into being.[42] Perhaps his real aim had been to gain a larger say in nuclear strategy and to close the gap between France and the UK as nuclear powers and Germany as a non-nuclear power.[43] However, Strauß's actions had caused him to have an international reputation as a nationalist with ideas similar to de Gaulle; at Cannes, Strauß obviously wished to improve his standing with an important audience in view of his own political future. As a result, Strauß stressed the German "determination to hold aloof from national nuclear weapons."[44]

The third proposal was advanced by Denis Healey. Healey rejected the multinational force proposed at Nassau because it was discriminatory. With respect to the MLF, he argued that it was very difficult to solve the puzzle of control, even if the United States was willing to give up its veto. For many European countries, it was easier to trust America than to trust each other. In Healey's view, the best solution therefore was to give "the Europeans a greater say in the use of the deterrent by increasing their knowledge in this field and intensifying joint consultation," something that was indeed done three years later with the creation of NATO's Nuclear Planning Group (NPG). Fritz Erler supported Healey, arguing that it was a waste of resources for Europe to spend a great deal of money on nuclear weapons that would merely duplicate the American deterrent.

Even if the discussions showed considerable support for a European nuclear force, this did not necessarily mean support for de Gaulle. Several speakers pointed out that de Gaulle was no more willing to give up his nuclear veto than the United States. Moreover, de Gaulle's rejection of British membership in the EEC and his diplomatic style were widely condemned. The Italian politician Mario Pedini openly accused the French president of "anti-Americanism."[45] But it was Spaak who used some of the most emotional language, calling the day of de Gaulle's press conference "the free world's black Monday." De Gaulle had shown a complete disregard for the interests

of his European allies and preferred the diplomacy of the "fait accompli."
By doing so, Spaak said, de Gaulle challenged "the principles which had
governed Western policy for fifteen years." Spaak expressed "vigorous opposition" to de Gaulle's insistence on a completely independent French nuclear
force.[46] The implied distrust of the American deterrent, he said, was dangerous. Even if some of France's complaints about American predominance
in the nuclear field were justified, he continued, they should be discussed in
the NATO framework. Moreover, mentioning the case of Czechoslovakia,
Spaak pointedly remarked that France's record of guaranteeing the security
of other countries was not particularly impressive.[47] "[T]he French," Spaak
concluded, "could not provide France's allies in continental Europe with the
guarantees offered by the United States deterrent."[48]

Edward Heath also launched a sharp attack on de Gaulle. He argued
that a solution to the nuclear problem could only be partial as long as no
European or Atlantic political authority existed. However, Heath said, partial solutions were only possible with greater willingness to compromise. At
the moment, France made no contribution to NATO, did not work towards
greater European unity, and did not contribute to the UN or to disarmament negotiations. France's partners were entitled to ask France "to play
her part."[49] With respect to the *force de frappe*, Heath added that "the question was not whether France would have a nuclear force or not but what that
country would do with it. In the absence of increased consultation within
NATO, certain anxieties might develop."[50] On the issue of the Common
Market, Heath did his best to show that Britain had been a reasonable negotiator and that the blame for the unilateral break-off resided solidly in Paris.

When Prince Bernhard asked a number of French and German participants to comment on the Franco-German Treaty, the Gaullist-Atlanticist
divide was again apparent. Strauß emphasized the historic character of
Franco-German reconciliation and attempted to diffuse concerns about its
impact on NATO. Erler, however, made clear that the treaty should only become effective "within the framework of Atlantic and European solidarity.
Any doubt in this regard should be removed when the time came to ratify
the treaty by including precise legal references." Mollet likewise warned that
the treaty, so reminiscent of the Fouchet Plan, "introduced within Six-Power
Europe a threat to smaller countries, more specifically in that it provided for
certain decisions to be reached between Germany and France, thereby tam-
pering with the operation of the Community."[51]

After the Cannes conference, Ernst van der Beugel told several friends
that it had been a useful meeting – not only because of the quality of the
participants and discussions, but especially because the goals of de Gaulle's
foreign policy and their incompatibility with the Atlantic alliance and
European integration had become so clear. In a letter to his friend Henry
Kissinger, Van der Beugel wrote:

> The French were absolutely impossible; the Gaullists stated their case
> and the others, amongst whom Faure, former Prime Ministers and

people like Fontaine and Baumgartner did not really dare to speak up. Since 1944 I never had the feeling that fascism was in a room where I was; now I had. If after the Bilderberg meeting anybody would have any illusion about their attitude they must be nuts.[52]

On the other hand, Van der Beugel was not satisfied with the American response to the Gaullist challenge. He thought both Ball and Nitze had been rather weak in their statements. As he told his friend Eric Warburg:

My strongest impressions are that the Americans are off balance and have no alternative policy after the breakdown of Brussels; that the Germans are more confused than ever and the British are in a very difficult position because of the domestic scene.[53]

Lamping added in a private memorandum

that the Gaullists felt their isolation, and that they were impressed in particular by the American contributions that expressed a heart-felt disappointment about the fact that de Gaulle's government obstructed the Atlantic security system that had been honestly and openly created by the US government.

The anti-Gaullist forces in France, meanwhile, had been given an opportunity to "put forward their objections against the President's policies in front of a high-quality international audience."[54]

Despite the success of the Cannes conference, the problem of French participation remained acute. Even anti-Gaullists like Mollet and Pleven had emphasized that "French prestige" should be taken into account. In addition, Lamping noted that certain psychological issues played a role:

The Frenchman, after all, doesn't feel at ease in an Anglo-Saxon atmosphere: these are two different worlds; the French find it difficult to call each other Jack or John instead of *Monsieur le Ministre* or *Monsieur le Président*; the mutual teasing (Healey – Jackson for example) doesn't come naturally to the Frenchman for whom discussions about political issues are sacredly earnest; the 'old-boys-milieu' he regards as difficult to understand with its misogynistic connotations; he is not used to cocktails before dinner; a lack in fluency in the English language causes the Frenchman never to feel fully included.[55]

After returning to Washington, George Ball reported to the National Security Council that the Bilderberg discussions had shown that:

De Gaulle is isolating himself more and more, and that he does not have a "grand design," or even a clear European policy. All de Gaulle can really do is to oppose the initiative of others by being negative. He cannot build the Europe he desires because his actions are conditioned by his overriding desire to build the predominance of France. As a result, he has nothing to offer other European states. [...] Ambassador Bohlen agreed with the analysis that de Gaulle cannot organize a European nuclear force. De Gaulle still yearns for a U.S./U.K./France directorate in which France would speak for all of Europe. However, Europeans are not prepared to have de Gaulle speak for them. Except for de Gaulle, most Europeans do not want the U.S. to get out of Europe.[56]

With regard to the general political situation in Europe, Ball saw little room for new initiatives. As long as de Gaulle was in power, British membership in the EEC was out of the question. Moreover, Ball said that "as a result of numerous informal conversations [...] he was impressed with the lame duck character of most of the member governments of NATO." The Macmillan Government was surrounded by an "air of death," and Adenauer was on his way out. Adenauer's departure would greatly reduce de Gaulle's power in Europe.[57]

The long-term danger, Ball emphasized, was that as a result of de Gaulle's policies and the general uncertainty of the political situation in Europe, a resurgence of nationalism could occur, particularly in Germany. However, the overall conclusion of the Cannes meeting was clear: although many Europeans shared de Gaulle's aim of a more independent Europe, they rejected his methods – at least for now.

Ball's assessment of the political situation in Germany soon found confirmation in the German debate concerning the ratification of the Franco-German Treaty. The Atlanticist group in the CDU – which, besides Birrenbach, also included Adenauer's likely successor Ludwig Erhard – decided to put its weight behind the idea of adding a special clause to the preamble of the treaty emphasizing the continuing German support for a close European-American partnership, for an integrated NATO defense, and for the existing European Communities. Birrenbach, Kohnstamm and Monnet were closely involved in the drafting of the preamble.[58]

In early April, Adenauer finally buckled under the combined pressure of the FDP, the SPD and the Atlanticists within his own party and agreed to the preamble. During the ratification of the Franco-German Treaty in the *Bundestag* in May 1963, the preamble received overwhelming support. The wording of the preamble – calling for a partnership between the United States and Europe – strikingly resembled President Kennedy's Independence Day speech, as well as the 1962 resolution of the Monnet Committee.[59]

The Gaullist-Atlanticist crisis provided the SPD with an excellent opportunity to prove that it had become a reliable supporter of the Atlantic alliance. Although the pro-Western stance of the party had been announced in 1960, doubts remained widespread about the real preferences of men such as Herbert Wehner. The SPD stance on the Franco-German Treaty now removed some of these doubts. In other words, the SPD had become a viable and – from the American point of view – safe alternative to Adenauer and the CDU. The SPD Bilderberg members used their Bilderberg connections to emphasize this point in Washington. During the 1963 Bilderberg conference in Cannes, Fritz Erler and Max Brauer asked George McGhee to arrange separate visits for them with President Kennedy.[60] The fact that the president agreed to see them both indicated the importance of the change in the political situation in West Germany. As Brauer told the SPD leadership: "[Kennedy] hopes that a SPD victory will improve the situation. He is done with Adenauer."[61]

Kennedy's visit to the Federal Republic (where he gave his famous "Ich bin ein Berliner" speech) in June 1963 did much to reinforce Germany's Atlantic orientation.[62] In contrast with de Gaulle's nationalist message, Kennedy publicly reinforced calls for an Atlantic partnership in front of record crowds and secured the support of Adenauer's soon-to-be successor Erhard. At the same time, the President found his reluctance to fully commit to the MLF confirmed by a number of German politicians who privately expressed doubts about its feasibility. Kennedy also did not hesitate to ignore German sensitivities later in the year as he negotiated a Limited Test Ban Treaty with the Soviet Union.

The 1964 Williamsburg conference

In the following years, the informal alliance continued to play an important role in the Gaullist-Atlanticist struggle. When Van der Beugel travelled to the United States in preparation for the 1964 Bilderberg conference in Williamsburg, Virginia (March 20–22) he was struck by "how strong the interest in the Bilderberg Conference is at the highest levels of the White House, the State Department and the Pentagon."[63] As he reported to Prince Bernhard, Secretary of State Rusk had even proposed hosting a reception for all Bilderberg participants, something Van der Beugel had rejected because it might lead to unnecessary publicity and set an unwanted precedent ("I'd be unwilling to bring my tailcoat to Bilderberg"). In the end, both Rusk and new President Lyndon Johnson used the Bilderberg meeting to set up a number of individual meetings with participants.

The conference itself featured a reprise of the Cannes debate on NATO's future, with two prominent Gaullists, Baumel and Christian de la Malène, present. As the hosting nation, the American group was larger than usual and included Dean Acheson, George Ball, McGeorge Bundy, Arthur Dean, Senator William Fulbright (D), Representative Chet Holifield (the Democratic chairman of the JAEC), C. D. Jackson, Senator Henry Jackson (D), Senator Jacob Javits (R), Henry Kissinger, John McCloy, George McGhee, and Shepard Stone. From Europe, a number of first-time Bilderbergers participated, including Gaston Deferre, the Socialist opponent of de Gaulle in the French presidential elections; Minister of State for Foreign Affairs Lord Dundee; Danish Foreign Minister Per Haekkerup; Dutch

Foreign Minister Joseph Luns; British diplomat (and future Bilderberg chairman) Eric Roll; General Hans Speidel (former commander of the NATO land forces in Central Europe); NATO Secretary General Dirk Stikker; and Ludger Westrick, one of Chancellor Erhard's most trusted aides.

The Williamsburg meeting began with one of the traditional Bilderberg discussions about recent changes in the Soviet Union and their wider significance for East-West relations. Marshall Shulman, a Soviet expert at Columbia University, held the introductory statement and argued that while the basic Soviet aims had not changed, the changes in short-term tactics were substantial and had become more deeply rooted than originally envisioned. The increasing Sino-Soviet tensions – which had escalated due to Soviet reluctance to help the Chinese to develop nuclear weapons – coupled with Soviet internal problems meant that the West could expect a prolonged period of peaceful coexistence. Moreover, the euphoria of the post-Sputnik years had evaporated, and Marxist-Leninist theory had difficulty explaining the period of economic growth and prosperity in the West.

Still, the Cold War would not end any time soon. Shulman concluded that the prospects for a real political settlement with the Soviet Union were not good. "It is sometimes thought," he said, "that Western countries should respond to this process of change [in the Soviet Union] by holding out opportunities for collaboration with the Soviet Union." This would be a mistake, Shulman argued. The past years had shown that the Soviet Union only reacted to Western strength and unity. "[W]hat is required [...]," Shulman concluded,

> is a policy which should not be defined on a simple linear scale from hard to soft, but a differentiated policy – one which [...] is firmly resistant to Soviet expansion and militant action, but at the same time seeks measures of collaboration [...] where there are mutual overlapping interests, particularly in seeking to introduce some safeguards into the military situation.[64]

As could be expected, left-leaning participants such as Healey, Deferre, and Paolo Vittorelli – the editor of *Avanti!* and the foreign affairs spokesman of the Nenni Socialists – emphasized the changes in the Soviet Union, whereas Ball, Senator Javits, and Assistant Secretary of the *Auswärtiges Amt* Franz Krapf highlighted "the stability of Soviet aims."[65] Ernst Majonica noted that many participants tended to "very optimistic forecasts" and felt it necessary to warn that the Soviet attitude on the German question remained the best way to predict Soviet intentions.[66] The Gaullist deputy Christian de la Malène, in turn, defended the French decision to officially recognize Communist China. According to Roll,

> His speech may well have been addressed to the Germans, as if to say 'here are the Anglo-Saxons worrying about Asia, Africa etc. and

whether the Chinese are worse than the Russians. We think all Communists are bad, and Central Europe is the real issue.[67]

On East-West Trade, George Ball gave a detailed statement regarding the
official US position. He distinguished between different communist areas.
On trade with the Soviet Union, the US maintained its opposition to selling
strategic goods. The recent US sales of wheat to the Soviet Union, therefore,
did not reflect a change of policy. With regard to Eastern Europe, Ball said,
the Johnson Administration favored a more flexible attitude, because of the
wider aim "to make them less dependent on the Soviet Union." With regard
to Communist China, North Korea and North Vietnam, on the other hand,
the US rejected any trade whatsoever. According to Ball, "the aggressive and
criminal behavior of China which threatened the West's vital interests" –
particularly in Vietnam – made a complete trade boycott imperative.[68]

Most participants agreed that an increase in East-West trade – particularly
with Eastern Europe – was to the advantage of the West. Otto Wolff expressed his delight that this taboo could at long last be realistically discussed in the United States. He warned, however, for too much optimism.
The ability of the communist countries to trade with the West was severely
limited because of the inferior quality of most of their goods. The only way
to offset this imbalance was to extend long-term credits (12 to 15 years), but
this was unacceptable since it amounted to "economic development aid."[69]
As Roll reported, most participants agreed that long-term credit "was the
one thing at which they drew the line."[70] Again, the British participants
were an exception, but they were completely isolated. Dean Acheson did not
attempt to hide his contempt for the British attitude on East-West trade and
reminded the conference that 25 years ago, the United States had agreed to
the British suggestion to impose economic sanctions against Adolf Hitler's
Germany.

In the discussion on NATO, Acheson presented his introductory report.
He compared NATO to a Mississippi steamboat – "going upstream it can't
go forward and blow the whistle at the same time" – and emphasized the
importance of Western unity in the face of the continued division of the
world. Central Europe, Acheson argued, still remained the crucial problem, if only because West Germany regarded it as such. Only if NATO possessed much stronger conventional forces, Acheson argued, would the West
be able to decisively influence events in that area. The Soviet Union would
be forced to act with considerable caution in the event of greater autonomy
of the satellites if they were faced with strong Western conventional forces
on the other side of the Iron Curtain. In other words, Moscow would thus
be forced to "ease up" its policy towards Eastern Europe. Also, in the event
of a "blow-up" in East-Germany or elsewhere, conventional forces would
be better able to prevent an escalation than forces wholly dependent on
the early use of tactical nuclear weapons. Acheson ended by endorsing the
MLF. He had become convinced that "it can be done"; that it was "hard to

overestimate the importance of moving toward closer partnership"; and that the MLF served a major political purpose in giving Germany a greater role in nuclear planning and control without the risk of national proliferation.[71]

Acheson's endorsement of the MLF, despite his earlier skepticism, was undoubtedly based on the fact that NATO had developed no other strategies for dealing with the nuclear question. Several other initial MLF-skeptics – including Van der Beugel and Erler – now agreed that the MLF, despite its obvious defects, was the best answer to Gaullist complaints about American domination and the best way to prevent national proliferation of nuclear forces.[72] This was exactly the line followed by the State Department's MLF Office, which had arranged special MLF briefings for most US participants.[73]

In a repeat of the Cannes scenario, Baumel attacked US nuclear and NATO policy in an hour-long speech.[74] But as Ernst Majonica noted in his diary, Baumel and his French colleagues were completely isolated.[75] Max Kohnstamm told the deputy assistant secretary of state for European affairs, J. Robert Schaetzel, that this time, in contrast to Cannes, more "Europeans were speaking up against the Gaullists and did not leave the task to Americans."[76] Eric Roll reported that

> apart from a short intervention by La Malene [sic], his Gaullist colleague, Baumel got no support from anyone in the subsequent discussion which was only divided between those who were wholeheartedly in favour of the M.L.F. as a means of strengthening the Alliance and those who were rather dubious about it.[77]

Those opposing Baumel on the European side included Bennett, Birrenbach, Deferre, Erler, Luns, and Snoy et d'Oppuers. Deferre made clear that he, along with many Frenchmen, disagreed most of all with de Gaulle's methods. If he came to power, Deferre would be willing "to negotiate and reach common decisions."[78] This was a welcome message, but Majonica was unimpressed by Deferre's speech, writing in his diary: "de Gaulle will beat him in his sleep."[79] Foreign Minister Luns replied to an accusation made by Baumel that Europe's lack of progress in political integration was due to the Dutch and Belgian rejection of the Fouchet Plan in 1962. Luns argued that the French refusal either to let Great Britain join the European Communities or to accept a greater degree of integration had been the cause of failure in 1962.

Skepticism about the MLF, however, was not limited to the Gaullists. Lord Dundee and Healey expressed their doubts about the expensive multilateral force, as did Henry Kissinger, who privately told Van der Beugel that he "had always opposed the MLF because I had thought it put too much strain on the German political fabric for a dubious objective."[80] Vittorelli, moreover, explained that the MLF had become an issue in Italian politics because it allowed the communists to portray the government as opposed to détente. Luns asked whether some other device for a greater European say and education in the nuclear field could not be found. The military value of the MLF was limited and it was expensive. The Netherlands, he said, would not be able to contribute much to the force.

Fritz Erler also called the MLF a second-best solution. Erler's statement, which Kohnstamm called "by far the best performance of the entire meeting," was a strong plea for the indivisibility of Western defense. The defense of Europe could only be Atlantic, not national or regional. However, Europe's economic resurgence and the end of the American nuclear monopoly necessitated a greater European contribution to the common deterrent. This contribution, Erler argued, should preferably be in the field of joint strategic planning. The MLF would divert resources away from the needed conventional buildup. However, if the MLF was the only alternative to national nuclear forces, Erler supported it. West Germany did not want to possess its own nuclear weapons, Erler concluded, but younger generations would not accept "permanent inferiority."[81]

On the American side, the response to the Gaullists was stronger than at Cannes. As Kohnstamm reported,

> Arthur Dean was so provoked by the French that he took them on openly. He said that a continuance of the kind of performance he had seen at Bilderberg could destroy the US-French friendship that had been built up over the past generations.[82]

Bundy also gave a sharp retort to Baumel and in particular denied the latter's accusation that de Gaulle's September 1958 memorandum on NATO reform had never received a real reply. Senator Fulbright and Dean Acheson, moreover, solemnly reaffirmed the American commitment to NATO.

After the Williamsburg conference, Van der Beugel told Henry Owen that

> [t]he American delegation showed great strength and cohesion and the five non-French members of the Common Market did very well, especially the Germans. It was also very important, that the congressional participants were convinced beyond any doubt about the positive attitude of the overwhelming majority of the Europeans towards the United States and NATO.[83]

The Gaullists, in other words, had failed to muster any support for their anti-NATO stance. The most vivid expression of European opposition to de Gaulle came from Carlo Schmid, who told Kohnstamm that "the Gaullist group was just like the *Gauleiters* of the Hitler period."[84]

The final day of the Williamsburg conference was spent discussing the one area of transatlantic relations where progress seemed possible: international trade. The general conclusion of the discussion was straightforward – the West should do all it could to lessen barriers to international trade in the Kennedy Round in GATT. The European Economic Community in particular had an obligation to avoid becoming a protectionist block – although Sicco Mansholt made clear that agricultural protection would be a most difficult problem to solve. The presence of Mansholt, Ball, US trade coordinator Christian Herter, GATT Secretary Eric Wyndham White, Senators Fulbright and Javits – both deeply involved in trade matters – the high OECD official Emile van Lennep, Snoy et d'Oppuers, Luns, and many others involved in international trade and finance, made the Bilderberg meetings into an important informal meeting place to ensure the success of the Kennedy Round.

The transatlantic relationship – three schools of thought

The second half of the 1960s was a frustrating period for all those who favored both further European integration and a deepening of transatlantic ties. During the 1965 empty chair crisis, President de Gaulle prevented the EEC from moving to a system of majority voting on most issues. Then, on March 7, 1966, de Gaulle announced France's withdrawal from NATO's integrated military structures. At the other side of the ocean, meanwhile, the choice of right-wing Senator Barry Goldwater to be the Republican nominee in the 1964 presidential elections rattled many European Bilderbergers, representing, as it seemed, a return to dangerous nationalist traditions in US foreign policy. Even after President Johnson's convincing victory, moreover, American leadership in Europe was in short supply – no doubt partly because of the Johnson Administration's increasing preoccupation with the war in Vietnam. As Van der Beugel told the Atlantic Council's Theodore Achilles in March 1965: "I belong to those Europeans who have no complex whatsoever as to strong American leadership and I deplore the lack of it especially during the last year."

During the Bilderberg conference that took place from April 2–4, 1965, at the Italian Villa d'Este, Lake Como, the conclusion seemed unavoidable that little could be done as long as de Gaulle remained in power.[85] Ernst van der Beugel contributed a paper on the State of the Alliance, asking whether the assumptions underlying the combined Cold War policy of European integration and collective security through NATO were still valid. He identified three (partly overlapping) schools of thought in the Gaullist-Atlanticist struggle. The first was the Gaullist school,

> inspired by a strong desire to increase the power and influence of Europe to such an extent that Europe could eventually have an independent policy in a world which till now was mainly dominated by the U.S. and the Soviet Union.

It challenged the *raison d'être* of NATO and "does not believe in the permanency of the U.S. political and military commitment to Europe." As a result, it insisted upon "its wish to provide Europe with its own nuclear force." It was not clear though, Van der Beugel noted, how "its European vision can be reconciled with the concept of the supremacy of the nation state."[86]

The second – and largest – school of thought "believes not only in the compatibility of European unity and Atlantic cohesion but it considers European unification as a prerequisite to Atlantic strength." It supported supranational European integration as the best way of tying Germany to the West and believed in the ultimate development of an Atlantic partnership. "Members of this school," Van der Beugel said, "were generally activists who considered any slowing down of European unification as being by definition detrimental to the cause of the West."[87]

The third, much smaller school of thought, to which Van der Beugel counted himself, had reached the conclusion that European integration and the Atlantic alliance were no longer mutually reinforcing. This school believed that "foreign policy on main issues and military policy in general are Atlantic functions and <u>not</u> European functions."[88] It was time to reject the idea of an equal partnership between Europe and the United States. Progress in the field of political integration, after all, was impossible because of the fundamental differences between de Gaulle and the other Five. The main task for the period ahead was to

> confine the efforts in Europe now to the economic field, to continue the struggle for the inclusion of the United Kingdom and other European countries in the continental group and to deepen and develop the military, economic and political integration, cooperation and consultation in the Atlantic Alliance.[89]

The New York Times columnist James Reston gave Van der Beugel's report a prominent (though anonymous) place in a long article in *The New York Times* and noted that "these sharp differences are found in all the Western European countries, and they indicate the magnitude of the task before the leaders of the alliance."[90] This much also became clear during the Bilderberg discussion on Van der Beugel's paper, which, not surprisingly, drew a lot of criticism.

Ball, a prominent proponent of the second school of thought, was the first to respond, in a passionate speech (quoted at the start of this book) simultaneously defending the concept of Atlantic partnership and attacking Gaullist nationalism. "The twelve years between 1950 and 1962 were the Golden Age of progress towards European unity and the Atlantic partnership," Ball said, "but at the beginning of 1963, one of the leading European nations had started to reverse the trend by a statement which had since been regarded as the first salvo in a nationalistic counter-revolution." Ball argued that this counter-revolution aimed at "a return to a 'fragmented' Western Europe" and the "national rivalry between European states which had caused so many tragedies in the past." Ball emphasized the

"deep anxiety which this trend aroused in him," and ended on an apoca-
lyptic note:

> Few of us consciously desired to return to the bad old days when the
> fate of mankind depended on rivalry, jealousy and the whims of Nation
> States which were not channeled through joint plans, co-operation
> agreements and solemnly contracted obligations. [...] we all knew that
> such a system was ineffective and would never function again. [Everyone
> should] recall that history could repeat itself and that, if it repeated it-
> self in the nuclear age, we would all vanish in a mushroom cloud.[91]

McGhee later reported that Ball's speech had made a big impression; the
subsequent discussion, however, confirmed Van der Beugel's basic analysis. Both within the United States and within most European countries,
members of the transatlantic elite were deeply divided between the three
schools of thought. And despite Ball's eloquence, it was also becoming
increasingly clear that the period when the United States, for political reasons, had swallowed its economic objections to the Common Market was
nearing its end, no doubt in part because of President de Gaulle's policies.
President Johnson's sudden turn away from the MLF in late 1964 seemed
to indicate a certain impatience with Europe in Washington, a desire to
move on from Europe to more urgent problems in the rest of the world.[92]
Tellingly, at the Villa d'Este conference Ball was asked to give a special
presentation on the situation in Vietnam, as James Reston reported in *The
New York Times*.

Spring was in the air at the Villa d'Este, which, situated at the southern
end of Lake Como, was probably the most beautiful spot where any of the
Bilderberg conferences had taken place. Yet those present at the conference
may have felt a twinge of melancholy. The Villa d'Este discussions set off
by Van der Beugel seemed to signify the end of a distinct era; 20 years after
the end of the Second World War, the era of the closest US involvement in
Europe appeared to be over.

Reston was attuned to this sentiment. "Yes," he wrote,

> Europe is worried about us. Having muddled through themselves, they
> are now concerned about our muddling through. They fear we are turn-
> ing away from Europe, that we are looking homeward and even east-
> ward to Asia, that we are blindly anti-Communist just as, in their eyes,
> we were blindly anti-colonial in our rush to break up the old empires.

Europe had liked Kennedy, Reston said, because "he was not a typical or
representative American." President Johnson was different, "because he
looks and acts like the popular European caricature of an American politician. Accordingly, since the election of Johnson and the bombing of North
Vietnam many of the old popular anti-American feelings have revived."[93]

In March 1966, de Gaulle provided further confirmation for this interpretation. Not only did he withdraw all French forces from NATO's integrated military command structure, he also announced his intention to seek
a Franco-Russian rapprochement, planning to visit Moscow in June 1966.[94]
De Gaulle's actions implied that, in his view, a unified Western alliance in
the Cold War was no longer necessary and perhaps even inhibited a relaxation of East-West tensions.

Although the German participants at the Bilderberg conference held in
Wiesbaden, West Germany (March 25–27, 1966) were especially shocked
and worried by de Gaulle's action, the overall result of the Bilderberg meeting was a feeling of almost relief that the alliance could get moving again
on the logjam of blocked issues.[95] Of course, few doubted the dangers of
de Gaulle's approach, but the Wiesbaden conference provided an opportunity of readjusting the alliance to these new circumstances. Prince Bernhard
specifically asked the members of the steering committee

> not to concentrate their remarks solely on the happenings of recent
> weeks (French Government's decisions). It was hoped that an important
> place would be allotted to changes aimed at a long-term improvement
> in the working of NATO with the door left open for France to return
> eventually.[96]

On the other hand, Van der Beugel told the Prince that frank talk and a
strong European contribution was crucial: "I do not believe that you need
to mask the seriousness of the situation in any way – to the contrary, with
NATO the aim of Bilderberg is at stake."[97]

The Johnson Administration realized the importance of a strong pres-
ence at Wiesbaden and was represented by George Ball, Robert Bowie (who
had been appointed advisor on NATO matters), George McGhee, John
McCloy (the Administration's point man for all German matters), and John
W. Tuthill, the US representative to the European Communities. The West
German government also saw the Wiesbaden conference as the first opportunity to forge a Western response to the Gaullist challenge. Apart from Abs,
Berg, Birrenbach, Erler, Schmid, and other Bilderberg regulars, Chancellor
Erhard decided to participate in part of the meeting. Another first-time participant was SPD parliamentarian and defense specialist Helmut Schmidt,
"who," Van der Beugel told Prince Bernhard, "in my opinion is the future
leader of the SPD."[98] Erhard used the Wiesbaden conference for private
conversations with John McCloy and George Ball. Manlio Brosio, Stikker's
successor as NATO secretary general, was also present.

The main conclusion of the Wiesbaden conference was that the NATO
crisis should be used to create a new sense of direction in the alliance. John
McCloy stated that de Gaulle's actions had the advantage of forcing NATO
to "face up to problems" that had existed for several years but could not be
addressed because of French opposition. The great danger, however, was

that de Gaulle's methods might win adherents in other European countries. Since "nationalism creates nationalism," there was a real risk of Europe going adrift, whereas the United States might become so disheartened by the "complexities of Europe" that it might disengage to some extent from European affairs. To avoid these dangers, "the highest form of statesmanship" was called for.[99]

Fritz Erler agreed that de Gaulle was "riding a tiger" – it was highly questionable whether the general could control the nationalistic forces he had set loose. George Ball used the occasion to reaffirm the US commitment to NATO and the alliance, much as he had done in the Villa d'Este. De Gaulle "seemed to be proposing to return to 1914." However, Ball said, the United States remained convinced that a nationalistic, fragmented West could never achieve the common objectives of defense, deterrence, and finding a settlement in Europe – only the combined and organized power of the West could do so.[100]

On the German side, both Erhard and Birrenbach indicated that they felt a solution of the nuclear question in NATO was now not only necessary but also possible because of the self-imposed French absence in NATO. Birrenbach showed greater willingness to compromise and abandoned his earlier insistence on a 'hardware solution' – involving co-ownership of nuclear submarines. In effect, he moved much closer to Erler's position, who favored a joint planning and development solution – the 'software solution.'[101]

The NATO crisis also led to greater flexibility on the part of the most important congressional representative in the nuclear question, JAEC Chairman Chet Holifield. Holifield indicated his willingness to consider amendments to the McMahon Act if the European allies could make a clear proposal of what they wanted. He argued that the McNamara Committee on nuclear strategy offered the most promising road forward.[102] A solution to the nuclear problem finally seemed in sight, although it would take another serious crisis in confidence between the US and Germany over non-proliferation and the matter of offset agreements and US troops in Germany before an agreement could be reached in 1967.[103] Secretary of State Dean Rusk's recommendation to President Johnson to turn the McNamara Committee into the Nuclear Planning Group, meanwhile, was based to a considerable extent on information gathered at the Wiesbaden conference. Rusk referred not just to Ball's talk with Erhard, but also to Holifield's changed position and to Erler's ideas about a solution to the nuclear problem.[104]

Birrenbach's change of heart at Wiesbaden probably did not reflect conviction as much as realism. During a trip to the United States in November 1965, he had received warnings from several high officials sympathetic to the German case that the political pressure for a US-Soviet non-proliferation treaty was mounting – partly as the result of the Gilpatric Report on non-proliferation.[105] It is indicative of the sensitivity of the Bilderberg organizers to such mood swings that they invited Roswell Gilpatric to the Wiesbaden conference, as well as Senator Fred Harris – one of 18 senators who had signed a statement in favor of non-proliferation negotiations – and Zbigniew Brzezinski, a Columbia professor and part-time White House consultant who favored a more active détente policy towards the Soviet Union.

Brzezinski argued at Wiesbaden that NATO should take a more active role in East-West relations and the relaxation of tensions with the Soviet Union. Most Bilderberg participants at Wiesbaden agreed that the threat of Soviet aggression in Europe was considerably smaller than only a few years ago (shortly after the Williamsburg conference Khrushchev had been forced to step back). The fact that this changed threat assessment came to be accepted in groups such as Bilderberg, paved the way for the 1967 NATO Harmel Exercise. The resulting Harmel Report introduced a new two-pillar concept of security for NATO, emphasizing the dual need for defense and détente.[106]

De Gaulle's challenge was by no means the only problem facing the alliance. The Vietnam War had increasingly become a strain on US-European relations, if only for the fear in Europe that America would become increasingly preoccupied with the war, with necessarily detrimental effects on the defense of Europe and the alliance as a whole. The high-level American presence at Wiesbaden was also an attempt to allay such European doubts. George Ball gave another special statement on the situation in Vietnam, meant both to inform the European allies and to win them over for a more active role outside the NATO area.[107] Ball was optimistic about the overall situation in Vietnam, arguing that the situation was improving because of the stepped-up US bombing campaign in North Vietnam and the increasing numbers of American forces. He expressed hope that the Viet-Cong would "find the rate of attrition intolerable" and that the US-supported actions to improve conditions in "pacified areas" would increase local support for the South Vietnamese government.[108]

There was some irony in Ball's presentation, however, because behind closed doors Ball was one of the strongest opponents of the Vietnam War in the Johnson Administration.[109] Another irony was that at the 1964 Williamsburg conference, the French participants had explicitly warned the United States about repeating the dangerous mistakes France had made during the Indochina war. These warnings, although based on years of French experience in the region, did not register in Washington, in part because Gaullist criticism could so easily be rejected as simply anti-American.[110] At Wiesbaden, meanwhile, Ball's pep-talk did not seem to convince the Europeans, who asked a series of probing questions about the possibility of escalation of the Vietnam War and about the willingness of the South Vietnamese to continue fighting.[111]

A new generation

The European response at Wiesbaden also reflected the mounting public opposition to the Vietnam War in much of Europe. In fact, the Bilderberg organizers had become seriously concerned about the effects of Vietnam and the upsurge of youth and student movements on public support for NATO.[112] Shortly after the Wiesbaden conference, Ernst van der Beugel wrote a memorandum for the Bilderberg Steering Committee in which he warned that the basic assumptions of "practically every participant in the Bilderberg conferences" – in Van der Beugel's words, the "need for European integration, need for a maximum of cohesion in the Atlantic world, need for a strong defensive posture towards the Eastern Bloc etc." – were no longer shared by large parts of the Western publics, "especially the young people." "I consider," Van der Beugel wrote, "the Gaullist deviation as much less dangerous than the complete ignorance of and indifference to our basic assumptions in the minds and hearts of such a substantial part of the population in our part of the world." The Bilderberg Steering Committee should discuss this development, to avoid becoming an "emeritus establishment group," stuck in the 1950s.[113]

Earlier attempts to prevent Bilderberg from ossifying had already led to the complete overhaul of the steering committee in 1964, but now a new sense of urgency was apparent – as it was in other organizations of the informal alliance such as the *Atlantik-Brücke*, the Atlantic Institute, the American Council on Germany, the CEDI, and the Ford Foundation.[114] As a result of Van der Beugel's memorandum, the steering committee decided to invite more participants under the age of 40 for the 1967 and 1968 Bilderberg conferences. The Ford Foundation assisted with a long list of potential younger participants in the United States and Europe.

The 1967 Bilderberg Conference in Cambridge (March 31–April 2) succeeded in bringing in a significant number of new faces.[115] However, with the escalating student unrest in 1968, Bilderberg's renewal remained a matter of great concern to the Bilderberg organizers. In September 1968, Van der Beugel again wrote a memorandum to the members of the Bilderberg steering committee, warning that

> from the point of view of age and from the point of view of opinion on basic matters of policy, we tend to be a rather one-sided group. In other words, to put it in the modern jargon we are very much 'establishment'.[116]

He added that by definition, the Bilderberg Group would always "have a strong establishment element," but he argued that the process of bringing in younger people should be continued and intensified:

> The Chairman and the two Secretaries rejected the notion that we should organize the Bilderberg Meeting as a sort of confrontation between two different groups but we found ourselves greatly in favour of an effort to increase the participation of much younger people who are much nearer to the views of the student generation in vital matters of foreign policy.

As an example, Van der Beugel mentioned the "[Eugene] McCarthy and younger [Robert] Kennedy people in the United States and the analogue groups in Europe."[117]

In an attempt to better grasp the generational changes that were rattling Western societies, the Bilderberg organizers also invited sociologists Daniel Bell and Ralf Dahrendorf and media guru Marshall McLuhan. Although Dahrendorf became a frequent participant, the effort seems to have had limited success. As Arthur Dean reported on a steering committee meeting in October 1969:

> There seemed to be general agreement among all of the members that we should not schedule another meeting of Bilderberg on "instability". Baron Edmond de Rothschild said that he recently attended a meeting at Geneva on a similar subject where in his opinion they had wasted about two days' time and he found the further discussion very boring. There also seemed to be a general consensus that we should not again invite sociologists to a Bilderberg meeting, but there was a general feeling that we should continue to invite younger persons in the fields that we decided upon to discuss.[118]

In a sense, the members of the informal alliance had become victims of the success of most Western societies. The perceived decline of the Soviet threat and the increasing wealth in the United States and Western Europe had removed some of the driving forces and motives that had led the World War II generation to develop the Marshall plan, NATO, and an integrated Europe.

The transatlantic crisis of the mid-1960s, meanwhile, did illustrate how the informal alliance could play a role in crisis management. Particularly, the debate in Germany between Gaullists and Atlanticists had been strongly influenced by members of the transatlantic elite. The Bilderberg meetings, moreover, managed to include Gaullist views, while making clear that the majority of Bilderberg participants remained committed to the basic aims of European integration and transatlantic cooperation. The combination of President de Gaulle's unilateral methods, the strongly nationalist, anti-integration message of Gaullism, and de Gaulle's unwillingness to accept a leading US role in Europe violated key norms held by most members of the transatlantic elite. The failure of de Gaulle's European designs was thus in part the failure to build a consensus amongst European members of the informal alliance. To the American participants, meanwhile, the Bilderberg meetings provided important moments to legitimize US positions and to counter the many Gaullist barbs in the Gaullist-Atlanticist struggle.

In all this, the limits of both the informal and the formal alliance were of course also apparent. As long as one crucial member of the alliance was unwilling to pursue an agenda of further integration and cooperation, there was no way the other members could force it. In addition, the fast-increasing importance of television and the democratization of foreign policy in the long 1960s appeared to chip away at the influence of the transatlantic elite.[119] The Bilderberg Group's indirect influence relied very much on the authority of its participants; however, it was precisely this authority that was questioned by the 1968 generation. Still, despite the sense that the 'golden era' of transatlantic cooperation was over, the Bilderberg Group successfully managed the transition to the 1970s and even survived the end of the Cold War. The transatlantic foreign policy elite, in other words, continued to value the informal alliance and what it stood for.

Notes

1 Quoted in James Reston, "Atlantic Unity is the Course of History," May 18, 1962, *The New York Times*, 30.
2 Report Saltsjöbaden Conference, 31, Box 20, Bilderberg Archives, NANL.
3 Ibid., 42.
4 Erler to Nitze, June 14, 1962, Box 157 A, Erler Papers, FES.
5 Joseph C. Harsch, "State of the Nations," *Christian Science Monitor*, May 22, 1962.
6 Report Saltsjöbaden Conference, 38, Box 20, Bilderberg Archives, NANL.
7 The declaration, which was agreed to by all members of the Action Committee representing most political parties in the Six, was published on June 26, 1962.
8 The groundwork of the speech had been laid by McGeorge Bundy during a December 1961 speech in Chicago. Both Bundy and Kennedy were in frequent contact with Monnet, as was Walt Rostow – one of the principal drafters of the Independence Day speech (the other was Henry Owen).
9 President John F. Kennedy, "Address at Independence Hall," Philadelphia, July 4, 1962.
10 On de Gaulle's veto, see Bozo, *Two Strategies*; Conze, *Gaullistische Herausforderung*, 257; Locher, *Crisis? What Crisis?*; Martin, *General de Gaulle's Cold War*; Münger, *Kennedy*, 250–257; Vaïsse, *Grandeur*, 220–224.
11 Press Conference by President de Gaulle, http://aei.pitt.edu/5777/1/5777.pdf. Accessed March 23, 2018.
12 On Nassau and the MLF, see Ashton, *Kennedy, Macmillan*; Costigliola, "Kennedy"; Gavin, *Nuclear Statecraft*; Haftendorn, *NATO*; Neustadt, *Report to JFK*; Priest, *Kennedy, Johnson and NATO*; Steinbrunner, *Cybernetic Theory*; Trachtenberg, *Constructed Peace*. On NATO during the 1960s more generally: Wenger, Nünlist and Locher, *Transforming NATO*.
13 See Gijswijt, "The Kennedy Administration."
14 Then again, the Kennedy Administration had tried to set up a meeting between Kennedy and de Gaulle since mid-1962 and had been put off several times.
15 "The U.S. and De Gaulle -- The Past and the Future," unsigned, January 30, 1963, Box 404, Bundy Chronological File, NSF, JFKL. Bundy identified himself as the author of this memorandum during a conference in 1992. See Trachtenberg, *Constructed Peace*, 284, Note 4.
16 On the treaty, see Baumann, *Begegnung*; Defrance and Pfeil, *Der Elysée-Vertrag*; Geiger, *Atlantiker gegen Gaullisten*; Granieri, *The Ambivalent Alliance*; Lappenküper, *Die deutsch-französische Beziehungen*; Schoenborn, "Chancellor Erhard's"; Steinkühler, *Der deutsch-französische Vertrag*.
17 As Costigliola rightly notes, President Kennedy himself did not inform his European allies of the secret deal to remove Jupiter missiles from Europe, which helped end the Cuban Missile Crisis. Costigliola, "Kennedy," 114–115.

18 See Schulz, "Die Politische Freundschaft," and Hoeres, *Außenpolitik und Öffen-tlichkeit*. On Erhard's role see Schoenborn, "Chancellor Erhard's."

19 In early February, Monnet and Kohnstamm met with the SPD's Herbert Wehner and Erich Ollenhauer, FDP leader Erich Mende, Ludwig Rosenberg and others to discuss the Franco-German Treaty. See the memoranda in Box 22, Kohnstamm Papers, EUI. Kohnstamm's diary shows that Kohnstamm was in almost daily telephone contact with Birrenbach in this period.

20 On Emmett's involvement, see Zetsche, "Quest for Atlanticism," 201–207.

21 James Reston, "What People Do They Think We Are?" January 21, 1963, *The New York Times*.

22 McCloy to Adenauer, February 4, 1963, Special Correspondence: John J. McCloy, POF, JFKL.

23 The conference was organized by Baumgartner (assisted by Wagon-Lits) and largely financed by the French government, with some assistance from Villiers' *Patronat*. Note that the official Cannes report wrongly lists May 29–31 as the conference dates.

24 Van der Beugel to Prince Bernhard (my translation), March 8, 1963, Box 67, Bilderberg Archives, NANL.

25 "Introductory Remarks," Box 1644, Carlo Schmid Papers, FES.

26 Joseph E. Johnson, Memorandum for the American Steering Committee, October 25, 1962, Box 76, Dean Papers, CUL. Johnson had met with Heinz, Nebolsine, and Stone to discuss de Gaulle's attitude: "There was concensus [sic] on the need to avoid any dictation by a government of the agenda of the private Bilderberg meetings."

27 See Chapter 4.

28 George Nebolsine, "Bilderberg Meeting at Soestdijk Palace, November 10, 1962," Box 76, Dean Papers, CUL.

29 "Meeting at Rijkens' house," January 29, 1963, Box 55, and Lamping, "After-thoughts over Cannes," July 11, 1963, Box 21, Bilderberg Archives, NANL.

30 Lamping, "Afterthoughts over Cannes," July 11, 1963, Box 21, Bilderberg Ar-chives, NANL.

31 See "Meeting at Rijkens' house," March 8, 1963, Box 55, Bilderberg Archives, NANL.

32 Healey and Callaghan were to become minister of defense and chancellor of the exchequer, respectively, in the 1964 Labour Government under Harold Wilson.

33 Summary Record of National Security Council Meeting, April 2, 1963, Box 314, NSF, JFKL.

34 Speech by Jacques Baumel, Box 116, POF, Countries, France: General 1963: March-October, JFKL. Van der Beugel provided Ball with a transcription of Baumel's speech made from a recording of the conference. The speech bears the signs of a hasty translation by the State Department. Quotes are from this translation.

35 The question of nuclear assistance was one of the most difficult the Kennedy Administration had to deal with. It considered the issue in the spring of 1961, in early 1962, in late 1962 as a result of the Nassau summit, and again in 1963 in the context of the limited test ban negotiations with the Soviet Union. Nitze was involved in several initial discussions with French officials, but the bridge to real cooperation was never crossed. Of course, Nitze and Ball were restricted in what they could tell the Cannes meeting about these attempts to find a solu-tion acceptable to de Gaulle. By 1963, President Kennedy became more and more convinced that relations with de Gaulle would have been far better if he had made "a clear offer of nuclear assistance to France in June of 1961." Bundy disagreed. See McGeorge Bundy, Memorandum for the Record, May 11, 1963,

Box 32, Folder 1963: July-May, White House Subject Files, McGeorge Bundy Papers, JFKL, 2.

36 "Brief Impressionistic Summary of Bilderberg Meeting," no author, Box 56-341, FFA.

37 Cannes Report, 21, Box 21, Bilderberg Archives, NANL.

38 Speech by Jacques Baumel, Box 116, POF, Countries, France: General 1963: March-October, JFKL.

39 McGeorge Bundy had recognized this problem two weeks after de Gaulle's press conference, writing:

> There remains one crucial question which we are still pushing ahead of us and on which it may be essential to make a decision, at least among ourselves, before long. This question is whether we are prepared to accept and support a real European requirement for a real European role, as and when that demand is presented. Our Nassau multilateral proposals are a major step forward, but they are presented still within the framework of a U.S. veto. Thus we still leave to General de Gaulle the chance to pose as the one true spokesman of real independence for Europeans.

Box 404, Bundy Chronological File, NSF, JFKL.

40 Max Kohnstamm Summary of the Cannes conference, Box 22, Kohnstamm Papers, EUI.

41 Cannes Report, 14, Box 21, Bilderberg Archives, NANL, and Max Kohnstamm Summary of the Cannes conference, Box 22, Kohnstamm Papers, EUIHA.

42 See Memcon Stikker Strauß, January 29, 1962, Box 56, Stikker Papers, NANL. Strauß told Stikker:

> Referring to present American nuclear policies and the idea of a limited war in Europe, Mr. Strauss [sic] stressed that Germany will some day have to draw certain consequences if this policy continued. It was unthinkable that she would remain without atomic armaments if the United States, the United Kingdom and even France possessed nuclear weapons.

43 For a recent overview of the Adenauer Government's attitude, see Geier, *Schwellenmacht.*

44 Max Kohnstamm Summary of the Cannes conference, Box 22, Kohnstamm Papers, EUI and Cannes Report, 19, Box 21, Bilderberg Archives, NANL.

45 Nitze Handwritten Notes, Box 61, Nitze Papers, LOC.

46 Cannes Report, 13 and 18, Box 21, Bilderberg Archives, NANL.

47 Arthur Dean Handwritten Notes Cannes, Box 76, Dean Papers, CUL.

48 Cannes Report, 18, Box 21, Bilderberg Archives, NANL.

49 Nitze Handwritten Notes Cannes, Box 61, Nitze Papers, LOC.

50 Cannes Report, 18, Box 21, Bilderberg Archives, NANL.

51 Cannes Report, 25, Box 21, Bilderberg Archives, NANL.

52 Van der Beugel to Kissinger, April 4, 1963, Box 7, Van der Beugel Papers, NANL.

53 Van der Beugel to Warburg, April 11, 1963, Box 7, Van der Beugel Papers, NANL.

54 Lamping, "Afterthoughts over Cannes," July 11, 1963, (my translation) Box 21, Bilderberg Archives, NANL.

55 Ibid.

56 Summary Record of National Security Council Meeting, 2 April 1963, Box 314, NSF, JFKL.

57 Ball drew several other conclusions from the Cannes meeting. First, the American attitude on East-West trade caused considerable irritation in Europe. As a result, Ball recommended that a revision of East-West trade policy should

be considered. Second, the American conventional forces strategy in NATO had not convinced the Europeans. "This strategy is being used effectively to undermine the European faith that the U.S. is resolved to use nuclear weapons when required." Third, many Europeans worried that without a nuclear weapons program, they would miss out on crucial developments in the peaceful use of nuclear energy. Ibid.

58 See Birrenbach to Monnet, March 16, 1963, Box 22, Kohnstamm Papers, EUI. Birrenbach told Monnet that he had done a legal study of the possibilities for the *Bundestag* to amend a treaty. There were two possibilities: a Bundestag declaration and a special clause in the preamble of the treaty. The second cause was "constitutionally unusual." But, Birrenbach added, this "does not disturb me at all."

59 A similar wording appears in Birrenbach's March 16 letter to Monnet, Ibid.

60 See McGhee to Secretary of State, April 1, 1963, Box 4141, Subject Numeric File 1963, RG 59, NARA.

61 Sitzung Parteivorstand, May 11, 1963, SPD Parteivorstand Protokolle, FES.

62 See Daum, *Kennedy in Berlin*; and Gijswijt, "Running for President."

63 Van der Beugel to Prince Bernhard, November 20, 1963, Box 67, Bilderberg Archives, NANL.

64 Marshall Shulman Statement, Box 36, Jackson Papers, DDEL. Lamping sent Jackson this transcript of a recording of the Williamsburg conference.

65 Eric Roll, Williamsburg 1964, Box 178959, FO 371, NAL.

66 Majonica Diary, Entry March 20, 1964 (my translation), Box 024/2, Majonica Papers, ACDP. I thank Christopher Beckmann of the *Konrad Adenauer Stiftung* for providing me with a transcript of the Majonica diary.

67 Eric Roll, Williamsburg 1964, Box 178959, FO 371, NAL.

68 Williamsburg Report, 23-24, Box 22, Bilderberg Archives, NANL, and Chet Holifield Handwritten Notes Williamsburg, 10-12, Box 43, Holifield Papers, USC.

69 See Otto Wolff's report on the East-West trade discussion and a copy of his own remarks, Box 188, KE 113, BDIA.

70 Eric Roll, Williamsburg 1964, Box 178959, FO 371, NAL.

71 Holifield Notes, Box 43, Holifield Papers, USC, and Williamsburg Report, 32–33, Box 22, Bilderberg Archives, NANL.

72 Van der Beugel told Henry Owen: "You convinced me about the multilateral force. I immediately went to work on this point and I hope and expect that a positive attitude will be taken [at the next Bilderberg meeting]." Van der Beugel to Owen, 25 November 1963, Box 7, Van der Beugel Papers, NANL. See also Van der Beugel to Kissinger, January 16, 1964, ibid. Van der Beugel now highlighted the anti-Gaullist element in the MLF: "The way to demonstrate that we are opponents of De Gaulle's policy is available in NATO and in eventually joining the multilateral force." Erler likewise told Walden Moore that he regarded the MLF as a "clumsy detour." However,

> I am not against MLF, because killing it, would open the way for uncontrolled proliferation. It would be a victory of Gaullist thinking not only in France but everywhere in the Western world. This would be disastrous for the coherence of the Alliance.

Erler to Moore, March 17, 1964, Box 156a, Erler Papers, FES.

73 See the briefing material, correspondence and memcons in Box 14, Office of the Special Assistant to the Secretary of State for Multilateral Force Negotiations, Lot 69D55 Entry 5250, NARA.

74 As a result of Baumel's speech – speakers were generally limited to five minutes speaking time – a traffic light was installed at subsequent Bilderberg meetings to signal when a speaker's time was up. The chairman of Bilderberg, Prince

Bernhard, later admitted in an interview that he especially enjoyed using the traffic light against Dutch Minister of Foreign Affairs Joseph Luns.

75 Majonica Diary, Entry March 20, 1964, Box 024/2, Majonica Papers, ACDP.

76 Conversation between Kohnstamm and Schaetzel, March 26, 1964, Box 14, Office of the Special Assistant to the Secretary of State for Multilateral Force Negotiations, Lot 69D55 Entry 5250, NARA.

77 Eric Roll, Williamsburg 1964, Box 178959, FO 371, NAL.

78 McGhee Notes Williamsburg, Box 2, series XIII, McGhee Papers, GUL.

79 Majonica Diary, Entry March 21, 1964, Box 024/2, Majonica Papers, ACDP.

80 Kissinger to Van der Beugel, January 25, 1965, Box 71, Bilderberg Archives, NANL. Kissinger's opposition to the MLF led to a falling out with his Harvard colleague Robert Bowie, and meant that Kissinger was not invited to the 1965 and 1966 conferences. Ibid.

81 McGhee Notes Williamsburg, Box 2, series XIII, McGhee Papers, GUL and Williamsburg Report, 38–39, Box 22, Bilderberg Archives, NANL.

82 Conversation between Kohnstamm and Schaetzel, March 26, 1964, Box 14, Office of the Special Assistant to the Secretary of State for Multilateral Force Negotiations, Lot 69D55 Entry 5250, NARA.

83 Van der Beugel to Owen, April 2, 1964, Box 7, Van der Beugel Papers, NANL.

84 Conversation between Kohnstamm and Schaetzel, March 26, 1964, Box 14, Office of the Special Assistant to the Secretary of State for Multilateral Force Negotiations, Lot 69D55 Entry 5250, NARA.

85 Gianni Agnelli financed and organized the conference.

86 Ernst van der Beugel, "The State of the Atlantic Alliance," February 1965, Box 56-341, FFA.

87 Ibid.

88 Ibid. (emphasis in original).

89 Ibid.

90 James Reston, "Challenge to Alliance," *The New York Times*, April 12, 1965.

91 Villa d'Este Report, 37–39, Box 23, Bilderberg Archives, NANL.

92 See Schwartz, *Lyndon Johnson and Europe*; and Priest, *Kennedy, Johnson*.

93 James Reston, "Lake Como: Europe on Johnson and Vietnam," *The New York Times*, April 4, 1965.

94 For a good overview see Ellison, "Defeating the General."

95 Otto Wolff was mainly responsible for organizing and financing the meeting.

96 Minutes Steering Committee, March 24–27, 1966, Box 73, Bilderberg Archives, NANL.

97 Van der Beugel to Prince Bernhard, March 16, 1966, (my translation), Box 73, Bilderberg Archives, NANL.

98 Van der Beugel to Bernhard, October 25, 1965, (my translation) Box 73, Bilderberg Archives, NANL.

99 David Bell Handwritten Notes, Box 34, Bell Papers, JFKL.

100 David Bell Handwritten Notes, Box 34, Bell Papers, JFKL and Fred Harris Handwritten Notes, Box 30, Folder 29, Harris Papers, CACUO.

101 See George McGhee to Dean Rusk, April 7, 1966, Box 14, Office of the Special Assistant to the Secretary of State for Multilateral Force Negotiations, Lot 69D55, Entry 5250, RG 59, NARA.

102 See also Birrenbach's report to Foreign Minister Gerhard Schröder of two private conversations with Holifield. The latter again confirmed that he saw the McNamara Committee as a realistic possibility. After much pressure from Birrenbach, Holifield thought that with strong unanimous support from the Johnson Administration, a hardware solution might be possible. However, he left no doubt that this would be politically difficult. Birrenbach to Schröder, April 4, 1966, Box 17/2, Birrenbach Papers, ACDP.

103 See Costigliola, "Lyndon B. Johnson,"; Kieninger, *Dynamic Détente*; and Bozo, Rey, Ludlow and Rother, *Visions of the End*.

104 Memorandum From Secretary of State Rusk to President Johnson, April 11, 1966, FRUS, 1964–1968, Vol. XIII, No. 155.

105 See Birrenbach to Schröder, November 13, 1965, Box 17/2, Birrenbach Papers, ACDP.

106 See Haftendorn, "The Adaptation," and Wenger, "Crisis and Opportunity."

107 Max Frankel, correspondent of *The New York Times*, was present at Wiesbaden and published an account of Ball's presentation: "U.S. Is Reassuring West on Vietnam," *The New York Times*, April 2, 1966.

108 Wiesbaden Report, 29, Box 24, Bilderberg Archives, NANL.

109 See Bill, *George Ball*, 164 ff.

110 On this point more generally, see Friedman, *Rethinking Anti-Americanism*, Chapter 5.

111 Wiesbaden Report, 26–31, Box 24, Bilderberg Archives, NANL.

112 On Bilderberg's rejuvenation, see also: Bloemendal, "Reframing the Diplomat," 216–228 and Philipsen, "Diplomacy with Ambiguity," 136–139. On the transnational dimensions of the 1960s' profound socio-political changes see Friedman, *Rethinking Anti-Americanism*, Chapter 6; Klimke, *The Other Alliance*; Suri, *Power and Protest*.

113 E.H. van der Beugel, "To the Members of the Steering Committee of Bilderberg," August 1966, Box 76, Dean Papers, CUL.

114 On the *Atlantikbrücke* and ACG, see Zetsche, "Quest for Atlanticism," 169–171; on Van der Beugel's involvement in reorganizing the Atlantic Institute, see Bloemendal, "Reframing the Diplomat," 210–216; on CEDI, see Großmann, *Die Internationale*, 259–271; on the Ford Foundation, see Berghahn, *America and the Intellectual*; Aubourg, "Problems of Transmission"; and Scott-Smith, "Maintaining Transatlantic Community."

115 Organized mainly by steering committee member Bennett.

116 E.H. van der Beugel, "To the Members of the Steering Committee of Bilderberg," September 24 1968, Box 5534, Schmidt Papers, FES.

117 Ibid. In the case of Germany, novelist Günter Grass and former ASTA-President Jens Litten were mentioned as potential participants.

118 Memorandum Arthur Dean, October 8, 1969, Box 22, Folder 13, Ball Papers, PUL.

119 See the introduction by Großmann and Miard-Delacroix, *Deutschland, Frankreich und die USA*.

Conclusion

When Joseph Retinger set out to create the Bilderberg Group, he relied on a simple, almost naive notion: that talking will lead to understanding, and that understanding is the basis of international cooperation. Almost seven decades later, the continued existence of the Bilderberg Group suggests that he was onto something.

Looking back at its early history, it is evident that the Bilderberg Group served an important function in transatlantic relations as an informal forum for consensus-building and conflict management, grappling with complex and interdependent issues such as European integration, the German question, nuclear strategy, decolonization, and East-West relations. The private nature of the meetings, their excellent organization, and their intimate atmosphere stimulated frank conversations inside and outside of the meeting rooms. For Bilderberg's participants the meetings served as a particularly sensitive international barometer, offering subtle indications of mood swings, changing perceptions, and attitudes on both sides of the Atlantic. Although the meetings represented only specific moments in time and were part of much wider debates, the Bilderberg discussions can provide us with important insights into the thinking of the emerging transatlantic foreign policy elite.

How the indirect influence of the meetings played out in the wider transatlantic relationship can be traced in how certain ideas gained traction, how disagreements were handled, and how certain norms and values came to define the habitus and worldviews of members of the informal alliance. Important examples include the case of European anti-Americanism in the early 1950s, when the Bilderberg Group's reports and discussions reached the highest levels of the Eisenhower Administration. In the case of the European Communities, the Bilderberg meetings provided a forum for discussing a European relaunch at a key moment in time, after the dramatic failure of the European Defense Community. In the aftermath of the Suez crisis, the Bilderberg meetings could be used to mend frayed ties and to discuss common responses to decolonization. In the case of the Gaullist challenge to the alliance, the Bilderberg meetings played an important role in the Gaullist-Atlanticist struggle and helped to maintain the internationalist approach behind the Atlantic alliance and the European Communities. In terms of American alliance leadership, finally, the Bilderberg meetings provided a space for the kind of informal diplomacy that could be more effective and legitimate than public threats or unilateral decisions.

Probably one of the most consequential effects of the Bilderberg meetings was the large increase in personal contacts and friendships among the transatlantic foreign policy elite, facilitated by the midcentury revolution in air travel and communications and eased by the cultural compatibility of those who regarded themselves as part of the West. Of course, participating in the meetings held different meanings for different people. Steering committee members valued the meetings differently than one-time participants. Convinced internationalists went to Bilderberg with a different attitude than Gaullist nationalists. Differences in language and culture, moreover, made it easier for some to flourish in the increasingly Anglo-Saxon, English-language milieus of the informal alliance than for others (explaining, perhaps, the remarkable success of the smaller European nations in being represented in both the formal and the informal alliance). For the majority of Bilderberg members, however, the meetings underscored the importance of the global mindset: the willingness to look past national loyalties and to devise new ways of international cooperation.

The result was a sense of community based on shared emotions, values, and the rhetoric of unity. The informal alliance thus contributed to a broader transatlantic political culture with a distinctly transnational public sphere. Since the Atlantic alliance ultimately depended on political and public support, it is safe to say that the informal alliance played an important role in its relative success, adaptability, and endurance. When scholars ask why NATO endures or how it adapts, the informal alliance should be part of the answer.[1]

More research of the informal alliance is therefore necessary. Important organizations such as the NATO Parliamentary Assembly, the Atlantic Institute, the Atlantic Council of the United States, the Munich Security Conference, the Monnet Committee, and the International Institute for Strategic Studies have hardly been studied. In addition, the transnational activities and connections of those most deeply involved in the informal alliance – transatlantic mediators such as George Ball, Kurt Birrenbach, Fritz Erler, Joseph Johnson, Denis Healey, Henry Kissinger, Max Kohnstamm, Guy Mollet, David Rockefeller, Paul-Henri Spaak, or Helmut Schmidt, to name just a few – deserve more attention. It is striking that even biographies of prominent Bilderberg members such as Kissinger and Schmidt ignore the informal alliance.

Although Bilderberg's history after 1968 remains largely hidden, some key moments can be identified. One concerned the decision not to open the group to membership from Japan, as David Rockefeller proposed in the early 1970s. A majority of the steering committee members (particularly in Europe) remained committed to the transatlantic orientation of Bilderberg and, as a result, Rockefeller and Brzezinski set out to create the Trilateral Commission – a development supported by most Bilderbergers.[2] Not surprisingly, the membership between the two organizations overlapped considerably.

Another key moment was the 1976 Lockheed scandal, concerning Prince Bernhard's acceptance of more than a million dollars in what appeared to be bribes. American Bilderbergers, probably still reeling from the Watergate scandal, were particularly indignant in their response and argued that Bilderberg should not be allowed to be associated with the scandal. The 1976 Bilderberg meeting was scheduled to take place in the United States and Arthur Dean warned of serious consequences if nothing was done. Eventually, Ernst van der Beugel had to tell Prince Bernhard that he had to resign as chairman.[3] Some Bilderbergers assumed that this would be the end of the group. Rockefeller and Brzezinski even discussed a plan to use the Trilateral Commission to launch an alternative Bilderberg.[4] Yet although the 1976 meeting was cancelled, a relaunch took place in 1977. German Chancellor Helmut Schmidt was one of those arguing strongly in favor of the continuation of the Bilderberg meetings.[5] Schmidt had also been a driving force behind the creation of the G7 meetings in 1975, perhaps inspired by his Bilderberg experiences. Many of the so-called G7 Sherpas responsible for coordinating the meetings were members of the informal alliance.[6]

After the end of the Cold War, the idea that the United States and Europe should, wherever possible, find joint responses to the major problems facing the world remained a powerful one. The continued US commitment to Europe's defense was visible in an expanding NATO. Of course, the fact that the Cold War was over did not necessarily mean that transatlantic relations were suddenly harmonious. The George W. Bush Administration's 2002 decision to invade Iraq caused a major transatlantic crisis. Based on the number of US officials present at the following year's Bilderberg meeting, and judging by press reports, the Bilderberg Group (like the more public Munich Security Conference) was one of the key venues where the transatlantic Iraq debate played out.[7] The limits of the Bilderberg method were apparent in the failure of major transatlantic partners to agree.

The Bilderberg Group has long been a favorite target of conspiracy theorists, stirred by Bilderberg's secretive nature and the quality of its participants. The group is frequently accused of fomenting war, disease, and financial crises around the world. Such conspiracy theories are typically based on a mix of conjecture and falsehoods and their authors care little for the historical record. Starting with Phyllis Schlafly writing about the 1957 St. Simons Island conference, many of these conspiracy theories have been driven by extreme right-wing nationalist forces such as the John Birch Society in the United States. With websites like *Infowars* and *Breitbart*, these forces have become influential voices in populist, anti-globalist movements reaching into the Trump White House.

Anti-establishment sentiment is an important component of these movements and finds frequent expression in the rejection of the global elites who meet at Bilderberg, Davos, or Munich. Anti-European groups have similarly used the Bilderberg meetings as proof that the European Communities were a secret elite project funded by the CIA. In recent years, Russian propagandists have also recognized the power of anti-establishment sentiment and have used the alleged misdeeds of the Bilderberg Group for their destabilizing purposes.[8] In many of these conspiracy theories, older, anti-Semitic tropes about high finance play a considerable role.

This book will not convince the conspiracy theorists, but it may help to steer public debates about Bilderberg and other transnational elite organizations in a more constructive direction. After all, even if Bilderberg is not a secret world government or capitalist plot, it is still legitimate to question its influence. Bilderberg contributed to complex processes of coordination and consensus building and it helped create a closely interconnected transatlantic elite, including a significant number of wealthy captains of industry and bankers. Democratically elected politicians who participated in the meetings were no more immune to this kind of indirect mutual influence than other Bilderberg members.

In the end, the question is whether the benefits of increased international understanding outweigh the risks that politicians are unduly influenced or democratic processes are subverted. Based on the history of Bilderberg's first decades, those risks appear to be small as long as the Bilderberg organizers ensure that different political and societal groups are sufficiently represented. The benefits of the Bilderberg Group are difficult to calculate, but at least for those who favor close transatlantic cooperation, the meetings seem to have served a useful purpose.

Notes

1 Johnston, *How NATO Adapts*, and Thies, *Why NATO Endures*.
2 Knudsen, *Trilateral Commission*, 37–40.
3 Bloemendal, "Reframing the Diplomat," 229–232.
4 Knudsen, *Trilateral Commission*, 64.
5 See Memorandum by Kliesow, April 25, 1977, Box 6790, Schmidt Papers, FES.
6 See Mourlon-Druol and Romero, *International Summitry*, and Spohr, *The Global Chancellor*.
7 See Martin Wolff, "A partnership heading for a destructive separation," *The Financial Times*, May 21, 2003. Wolff's language is strikingly similar to the rhetoric of the early Bilderberg meetings.
8 See Jim Rutenberg, "RT, Sputnik and Russia's New Theory of War," *The New York Times*, September 13, 2017.

Appendix – List of Bilderberg Conferences, 1954–1968

1   Hotel de Bilderberg, Oosterbeek, the Netherlands (May 29–31, 1954)

   a   The attitude towards communism and the Soviet Union;
   b   The attitude towards dependent areas and peoples overseas;
   c   The attitude towards economic policies and problems;
   d   The attitude towards European integration and the European Defense Community.

2   Barbizon, France (March 18–20, 1955)

   a   Survey of Western European-USA relations since the first Bilderberg conference;
   b   Communist infiltration in various Western countries;
   c   The uncommitted peoples:
        1   Political and ideological aspects;
        2   Economic aspects.

3   Garmisch-Partenkirchen, Germany (September 23–25, 1955)

   a   Review of events since the Barbizon conference;
   b   Article 2 of the North Atlantic Treaty Organization;
   c   The political and strategic aspects of atomic energy;
   d   The reunification of Germany;
   e   European unity;
   f   The industrial aspects of atomic energy;
   g   Economic problems:
        1   East-West trade;
        2   The political aspects of convertibility;
        3   Expansion of international trade.

4   Fredensborg, Denmark (May 11–13, 1956)

   a   Review of developments since the last conference;
   b   The causes of the growth of anti-Western blocs, in particular in the United Nations;
   c   The role played by anti-colonialism in relations between Asians and the West;
   d   A common approach by the Western world towards China and the emergent nations of South and East Asia;

    e The communist campaign for political subversion or control of the newly emancipated countries of Asia;

    f How the West can best meet Asian requirements in the technical and economic fields.

5 St. Simons Island, United States (February 15–17, 1957).

    a Review of events since the fourth Bilderberg meeting in May 1956;

    b Nationalism and neutralism as disruptive factors inside the Western Alliance;

    c The Middle East;

    d The European policy of the Alliance, with special reference to the problems of Eastern Europe, German reunification and military strategy.

6 Fiuggi, Italy (October 4–6, 1957)

    a Survey of developments since the last conference;

    b Modern weapons and disarmament in relation to Western security;

    c Are existing political and economic mechanisms within the Western community adequate?

7 Buxton, United Kingdom (September 13–15, 1958)

    a Survey of events since the last conference;

    b The future of NATO defense;

    c Western economic cooperation;

    d The Western approach to Soviet Russia and communism.

8 Enlarged Steering Committee Meeting, Oosterbeek, The Netherlands (April 25–26, 1958)
    Neutralism and East-West Negotiations

9 Enlarged Steering Committee Meeting, Oosterbeek, The Netherlands (January 19–20, 1959)
    The Free Trade Area

10 Enlarged Steering Committee Meeting, Knokke, Belgium (March 20–21, 1959)
    The Berlin Crisis

11 Yeşilköy, Turkey (September 18–20, 1959)

    a Review of developments since the last conference;

    b Unity and division in Western policy.

12 Bürgenstock, Switzerland (May 28–29, 1960)

    a State of the world situation after the failure of the Summit Conference;

    b New political and economic developments in the Western World.

13 St. Castin, Canada (April 21–23, 1961)

    a   What initiatives are required to bring about a new sense of leader-
        ship and direction within the Western community?
    b   The implications for Western unity of changes in the relative eco-
        nomic strength of the United States and Western Europe.

14 Saltsjöbaden, Sweden (May 18–20, 1962)

    a   The political implications for the Atlantic community of its mem-
        bers' policies in the United Nations;
    b   Implications for the Atlantic community of prospective developments.

15 Cannes, France (March 29–31, 1963)

    a   The balance of power in the light of recent international developments;
    b   Trade relations between the U.S.A. and Europe in the light of the
        negotiations for Britain's entry into the Common Market;
    c   Trade relations between the Western world and the developing
        countries.

16 Williamsburg, United States (March 20–22, 1964)

    a   The consequences for the Atlantic Alliance of apparent changes in
        the communist world
        1   Soviet internal development;
        2   The Communist Bloc;
    b   Possible changes in the attitude of the USSR to the West;
    c   Recent developments within the Western world.

17 Villa d'Este, Italy (April 2–4, 1965)

    a   Monetary cooperation in the Western world;
    b   The State of the Atlantic Alliance.

18 Wiesbaden, Germany (March 25–27, 1966)

    a   Should NATO be reorganized and if so how?
    b   The future of world economic relations especially between indus-
        trial and developing countries.

19 Cambridge, United Kingdom (March 31-April 2, 1967)

    a   Do the basic concepts of Atlantic cooperation remain valid for the
        evolving world situation? If not, what concepts could take their
        place?
    b   The technological gap between America and Europe with special
        reference to American investments in Europe.

20 Mont-Tremblant, Canada (April 26–28, 1968)

    a   The relations between the West and the Communist countries;
    b   Internationalization of business.

Unpublished sources and interviews

Belgium

Archives Université Catholique de Louvain (AUCL)
Zeeland, Paul van. Papers

Fondation Paul-Henri Spaak (FPHS)
Spaak, Paul-Henri. Papers

France

L'Office Universitaire de Recherche Socialiste, Paris (OURS)
Mollet, Guy. Papers

Germany

Archiv der sozialen Demokratie, Friedrich Ebert Stiftung, Bonn (FES)
Erler, Fritz. Papers
Schmid, Carlo. Papers
Schmidt, Helmut. Papers
SPD Parteivorstand

Archiv für Christlich-Demokratische Politik, St. Augustin (ACDP)
Birrenbach, Kurt. Papers
Kiesinger, Kurt Georg. Papers
Krone, Heinrich. Papers
Majonica, Ernst. Papers

Bundesverband der Deutschen Industrie Archives, Berlin (BDIA)
BDI Präsidium
Bilderberg Files

Bundesarchiv Koblenz (BAK)
Blankenhorn, Herbert. Papers
Hallstein, Walter. Papers

Politisches Archiv des Auswärtigen Amtes, Berlin (AA)
B1 Ministerialbüro

B2 Büro Staatssekretäre
B10 Politische Abteilung 2
B14 NATO
B24 France
B32 USA

Rheinisch-Westfälische Wirtschaftsarchiv zu Köln (RWA)
Wolff von Amerongen, Otto. Papers

Staatsarchiv Hamburg (SH)
Brauer, Max. Papers

Italy

European University Institute, Historical Archives (EUI)
ECSC Archives
European Movement Archives
Kohnstamm, Max. Papers

The Netherlands

Internationaal Instituut voor Sociale Geschiedenis (IISG), Amsterdam
Mansholt, Sicco. Papers

Dutch National Archives, The Hague (NANL)
Beugel, Ernst H. van der. Papers
Bilderberg Archives
Ministerie van Algemene Zaken
Stikker, Dirk. Papers

Roosevelt Study Center, Middelburg (RSC)
Eisenhower Administration, Microfilm Collection

United Kingdom

The National Archives, London (NAL)
Public Record Office (PRO):
CAB 21
FO 371
PREM 11
PREM 13
Treasury 337

The Polish Library, London
Retinger, Joseph H. Papers

University College London (UCL)
Gaitskell, Hugh. Papers

United States

The Carl Albert Center, Congressional Research and Studies, The University of Oklahoma (CACUO)
Harris, Senator Fred. Papers

Cornell University Library, Division of Rare and Manuscript Collections (CUL)
Dean, Arthur H. Papers

Dwight D. Eisenhower Library, Abilene (DDEL)
Ann Whitman File: International Series
Ann Whitman File: National Security Council Series
Gruenther, Alfred M. Papers
Jackson, Charles D. Papers
Norstad, Lauris. Papers
Smith, Gerard C. Papers
Smith, Walter Bedell. Papers
U.S. Council on Foreign Economic Policy Office of the Chairman Records

Ford Foundation Archives, New York City (FFA)
Grant File 55–79, Bilderberg Meetings
Grant File 56–341, Bilderberg Meetings

Georgetown University Library (GUL)
McGhee, George W. Papers

Hoover Institution, Stanford University
Murphy, Robert D. Papers

Lyndon B. Johnson Library, Austin (LBJL)
Ball, George W. Papers
Bator, Francis M. Papers
National Security Files
White House Central Files

John F. Kennedy Library, Boston (JFKL)
Ball, George W. Papers
Bell, David. Papers
Bundy, McGeorge. Papers
National Security Files (NSF)
Neustadt, Richard E. Papers
Presidential Office Files (POF)

Library of Congress, Washington (LOC)
Harriman, W. Averell Papers
Nitze, Paul H. Papers

National Archives and Records Administration, College Park, Maryland (NARA)
Record Group 59: Department of State

Central Files:
Decimal Files
Subject Numeric Files
Lot Files:
Bureau of European Affairs Deputy Assistant Secretary
Conference Files 1949–1963
Memoranda of Conversation Secretary and Under Secretary
Office of Atlantic Political and Economic Affairs
Office of the Special Assistant to the Secretary of State for Multilateral
    Force Negotiations
Office of the Under Secretary of State for Political Affairs
Policy Planning Staff
Records of Ambassador Charles E. Bohlen
Records of Under Secretary of State George W. Ball

Princeton University Library, Department of Rare Books and Special Collec-
    tions (PUL)
Ball, George W. Papers
Dulles, Allen W. Papers

Rockefeller Foundation Archives (RFA)
Record Group 1.2 (Bilderberg Grant)

Stony Brook University, Special Collections and University Archives
Javits, Senator Jacob K. Papers

University of Southern California, Doherny Memorial Library (USC)
Holifield, Chester (Chet) Earl. Papers

Wisconsin Historical Society (WHS)
Harsch, Joseph C. Papers

Interviews

Ball, George. Oral History Interview, April 12, 1965, John F. Kennedy
    Library.
Beugel, Ernst van der. Oral History Interview, Nationaal Archief, The
    Hague.
Beugel, Ernst van der. Interview by the author, The Hague, 2003.
Kiesinger, Kurt Georg. Oral History Interview, Archiv für Christlich-
    Demokratische Politik.
Pomian, John. Interview by the author, London, January 14, 2004.

Bibliography

Acharya, Amitav. *East of India, South of China. Sino-Indian Encounters in Southeast Asia.* Oxford: Oxford University Press, 2017.

Agee, Philip, and Louis Wolf. *Dirty Work: The CIA in Western Europe.* Secaucus, NJ: L. Stuart, 1978.

Aldrich, Richard J. "European Integration: An American Intelligence Connection." in: *Building Postwar Europe. National Decision-Makers and European Institutions, 1948–1963,* edited by Anne Deighton, 159–179, New York: St. Martin's Press, 1995.

Aldrich, Richard J. "OSS, CIA and European Unity: The American Committee on United Europe, 1948–1960." *Diplomacy and Statecraft* 8, no. 1 (1997): 184–227.

Aldrich, Richard J. *The Hidden Hand: Britain, America, and Cold War Secret Intelligence.* London: John Murray, 2001.

Ambrose, Stephen E. *Eisenhower. Soldier and President.* New York: Simon and Schuster, 1990.

Angster, Julia. *Konsenskapitalismus und Sozialdemokratie. Die Westernisierung von SPD und DGB.* Munich: Oldenbourg, 2003.

Aron, Raymond, and Daniel Lerner. *La Querelle de la C.E.D. Essais d'analyse sociologique.* Paris: Colin, 1956.

Asbeek, Brusse Wendy. *Tariffs, Trade and European Integration 1947–1957. From Study Group to Common Market.* Basingstoke: Macmillan, 1997.

Ashton, Nigel John. *Eisenhower, Macmillan and the Problem of Nasser. Anglo-American Relations and Arab Nationalism, 1955–59.* Houndmills: Macmillan Press, 1996.

Ashton, Nigel John. *Kennedy, Macmillan, and the Cold War. The Irony of Interdependence.* Houndmills: Palgrave Macmillan, 2002.

Aubourg, Valérie. "The Atlantic Congress of 1959: An Ambiguous Celebration of the Atlantic Community." in: *A History of NATO: The First Fifty Years. Volume 3,* edited by Gustav Schmidt, 341–357, Basingstoke: Palgrave, 2001.

Aubourg, Valérie. "Organizing Atlanticism: The Bilderberg Group and the Atlantic Institute, 1952–1963." in: *The Cultural Cold War in Western Europe, 1945–1960,* edited by Giles Scott-Smith and Hans Krabbendam, 92–105, London: Frank Cass, 2003.

Aubourg, Valérie. "Le groupe de Bilderberg et l'intégration européenne jusqu'au milieu des années 1960. Une influence complexe." in: *Réseaux économiques et construction européenne. Economic Networks and European Integration,* edited by Michel Dumoulin, 411–430, Brussels: Peter Lang, 2004.

Aubourg, Valérie. "The Bilderberg Group: Promoting European Governance Inside an Atlantic Community of Values." in: *Transnational Networks in Regional Integration: Governing Europe, 1945–83*, edited by Wolfram Kaiser, Brigitte Leucht, and Michael Gehler, 38–60, Basingstoke: Palgrave Macmillan, 2010.

Aubourg, Valérie. "Problems of Transmission: The Atlantic Community and the Successor Generation as Seen by US Philanthropy, 1960s–1970s." in: *Atlantic, Euratlantic, or Europe-America: The Atlantic Community and the European Idea from Kennedy to Nixon*, edited by Giles Scott-Smith and Valérie Aubourg, 416–443, Paris: Soleb, 2011.

Ball, George. *The Past Has Another Pattern*, New York: W.W. Norton, 1982.

Banyan, Will. "The Bilderberg Connection: Did the Bilderberg Group Send Nixon to China?" Conspiracy Archive, October 3, 2015. Accessed March 10, 2018. www.conspiracyarchive.com/2015/10/04/the-bilderberg-connection-did-the-bilderberg-group-send-nixon-to-china/.

Bariéty, Jacques. "Die deutsche Frage aus französischer Sicht, 1945–1955." in: *Die deutsche Frage in der Nachkriegszeit*, edited by Wilfried Loth, 172–194, Berlin: Akademie Verlag, 1994.

Bar-on, Mordechai. "Three Days in Sèvres, October 1956." *History Workshop Journal* 62, (2006): 172–186.

Baston, Lewis. *Reggie. The Life of Reginald Maudling*. Sutton Publishing, 2004.

Baumann, Ansbert. *Begegnung der Völker? Der Elysée-Vertrag und die Bundesrepublik Deutschland. Deutsch-französische Kulturpolitik von 1963 bis 1969*. Frankfurt am Main: Lang, 2003.

Baylis, John. *Ambiguity and Deterrence: British Nuclear Strategy, 1945–1964*. Oxford: Clarendon Press, 1995.

Behrends, Jan C., Árpád von Klimó, and Patrice G. Poutrus. *Anti-Amerikanismus im 20. Jahrhundert*, Bonn: Verlag Dietz, 2005.

Behrman, Greg. *The Most Noble Adventure. The Marshall Plan and the Time When America Helped Save Europe*. New York: Free Press, 2007.

Belmonte, Laura A. *Selling the American Way. U.S. Propaganda and the Cold War*. Philadelphia, PA: University of Pennsylvania Press, 2008.

Berghahn, Volker R., *America and the Intellectual Cold Wars in Europe. Shepard Stone between Philanthropy, Academy, and Diplomacy*. Princeton: Princeton University Press, 2001.

Berghahn, Volker R. "Zur Soziologie der deutsch-amerikanischen Beziehungen nach dem Zweiten Weltkrieg: die Netzwerke von Shepard Stone." in: *Deutschland und die USA in der internationalen Geschichte des 20. Jahrhundert. Festschrift für Detlef Junker*, edited by Philipp Gassert and Manfred Berg, 407–422, Stuttgart: Franz Steiner Verlag, 2004.

Berman, Maureen R., and Joseph E. Johnson. *Unofficial Diplomats*. New York: Columbia University Press, 1977.

Beschloss, Michael R. *The Crisis Years. Kennedy and Khrushchev, 1960–1963*. New York: Edward Burlingame Books, 1991.

Beugel, Ernst H. van der. *From Marshall Aid to Atlantic Partnership. European Integration as a Concern of American Foreign Policy*. Amsterdam: Elsevier, 1966.

Bill, James A. *George Ball. Behind the Scenes in US Foreign Policy*. New Haven, CT: Yale University Press, 1997.

Bird, Kai. *The Chairman. John J. McCloy and the Making of the American Establishment*. New York: Simon & Schuster, 1992.

Bischof, Anna, and Zuzana Jürgens, eds. *Voices of Freedom – Western Interference? 60 Years of Radio Free Europe.* Göttingen: Vandenhoeck & Ruprecht, 2015.

Biskupski, M.B.B. "Spy, Patriot, or Internationalist? The Early Career of Józef Retinger, Polish Patriarch of European Union." *The Polish Review* 43, no. 1 (1998): 23–67.

Biskupski, M.B.B. *War and Diplomacy in East and West: A Biography of Józef Retinger.* London: Routledge, 2017, Kindle edition.

Bissell, Richard M. *Reflections of a Cold Warrior: From Yalta to the Bay of Pigs.* New Haven, CT: Yale University Press, 1996.

Black, Eugene R. *The Diplomacy of Economic Development.* Cambridge: Harvard University Press, 1960.

Black, Lawrence. "'The Bitterest Enemies of Communism': Labour Revisionists, Atlanticism and the Cold War." *Contemporary British History* 15, no. 3 (2001): 26–62.

Bleiker, Roland and Emma Hutchinson. "Fear No More: Emotions and World Politics." *Review of International Studies* 34, no. S1 (2008): 115–135. doi:10.1017/S0260210508007821.

Bloemendal, Albertine. "Reframing the Diplomat. Ernst van der Beugel and the Cold War Atlantic Community." PhD diss., Leiden University, 2017.

Bossuat, Gérard. *La France, l'aide américaine et la construction européenne 1944–54,* Vol. 1, Paris, 1992.

Bossuat, Gérard. *L'Europe des Français 1943–1959. La IV République aux sources de l'Europe communautaire.* Paris: Publications de la Sorbonne, 1997.

Bossuat, Gérard, ed. *Inventer l'Europe. Histoire nouvelle des groupes d'influence et des acteurs de l'unité européenne.* Brussels: Peter Lang, 2003.

Botts, Joshua. "'Nothing to Seek and … Nothing to Defend': George F. Kennan's Core Values and American Foreign Policy, 1938–1993." *Diplomatic History* 30, no. 5 (2006): 839–866.

Bourdieu, Pierre. "Social Space and Symbolic Power." *Sociological Theory* 7, no. 1 (1989): 14–25.

Bowie, Robert R., and Richard H. Immerman. *Waging Peace: How Eisenhower Shaped an Enduring Cold War Strategy.* Oxford: Oxford University Press, 1997.

Boyle, Peter G., ed. *The Eden-Eisenhower Correspondence, 1955–1957.* Chapel Hill, NC: The University of North Carolina Press, 2005.

Bozo, Frédéric. *Two Strategies for Europe: De Gaulle, the U.S., and the Atlantic Alliance.* Lanham, MD: Rowman & Littlefield, 2001.

Bozo, Frédéric, Marie-Pierre Rey, N. Piers Ludlow, and Bernd Rother, eds. *Visions of the End of the Cold War, 1945–1990.* New York: Berghahn Books, 2012.

Brands, H.W. *Cold Warriors. Eisenhower's Generation and American Foreign Policy.* New York: Columbia University Press, 1988.

Brogi, Alessandro. *Confronting America. The Cold War between the United States and the Communists in France and Italy.* Chapel Hill, NC: University of North Carolina Press, 2011.

Buchstab, Günter, ed. *Adenauer: "Wir haben wirklich etwas geschaffen." Die Protokolle des CDU-Bundesvorstands 1953–1957.* Düsseldorf: Droste, 1990.

Bułhak, Władysław. "The Foreign Office and the Special Operations Executive and the Expedition of Józef Hieronim Retinger to Poland, April-July 1944." *The Polish Review* 61, no. 3 (2016): 33–57.

Callahan, David. *Dangerous Capabilities: Paul Nitze and the Cold War.* New York: Harper & Row, 1990.

Camps, Miriam. *Britain and the European Community 1955–1963*. London: Oxford University Press, 1964.

Catteral, Peter, ed. *The Macmillan Diaries: The Cabinet Years, 1950–1957*. London: Pan, 2004.

Celt, Marek. *Parachuting into Poland: Memoir of a Secret Mission with Jósef Retinger*. Jefferson, NC: McFarland, 2013.

Charman, Sarah and Keith Williams. *The Parliamentarians' Role in the Alliance. The North Atlantic Assembly 1955–1980*. Brussels: North Atlantic Assembly, 1981.

Checkel, Jeffrey, T. "International Institutions and Socialization in Europe: Introduction and Framework." *International Organization* 59, no. 4 (2005): 801–826.

Citino, Nathan J. *Envisioning the Arab Future. Modernization in US-Arab Relations, 1945–1967*. New York: Cambridge University Press, 2017.

Cohen, Antonin. "Constitutionalism without Constitution: Transnational Elites between Political Mobilization and Legal Expertise in the Making of a Constitution for Europe (1940s–1960s)." *Law & Social Inquiry* 32, no. 1 (2007): 109–135.

Cohen, Warren I. *Dean Rusk*. Totowa, NJ: Cooper Square, 1980.

Cohen, Warren I. *The New Cambridge History of American Foreign Relations. Challenges to American Primacy, 1945 to the Present*. Cambridge: Cambridge University Press, 2013.

Coleman, Peter. *The Liberal Conspiracy. The Congress for Cultural Freedom and the Struggle for the Mind of Postwar Europe*. New York: Free Press, 1989.

Colen, José, and Élisabeth Dutartre-Michaut, eds. *The Companion to Raymond Aron*. New York: Palgrave Macmillan, 2015.

Connelly, Matthew. "Taking off the Cold War Lens: Visions of North South Conflict during the Algerian War for Independence." *American Historical Review* 105, no. 3 (2000): 739–769.

Conway, Martin. "Legacies of Exile: The Exile Governments in London during the Second World War and the Politics of Post-War Europe." in: *Europe in Exile: European Exile Communities in Britain, 1940–1945*, edited by Martin Conway and José Gotovich, 255–276, New York: Berghahn Books, 2001.

Conze, Eckart. *Die Gaullistische Herausforderung. Die deutsch-französischen Beziehungen in der amerikanischen Europapolitik, 1958–1963*. Munich: Oldenbourg, 1995.

Conze, Vanessa. *Das Europa der Deutschen. Ideen von Europa in Deutschland zwischen Reichstradition und Westorientierung (1920–1970)*. Munich: Oldenbourg, 2005.

Costigliola, Frank. "Lyndon B. Johnson, Germany and 'the End of the Cold War.'" in: *Lyndon Johnson Confronts the World: American Foreign Policy, 1963–1968*, edited by Warren I. Cohen and Nancy B. Tucker, 173–210, Cambridge: Cambridge University Press, 1994.

Costigliola, Frank. "Kennedy, the European Allies, and the Failure to Consult." *Political Science Quarterly* 110, no. 1 (1995): 105–123.

Costigliola, Frank. *Roosevelt's Lost Alliances. How Personal Politics Helped Start the Cold War*. Princeton: Princeton University Press, 2012.

Craig, Campbell. *Destroying the Village: Eisenhower and Thermonuclear War*. New York: Columbia University Press, 1999.

Craig, Campbell. "The Illogic of Henry Kissinger's Nuclear Strategy." *Armed Forces & Society* 29, no. 4 (2003): 547–568.

Craig, Campbell, and Fredrik Logevall. *America's Cold War. The Politics of Insecurity*. Cambridge, MA: Belknap Press of Harvard University Press, 2009.

Cresswell, Michael and Marc Trachtenberg. "France and the German Question, 1945–1955." *Journal of Cold War Studies* 5, no. 3 (2003): 5–25.

Crosswell, D. K. R. *Beetle. The Life of General Walter Bedell Smith*. Lexington, KY: University Press of Kentucky, 2010.

Cumings, Bruce. *The Korean War: A History*. New York: Modern Library, 2010.

Daalder, Hans. *Drees en Soestdijk: over de zaak-Hofmans en andere crises 1948–1958*. Amsterdam: Balans, 2006.

Daddow, Oliver J. *Britain and Europe since 1945: Historiographical Perspectives on Integration*. Manchester: Manchester University Press, 2004.

Daum, Andreas W. *Kennedy in Berlin. Politik, Kultur und Emotionen im Kalten Krieg*. Paderborn: Schöningh, 2003.

Davies, Norman. *Rising '44. The Battle for Warsaw*. London: Pan Books, 2004.

Defrance, Corine, and Ulrich Pfeil, eds. *Der Elysée-Vertrag und die deutsch-französischen Beziehungen 1945–1963–2003*. Munich: Oldenbourg, 2005.

Defty, Andrew. *Britain, America and Anti-Communist Propaganda 1945–53: The Information Research Department*. London: Routledge, 2004.

De Grazia, Victoria. *Irresistible Empire. America's Advance through Twentieth-Century Europe*. Cambridge, MA: Belknap Press of Harvard University Press, 2005.

Derix, Simone. *Bebilderte Politik. Staatsbesuche in der Bundesrepublik Deutschland 1949–1990*. Göttingen: Vandenhoeck & Ruprecht, 2009.

Deutsch, Karl W. *Political Community and the North Atlantic Area: International Organization in the Light of Historical Experience*. Princeton: Princeton University Press, 1957.

DiLeo, David. "George Ball and Jean Monnet: Advocates for a Wider Europe." in: *Courting the Common Market. The First Attempt to Enlarge the European Community, 1961–1963*, edited by Richard T. Griffiths and S. Ward, 179–194, London: Lothian Foundation Press, 1996.

Divine, Robert A. *The Sputnik Challenge. Eisenhower's Response to the Soviet Satellite*. New York: Oxford University Press, 1993.

Dockrill, Saki. *Eisenhower's New-Look National Security Policy, 1953–61*. Basingstoke: Macmillan, 1996.

Doering-Manteuffel, Anselm. *Wie Westlich sind die Deutschen? Amerikanisierung und Westernisierung im 20. Jahrhundert*. Göttingen: Vandenhoeck & Ruprecht, 1999.

Dongen, Luc Van, Stéphanie Roulin, and Giles Scott-Smith, eds. *Transnational Anti-Communism and the Cold War: Agents, Activities, and Networks*. Palgrave Macmillan Transnational History Series. Basingstoke: Palgrave Macmillan, 2014.

Dorril, Stephen. *MI6. Inside the Covert World of Her Majesty's Secret Intelligence Service*. New York: Simon and Schuster, 2002.

Dröge, Philip. *Beroep, meesterspion: Het geheime leven van Prins Bernhard*. Amsterdam: Vassallucci, 2002.

Duchêne, François. *Jean Monnet. The First Statesman of Interdependence*. New York: W.W. Norton, 1994.

Dujardin, Vincent and Michel Dumoulin. *Paul van Zeeland*. Brussels: Racine, 1997.

Dulles, John Foster. "Policy for Security and Peace." *Foreign Affairs* 32, no. 3 (1954): 353–364.

Dulles, John Foster. "Challenge and Response in United States Policy." *Foreign Affairs* 36, no. 1 (1957): 25–43.

Dumoulin, Michel, ed. *Réseaux économiques et construction européenne. Economic Networks and European Integration.* Brussels: Peter Lang, 2004.

Dumoulin, Michel and A.-M. Dutrieue. *La Ligue Européenne de Coopération Économique (1946–1981): Un Group d'étude et de Pression dans la Construction Européenne.* Berne: Peter Lang, 1993.

Eckardt, Felix von. "Konrad Adenauer – Eine Charakterstudie." in: *Konrad Adenauer und Seine Zeit. Politik und Persönlichkeit des ersten Bundeskanzlers. Beiträge von Weg- und Zeitgenossen,* edited by Dieter Blumenwitz, 137–148, Stuttgart: Deutsche Verlags-Anstalt, 1976.

Eisermann, Daniel. *Außenpolitik und Strategiediskussion. Die Deutsche Gesellschaft für Auswärtige Politik 1955 bis 1972.* Munich: Oldenbourg, 1999.

Ellison, James. "Defeating the General: Anglo-American Relations, Europe and the NATO Crisis of 1966." *Cold War History* 6, no. 1 (2006): 85–111.

Ellison, James. *The United States, Britain and the Transatlantic Crisis: Rising to the Gaullist Challenge.* Basingstoke: Palgrave Macmillan, 2007.

Ellwood, David W. *Rebuilding Europe: Western Europe, America, and Postwar Reconstruction.* London: Longman, 1992.

Ellwood, David W. *The Shock of America. Europe and the Challenge of the Century.* Oxford: Oxford University Press, 2012.

Engerman, David C. *Staging Growth. Modernization, Development, and the Global Cold War.* Amherst, MA: University of Massachusetts Press, 2003.

Engerman, David C. "The Romance of Economic Development and New Histories of the Cold War." *Diplomatic History* 28, no. 1 (2004): 23–54.

Erdman, Andrew P.N. "'War No Longer Has Any Logic Whatever': Dwight D. Eisenhower and the Thermonuclear Revolution." in: *Cold War Statesmen Confront the Bomb. Nuclear Diplomacy since 1945,* edited by John Lewis Gaddis, 87–119, Oxford: Oxford University Press, 1999.

Felken, Detlef. *Dulles und Deutschland. Die amerikanische Deutschlandpolitik 1953–1959.* Bonn: Bouvier Verlag, 1993.

Ferguson, Niall. *Kissinger. The Idealist. Volume I, 1923–1968.* New York: Penguin Books, 2015.

Ferguson, Niall. *The Square and the Tower. Networks and Power, from the Freemasons to Facebook.* New York: Penguin Press, 2018.

Flockhart, Trine. "'Masters and Novices': Socialization and Social Learning through the NATO Parliamentary Assembly." *International Relations* 18, no. 3 (2004): 361–380.

Førland, Tor Egil. "'Selling Firearms to the Indians': Eisenhower's Export Control Policy, 1953–54." *Diplomatic History* 15, no. 2 (1991): 221–244.

Freedman, Lawrence. *The Evolution of Nuclear Strategy.* Basingstoke: Palgrave Macmillan, 2003.

Friedman, Max Paul. *Rethinking Anti-Americanism. The History of an Exceptional Concept in American Foreign Relations.* Cambridge: Cambridge University Press, 2012.

Friedrich, Carl J. *Man and His Government. An Empirical Theory of Politics.* New York: McGraw-Hill, 1963.

Gaddis, John Lewis. *Strategies of Containment. A Critical Appraisal of Postwar American National Security Policy.* New York: Oxford University Press, 1982.

Gaddis, John Lewis. "The Unexpected John Foster Dulles." in: *John Foster Dulles and the Diplomacy of the Cold War,* edited by Richard H. Immerman, 47–77, Princeton: Princeton University Press, 1990.

Gaddis, John Lewis. *We Now Know. Rethinking Cold War History.* Oxford: Clarendon Press, 1997.

Gaddis, John Lewis. *The Cold War.* London: Allen Lane, 2006.

Gassert, Philipp. "Amerikanismus, Antiamerikanismus, Amerikanisierung. Neue Literatur zur Sozial-, Wirtschafts- und Kulturgeschichte des amerikanischen Einflusses in Deutschland und Europa." *Archiv für Sozialgeschichte* 39, (1999): 531–561.

Gavin, Francis J. *Nuclear Statecraft. History and Strategy in America's Atomic Age.* Ithaca, NY: Cornell University Press, 2012.

Gavin, Victor. "Power through Europe? The Case of the European Defence Community in France (1950–1954)." *French History* 23, no. 1 (2009): 69–87.

Geelhoed, E. Bruce, and Anthony O. Edmonds. *Eisenhower, Macmillan and Allied Unity, 1957–1961.* Houndmills: Macmillan, 2003.

Gehler, Michael, and Wolfram Kaiser, eds. *Transnationale Parteienkooperation der europäischen Christdemokraten. Dokumente 1945–1965.* Munich: K.G. Saur, 2004.

Geier, Stephan. *Schwellenmacht. Bonns heimliche Atomdiplomatie von Adenauer bis Schmidt.* Paderborn: Schöningh, 2013.

Geiger, Tim. *Atlantiker gegen Gaullisten. Außenpolitischer Konflikt und innerparteilicher Machtkampf in der CDU/CSU 1958–1969.* Munich: Oldenbourg, 2008.

Gemelli, Giuliana, and Roy MacLeod, eds. *American Foundations in Europe. Grant-Giving Policies, Cultural Diplomacy and Trans-Atlantic Relations, 1920–1980.* Brussels: Peter Lang, 2003.

Gerbet, Pierre. *La naissance du Marché Commun.* Brussels: Complexe, 1987.

Geven, Ruud. "Transnational Networks and the Common Market: Business Views on European Integration, 1950–1980." PhD Diss., University of Maastricht, 2014.

Giauque, Jeffrey Glen. *Grand Designs and Visions of Unity. The Atlantic Powers and the Reorganization of Western Europe.* Chapel Hill, NC: University of North Carolina Press, 2002.

Gienow-Hecht, J. C. E. "Always Blame the Americans: Anti-Americanism in Europe in the Twentieth Century." *The American Historical Review* 111, no. 4 (2006): 1067–1091.

Gijswijt, Thomas W. "Beyond NATO: Transatlantic Elite Networks and the Atlantic Alliance," in: *Transforming NATO in the Cold War. Challenges Beyond Deterrence in the 1960s,* edited by Andreas Wenger, Christian Nünlist, and Anna Locher, 50–63, London: Routledge, 2007.

Gijswijt, Thomas W. "The Bilderberg Group and Dutch-American Relations." in: *NL-US. Four Centuries of Dutch-American Relations,* edited by Hans Krabbendam, Cornelis A. van Minnen, and Giles Scott-Smith, 808–818, Amsterdam: Boom, 2009.

Gijswijt, Thomas W. "Running for President of the West: Kennedy's European Trip in June 1963." in: *Atlantic, Euratlantic, or Europe-America: The Atlantic Community and the European Idea from Kennedy to Nixon,* edited by Giles Scott-Smith and Valérie Aubourg, 152–172, Paris: Soleb, 2011.

Gijswijt, Thomas W. "The Bilderberg Group and the end of the Cold War: The Disengagement Debates of the 1950s." in: *Visions of the End of the Cold War, 1945–1990,* edited by Frédéric Bozo, Marie-Pierre Rey, N. Piers Ludlow, and Bernd Rother, 30–43, New York: Berghahn Books, 2012.

Gijswijt, Thomas W. "The Kennedy Administration, Alliance Politics and Informal Diplomacy during the Transatlantic Crisis of 1962/63." in: *Deutschland, Frankreich und die USA in den 'langen' 1960er Jahren. Ein transatlantisches*

Dreiecksverhältnis, edited by Johannes Großmann and Hélène Miard-Delacroix, 147–162, Stuttgart: Franz Steiner Verlag, 2018.

Gill, Stephen. *American Hegemony and the Trilateral Commission.* Cambridge: Cambridge University Press, 1990.

Gillingham, John R. *European Integration, 1950–2003. Superstate or New Market Economy?* Cambridge: Cambridge University Press, 2003.

Gillingham, John R. "The German Problem and European Integration." in: *Origins and Evolution of the European Union*, edited by Desmond Dinan, 55–82, Oxford: Oxford University Press, 2006.

Grabbe, Hans-Jürgen. *Unionsparteien, Sozialdemokratie und Vereinigten Staaten von Amerika 1945–1966.* Düsseldorf: Droste, 1983.

Granieri, Ronald J. *The Ambivalent Alliance. Konrad Adenauer, the CDU/CSU, and the West, 1949–1966.* New York: Berghahn Books, 2002.

Greenberg, Udi. *The Weimar Century. German Émigrés and the Ideological Foundations of the Cold War.* Princeton: Princeton University Press, 2014.

Greiner, Bernd. "'Test the West'. Über die Amerikanisierung der Bundesrepublik Deutschland." In: *Westbindungen: Amerika in der Bundesrepublik*, edited by Heinz Bude and Bernd Greiner, 16–54, Hamburg: Hamburger Edition, 1999.

Greiner, Bernd, Christian Th. Müller, and Dierk Walter, eds. *Angst im Kalten Krieg.* Hamburg: HIS Verlag, 2009.

Greiner, Christian. "Die Entwicklung der Bündnisstrategie 1949 bis 1958." in: *Die NATO als Militärallianz. Strategie, Organisation und nukleare Kontrolle im Bündnis 1949 bis 1959*, edited by Bruno Thoß, 19–174, Munich: Oldenbourg, 2003.

Groeben, Hans von der. *The European Community. The Formative Years. The Struggle to Establish the Common Market and the Political Union (1958–66).* Luxemburg: Office for Official Publications of the European Communities, 1987.

Grosbois, Thierry. "L'action de Józef Retinger en faveur de l'idée européenne 1940–46." *European Review of History* 6, no. 1 (1999): 59–82.

Grosbois, Thierry and Yves Stelandre. "Belgian Decision-Makers and European Unity, 1945–63." in: *Building Postwar Europe. National Decision-Makers and European Institutions, 1948–1963*, edited by Anne Deighton, 127–140, New York: St. Martin's Press, 1995.

Großmann, Johannes. *Die Internationale der Konservativen. Transnationale Elitenzirkel und private Außenpolitik in Westeuropa seit 1945.* Munich: Oldenbourg, 2014.

Großmann, Johannes. "Winning the Cold War: Anti-Communism, Informal Diplomacy, and the Transnational Career of Jean Violet." *New Global Studies* 8, no. 1 (2014): 87–101.

Großmann, Johannes. "Die "Grundtorheit unserer Epoche"? Neue Forschungen und Zugänge zur Geschichte des Antikommunismus." *Archiv für Sozialgeschichte* 56 (2016): 549–590.

Großmann, Johannes, and Hélène Miard-Delacroix, eds. *Deutschland, Frankreich und die USA in den 'langen' 1960er Jahren. Ein transatlantisches Dreiecksverhältnis.* Stuttgart: Franz Steiner Verlag, 2018.

Guieu, Jean-Michel, and Christophe le Dréau, eds. *Le "Congrès de l'Europe" à La Haye (1948–2008).* Brussels: Peter Lang, 2008.

Guillen, Pierre. "The Role of the Soviet-Union as a Factor in the French Debates on the European Defence Community." *Journal of European Integration History* 2, no. 1 (1996): 71–83.

Haase, Christian. *Pragmatic Peacemakers. Institutes of International Affairs and the Liberalization of West Germany 1945–73.* Augsburg: Wissner, 2007.

Haftendorn, Helga. *NATO and the Nuclear Revolution. A Crisis of Credibility, 1966–1967.* Oxford: Clarendon Press, 1996.

Haftendorn, Helga. "The Adaptation of the NATO Alliance to a Period of Détente: The 1967 Harmel Report." In: *Crises and Compromises: The European Project, 1963–1969,* edited by Wilfried Loth, 285–322, Baden-Baden: Nomos, 2001.

Hahn, Peter L. *The United States, Great Britain, and Egypt, 1945–1957. Strategy and Diplomacy in the Early Cold War.* Chapel Hill, NC: The University of North Carolina Press, 1991.

Hahnimäki, Jussi. *The Flawed Architect. Henry Kissinger and American Foreign Policy.* Oxford: Oxford University Press, 2004.

Halperin, Morton A. "The Gaither Committee and the Policy Process." *World Politics* 13, no. 3 (1961): 360–384.

Harris, Sarah Miller. *The CIA and the Congress for Cultural Freedom in the Early Cold War.* London: Routledge, 2016.

Hatch, Alden. *HRH Prince Bernhard of the Netherlands: An Authorised Biography.* London: George G. Harrap, 1962.

Healey, Denis. *The Time of My Life.* London: Michael Joseph, 1989.

Hemmer, Christopher, and Peter J. Katzenstein. "Why Is There No NATO in Asia? Collective Identity, Regionalism, and the Origins of Multilateralism." *International Organization* 56, no. 3 (2002): 575–607.

Hinrichsen, Hans-Peter. *Der Ratgeber. Kurt Birrenbach und die Außenpolitik der Bundesrepublik Deutschland.* Berlin: Verlag für Wissenschaft und Forschung, 2002.

Hitchcock, William I. *France Restored. Cold War Diplomacy and the Quest for Leadership in Europe, 1944–1954.* Chapel Hill: The University of North Carolina Press, 1998.

Hixson, Walter L. *George F. Kennan. Cold War Iconoclast.* New York: Columbia University Press, 1989.

Hixson, Walter L. *Parting the Curtain. Propaganda, Culture, and the Cold War, 1945–1961.* Basingstoke: Macmillan, 1997.

Hochgeschwender, Michael. *Freiheit in der Offensive? Der Kongreß für Kulturelle Freiheit und die Deutschen.* Munich: Oldenbourg, 1998.

Hoeres, Peter, *Außenpolitik und Öffentlichkeit: Massenmedien, Meinungsforschung und Arkanpolitik in den deutsch-amerikanischen Beziehungen von Erhard bis Brandt.* Munich: Oldenbourg, 2013.

Hogan, Michael J. *The Marshall Plan: America, Britain, and the Reconstruction of Western Europe, 1947–1952.* Cambridge: Cambridge University Press, 1987.

Hollander, Paul. *Anti-Americanism. Critiques at Home and Abroad, 1965–1990.* New York: Oxford University Press, 1992.

Honeck, Mischa, and Gabriel Rosenberg. "Transnational Generations: Organizing Youth in the Cold War." *Diplomatic History* 38, no. 2 (2014): 233–239. doi:10.1093/dh/dhu011.

Hopkins, Michael F. *Oliver Franks and the Truman Administration: Anglo-American Relations, 1948–1952.* London: Routledge, 2003.

Ikenberry, G. John. *After Victory. Institutions, Strategic Restraint, and the Rebuilding of Order after Major Wars.* Princeton: Princeton University Press, 2001.

Ingimundarson, Valur. "Containing the Offensive: The 'Chief of the Cold War' and the Eisenhower Administration's German Policy." *Presidential Studies Quarterly* 23, no. 3 (1997): 480–495.

Iriye, Akira. *Global Community. The Role of International Organizations in the Making of the Contemporary World*. Berkeley: University of California Press, 2002.

Iriye, Akira, and Pierre-Yves Saunier, eds. *The Palgrave Dictionary of Transnational History*. Basingstoke: Palgrave Macmillan, 2009.

Jackson, Ian. *The Economic Cold War: America, Britain and East-West Trade, 1948–63*. Basingstoke: St. Martin's Press, 2001.

Johnston, Andrew M. "Mr. Slessor Goes to Washington: The Influence of the British Global Strategy Paper on the Eisenhower New Look." *Diplomatic History* 22, no. 3 (1998): 361–398.

Johnston, Seth A. *How NATO Adapts. Strategy and Organization in the Atlantic Alliance since 1950*. Baltimore, MD: Johns Hopkins University Press, 2017.

Jones, Matthew. "Targeting China: U.S. Nuclear Planning and 'Massive Retaliation' in East Asia, 1953–1955." *Journal of Cold War Studies* 10, no. 4 (2008): 37–65.

Judt, Tony. *Postwar. A History of Europe since 1945*. London: Pimlico, 2007.

Junker, Detlef. *The Manichaean Trap: American Perceptions of the German Empire, 1871–1945*. Washington, D.C.: German Historical Institute, 1995.

Kaelble, Hartmut. *A Social History of Europe, 1945–2000. Recovery and Transformation after Two World Wars*. New York: Berghahn, 2013.

Kaiser, Wolfram. *Using Europe, Abusing the Europeans. Britain and European Integration, 1945–63*. Basingstoke: Macmillan, 1996.

Kaiser, Wolfram. "From State to Society? The Historiography of European Integration." in: *European Union Studies*, edited by Michelle Cini and Angela K. Bourne, 190–208, Basingstoke: Palgrave Macmillan, 2006.

Kaiser, Wolfram. *Christian Democracy and the Origins of European Union*. Cambridge: Cambridge University Press, 2007.

Kaiser, Wolfram, Brigitte Leucht, and Michael Gehler, eds. *Transnational Networks in Regional Integration: Governing Europe, 1945–83*. Basingstoke: Palgrave Macmillan, 2010.

Kaiser, Wolfram, Brigitte Leucht, and Morten Rasmussen. *The History of the European Union: Origins of a Trans- and Supranational Polity, 1950–1972*. London: Routledge, 2008.

Kaiser, Wolfram, and Peter Starie, eds. *Transnational European Union: Towards a Common Political Space*. London: Routledge, 2005.

Kaplan, Frederic M. *The Wizards of Armageddon*. New York: Simon and Schuster, 1983.

Kaplan, Lawrence S. *NATO 1948. The Birth of the Transatlantic Alliance*. Lanham, MD: Rowman & Littlefield, 2007.

Katzenstein, Peter J., and Robert O. Keohane, eds. *Anti-Americanisms in World Politics*. Ithaca, NY: Cornell University Press, 2007.

Kempe, Frederick. *Berlin 1961. Kennedy, Khrushchev, and the Most Dangerous Place on Earth*. New York: G.P. Putnam's Sons, 2011.

Kennedy, John F. "A Democrat Looks at Foreign Policy." *Foreign Affairs* 36, no. 1 (1957): 44–59.

Keohane, Robert, and Joseph Nye. *Transnational Relations and World Politics*. Cambridge, MA: Harvard University Press, 1971.

Kieninger, Stephan. *Dynamic Détente: The United States and Europe, 1964–1975.* Lanham, MD: Rowman & Littlefield, 2016.

Kilian, Werner. *Adenauers Reise nach Moskau.* Freiburg: Herder, 2005.

Kilmuir, David Patrick Maxwell Fyfe, Earl of. *Political Adventure. The Memoirs of the Earl of Kilmuir.* London: Weidenfeld and Nicolson, 1964.

Kissinger, Henry A. "Missiles and the Western Alliance." *Foreign Affairs* 36, no. 3 (1958): 383–400.

Kissinger, Henry A. *The Necessity for Choice. Prospects of American Foreign Policy.* London: Chatto and Windus, 1960.

Klimke, Martin. *The Other Alliance. Student Protest in West Germany and the United States in the Global Sixties.* Princeton: Princeton University Press, 2010.

Klitzing, Holger. *The Nemesis of Stability. Henry A. Kissinger's Ambivalent Relationship with Germany.* Trier: WVT, 2007.

Knudsen, Dino. *The Trilateral Commission and Global Governance. Informal Elite Diplomacy, 1972–1982.* Routledge: London, 2016, Kindle edition.

Kochavi, Noam. *A Conflict Perpetuated. China Policy during the Kennedy Years.* Westport, CT: Praeger, 2002.

Kotek, Joël. "Youth Organizations as a Battlefield in the Cold War." *Intelligence and National Security* 18, no. 2 (2003): 168–191.

Kroes, Rob. *If You've Seen One, You've Seen the Mall. Europeans and American Mass Culture.* Urbana, IL: University of Illinois Press, 1996.

Krüger, Dieter. *Sicherheit durch Integration? Die wirtschaftliche und politische Zusammenarbeit Westeuropas 1947 bis 1957/58.* Munich: Oldenbourg, 2003.

Kuisel, Richard. *Seducing the French. The Dilemma of Americanization.* Berkeley, CA: University of California Press, 1993.

Kuklick, Bruce. *Blind Oracles. Intellectuals and War from Kennan to Kissinger.* Princeton: Princeton University Press, 2006.

Kunz, Diane. *The Economic Diplomacy of the Suez Crisis.* Chapel Hill, NC: The University of North Carolina Press, 1991.

Küsters, Hanns-Jürgen. *Die Gründung der Europäischen Wirtschaftsgemeinschaft.* Baden-Baden: Nomos, 1982.

Kyle, Keith. *Suez.* London: Weidenfeld and Nicolson, 1991.

Lacouture, Jean. *De Gaulle. Vol. 3. Le Souverain, 1959–1970.* Paris: Éditions du Seuil, 1986.

Lane, A. T., and Marian Wolański. *Poland and European Integration: The Ideas and Movements of Polish Exiles in the West, 1939–91.* Houndmills: Palgrave Macmillan, 2009.

Lappenküper, Ulrich. *Die deutsch-französische Beziehungen 1949–1963. Von der 'Erbfeindschaft' zur 'Entente élementaire.' Vol. 1: 1949–1958.* Munich: Oldenbourg, 2001.

Larres, Klaus. *Churchill's Cold War: The Politics of Personal Diplomacy.* New Haven, CT: Yale University Press, 2002.

Laron, Guy. *Origins of the Suez Crisis: Postwar Development Diplomacy and the Struggle Over Third World Industrialization, 1945–1956.* Washington, D.C.: Johns Hopkins University Press, 2013.

Laville, Helen, and Hugh Wilford, eds. *The US Government, Citizen Groups, and the Cold War. The State-Private Network.* London: Routledge, 2006.

Lefèbvre, Denis. *Guy Mollet. Le Mal Aimé.* Paris: Plon, 1992.

Leffler, Melvyn P. *For the Soul of Mankind. The United States, the Soviet Union, and the Cold War.* New York: Hill and Wang, 2007.

Lennep, Emile van. *Emile van Lennep in de wereldeconomie: herinneringen van een internationae Nederlander*. Leiden: Stenfert Kroese, 1991.

Lett, Brian. *SOE's Mastermind. An Authorized Biography of Major General Sir Colin Gubbins*. Barnsley: Pen & Sword Military, 2016.

Lipgens, Walter. *Die Anfänge der europäischen Einigungspolitik 1945–1950. Vol. 1: 1945–1947*. Stuttgart: Klett, 1977.

Lipgens, Walter, and Wilfried Loth, eds. *Documents on the History of European Integration. Volume 4*. Berlin: De Gruyter, 1991.

Little, Douglas. *American Orientalism. The United States and the Middle East since 1945*. Chapel Hill, NC: The University of North Carolina Press, 2002.

Locher, Anna. *Crisis? What Crisis?: NATO, de Gaulle, and the Future of the Alliance, 1963–1966*. Baden-Baden: Nomos, 2010.

Loth, Wilfried. "Beiträge der Geschichtswissenschaft zur Deutung der Europäischen Integration." in: *Theorien europäischer Integration*, edited by Wilfried Loth and Wolfgang Wessels, 87–106, Opladen: Leske and Budrich, 2001.

Loth, Wilfried. *Building Europe: A History of European Unification*. Berlin: De Gruyter, 2015.

Louis, W. R., and Roger Owen, eds. *Suez 1956: The Crisis and Its Consequences*. Oxford: Clarendon Press, 1989.

Lowe, Peter. "The Frustrations of Alliance: Britain, the United States, and the Korean War, 1950–51." in: *The Korean War in History*, edited by James Cotton and Ian Neary, 80–99, Manchester: Manchester University Press, 1989.

Lucas, W. Scott. *Divided We Stand: Britain, the United States and the Suez Crisis*. London: Hodder & Stoughton, 1991.

Lucas, W. Scott. *Freedom's War: The American Crusade against the Soviet Union*. New York: New York University Press, 1999.

Ludlow, N. Piers. *Dealing with Britain. The Six and the First UK Application to the EEC*. Cambridge: Cambridge University Press, 1997.

Luff, Jennifer. *Commonsense Anticommunism. Labor and Civil Liberties between the World Wars*. Chapel Hill, NC: University of North Carolina Press, 2012.

Lundestad, Geir. *"Empire" by Integration. The United States and European Integration, 1945–1997*. Oxford: Oxford University Press, 1998.

Lundestad, Geir. *The United States and Europe since 1945. From "Empire by Invitation" to Transatlantic Drift*. Oxford: Oxford University Press, 2003.

Lüthy, Herbert. "De Gaulle: Pose and Policy." *Foreign Affairs* 43, no. 4 (1965): 561–573.

Lynch, Frances M. B. *France and the International Economy: From Vichy to the Treaty of Rome*. London: Routledge, 1997.

Lynch, Frances M. B. "De Gaulle's First Veto: France, the Rueff Plan and the Free Trade Area." *Contemporary European History* 9, no. 1 (2000): 111–135.

Lynn, Katalin Kádár, ed. *The Inauguration of Organized Political Warfare. Cold War Organizations Sponsored by the National Committee for a Free Europe/Free Europe Committee*. Saint Helena, CA: Helena History Press, 2013.

Macmillan, Harold. *Tides of Fortune, 1945–1955*. London: Macmillan, 1969.

Maier, Charles S. *Among Empires. American Ascendancy and Its Predecessors*. Cambridge, MA: Harvard University Press, 2006.

Maier, Charles S. "Privileged Partners: The Atlantic Relationship at the End of the Bush Regime." in: *Just Another Major Crisis? The United States and Europe since 2000*, edited by Geir Lundestad, 17–33, Oxford: Oxford University Press, 2008.

Mangold, Peter. *The Almost Impossible Ally. Harold Macmillan and Charles de Gaulle.* London: I.B. Tauris, 2006.

Mariano, Marco, ed. *Defining the Atlantic Community. Culture, Intellectuals, and Policies in the Mid-Twentieth Century.* London: Routledge, 2010.

Marjolin, Robert. *Le Travail d'une Vie. Mémoires, 1911–1986.* Paris: Laffont, 1986.

Markovits, Andrei S. *Uncouth Nation. Why Europe Dislikes America.* Princeton: Princeton University Press, 2007.

Martin, Garret. *General De Gaulle's Cold War. Challenging American Hegemony, 1963–1968.* New York: Berghahn Books, 2013.

Masuda, Hajimu. *Cold War Crucible. The Korean Conflict and the Postwar World.* Cambridge, MA: Harvard University Press, 2014.

May, Ernest, ed. *American Cold War Strategy: Explaining NSC 68.* Boston, MA: St. Martin's Press, 1993.

Mazlish, Bruce. *Reflections on the Modern and the Global.* New Brunswick: Transaction, 2013.

McKenzie, Brian A. "The European Youth Campaign in Ireland: Neutrality, Americanization, and the Cold War 1950 to 1959." *Diplomatic History* 40, no. 3 (2016): 421–444. doi:10.1093/dh/dhv010.

McMahon, Robert J., ed. *The Cold War in the Third World.* Oxford: Oxford University Press, 2013.

Melissen, Jan. *The Struggle for Nuclear Partnership. Britain the United States and the Making of an Ambiguous Alliance, 1952–1959.* Groningen: Styx Publications, 1993.

Milloy, John C. *The North Atlantic Treaty Organization, 1948–1957. Community or Alliance?* Montreal: McGill-Queen's University Press, 2006.

Milne, David. *Worldmaking. The Art and Science of American Diplomacy.* New York: Farrar, Straus and Giroux, 2017.

Milward, Alan S. *The European Rescue of the Nation-State.* London: Routledge, 1992.

Milward, Alan S. *The Rise and Fall of a National Strategy, 1945–1963.* London: Whitehall History Publishing, 2005.

Mistry, Kaeten. "Approaches to Understanding the Inaugural CIA Covert Operation in Italy: Exploding Useful Myths." *Intelligence and National Security* 26, nos. 2–3 (2011): 246–268. doi:10.1080/02684527.2011.559318.

Mourlon-Druol, Emmanuel, and Federico Romero, eds. *International Summitry and Global Governance: The Rise of the G7 and the European Council, 1974–1991.* London: Routledge, 2014.

Müller, Jan-Werner, ed. *Memory and Power in Post-War Europe.* Cambridge: Cambridge University Press, 2002.

Münger, Christoph. *Kennedy, die Berliner Mauer und die Kubakrise. Die westliche Allianz in der Zerreißprobe 1961–1963.* Paderborn: Ferdinand Schöningh, 2003.

Murphy, Craig. *The United Nations Development Programme. A Better Way?* Cambridge: Cambridge University Press, 2006.

Muschik, Eva-Maria. "Managing the World: The United Nations, Decolonization, and the Strange Triumph of State Sovereignty in the 1950s and 1960s." *Journal of Global History* 13, (2018): 121–144.

Nash, Philip. "Eisenhower, Nuclear Weapons and Arms Control." in: *A Companion to Dwight D. Eisenhower,* edited by Chester Pach, 327–349, Malden, MA: Wiley-Blackwell, 2017.

Nehring, Holger. *Politics of Security. British and West German Protest Movements and the early Cold War, 1945–1970.* Oxford: Oxford University Press, 2013.

Neuss, Beate. *Geburtshelfer Europas? Die Rolle der Vereinigten Staaten im europäischen Integrationsprozess 1945–1958.* Baden-Baden: Nomos Verlag, 2000.

Neustadt, Richard E. *Report to JFK: The Skybolt Crisis in Perspective.* Ithaca, NY: Cornell University Press, 1999.

Nichols, David A. *Eisenhower 1956. The President's Year of Crisis: Suez and the Brink of War.* New York: Simon & Schuster, 2011.

Nitze, Paul H. "Atoms, Strategy and Policy." *Foreign Affairs* 34, no. 2 (1956): 187–199.

Nitze, Paul H. with Ann M. Smith and Steven L. Rearden. *From Hiroshima to Glasnost. At the Center of Decision - A Memoir.* New York: Grove Weidenfeld, 1989.

Norwig, Christina. "A First European Generation? The Myth of Youth and European Integration in the Fifties." *Diplomatic History* 38, no. 2 (2014): 251–260. doi:10.1093/dh/dhu006.

Norwig, Christina. *Die erste europäische Generation. Europakonstruktionen in der europäischen Jugendkampagne 1951–1958.* Göttingen: Wallstein Verlag, 2016.

Nünlist, Christian, Anna Locher, and Garret Martin, eds. *Globalizing De Gaulle. International Perspectives on French Foreign Policies, 1958–1969.* Lanham, MD: Lexington Books, 2010.

Nye, Joseph S. *Soft Power: The Means to Success in World Politics.* New York: Public Affairs, 2004.

Orlow, Dietrich. *Common Destiny. A Comparative History of the Dutch, French, and German Social Democratic Parties, 1945–1969.* New York: Berghahn Books, 2000.

Osgood, Kenneth A. "Form before Substance: Eisenhower's Commitment to Psychological Warfare and Negotiations with the Enemy." *Diplomatic History* 24, no. 3 (2000): 405–433.

Osgood, Kenneth A. *Total Cold War: Eisenhower's Secret Propaganda Battle at Home and Abroad.* Lawrence, KS: University of Kansas Press, 2006.

Osgood, Robert E. *NATO. The Entangling Alliance.* Chicago, IL: University of Chicago Press, 1962.

Pagedas, Constantine A. *Anglo-American Strategic Relations and the French Problem, 1960–1963: A Troubled Partnership.* London: Frank Cass, 2000.

Palayret, Jean Marie. "Eduquer les jeunes à l'union: La Campagne européenne de la jeunesse 1951–1958." *Journal of European Integration History* 1 (1995): 47–60.

Parker, Jason. "Cold War II: The Eisenhower Administration, the Bandung Conference, and the Reperiodization of the Postwar Era." *Diplomatic History* 30, no. 5 (2006): 867–892.

Parmar, Inderjeet. *Foundations of the American Century. The Ford, Carnegie, & Rockefeller Foundations in the Rise of American Power.* New York: Columbia University Press, 2012.

Parsons, Craig. *A Certain Idea of Europe.* Ithaca, NY: Cornell University Press, 2003.

Paxton, Robert O., and Nicholas Wahl, eds. *De Gaulle and the United States. A Centennial Reappraisal.* Oxford: Berg, 1994.

Pedlow, Gregory W. *Nato Strategy Documents 1949–1969.* NATO Website, 1998. Accessed February 3, 2018. www.nato.int/archives/strategy.htm.

Philipsen, Ingeborg. "Diplomacy with Ambiguity: The History of the Bilderberg Organisation 1952–1977." PhD diss., University of Copenhagen, 2009.

Pieczewski, Andrzej. "Joseph Retinger's Conception of and Contribution to the Early Process of European Integration." *European Review of History* 17, no. 4 (2010): 581–604.

Pineau, Christian and Christiane Rimbaud. *Le Grand Pari. L'Aventure du traité de Rome.* Paris: Fayard, 1991.

Polonsky, A. B. "Polish Failure in Wartime London: Attempts to Forge a European Alliance, 1940–1944." *The International History Review* 7, no. 4 (1985): 576–591.

Pomian, John, ed. *Joseph Retinger. Memoirs of an Eminence Grise.* Brighton: Sussex University Press, 1972.

Price, Harry Bayard. *The Marshall Plan and Its Meaning.* Ithaca, NY: Cornell University Press, 1955.

Priest, Andrew. *Kennedy, Johnson and NATO. Britain, America and the Dynamics of Alliance, 1962–68.* London: Routledge, 2006.

Rearden, Steven L. *The Evolution of American Strategic Doctrine: Paul H. Nitze and the Soviet Challenge.* Boulder, CO: Westview Press, 1984.

Rearden, Steven L. "Feature Review: Reassessing the Gaither Report's Role." *Diplomatic History* 25, no. 1 (2001): 153–157.

Rebattet, F. X. "The European Movement, 1945–1953: A Study in National and International Non-governmental Organisations Working for European Unity." PhD diss., Oxford University, 1963.

Retinger, Joseph. *Conrad and His Contemporaries.* London: Minerva Publishers, 1941.

Richardson, Ian, Andrew Kakabadse, and Nada Kakabadse. *Bilderberg People. Elite Power and Consensus in World Affairs.* Abingdon: Routledge, 2011.

Rijkens, Paul. *Handel en wandel: nagelaten gedenkschriften, 1888–1965.* Rotterdam: Donker, 1965.

Risso, Linda. *Propaganda and Intelligence in the Cold War. The NATO Information Service.* London: Routledge, 2014.

Roberts, Chalmers M. *The Nuclear Years. The Arms Race and Arms Control, 1945–1970.* New York: Praeger Publishers, 1970.

Roberts, Frank. *Dealing with Dictators. The Destruction and Revival of Europe 1930–1970.* London: Weidenfeld & Nicolson, 1991.

Roberts, Priscilla. "The Transatlantic American Foreign Policy Elite: Its Evolution in Generational Perspective." *Journal of Transatlantic Studies* 7, no. 2 (2009): 163–183.

Rockefeller, David. *Memoirs.* New York: Random House, 2002.

Rodgers, Daniel T. *Atlantic Crossings. Social Politics in a Progressive Age.* Cambridge, MA: Belknap Press of Harvard University Press, 1998.

Roger, Philippe. *The American Enemy. A Story of French Anti-Americanism.* Chicago, IL: University of Chicago Press, 2005.

Roman, Peter J. *Eisenhower and the Missile Gap.* Ithaca, NY: Cornell University Press, 1995.

Romero, Federico. "Cold War Anti-Communism and the Impact of Communism on the West." in: *The Cambridge History of Communism. Volume II. The Socialist Camp and World Power 1941–1960s,* edited by Norman Naimark, Silvio Pons, and Sophie Quinn-Judge, 291–314, Cambridge: Cambridge University Press, 2017.

Rosenberg, David. "The Origins of Overkill: Nuclear Weapons and American Strategy, 1945–1960." *International Security* 7, no. 4 (1983): 3–71.

Rosenberg, Emily S., ed. *A World Connecting, 1870–1945.* Cambridge, MA: Belknap Press of Harvard University Press, 2012.

Rosenboim, Or. *The Emergence of Globalism. Visions of World Order in Britain and the United States, 1939–1950.* Princeton, NJ: Princeton University Press, 2017.

Rougemont, Denis de. "Esquisse d'une biographie: J. H. Retinger." in: *Oeuvres complètes de Denis de Rougemont. III Écrits sur L'Europe. Volume Premier 1948–1961,* edited by Denis de Rougemont and Christophe Calame, 460–483, Paris: Éditions De La Différence, 1994.

Roussel, Éric. *Charles de Gaulle.* Paris: Gallimard, 2002.

Rusk, Dean. *As I Saw It.* New York: Norton, 1990.

Saunders, Frances Stonor. *The Cultural Cold War: The CIA and the World of Arts and Letters.* New York: New Press, 2000.

Schlaack, Susanne. *Walter Lippmann und Deutschland. Realpolitische Betrachtungen im 20. Jahrhundert.* Frankfurt am Main: Lang, 2004.

Schmid, Carlo. *Erinnerungen.* Bern: Scherz, 1979.

Schmidt, Gustav. "'Tying' (West) Germany to the West – But to What? NATO? WEU? The European Community?" in: *Western Europe and Germany. The Beginnings of European Integration 1945–1960,* edited by Clemens A. Wurm, 137–174, Oxford: Berg, 1995.

Schmidt, Helmut, *Menschen und Mächte.* Berlin: Siedler, 1987.

Schoenborn, Benedikt. "Chancellor Erhard's Silent Rejection of de Gaulle's Plans: The Example of Monetary Union." *Cold War History* 14, no. 3 (2014): 377–402.

Schrecker, Ellen. *Many Are the Crimes. McCarthyism in America.* Boston, MA: Little, Brown, 1998.

Schulz, Matthias. "Die politische Freundschaft Jean Monnet-Kurt Birrenbach, die Einheit des Westens und die 'Präambel' zum Elysée-Vertrag von 1963." in: *Interessen verbinden: Jean Monnet und die europäische Integration der Bundesrepublik Deutschland,* edited by Andreas Wilkens, 299–327, Paris: Bouvier, 1999.

Schwabe, Klaus. *Jean Monnet. Frankreich, die Deutschen und die Einigung Europas.* Baden-Baden: Nomos, 2016

Schwartz, Thomas Alan. *America's Germany: John J. McCloy and the Federal Republic of Germany.* Cambridge, MA: Harvard University Press, 1991.

Schwartz, Thomas Alan. *Lyndon Johnson and Europe. In the Shadow of Vietnam,* Cambridge, MA: Harvard University Press, 2003.

Schwarz, Hans-Peter. *Adenauer. Der Staatsmann.* Stuttgart: Deutsche Verlags-Anstalt, 1991.

Scott-Smith, Giles. *The Politics of Apolitical Culture: The Congress for Cultural Freedom, the CIA and Post-War American Hegemony.* London: Routledge, 2002.

Scott-Smith, Giles. *Networks of Empire. The US State Department's Foreign Leader Program in the Netherlands, France, and Britain 1950–70.* Brussels: Peter Lang, 2008.

Scott-Smith, Giles. *Western Anti-Communism and the Interdoc Network: Cold War Internationale.* Basingstoke: Palgrave Macmillan, 2012.

Scott-Smith, Giles. "Maintaining Transatlantic Community: US Public Diplomacy, the Ford Foundation and the Successor Generation Concept in US Foreign Affairs, 1960s–1980s." *Global Society* 28, no. 1 (2014): 90–103. doi:10.1080/13600826.2013.848189.

Scott-Smith, Giles and David Snyder. "'A Test of Sentiments': Civil Aviation, Alliance Politics, and the KLM Challenge in Dutch-American Relations." *Diplomatic History* 37, no. 5 (2013): 917–945. doi:10.1093/dh/dht065.

Scott-Smith, Giles, and Hans Krabbendam, eds. *The Cultural Cold War in Western Europe, 1945–1960*. London: Frank Cass, 2003.

Scott-Smith, Giles, and Valérie Aubourg eds. *Atlantic, Euratlantic, or Europe-America: The Atlantic Community and the European Idea from Kennedy to Nixon*. Paris: Soleb, 2011.

Scott-Smith, Giles, Valérie Aubourg, and Gérard Bossuat, eds. *European Community, Atlantic Community? The Atlantic Community and Europe*. Paris: Soleb, 2008.

Segers, Mathieu L. L. *Deutschlands Ringen mit der Relance. Die Europapolitik der BRD während der Beratungen und Verhandlungen über die Römischen Verträge*. Frankfurt am Main: Lang, 2008.

Segers, Matthieu L. L. "De Gaulle's Race to the Bottom: The Netherlands, France and the Interwoven Problems of British EEC Membership and European Political Union, 1958–1963." *Contemporary European History* 19, no. 2 (2010): 111–132.

Serra, Enrico, ed. *Il Rilancio dell'Europa e i Tratti di Roma. La Relance Européenne et les traités de Rome. The Relaunching of Europe and the Treaties of Rome*. Baden-Baden: Nomos, 1989.

Shaw, Martin. "The Political Structure of a Global World: The Role of the United States." in: *The Paradox of a Global USA*, edited by Bruce Mazlish, Nayan Chanda, and Kenneth Weisbrode, 16–30, Stanford: Stanford University Press, 2007.

Sheehan, James J. *Where Have All the Soldiers Gone? The Transformation of Modern Europe*. Boston, MA: Houghton Mifflin, 2008.

Shoup, Lawrence. *Wall Street's Think Tank: The Council on Foreign Relations and the Empire of Neoliberal Geopolitic, 1976–2014*. New York: Monthly Review Press, 2015.

Slessor, Sir John. "Air Power and World Strategy Today." *Foreign Affairs* 33, no. 1 (1954): 43–53.

Small, Melvin. "The Atlantic Council – The Early Years." NATO Website, June 1998. Accessed February 3, 2018. www.nato.int/acad/fellow/96-98/small.pdf.

Smith, Gerard C. *Disarming Diplomat. The Memoirs of Gerard C. Smith, Arms Control Negotiator*. Lanham, MD: Madison Books, 1996.

Smyser, W. R. *From Yalta to Berlin. The Cold War Struggle Over Germany*. New York: St. Martin's Press, 1999.

Snead, David L. *The Gaither Committee, Eisenhower, and the Cold War*. Columbus, OH: Ohio State University Press, 1999.

Soell, Hartmut. *Fritz Erler. Eine politische Biographie*. Berlin: Dietz, 1976.

Soell, Hartmut. *Helmut Schmidt. 1918–1969. Vernunft und Leidenschaft*. Munich: Deutsche Verlags-Anstalt, 2003.

Spaak, Paul-Henri. *Combats inachevés. De l'espoir aux déceptions*. Paris: Fayard, 1969.

Spaak, Paul-Henri. *The Continuing Battle. Memoirs of a European, 1936–1966*. Boston, MA: Little Brown, 1971.

Spaulding Jr., Robert Mark. "'A Gradual and Moderate Relaxation': Eisenhower and the Revision of American Export Control Policy, 1953–1955." *Diplomatic History* 17, no. 2 (1993): 223–249.

Spohr, Kristina. *The Global Chancellor: Helmut Schmidt and the Reshaping of the International Order*. Oxford: Oxford University Press, 2016.

Steel, Ronald. *Walter Lippmann and the American Century*. Boston, MA: Little, Brown, 1980.

Steinbrunner, John. *The Cybernetic Theory of Decision. New Dimensions of Political Analysis*. Princeton: Princeton University Press, 1974.

Steinkühler, Manfred. *Der deutsch-französische Vertrag von 1963. Entstehung, diplomatische Anwendung und politische Bedeutung in den Jahren von 1958 bis 1969.* Berlin: Duncker & Humblot, 2002.

Stephan, Alexander. *The Americanization of Europe. Culture, Diplomacy, and Anti-Americanism after 1945.* New York: Berghahn Books, 2006.

Storrs, Landon R. Y. *The Second Red Scare and the Unmaking of the New Deal Left.* Princeton: Princeton University Press, 2013.

Stueck, William Whitney. *The Korean War. An International History.* Princeton: Princeton University Press, 1995.

Suri, Jeremi. *Henry Kissinger and the American Century.* Cambridge, MA: Belknap Press of Harvard University Press, 2007.

Suri, Jeremi. *Power and Protest. Global Revolution and the Rise of Detente.* Cambridge, MA: Harvard University Press, 2003.

Thiemeyer, Guido. *Vom "Pool Vert" zur Europäischen Wirtschaftsgemeinschaft: europäische Integration, kalter Krieg und die Anfänge der gemeinsamen europäischen Agrarpolitik 1950–1957.* Munich: Oldenbourg, 1999.

Thies, Wallace J. *Why NATO Endures.* Cambridge: Cambridge University Press, 2009.

Thomas, Evan. *The Very Best Men. Four Who Dared: The Early Years of the CIA.* New York: Simon & Schuster, 1995.

Thomas, Martin. "Defending a Lost Cause? France and the United States Vision of Imperial Rule in French North Africa, 1945–1956." *Diplomatic History* 26, no. 2 (2002): 215–247.

Thompson, Nicholas. *The Hawk and the Dove. Paul Nitze, George Kennan, and the History of the Cold War.* New York: Henry Holt, 2009.

Thoß, Bruno. "Sicherheits- und deutschlandpolitische Komponenten der europäischen Integration zwischen EVG und EWG, 1954–1957." in: *Vom Marshallplan zur EWG: Die Eingliederung der Bundesrepublik Deutschland in die westliche Welt*, edited by Ludolf Herbst, 475–500, Munich: Oldenbourg, 1990.

Thoß, Bruno. *NATO-Strategie und nationale Verteidigungsplanung. Planung und Aufbau der Bundeswehr unter den Bedingungen einer massiven atomaren Vergeltungsstrategie 1952 bis 1960.* Munich: Oldenbourg, 2006.

Trachtenberg, Marc. *A Constructed Peace: The Making of the European Settlement 1945–1963.* Princeton, NJ: Princeton University Press, 1999.

Trachtenberg, Marc, and Christopher Gehrz. "America, Europe, and German Rearmament, August-September 1950: A Critique of a Myth." in: *Between Empire and Alliance. America and Europe during the Cold War*, edited by Marc Trachtenberg, 1–32, Lanham, MD: Rowman & Littlefield, 2003.

Tucker, Nancy Bernkopf. *The China Threat. Memories, Myths, and Realities in the 1950s.* New York: Columbia University Press, 2012.

Unrue, Darlene Harbour. *Katherine Anne Porter Remembered.* Tuscaloosa, AL: University of Alabama Press, 2010.

Vaïsse, Justin. "Zbig, Henry, and the New Foreign Policy Elite." in: *Zbig. The Strategy and Statecraft of Zbigniew Brzezinski*, edited by Charles Gati, 3–26, Baltimore, MD: The Johns Hopkins University Press, 2013.

Vaïsse, Maurice, ed. *La France et l'opération de Suez de 1956.* Paris: Centre d'Études d'Histoire de la Défense, 1997.

Vaïsse, Maurice. *La grandeur. Politique étrangère du général de Gaulle 1958–1969.* Paris: Fayard, 1998.

Vanke, Jeffrey W. "An Impossible Union: Dutch Objections to the Fouchet Plan, 1959–1962." *Cold War History* 2, no. 1 (2001): 95–112.

Van Vleck, Jenifer L. "The 'Logic of the Air': Aviation and the Globalism of the 'American Century'." *New Global Studies* 1, no. 1 (2007): 1–37.

Vayssière, Bertrand. *Vers une Europe fédérale?: les espoirs et les actions fédéralistes au sortir de la Seconde Guerre mondiale.* Brussels: Peter Lang, 2007.

Wall, Irwin. *France, the United States, and the Algerian War.* Berkeley, CA: University of California Press, 2001.

Warner, Michael. "The CIA's Office of Policy Coordination: From NSC 10/2 to NSC 68." *International Journal of Intelligence and Counterintelligence* 11, no. 2 (1998): 211–220.

Weber, Petra. *Carlo Schmid 1896–1976. Eine Biographie.* Munich: Beck, 1996.

Weenink, W. H. *Bankier van de wereld. Bouwer van Europa. Johan Willem Beyen, 1897–1976.* Amsterdam: Prometheus/NRC Handelsblad, 2005.

Weisbrode, Kenneth. *The Atlantic Century. Four Generations of Extraordinary Diplomats Who Forged America's Vital Alliance with Europe.* Cambridge, MA: Da Capo Press, 2009.

Wendt, Björn. *Die Bilderberg-Gruppe. Wissen über die Macht gesellschaftlicher Eliten.* Göttingen: Optimus, 2015.

Wendt, Björn, Marcus B. Klöckner, Sascha Pommrenke, and Michael Walter, eds. *Wie Eliten Macht organisieren. Bilderberg & Co.: Lobbying, Thinktanks und Mediennetzwerke.* Hamburg: VSA Verlag, 2016.

Wenger, Andreas. "Crisis and Opportunity: NATO's Transformation and the Multilateralization of Détente, 1966–1968." *Journal of Cold War Studies* 6, no. 1 (2004): 22–74.

Wenger, Andreas, Christian Nünlist, and Anna Locher, eds. *Transforming NATO in the Cold War. Challenges beyond Deterrence in the 1960s.* London: Routledge, 2007.

Westad, Odd Arne. *The Global Cold War. Third World Interventions and the Making of Our Times.* Cambridge: Cambridge University Press, 2007.

Wilford, Hugh. *The CIA, the British Left and the Cold War. Calling the Tune?* London: Frank Cass, 2003.

Wilford, Hugh. "CIA Plot, Socialist Conspiracy, or New World Order? The Origins of the Bilderberg Group, 1952–1955." *Diplomacy and Statecraft* 14, no. 3 (2003): 70–82.

Wilford, Hugh. *The Mighty Wurlitzer: How the CIA Played America.* Cambridge, MA: Harvard University Press, 2008.

Wilkinson, Peter, and Joan Bright Astley. *Gubbins and SOE.* London: Leo Cooper, 1993.

Williams, Geoffrey, and Bruce Reed. *Denis Healey and the Policies of Power.* London: Sidgwick & Jackson, 1971.

Williams, Philip M., ed. *The Diary of Hugh Gaitskell, 1945–1956.* London: Jonathan Cape, 1983.

Winand, Pascaline. *Eisenhower, Kennedy, and the United States of Europe.* New York: St. Martin's Press, 1993.

Wittner, Lawrence S. *Resisting the Bomb. A History of the World Nuclear Disarmament Movement, 1954–1970.* Stanford, CA: Stanford University Press, 1997.

Wohlstetter, Albert. "The Delicate Balance of Terror." *Foreign Affairs* 37, no. 1 (1959): 211–256.

Wohlstetter, Albert. "Nuclear Sharing: NATO and the N+1 Country." *Foreign Affairs* 39, no. 3 (1961): 355–387.

Wolff von Amerongen, Otto. *Der Weg nach Osten. Vierzig Jahre Brückenbau für die deutsche Wirtschaft*. Munich: Droemer Knaur, 1992.

Zetsche, Anne. "The Quest for Atlanticism: German-American Elite Networking, the Atlantik-Brücke and the American Council on Germany, 1952–1974." PhD diss., Northumbria University, 2016.

Zipp, Samuel. "When Wendell Willkie Went Visiting: Between Interdependency and Exceptionalism in the Public Feeling for *One World*." *American Literary History* 26, no. 3 (2014): 484–510.

Index

Membership in the Bilderberg steering committee (SC) and the years of participation in the Bilderberg conferences during the period 1954–1969 is noted in parentheses for all Bilderberg participants in the index. In the years 1955 and 1957, two Bilderberg conferences took place, identified as 1955–1, 1955–2, 1957–1, and 1957–2.